D1355999

C153792234

VICTORIA'S
GENERALS

In loving memory of Elizabeth Blinkhorn Corvi

VICTORIA'S
GENERALS

Edited by
STEVEN J CORVI
& IAN F W BECKETT

Pen & Sword
MILITARY

First published in Great Britain in 2009 by
Pen & Sword Military
An imprint of
Pen & Sword Books Ltd
47 Church Street
Barnsley
South Yorkshire
S70 2AS

ISBN 978 1 84415 918 5

Typeset in 10.5pt Ehrhardt
by S.L. Menzies-Earl

Printed and bound in England
by CPI UK

Pen & Sword Books Ltd incorporates the imprints of
Pen & Sword Aviation, Pen & Sword Maritime, Pen & Sword Military, Wharncliffe
Local History, Pen & Sword Select,
Pen & Sword Military Classics and Leo Cooper.

For a complete list of Pen & Sword titles please contact
PEN & SWORD BOOKS LIMITED
47 Church Street, Barnsley, South Yorkshire, S70 2AS, England
E-mail: enquiries@pen-and-sword.co.uk
Website: www.pen-and-sword.co.uk

Contents

List of Maps

1. Plan of the battles of Tel-el-Kebir and Kassassin, 1882. (From Sir Evelyn Wood, *British Battles on Land and Sea*, London: Cassell & Co., 1915)
2. Plan of the battle of Khambula, 1879. (From Sir Evelyn Wood, *British Battles on Land and Sea*, London: Cassell & Co., 1915)
3. Plan of the battle of Colenso, 1899. (From W Baring Pemberton, *Battles of the Boer War*, London: Batsford, 1964)
4. Plan of the battle of Majuba, 27 February 1881.
5. Plan of the battles of Laing's Nek, Schuinshootge and Majuba, 1881.
6. Plan of the Isandlwana campaign, 1879. (With permission of the University of KwaZulu-Natal Press)
7. Map to illustrate General Gordon's Journals. (From A Egmont Hake, *The Journals of Major-General C G Gordon CB, at Khartoum*, London: Kegan Paul, Trench, 1885)
8. Khartoum and environs.
9. Plan of the north-west frontier and Afghanistan. (From G Forrest, *The Life of Lord Roberts, KG, VC*, London: Cassell & Co., 1914)
10. Plan of the battle of Paardeberg, 1900. (From David James, *Lord Roberts*, London: Hollis & Carter, 1954)
11. Plan of the north-west frontier of India. (From David James, *Lord Roberts*, London: Hollis & Carter, 1954)
12. The South African War, 1899–1902.
13. The battle of Omdurman, phase one, 2 September 1898.
14. The battle of Omdurman, phase two, 2 September 1898.
15. The battle of Omdurman, phase three, 2 September 1898.

List of Plates

Acknowledgements

Quotations from the Royal Archives appear by gracious permission of Her Majesty the Queen. Quotations from Crown copyright material in The National Archives appear by permission of Her Majesty's Stationery Office. The editors and authors also give their thanks to the following for allowing them to consult and quote from archives in their possession and/or copyright: The Trustees of the Liddell Hart Centre for Military Archives, King's College, London; The Trustees of the British Library Board; The Trustees of the Imperial War Museum; The National Army Museum; The Royal Pavilion Libraries and Museums (Hove Reference Library); The National Library of Scotland; The Sudan Archive of the University of Durham; The Killie Campbell Library of the University of KwaZulu-Natal; The KwaZulu-Natal Archives; South Lanarkshire Council Museum; and The William Perkins Library of the University of Durham, North Carolina.

List of Contributors

Professor Ian Beckett was formerly Professor of History at the University of Northampton. He is Chairman of the Army Records Society. His publications include *The Victorians at War* (2003) and the forthcoming *Wolseley and Ashanti: The Asante War Journal and Correspondence of Major General Sir Garnet Wolseley, 1873–74* for the Army Records Society.

Dr Steven Corvi is Assistant Professor at the American Military University and is Northeast Chairman for Military History in the Popular Culture Association. His PhD was on Sir Horace Smith-Dorrien and he has contributed an article on the Royal Army Veterinary Corps to *JSAHR*. He has previously co-edited *Haig's Generals* (2006) with Ian Beckett.

Gerald H Herman is Assistant Professor of History at Northeastern University, Boston. His publications include *The Pivotal Conflict: Comprehensive Chronology of the First World War* (1992) and a multi-media exploration of that war's cultural impacts called *World War I: the Destroying Fathers Confirmed*. He also co-edited *The Media, the Academy and the Law: Assessing the Truth from the Protocols of Zion to Holocaust Denial* (2005).

Professor John Laband is Professor of History at Wilfrid Laurier University, Waterloo, Ontario, and an Associate of the Laurier Centre for Military, Strategic and Disarmament Studies. His many publications include *The Transvaal Rebellion: The First Boer War* (2005), *Lord Chelmsford's Zululand Campaign, 1878–79* (1994), *The Rise and Fall of the Zulu Nation* (1997) and *Kingdom in Crisis: The Zulu Response to the British Invasion of 1879* (1992).

Dr Stephen Manning is a visiting Professor of History at the University of Exeter, where he occasionally lectures on colonial warfare. He is the author of *Evelyn Wood VC: Pillar of Empire* (2007) and the forthcoming *Soldiers of the Queen*.

Dr Stephen Miller is Assistant Professor of History at the University of Maine. His publications include *Volunteers on the Veld: Britain's Citizen Soldiers and the South African War* (2007) and *Lord Methuen and the British Army* (1999). He is the editor of the forthcoming *Soldiers and Settlers in South Africa, 1850-1918* and is now working on discipline and punishment in the late Victorian army.

Dr Keith Surridge teaches on various American university programmes in London. His publications include *Managing the South African War, 1899–1902: Politicians versus Generals* (1998) and (with Denis Judd) *The Boer War* (2002). He has also contributed articles on Kitchener and on the South African War to academic journals.

Professor André Wessels is Professor of History at the University of the Orange Free State, Bloemfontein, South Africa. His publications include two volumes for the Army Records Society, *Lord Roberts and the War in South Africa, 1899–1902* (2000) and *Lord Kitchener and the War in South Africa, 1899–1902* (2006), as well as more than fifty articles in academic journals and several chapters in books.

Introduction

The senior British generals of the Victorian era – men like Garnet Wolseley, Frederick Roberts, Charles Gordon and Herbert Kitchener – were heroes of their time. As soldiers, administrators and battlefield commanders they represented the empire at the height of its power. But they were a disparate, sometimes fractious group of men. They exhibited many of the failings as well as the strengths of the British army of the nineteenth century. Now, when the Victorian period is being looked at more critically than before, the moment is right to reassess them as individuals and as military leaders. For this study, a group of military historians has come together to explore the personalities and the careers of a number of leading commanders. The contributors consider how they met the challenges created by the low-intensity colonial conflicts they faced. They assess how they coped with the emerging industrial military technologies of their age, such as smokeless powder, magazine breech-loading rifles, breech-loading rifled artillery and the machine-gun that heralded a new age in the history of warfare and required considerations of new doctrinal application.

Throughout the emphasis is on the leadership skills these men exhibited, and on their style of command. Key campaigns in their careers are analysed in detail, to show clearly the personal qualities that brought them to prominence and to illustrate the range of colonial wars in which they took part. This balanced reconsideration of these eminent military men gives a fascinating insight into their careers, into the British army of their day and into a now-remote period when Britain was a world power and the army the effective spade that ploughed the fertile field of imperial expansion.

The goal of this study is to illustrate each personality within the broader spectrum of the social and political environment of the late Victorian period, utilising the chronological parameters of the reforms of Edward Cardwell as Secretary State for War between 1868 and 1874 and the Second South African (Anglo–Boer) War of 1899 to 1902. Apart from Wolseley, Roberts, Kitchener and Gordon, therefore, the other generals considered are three of Wolseley's associates – Redvers Buller, George Colley and Evelyn Wood – and the unfortunate Lord Chelmsford. By continental standards, the British army was a small one, the largest number of men put into the field between the end of the Crimean War in 1856 and the opening of the South African War in 1899 being the 35,000 men directed by Wolseley in the occupation of Egypt in 1882. Even at the height of the South African War, Britain fielded only 450,000 men. This did not mean that considerable professional demands were not being made upon them. For one thing, as the military theorist of 'small wars', Charles Callwell, suggested, such campaigns required the conquest of nature as much as the conquest of indigenous opponents.[1] Having needed to cross 600 miles of Canadian wilderness before the lakes froze during his Red River expedition in 1870, it was understandable that, confronted with the need to complete operations in Asante in 1873–74 before the climate took its toll of his European troops, Wolseley wrote 'I always seem to be condemned to command in expeditions which must be accomplished before a certain season of the year begins.'[2] These considerations of terrain and climate are clear in Steven Corvi's account of Wolseley's campaigns. In advancing over 400 miles from the Red Sea coast to Magdala in Abyssinia in 1867–68 Sir Robert Napier's expeditionary force of 13,000 men required the logistic support of 14,500 followers and 36,000 draught animals. Even the small Duffla expedition on the heavily forested north-eastern frontier of India in 1874–75 needed 1,200 coolies while, in Zululand in 1879, it was painfully difficult for Lord Chelmsford to assemble the 977 wagons, 10,023 oxen, 803 horses and 398 mules he utilised to support his columns and all but impossible to make more than 10 miles a day. Indeed, Wolseley was to note that, when fully deployed on the march, Chelmsford's baggage train was 3 or 4 miles longer than it could actually travel in a day.[3]

Railways could help in certain circumstances, as at Suakin in 1885 and in the reconquest of the Sudan in 1896–98. Indeed, as Keith Surridge reminds us, G W Steevens, the military correspondent of the *Daily Mail* aptly described the Sudan Military Railway as 'the deadliest weapon . . . ever used against Mahdism',[4] the 230 miles of single track across the desert from Wadi Halfa to Abu Hamed shortening the journey time from 24 hours by camel and steamer to but 18 hours. On the other hand, as in the South African War, dependence upon the relatively few railways could limit strategic options and, in advancing upon the capital of the Orange Free State at Bloemfontein, Lord Roberts was forced to leave the highly vulnerable line of the railway to fall back upon oxen, horses and mules, only for the Boers to almost wreck his efforts by stampeding over 3,000 of his oxen at Waterval Drift in February 1900.

In terms of the indigenous opponents, however, the sheer variety encountered was itself extraordinary, ranging from European-trained opponents such as the Egyptian army in 1882 to disciplined native armies such as the Zulu, fanatics like the Dervishes of the Sudan, or, almost in a category of their own, mounted Boers armed with modern weapons. Of course, even primitive native opponents could defeat a trained modern army, as the Zulu proved at Isandlwana in 1879, but in many respects, of course, it must be acknowledged that none of the leading Victorian commanders faced a truly modern opponent with the exception of the Boers and it was against the Boers that Buller and Colley failed, and Roberts and Kitchener faced their greatest challenge. As Major General the Hon Neville Lyttelton observed of commanding the 4th (Light) Brigade at Colenso in December 1899, following his experience as a brigade commander in the Sudan a year earlier: 'In the first [Omdurman] 50,000 fanatics streamed across the open regardless of cover to certain death, while at Colenso I never saw a Boer all day till the battle was over, and it was our men who were the victims.'[5] Indeed, whereas the army had lost over 100 men killed or died of wounds in a single action only twice between 1857 and 1899 – at Isandlwana in January 1879 and at Maiwand in Afghanistan in July 1880 – those killed or died of wounds between 28 November 1899 and 24 January 1900 totalled 102 at the Modder River, 205 at Magersfontein, 171 at Colenso, 348 (over two days) at Paardeburg and 383 at Spion Kop. As John Laband indicates, Chelmsford was resistant to changing orthodox military methods in Zululand, when they had appeared to work satisfactorily in the Ninth Kaffir (Cape Frontier) War of 1877–78 but, as both André Wessels and Keith Surridge show, Roberts and Kitchener were prepared to adapt new methods to defeat the Boers, albeit what became known as 'methods of barbarism'. In a sense, however, these were not so different from the 'total war' that both Stephen Manning and Stephen Miller suggest Wood and Buller waged against the Zulu while neither Roberts nor Kitchener had displayed any squeamishness in Afghanistan or the Sudan. As Ian Beckett indicates, Colley, too, had little regard for his opponents, be they Afghans or Boers, and Wolseley was as prejudiced as any of his contemporaries when it came to native opponents. Indeed, as Gerald Herman suggests, perhaps only Gordon truly had any real feeling for indigenous peoples.

Apart from nature and indigenous opponents, British commanders certainly had to contend with politicians with the increasing extension of the submarine telegraph cable through the 1870s and 1880s rendering them liable to the vagaries of political indecision in London, one general officer noting of Wolseley's failure to save Gordon in 1884–85 that 'it is ungenerous to forget that nowadays military methods are too often the slaves of political expediency'.[6] In any case, commanders increasingly needed to exercise both military and political judgement, Wolseley playing the game astutely while, as Wessels notes, Frederick Roberts learned the hard way, erring in issuing a proclamation in December 1878 suggesting the annexation of the Kurram valley and then mishandling the summary executions in Kabul in January 1880 of those suspected of complicity in the massacre of the British mission of Louis Cavagnari. By the time of the South African War, however, Roberts was a practised exponent of political skills to the extent that he and Kitchener, as Surridge shows, seized effective control of policy, the debt the government owed them in securing its political survival after the exigencies of 'Black Week' also enabling them to dictate the eventual political settlement. As Beckett and Manning demonstrate, Colley and Wood were both bedevilled by the contradictory and uncertain policy of the Gladstone administration during the Anglo-Transvaal War of 1880–81. Equally, the culpability of Gladstone's government in the failure to reach Khartoum in time to save Gordon is clear from Corvi's account of Wolseley, albeit that, as Herman shows, throughout his career, Gordon was a dangerously loose cannon so far as politicians and even his fellow soldiers were concerned. Furthermore, Laband shows the poor civil-military relationship to which Chelmsford contributed in the conduct of policy in Zululand and Miller the difficulties under which Buller laboured as the Conservative Secretary of State for War, Lord Lansdowne, undermined his command in the South African War.

Political considerations intruded largely due to the growing recognition that there was a need to take account of public opinion in an age of popular journalism. Thus, when Lieutenant General Sir Edward Selby Smyth, who had previously served at the Cape, offered his services in the Zulu War, the Secretary of State for War immediately rejected the appointment of a soldier who was 'hardly well enough known' to take on the job of reversing Isandlwana.[7] Similarly, the feeble Lieutenant General the Hon Sir Leicester Smyth, sent to command at the Cape after the Zulu War was safely over and no new crises were anticipated, was pointedly instructed not to interfere with George Colley in Natal in 1880; ignored when Evelyn Wood was sent out to be Colley's deputy in February 1881; passed over when Colley was killed at Majuba later that month, at which time the public's new hero, Roberts, was sent out to take command; and again overlooked when Sir Charles Warren was appointed to command the expedition to Bechuanaland in October 1884.

Most commanders were hostile to the press, Kitchener famously having supposed to have swept out of his tent past the assembled correspondents on one occasion in the Sudan exclaiming, 'Get out of my way, you drunken swabs!'[8] As Surridge points out, Kitchener's relations with the ubiquitous 'specials' remained poor and it was only the intervention of the government that compelled him to allow correspondents south of Assouan during the campaign. Again, as Wessels reminds us, during the Second Afghan War, Roberts had Maurice Macpherson of the *Standard* removed from the Kurram Field Force for eluding press controls and, in South Africa, he and Kitchener imposed tight regulations in comparison to the somewhat lazy approach of Redvers Buller.

If commanders faced a range of external pressures, there were also internally generated difficulties in terms of the generally casual attitude towards the emergence of a general staff. In part, the persistence of this tendency derived from the older conflict between the relative importance accorded 'character' and intellect in the army. It can be noted that one of Wolseley's leading adherents, Frederick Maurice, maintained in 1872 that the British officer 'hates . . . literary work even in the form of writing letters', while another partial associate of Wolseley, Sir John Ardagh, was contemptuous of what he perceived to be the idea that 'the "athletic duffer", who is useful in a football team, must necessarily be a better soldier than the man who comes first in any examination'.[9] Certainly, courage was routinely expected of a Victorian commander. Buller, Roberts and Wood had all won the VC. Wolseley lost the sight of his right eye in the Crimea – as Wessels notes, Roberts also had no sight in his right eye following an attack of brain fever in his youth – and, as Manning tells us, Wood was frequently wounded as well as plagued by an extraordinary range of illnesses and freak accidents.

In reality, matters were changing for as Brian Bond has noted, while the army 'succeeded to a remarkable degree in preserving an essentially eighteenth-century mode of life and in excluding all but a handful of officers from the lower-middle and working classes', it also 'reduced the influence of wealth and social position and substituted objective educational tests for entry and a regularised system for professional advancement'.[10] As Corvi, Wessels and Manning all demonstrate, Wolseley, Roberts and Wood were all highly professional and reform-minded, though Roberts in a somewhat conservative fashion. Certainly, the Staff College gradually came to be sufficiently accepted to begin to provide real intellectual foundation for tactical and logistical reform. Wolseley, for example, favoured Staff College graduates in all his campaigns. A total of 34 PSCs (Passed Staff College) served in Egypt in 1882, including 14 in the headquarters and 5 out of 7 in the intelligence section; 20 on the Gordon Relief Expedition in 1884–85, including 6 in the headquarters and 7 on lines of communication; and no less than 80 PSCs were appointed to the staff or dispatched on special service to South Africa in 1899, 33 being named to the staff of the army corps and the first three divisions. Wolseley, however, did tend to employ larger staffs than many of his contemporaries.[11] In Zululand, for example, though actually dedicated to his profession, as Laband indicates, Chelmsford had just 14 individuals on his headquarters staff for a force of almost 18,000 men, although each of the 5 columns employed also had about 7 staff officers. Nor did Chelmsford employ any intelligence staff, utilising only one civilian in an intelligence capacity. Wolseley by contrast immediately allocated Major General the Hon Henry Clifford nine assistants on the lines of communication and placed Frederick Maurice in charge of intelligence. There were a further seventeen officers on Wolseley's personal and headquarters staffs for a substantially reduced establishment of troops.[12] Compared to continental standards, of course, all British staffs remained small and it must be recognised that much of the army's operational leadership derived from individual skill and bravado rather than a clear-cut application of doctrine on the battlefield. In one sense, however, this might have actually been preferable to too theoretical a military knowledge since arguably, as recounted by Laband and Beckett, some of the greatest failures of leadership were those of able administrators such as Chelmsford at Isandlwana and Colley at Majuba. Inevitably perhaps, luck also had something to do with it. In the end Wolseley's luck ran out in the Sudan in 1884–85, while, as Manning shows, Wood's reputation as a successful field commander owed much to the memory of his near catastrophic defeat by the Zulu at Hlobane in March 1879 being conveniently erased by the great victory at Khambula the following day. As Wessels makes clear, Roberts was also an exceedingly lucky general.

The personalised approach to command and leadership also fuelled the rivalry of the so-called 'rings' around commanders. The struggle ranged widely over issues of imperial strategy and military reform, though neither particular issues nor the positions assumed by individuals with respect to them were necessarily constant as the factions attempted to manoeuvre adherents into particular commands. As Corvi demonstrates, Wolseley's 'Ashanti Ring', known to some as the 'Mutual Admiration Society', was the best known, and the essays by Beckett, Manning and Miller all illustrate the centrality of the 'ring' to the careers of Colley, Wood and Buller. Roberts, too, however, had his adherents as, subsequently, did Kitchener, Wessels and Surridge both illustrating the operation of their groups in India and the Sudan respectively. Moreover, the Duke of Cambridge as the army's Commander in Chief from 1856 to 1895 was equally determined to have his own way with regard to appointments, favouring seniority over 'selection' even after the establishment of a selection board in 1891 to enforce promotion by selection. To some extent, Chelmsford as one of the 'old school' typified those favoured by Cambridge, although, as Laband shows, Chelmsford's manifold failures ultimately cost him the Duke's support. Gordon, of course, was too much of a maverick to belong to any particular group. There was often an element of vindictiveness in the working of the rings but in the criticism of them there was equally a large measure of resentment on the part of those excluded from campaigns and the glory and honour that might derive from them.

Of course, the constant employment of a relatively small number of officers did restrict the development of others, Wolseley in particular becoming something of a prisoner of the initial success of his ring in feeling it desirable to employ the same men lest his rejection of them might reflect adversely on his earlier choice. Indeed, Wolseley continued to employ the same men despite his own increasing criticism of their failings. Wood, for example, was never forgiven for signing the peace treaty with the Boers after Colley's death at Majuba in February 1881, while Henry Brackenbury's advocacy of the creation of a general staff was regarded by Wolseley as evidence of Brackenbury's own ambition. Certainly, as the prominent members of Wolseley's ring became more senior, their willingness to work together was subordinated to their own ambitions, even Buller, as Miller shows, being regarded with suspicion by Wolseley for his apparent willingness to accept the office of Commander in Chief from the Liberal government ahead of Wolseley in 1895, the subsequent change of government granting Wolseley his long-sought prize. Individuals manoeuvring for preferment was hardly unusual, however, Buller noting after visiting Roberts in Pretoria in July 1900: 'I found Roberts sitting in one building with his Hindu staff, Kitchener in another with his Egyptian staff, and [Lieutenant General Sir Thomas] Kelly-Kenny in a third with an English staff, all pulling against each other.'[13]

Yet, while Wolseley's command system, was highly personalised, he did plan carefully in advance, in contrast to Roberts who was an indifferent organiser.

Wolseley relied fairly heavily on his chiefs of staff for routine administration but they were not intended to share in decision-making. Buller, for example, who acted in this capacity on the Gordon Relief Expedition, saw Wolseley for only eight hours in two months once Wolseley went forward to Wadi Halfa in December 1884, leaving Buller 360 miles behind at Korti.[14] Miller illustrates the problems that resulted. Generally, Wolseley allowed little latitude to his subordinates in field command, the problem in the Sudan being that of scale. Wolseley was not allowed as far forward as he would have liked by the government, being instructed to go no further than Korti, and the sheer distances involved – it was 1,600 miles from Cairo to Khartoum – proved too great for personal control to be exercised. Moreover, the very way Wolseley operated had militated against the development of initiative in his subordinates and, without him, they often floundered. The problem was that improvisation was no substitute for a proper general staff and Wolseley's capacity to manage affairs decreased in proportion to the growth in the scale of operations.

Of course, in such a personalised system, personality itself also counted. Wolseley was admired rather than liked. He certainly never had the same rapport with the rank and file as Buller, Roberts or even Chelmsford, which is clearly evident in the essays by Miller, Wessels and Laband. Kitchener was very much a loner and, as Surridge suggests, a man of great insecurities, while, as Beckett shows, Colley also tended towards somewhat empty rhetoric in his dealings with those under his command. Despite his personal vanity, Wood, as Manning illustrates, was always prepared in his later training role to allow his subordinates the opportunity to think seriously about their profession but, as Herman suggests, Gordon was the most charismatic as well as arguably the most enigmatic. Though so very different one from another, however, all these men shared a devotion to their chosen profession and a determination to succeed in it. In the process they contributed immeasurably to the story of the late Victorian army.

Notes

1. Ian F W Beckett, 'Another British Way in Warfare: Charles Callwell and Small Wars', in Ian F W Beckett, ed., *Victorians at War: New Perspectives* (Society for Army Historical Research Special Publication No. 16, 2007), pp. 89–102.
2. Hove, Wolseley Mss, W/P 3/17, Wolseley to wife, 16 Dec. 1873.
3. Ian F W Beckett, 'Command in the Late Victorian Army', in Gary Sheffield, ed., *Leadership and Command: The Anglo-American Experience since 1861* (London: Brassey's, 1997), pp. 37–56; idem, 'Command in South Africa', in Peter Boyden, Alan Guy and Marion Harding, eds, *Ashes and Blood: The British Army in South Africa, 1795-1914* (London: National Army Museum, 1999), pp. 60–71.
4. G W Steevens, *With Kitchener to Khartoum* (Edinburgh: Blackwood & Sons, 1898), p. 22.
5. General Sir Neville Lyttelton, *Eighty Years Soldiering, Politics, Games* (London: Hodder & Stoughton, 1927), p. 212.
6. Royal Archives, VIC/MAIN/ N/41/78, Hardinge to the Queen, 12 Feb. 1885.

7. Royal Archives, Cambridge Mss, VIC/AddE/1/8596, Stanley to Cambridge, 20 Mar. 1879.

8. E N Bennett, *The Downfall of the Dervishes: Being a Sketch of the Final Sudan Campaign of 1898* (Methuen, London, 1898), p. 70.

9. Ian F W Beckett, 'Victorians at War: War, Technology and Change', *Journal of the Society for Army Historical Research*, 81 (2003), 330–38; idem, *The Victorians at War* (London: Hambledon, 2003), p. 180.

10. Brian Bond, *The Victorian Army and the Staff College* (London: Eyre Methuen, 1972), p. 29.

11. Beckett, *Victorians at War*, pp. 8–9.

12. *Narrative of the Field Operations connected with the Zulu War of 1879* (London: War Office Intelligence Branch, 1881), pp. 152–54.

13. Earl of Midleton, *Records and Recollections, 1856–1939* (London: John Murray, 1939), p. 120.

14. Beckett, *Victorians at War* p. 11.

Chapter 1

Garnet Wolseley

Steven J Corvi

'I am the Very Model of a Modern Major General' was the line from the famous Gilbert and Sullivan operetta, *The Pirates of Penzance* (1879). Some can draw the similarities between the Gilbert and Sullivan's character Major General Stanley and Garnet Wolseley, who also permeated Victorian popular culture and slang with the then contemporary term 'All Sir Garnet', meaning everything is in good order. The Victorian Imperial period was dominated by two major military figures, Wolseley and Roberts. Where Roberts was the hero in the field, Wolseley was more of the reforming intellectual general. This of course does not discount Wolseley's vast experience in Victorian campaigns: Crimea, China, Canada, Asante, Egypt and the Sudan. His productive association with Edward Cardwell (Secretary of State for War, 1868–74) proved to be an important step in producing a more professional and highly trained British army. Wolseley said of Cardwell, 'no British war minister ever responded more readily to demands made upon him by his military advisers'.[1] Wolseley was considered the most influential reforming soldier of the Victorian age, with his firm support of Cardwell's reforms and his practical battlefield experiences, which left an indelible mark on the British army.

Garnet Wolseley was born on 4 June 1833 in Dublin. He was one of seven children, which included three brothers (Richard, Frederick and George) and three sisters (Matilda, Frances and Caroline). Garnet's father died when he was only 7 years old and this profoundly affected his life. The family was forced to struggle on a meagre army pension. This poverty had an obvious immediate impact on Garnet's life and it was also to cause hardship in his then future army career. Garnet Wolseley was forced by circumstances to excel by sheer ability and competency. Since he was not afforded a public-school education, his mother and then, later, tutors educated him. He was forced at 14 to leave school and become a land surveyor in a Dublin office. Garnet considered a life in the Protestant clergy, but could not afford the education to pursue such a career. He then turned to the army and sought commission via a nomination from the Commander in Chief, the Duke of Wellington. He was at first ignored, but finally was gazetted an ensign in the 12th Foot in 1852.

Chronology

4 June 1833	Garnet Joseph Wolseley born at Golden Bridge House, Co. Dublin Educated in Dublin
12 March 1852	Commissioned as Ensign in 12th Foot
13 April 1852	Transferred to 80th Foot
1852–53	Service in Burma
19 March 1853	Severely wounded at Kyault Azein
16 May 1853	Promoted Lieutenant
27 January 1854	Transferred to 84th Foot
24 February 1854	Transferred to 90th Foot
1854–56	Service in Crimea
26 January 1855	Promoted Captain
30 August 1855	Severely wounded at Sebastopol
1857–58	Service in India
24 March 1858	Promoted Brevet Major
26 April 1859	Promoted Brevet Lieutenant Colonel
1860–61	Service in China
15 February 1861	Promoted Major (Unattached)
6 August 1861	Promoted Major in regiment
11 January 1862	Appointed AQMG, Canada
5 June 1865	Promoted Brevet Colonel
4 June 1867	Married Louisa Erskine
1 October 1867	Appointed DQMG, Canada
5 April 1870	Appointed to lead Red River expedition
1 May 1871	Appointed AAG, Horse Guards
6 September 1873	Appointed to command Asante expedition as Local Major General
1 April 1874	Promoted Major General, antedated to 6 March 1868
April 1874	Appointed Inspector General of Auxiliary Forces
16 February 1875	Appointed High Commissioner and GOC, Natal
25 November 1876	Appointed Member of Council of India
25 March 1878	Promoted Lieutenant General
22 July 1878	Appointed High Commissioner and Governor General, Cyprus
23 June 1879	Appointed High Commissioner and Governor, Natal and Transvaal as Local General
1 July 1880	Appointed QMG, War Office
1 April 1882	Appointed AG, War Office
4 August 1882	Appointed C in C, Egyptian expedition as Temporary General
13 September 1882	Victory of Tel-el-Kebir
18 November 1882	Promoted General and created Baron Wolseley of Cairo and Wolseley
1884–85	Commanded Gordon Relief Expedition
19 August 1885	Elevated to Viscount
1 October 1890	Appointed GOC, Ireland
26 May 1894	Promoted Field Marshal
1 November 1895	Appointed C in C of the British army
30 November 1900	Retired as C in C
25 March 1913	Died at Menton, France
31 March 1913	Buried in St Paul's Cathedral

Appointed CB, 1870; KCMG, 1870; KCB, 1874; GCMG, 1874; GCB, 1880; KP, 1885

The army that Wolseley was commissioned into was one that had seemingly declined since the Napoleonic Wars, though some reforms were underway by the late 1840s and early 1850s. The conditions of enlisted service remained substandard, however, and the 'army life' only attracted the man without means. Wellington referred to his army as the 'scum of the earth'. This scum was what Wolseley would inherit and later greatly improve. Caught at a moment of transition, the army would be severely tested in the Crimea and forced to reform further under more modern lines. This was a fortuitous time for Wolseley to enter the army and be a formative edifice for reform.[2]

Garnet's career began with active duty in the Second Burma War and he was badly wounded at Kyault Azein, leading an attack on a stronghold. This valorous act earned him a mention in dispatches and a promotion. Wolseley commented in his published biography, 'I have never experienced the same unalloyed and elevating satisfaction, or known again the joy I then felt as I ran for the enemy's stockade . . .'.[3] He received, however, a fierce leg wound, which would take him out of action in Burma. He luckily recovered quickly, for he could have just have easily died from this wound or at least have lost his leg, which would have effectively ended his active military career. Wolseley was shipped home to convalesce, and this was just in time for the Crimean War.[4]

Garnet had transferred to the 90th Perthshire Light Infantry (later the Cameronians) in February 1854. Wolseley arrived after the major battles of the war, Alma, Balaclava and Inkerman, had been bungled by Lord Raglan: 'The first object that greeted Wolseley's eyes as he stepped out of the boat on to the inhospitable shores of the Crimea, was a firelock which lay half in and half out of the water.'[5] This was an eerie precursor to the later siege of Sebastopol, the incompetent handling of troops and the use of archaic weapon technology by Wolseley's regiment. Lieutenant Wolseley volunteered for dangerous duty with the Royal Engineers, which was the best opportunity for action and promotion. During his service with them in the trenches, he started a friendship with young Charles Gordon, whom he would later lead an expedition to save during Gordon's ill-fated defence of Khartoum (1884–85). He served in 'Gordon's Battery' on 4 January 1855, which inculcated a lasting relationship and earned him a promotion to Captain for his front-line duty.[6] Wolseley was badly wounded while working on a sap trench with two other Sergeant Sappers, who were killed by the artillery fire. He slowly convalesced at a hospital near Balaclava. He stayed in the Crimea until the Peace of Paris was signed in April 1856.

The origins of the Indian Mutiny of 1857 had deep roots, but it stemmed from the basic principle that the British were trying to convert the Muslim and Hindu soldiers to Christianity. Rumours were circulated that cartridges were greased with beef and pork fat and that the powdered bones of pigs and cows were added to the ration flour, which of course offended both Muslim and Hindus alike serving in native Sepoy regiments. The Mutiny began in Meerut and spread rapidly across British military installations from Agra, Lucknow and the infamous Cawnpore. Wolseley participated in the relief of Lucknow and garnered admiration for his composure under fire in a few engagements. This was to mark Wolseley's last service as a regimental officer, for he was to serve as a staff officer or commander on future campaigns. He was also promoted to Brevet Major in 1858 and served as Quartermaster General to Major General Sir Hope Grant. At the conclusion of the Indian mutiny campaign, Wolseley was promoted to Brevet Lieutenant Colonel, which made him the youngest colonel in the British army, and the most rapidly promoted officer of this time period.[7]

Wolseley was called upon for an expedition to China, which was initiated to ratify the Treaty of Tientsin that had been agreed after the siege of Canton in June of 1858. Sir Hope Grant commanded the expedition and Wolseley again served on his staff as Quartermaster General. The campaign was a joint venture between British and French forces, focussing on the Taku forts, which fell after a brief engagement. Wolseley was engrossed in logistical planning of the campaign and especially the aftermath.[8] The peace treaty was finally signed in 1861, but there was another threat that was rising, the Taiping Rebellion, later crushed by Wolseley's friend Charles Gordon.[9]

After China, Garnet took eighteen months' leave, and took care of family affairs. He was then ordered to Canada by the War Office and given the duty of Assistant Quartermaster General. Wolseley reached Halifax on 5 January 1862. The American Civil War was raging in the United States and this interested Wolseley very much, especially in the prosecution of a modern industrialised war on such a large scale. Wolseley used his time wisely and took two months' leave to observe the Confederate armies close up. He had a letter of introduction and travelled with *The Times* correspondent Frank Lawley, meeting up with the Confederate army at Fredericksburg. Wolseley visited Robert E Lee's headquarters at Winchester, where he met Lee himself, and his two Corps commanders, 'Stonewall' Jackson and Longstreet. This made quite the impression on the young Colonel. He wrote an article for *Blackwood's Magazine* about his visit to Lee's army. This led to later biographical works on Union General William Sherman and Confederate General Nathan Forest. He learned many valuable lessons during his visit of American Civil War battles, which was the only major industrialised war that he witnessed in person. However, Garnet mistakenly still held his belief in the use of cavalry in large-scale operations on Civil War battlefields, a stalwart concept in the *arme blanche* school that prevailed in many quarters until the First World War.[10] Wolseley himself later switched his ideas on cavalry and derived an immensely more practical idea on the use of horses on the modern battlefield, which was more in line with Havelock and Denison's theories[11] on mounted infantry.[12] There was a scare that the Union forces would invade Canada after they defeated the Confederate forces. This was quickly dispelled when it was realised this was not the intention of the North.

Wolseley wrote the first edition of his *The Soldiers Pocket Book for Field Service* during his time in Canada, a work that was greatly improved by his new wife's grammatical input, Wolseley having married Louisa Erskine in 1867. Wolseley was able to put his theories to practical work when he was given command of the Red River expedition on 5 April 1870. In November 1869 French-Canadian residents rose up in rebellion to British rule and the Hudson Bay Company in Fort Garry, Manitoba under the leadership of Louis Riel. This afforded Wolseley his first independent command. He commanded the British regular force of the 1st Battalion, 60th Rifles and a battery of Royal Field Artillery and the Canadian Militia, which consisted of the 1st Ontario Rifles and 2nd Quebec Rifles. The expedition was meticulously planned and it succeeded with the bloodless capitulation of Riel. This expedition was the origin of the first 'Wolseley Ring',[13] which was to be a powerful clique in the late Victorian army. Initially, it included Colonel John McNeill, Captain Redvers Buller, Lieutenant William Butler and Lieutenant Hugh McCalmont. Wolseley would widen his circle to other officers such as Henry Brackenbury, George Colley, Frederick Maurice and Evelyn Wood in the Asante campaign, which more properly marked the real beginning of the 'Wolseley Ring' and its arguably undue influence on the late Victorian army.

Returning to England to become Assistant Adjutant General at Horse Guards under the Crimean veteran Adjutant General Sir Richard Airey, Wolseley's arrival coincided with the reform-oriented administration of the Liberal Secretary of State for War, Edward Cardwell. Cardwell faced the monumental task of improving the efficiency, organisation and social strata of the army, while simultaneously reducing the overall budget. Wolseley's position was potentially influential since, under the then present structure of the British army, the most important staff officers under the Commander in Chief were the Military Secretary and Adjutant General.[14] Some of the major reforms that were implemented were the abolition of purchased commissions, the adoption of short service, the creation of a more efficient reserve system, and the localisation and linking of battalions. The Commander in Chief, the Duke of Cambridge, and also the Queen herself opposed these reforms. Wolseley, who became associated with Cardwell, believed that the army was a naturally conservative institution and by its nature tended to resist reform due to its myriad of inhibitions such as adherence to discipline, deference to civil authority and respect for tradition, especially regimental tradition.[15] Wolseley declared that reforms would only go forward after temporary setbacks, 'Discipline is apt to make parrots of us all; we have much less individuality than the members of civil professions.'[16] Wolseley and his 'ring' were linked to reforms in the army but not without other competitive 'rings', such as that soon associated with Roberts. The further rivalry and competition for staff appointments between the 'rings' supporting Roberts and Wolseley merely emphasised that the army was not a monolithic body. The movements in favour of reform were split, with Roberts advocating proposals that differed radically from those of Wolseley inasmuch as they reflected his own military experience and strategic priorities shaped by (Roberts') service on the Indian sub-continent.[17]

Wolseley made an impact on army reform but, more importantly, he was the impetus to further propel this reform movement after Cardwell's tenure as

Secretary. He pushed further for professionalisation of the army and went loggerheads with the Duke of Cambridge on many occasions. Wolseley no doubt was in favour of Cardwell's reforms and he rarely agreed with the Duke of Cambridge's opinions. In fact, he challenged the Duke's leadership, position, values and stalwart conservatism, which Wolseley felt stagnated the growth of the army in a very dynamic period of industrial growth and rapid change in the application of technology on the battlefield. Wolseley understood that modern weapons made the defensive more favourable than the offensive and the ignorance of these principles would incur unacceptable casualties on the battlefield. He also urged the use of defensive entrenchment, and indirect fire in artillery, so as not to expose the artillery battery to counter fire from both the opposing artillery and infantry. Wolseley understood modern massed rifle firepower and its increasing killing range, which was ever expanding from 1870 to 1900. However, not all his prescience was readily accepted and only after some sore defeats and heavy casualties were Wolseley's reform ideas adopted into the army, after the Anglo-Boer War (1899–1902), which was indicative of a steep learning curve in staff work.[18] The Wolseley 'ring' was said to be the 'young school with advanced ideas', and this propelled many of its members on to successful careers, such as Wood, Brackenbury, Colley and Maurice. However, this personal ambition could vitiate the enthusiasm for reform and in some cases the 'ring' members would placate the conservative establishment, the Duke of Cambridge.[19]

The Asante campaign was considered the campaign that made Wolseley's name familiar in the Victorian household,

> But the name and services of Sir Garnet Wolseley would have remained in comparative obscurity had not one of those crises arisen which this country, with her vast colonies and dependencies, has so frequently been called upon to meet, and once again 'the hour brought forth the man'.[20]

The Asante king, Kofi Karikari, ordered his army to attack the British protectorate at Elmina, which would provide the Asante access to the ocean. This attack was considered intolerable and the Gladstone government was determined to drive the Asante back to their own country. Wolseley put forward a plan to expel the Asante from British territory which was approved by both Cardwell and the Colonial Secretary, Lord Kimberley. Wolseley had a succinct and precise plan with clear-cut objectives, as outlined in his memorandum of August 1873:

> The first object to be attained, as I understand the circumstances existing on the Gold Coast at present, is to free the Protectorate of its Ashanti invaders; and secondly, having accomplished this, to advance into the Ashanti territory, and by the seizure and destruction of Coomassie, strike a decisive blow at the Ashanti power, not only directly by the loss and secure punishment inflicted upon its Government, but, by the moral effects of a great victory, to destroy for ever it military prestige and influence over the neighbouring nations.[21]

He arrived in Cape Coast Castle on 2 October 1873 and went straight into preparing logistically for the military campaign. He raised two regiments of native soldiers under the command of Colonel Evelyn Wood (90th Foot) and Major Baker Russell (13th Hussars). Wolseley's selection of his staff is considered the origin of the Asante or Wolseley 'ring', with Buller, Wood, McNeill, Butler, Brackenbury, Colley and Maurice all participating. They were a competent group of men that proved themselves in battle but were not always the best in command of soldiers themselves. Colley comes to mind as a great military mind but a not so competent leader at Majuba Hill. The 'ring' was a high-quality staff, which was essential for success due to the fact that Wolseley had very little information on the terrain, and the few surviving members of the expedition of 1864 could only give scant details of the country and the enemy's numbers and capacities.[22]

Wolseley began the campaign against the Asante-controlled villages on 13 October and moved forward with reasonable rapidity. The native troops (Fante tribesmen and 'Hausa') employed proved to be unreliable in battle and created problems so that Wolseley sent an expected message to Cardwell that British troops would be needed to reach the Asante capital of Kumase. Wolseley requested two (later three) battalions of infantry, and a detachment of Royal Artillery and Royal Engineers, the whole amounting to approximately 1,450 men. Wolseley stated:

> There is, but one method of freeing these settlements from the continued menace of Ashanti invasion; and this is to defeat the Ashanti army in the field, to drive it from the protected territories, and, if necessary, to pursue it into its own land, and to march victorious on the Ashanti capital.[23]

The Cabinet met and dispatched the 2/23rd Foot (Royal Welsh Fusiliers); the 42nd Royal Highlanders (Black Watch) made up to strength with 170 men from the 79th Highlanders; and the 2nd Rifle Brigade. One of the main problems was the desertion of the native carriers and this had to be overcome on the spot. Wolseley reluctantly imposed his power to enforce conscript labour, through his position as Civil Governor. Now that transportation was more secure the campaign was able to move ahead in January. The largest battles were for Kumase. Wolseley made careful preparations with a halt at Fommanah to replenish his supplies and ready his men; it also gave King Kofi Karikari time to sue for peace as he inferred he would do.

The battle at Amoaful on 31 January 1874 was the battle that enabled Wolseley to advance through to Kumase and the final defeat of the Asante. The 42nd Highlanders took the brunt of action and casualties at Amoaful, and were highly praised by Wolseley:

> It is impossible for me to speak in too high terms of that magnificent regiment the 42nd Highlanders; their steadiness and discipline, the admirable way in which they were kept in hand by their officers, and the enthusiastic gallantry with which each charge was executed exceed all praise.[24]

He occupied and then destroyed Kumase, completing what he outlined as a successful campaign,

> I believe that the main object of my expedition has been perfectly secured. The territories of the Gold Coast will not again be troubled with warlike ambition of this restless Power [Ashanti]. I may add that the Flag of England from this moment will be received throughout western Africa with respectful awe.[25]

Wolseley's return to Britain was triumphant and it secured his reputation as a highly successful field commander: he was promoted to Major General and given £25,000 from Parliament for his services in Africa. However, the question of reform was still of paramount concern to Wolseley, and he felt that, with the resignation of Cardwell, after Disraeli's government took over in early 1874, reform would not be implemented and most likely blocked by the Duke of Cambridge. The new Secretary of State for War, Gathorne Hardy, played into the Duke's hands and Wolseley thought that India might now be the best location for him to improve and reform the British army, but he was appointed Inspector General of Auxiliary Forces at home. His principal job was to organise the Militia, Volunteers and the Yeomanry units. The goal was to prepare these home defence units to defend Britain. After less than a year as Inspector General, Wolseley was sent to the Natal Colony as High Commissioner and GOC to further the government's plan for a federation between the British and Afrikaner colonies in southern Africa by securing amendment to the Natal constitution. The largest perceived threat to Natal was from the highly militaristic and organised tribe of the Zulu. Wolseley brought his 'ring' officers with him to form his staff, principally Colley, Brackenbury and Butler. Colley was sent out to reconnoitre the Transvaal and the Boer frontier settlements. Butler was sent to the Orange Free State, the other independent Boer republic, to surmise the native problem. Having secured the constitutional arrangements, Wolseley returned to England after a short time, and Colley was posted to India as Military Secretary to Viceroy Lord Lytton: Colley would be back in South Africa fighting the Boers with tragic results at Majuba Hill.[26]

With the possibility of war with Russia looming in 1878 over Russia's Balkan ambitions, Wolseley was designated as chief of staff to any potential British expeditionary force but was then sent to the island of Cyprus, which had been recently ceded by the Sultan of Ottoman Turkey to Britain in preparation for any conflict with Tsarist Russia. It proved a quiet posting as the possibility of conflict was brought to an end at the Congress of Berlin in July 1878. Meanwhile, conflict started to flare up in South Africa with the Zulu and Lord Chelmsford led British forces into Zululand in January 1879, two members of the 'ring', Wood and Buller, serving under him: Buller commanded the Frontier Light Horse, an irregular volunteer unit, and Wood one of Chelmsford's columns. Chelmsford's own column came under a devastating attack from a Zulu army 10,000 strong at

Isandlwana with disastrous results. Wolseley was sent out in April 1879 to supersede Chelmsford. He landed in Cape Town on 23 June 1879 and was greeted with two alarming pieces of news. The first was that a Zulu raiding party had killed the Prince Imperial of France, serving with the British forces in an ambiguous semi-official capacity. The other was that Chelmsford's second invasion force was nearing the Zulu capital at Ulundi. Wolseley wanted to consolidate his forces, but Chelmsford had disobeyed orders to wait for Wolseley to arrive before engaging in any battles and moved on Ulundi. Chelmsford defeated a much larger Zulu army with his force of 5,000 men. This was a much-welcomed victory for Chelmsford if not for Wolseley, who wanted to conclude the campaign himself, but Chelmsford did not follow up and capture the Zulu chief, Cetshwayo. Thus, Wolseley set up camp at Ulundi and finally captured Cetshwayo on 28 August 1879. This was to mark the end of the Zulu War but with its end came new problems with the Boers. Imposing a settlement on Zululand, Wolseley left the Transvaal question and pending Boer issues in 1880 to his friend, Colley. This was to lead, of course, to some dire circumstances at Majuba Hill a year later.[27]

Wolseley was hoping to secure the chief command in India, but was offered instead a War Office position as Quartermaster General. Moreover, he only received the GCB for concluding the Zulu War, which was the same award given to Lord Chelmsford. Wolseley was hoping to at least maintain the local rank of General which was conferred upon him when he went to the Natal Colony, but this was not retained for reasons that did not reflect his service and professionalism as a soldier, but rather the political and highly personal nature of the British army of this era. As Quartermaster General, Wolseley attended the German autumn military manoeuvres. This was considered an honour for Wolseley and he met the German Emperor Wilhelm I, the Crown Prince, and Count von Moltke (the Elder). This was thought-provoking after the recent Franco-Prussian War victories, considering the interest Wolseley had in modern warfare.[28]

However, 1881 proved to be a disastrous year for the British army in the Transvaal. Colley suffered a defeat at Laing's Nek on 28 January 1881. The Colonial Office ordered Colley to either defeat the Boers succinctly or end hostilities before the war spread throughout the region. Colley was defeated and killed at Majuba Hill on 27 February 1881, news that echoed loudly throughout the British empire. Wolseley had lost a good friend and felt the government-negotiated peace was an insult to Colley and his men. Wolseley was not happy with Wood, who had signed the Pretoria Convention Peace Treaty,

> I feel sure we should never have relinquished our hold over the Transvaal. If we were to have a fight upon the question, how much better it would have been to have had it when the Boers possessed no artillery, were only armed with bad sporting rifles, had very little ammunition and still less money than in 1899.[29]

This was an erudite assessment that shows prescience of the military-political situation of this period and would weigh heavy upon the British army in the Second Anglo-Boer War (1899–1902).

Wolseley showed great dedication to army reform, as is reflected in the following extract:

> The depth of Wolseley's commitment to army reform and his recognition of the importance of mobilizing the public are at no point clearer than when considering the proposal he put forward after the government had all but abandoned the idea of making him a peer. On hearing of the postponement of the matter, he indicated to Childers that, if the argument still centred round the inadvisability of having the Quarter-Master General sit in the House of Lords, he was prepared to resign his position and accept a peerage and the position of Governor-General of Gibraltar in succession to Lord Robert Napier. He would then be able to support the government in its programme of [army] reform . . .[30]

The government backed down on making Wolseley a peer and offered him the job of Adjutant General. This position had a condition brought down from the Duke of Cambridge by which Wolseley had to promise not to publish publicly anything on military affairs that would oppose the Duke's views. This was an assurance that Wolseley had no intention of keeping and he showed great resistance to the Duke's views and, in his position as Adjutant General, pressed his own opinions readily forward, especially in the case of much-needed army reform issues. Wolseley in his new position was appointed president to the Colour Committee, which decided to change the colour of the British Army uniform from red to khaki: 'After red had proved such a conspicuous target at Majuba Hill in 1881 the Adjutant-General, Garnet Wolseley, threw his weight behind efforts to modernise and improve the army uniform. In 1883 a committee of which he was chairman suggested the adoption of grey for service dress. Yet significant clothing reforms were not brought about much before 1900.'[31] This issue would take some time to be concluded but the practicality of the colour change would of course be the deciding factor, even in the face of royal opposition by the Duke of Cambridge and Queen Victoria herself.

Tel-el-Kebir and the Egyptian Campaign, 1882

Unrest in Egypt and the eventual collapse of the Egyptian government led to the military taking over the government in April 1882. Wolseley's task was purely militaristic and he was to defeat and disperse the forces under Arabi Pasha, which were in rebellion to the Khedive Tewfik. He was then subsequently to restore the prince to the throne in Egypt. Prime Minister Gladstone in a breakfast meeting with Wolseley had told him that the British government is 'bound to protect Tewfik'.[32] Wolseley was appointed Commander in Chief of all land forces in Egypt and was sent with an army of 24,000 men from Malta and Cyprus and a further

7,000 from India. The operation was originally to be a joint venture between France and Great Britain. France had been eager not to allow rebellion to foment across North Africa, especially since they had recently acquired Tunis. The French Chamber of Deputies refused the vote to the Freycinet administration and the ministry fell from power. The Ottoman Turkish government was also content to watch from the sidelines. It was apparent by July 1882 that Britain would be acting alone. It was imperative that the flow of shipping through the Suez Canal to Port Said not be disrupted. This was of vital interest to British trade, especially routes to India and China.[33]

Wolseley perceived this campaign as a logistical problem rather than tactical or strategic. The problem was the desert and supply of an army in the desert. The most important provision for men and animals was water. Horses require on average 8 gallons of water a day, and since transportation was vital this was an element that had to be well planned in the summer heat of the Sahara. Lieutenant General Wolseley was given the local rank of General and was given command of the full operation. As usual, he managed to bring many of the 'ring' with him: Wood was in command of an infantry brigade; Buller was in the intelligence department; Baker Russell commanded the 1st Cavalry Brigade; and Butler and Maurice received appointments on Wolseley's staff. These selections created a bit of a stir with the Duke of Cambridge and other detractors of Wolseley, but nevertheless he went forward with what he perceived to be the best men for the jobs.[34] Wolseley received two divisions of infantry and a brigade of cavalry with full transportation and, since animals would not be available in Egypt, he also asked for mules to be shipped from America and he wanted five steam locomotives to expedite all transportation of men, animals and supplies. He also put in a request for open rail stock to repair anticipated demolition by the enemy. The ready supply of water was paramount in an operation in the Sahara and Wolseley wanted to be prepared for every contingency.[35] Wolseley's concern for transportation is interestingly observed in his earlier diary entry of May 1882 when he was still back in the War Office.

> Discussed transport with Adye, Maurice and Reeve. Adye is unsafe on such points & very ignorant of practical war: he thinks because he has mules, carts & a collection of Levantine ruffians whom he calls drivers that he has an effective transport: he might as well imagine he had secured a painter, when he purchased a canvas & a paint box.[36]

The plan was to have separate forces to attack and secure the Suez Canal and Cairo. Wolseley had another Asante veteran, though one he did not entirely like, Major General Alison, command two battalions of infantry and a company of Naval Engineers from Cyprus. They were prepared to go forward within 24 hours of given notice, a sort of modern-day rapid deployment force. Wolseley planned to move forward on the Canal Zone and Ismailia and then to Tel-el-Kebir and then eventually to Cairo. Secrecy was maintained since there were many foreign correspondents and Egyptian spies and even the French designer of the Suez Canal was considered hostile to British plans. After Wolseley landed and took Alexandria on 21/22 August 1882, his first point of action was to take Tel-el-Mahuta, since there was a large force of infantry there and the dams there were making the water supply at the Sweetwater canal dangerously low. He left behind his main force to repair the railways and to secure logistical supplies from the ships to supply the main body of troops. Wolseley made a bold move to attack and take Tel-el-Mahuta with a small force. This was important to secure the water supply and to catch Arabi Pasha's men off guard. The move paid off and Wolseley was able to take Tel-el-Mahuta. After this action Wolseley meticulously brought up his dispersed forces. It was important that supply lines be maintained and secured before any forces moved forward. There was pressure in early September from the press and home government for Wolseley to move forward, but he needed to wait for supplies to be concentrated at Kassassin. They had to come up through rail and land transportation via Ismailia, Tel-el-Mahuta to Kassassin. This was essential for a successful campaign to be launched on Tel-el-Kebir. Wolseley had followed the age-old lesson of securing lines of supply before advancing tactically into battle. Since he was in the largest desert in the world this was very prudent.[37] Wolseley made his headquarters at Kassassin on 8 September 1882 and began a plan to take Tel-el-Kebir.

Since the advance to Tel-el-Kebir would be across open desert with no cover and the Egyptian forces were armed with modern breech-loading rifles (equal to the British rifles), Wolseley decided on a daring night march with a dawn attack on Tel-el-Kebir. The attack proceeded at 0450 on 13 September when his force was detected by Egyptian sentries, then Wolseley's whole force moved forward to attack and overwhelmed the Egyptian forces in a short time. The whole of Tel-el-Kebir and the railway station had been taken by 0700. This was a lightning attack that was dominated by artillery support and finally fell to a lot of hand-to-hand combat. Wolseley spoke highly of the fighting men in a telegram to Secretary of State for War, Hugh Childers, and his diary entry read, 'All rendezvous at 5 AM and heard first shot on Tel-el-Kebir by 6:45 and send off telegram to Childers at 7AM. Our loss not as heavy as I expected.'[38] He followed up with a gleaming telegram to Childers, 'I can say emphatically, that I never wish to have under my orders better Infantry Battalions than those which I am proud to have commanded at Tel-el-Kebir.'[39]

Wolseley, true to his word, achieved his objective from the beginning until the end of the Egyptian campaign in 1882. His job was simple, to maintain the flow of shipping through the Suez Canal to Port Said without major disruptions and to capture Cairo intact. The campaign needed to be planned quickly and efficiently, since the terrain provided many challenges, and Wolseley did not want this campaign to descend into a battle of attrition in which heat exhaustion and sickness would have taken there toll.[40] Wolseley finally went home on 21 October 1882 after all loose ends were tied up. A garrison of 12,000 British soldiers were

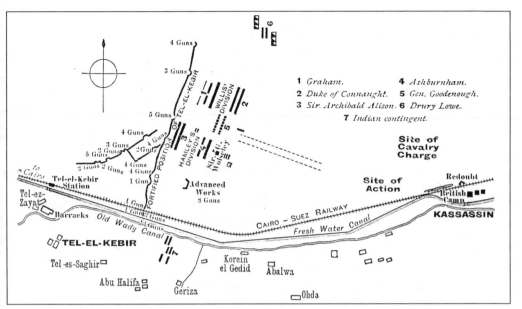

Plan of the battles of Tel-el-Kebir and Kassassin, 1882. (From Sir Evelyn Wood, *British Battles on Land and Sea*, London: Cassell & Co., 1915)

left behind under the command of Alison, who had come from Cyprus at the beginning of the campaign. Evelyn Wood, a prominent Wolseley 'ring' member became Sirdar of the Egypt army in December 1882. Wolseley was awarded his much-deserved peerage and attained the rank of full General for his duties in Egypt.[41]

The next question of debate was the Sudan issue (1884–85). Since Egypt controlled the southern province of Sudan, it seemed Egypt and Britain inherited the problems of the region. Since Britain had a considerable military presence in Egypt it seemed to exacerbate the problems in Sudan. There was a Muslim uprising led by Mohammed Ahmed, who was the self-proclaimed Mahdi or 'Chosen One', who was to regenerate the faith of Islam and to expel the infidels or convert them into the folds of Islam. The Egyptian government decided to evacuate the Sudan and hopefully contain the spread of Mahdist teachings north. The British government did not want to intervene militarily after the defeat of Colonel Hicks's forces at El Obeid by the Mahdist forces. It was then decided to send Charles Gordon to the Sudan to expedite the evacuation and ensure the loyalty of the tribes not swayed by the Mahdi. Though Wolseley was instrumental in getting Gordon to go to the Sudan, he was slightly untrusting of Gordon's methods but he did see much worth in the man as a military leader. He also felt that the convictions Gordon brought with him would be helpful in maintaining the loyalty of the populace in Khartoum and the Sudan. Gordon's mission had turned into a disaster and the government was begrudgingly forced to send a relief expedition to save Gordon in Khartoum. Wolseley was to be in command of this expedition. There were two factors that dominated this relief expedition and doomed it to ultimate failure: procrastination by Gladstone's government, which perceived Gordon as disobeying orders, and the flow of events in the Sudan. Wolseley pressed for an immediate relief expedition to be sent in the autumn and wanted to start making logistical plans for this expedition. The Cabinet delayed and did not make any decisions on this mission. It was not until 5 August 1884 that the government allowed a budget and made plans to send a relief expedition to Khartoum. Wolseley was put in command and dispatched to Egypt, arriving in Cairo on 9 September 1884.

There was a large effort made by Wolseley to move from Wadi Halfa, and build up men and supplies and there was also the much-famed battle of Abu Klea, but this was all in vain as on 4 February 1885 Wolseley read the news that Khartoum had fallen and Gordon was dead. The expedition's failure weighed heavily upon Wolseley's shoulders. He squared the blame on Gladstone and subsequently Gladstone's government fell in the aftermath of Gordon's death. The Gordon relief expedition was the real first failure in Wolseley's career as a commander in the field. It would prove to be his last field command. It seemed that Wolseley's career was in the doldrums but this was not the case, as outlined by his most recent biographer, Halik Kochanski,

> Wolseley returned from the Sudan chastened, but determined to devote his attention to turning the British army into a professional force capable of meeting and defeating any enemy, colonial or European, on the battlefield. The ingrained conservatism of the Duke of Cambridge meant that his efforts were frequently hampered, and in many areas he could do little more than prepare ground for the time when, he hoped, he would succeed the Duke and create his model of a modern British army.[42]

Wolseley was a stalwart if not personal commander and many have written on his abilities as a commander. Ian Hamilton said, 'Wolseley was the most impersonal commander I have ever met . . . a soldier of quality',[43] and the Queen's secretary Sir Henry Ponsonby wrote, 'he does not inspire any love among those who serve under him though I think they have confidence in him. He thoroughly believes in himself and this makes others believe in him. He is hard and very likely unfeeling but this is useful if unpleasant in a general.'[44] Wolseley was an intellectual general and perhaps a bit distant to the colloquial club atmosphere of the late Victorian army. He was certainly effective as a commander and successful as an army reformer. He seemed to inspire by example and duty rather than camaraderie.

Wolseley was a keen army reformer and put forth many schemes and ideas in the British army when he returned to the War Office in 1885 as Adjutant General. Wolseley believed that much of the training in the British army was for the benefit of show and parade ground, and that this was of little use in actual battlefield conditions. Wolseley was known for stating that a 'good battalion' is one that can shoot well under fire, efficient in outpost colonial duties, capable of night marches and studied in the tactical realities of modern battlefields. This in many ways flew in the face of the notion of army life during this period. The highly personal and fraternal nature of the late Victorian army could be the antithesis to the goals outlined by Wolseley. During his tenure in office as AG (1885–90) Wolseley wanted the British army to have the best possible rifle and he put forth the adoption of the Lee-Metford magazine rifle in 1888.[45] This was the precursor to the famous Lee-Enfield rifle, which would serve in two world wars. The Lee-Metford, although it did not use the more-advanced smokeless powder, produced a superior rate of fire and accuracy than the Martini-Henry and Martini-Enfield rifles. Wolseley influenced many upcoming field commanders in both 'rings' – his own as well as that of Roberts, such as Kitchener, Hamilton and Smith-Dorrien – on the importance of rifle firepower, musketry accuracy and covered-position field firing.

Wolseley was a deep and strong proponent of the machine-gun. He had employed both the Gardner and Nordenfeld guns on campaign in various situations with a variety of results. The failure of the Gardner gun at Abu Klea did not deter his enthusiasm for this new weapon system. When the Maxim machine-gun was introduced in 1887 it was Wolseley who became a strong proponent of this weapon. He had spoken on the Maxim at a United Service meeting,

> the machine gun [Maxim] will take the place of considerable bodies of men . . . I believe there is a very great future for [it], and that the general of that nation which knows how to develop or make use of it will in the future have a very great opportunity – an opportunity that has never been made use of by anyone before.[46]

As has been remarked, 'Garnet Wolseley, who would die one year before World War One began, was surely astounded by the British lack of interest in machine-guns.'[47]

Since the new Maxim machine-gun was not hand-crank operated like the previous machine-guns (Gatling, Gardner and Nordenfeld), it provided a much higher rate of fire with less likelihood of jamming since it was belt loaded. The tactical implication of this weapon on the burgeoning colonial battlefields was attracting much interest. Wolseley was also enthusiastic about the new weapon: 'the fire of this small arm, firing from a fixed carriage [or position] at ascertained ranges of 2000 up to 3000 yards and beyond will be most effective'.[48] Wolseley also pushed forward the establishment of a Promotion Board in 1890 for the promotion of officers. Two areas that Wolseley failed in were in the establishment of a new modern drill book and regular large-scale manoeuvres, which were prevalent in continental armies. This posed problems in the future since the commanders at Aldershot and Salisbury had little or no experience in handling troops in sizes above brigade levels. Corps and army level manoeuvres were not even considered and divisional manoeuvres were carried out with a very artificial level of organisation and not indicative of a modern battlefield. This of course would prove very detrimental in 1914.[49]

The Duke of Cambridge finally retired as Commander in Chief in 1895 but the post was first offered to Buller, who was not a boat-rocker and would not implement much or any reform in the army. This is what the outgoing Duke of Cambridge wanted. When the Liberal government that had nominated Buller resigned, however, the incoming Secretary of State for War, Lord Landsowne, put forth Wolseley's name for the position to the Queen. There was much debate between the Queen and the government but Victoria finally conceded Wolseley's appointment. It was feared by the Queen that Wolseley would make many changes and was 'full of fancies' and had a 'clique of his own'. Wolseley found that his position as Commander in Chief was a much-watered down version of what the position had been under Cambridge. This of course troubled Wolseley, who wanted to make some much-needed reforms and changes to the British army. Relations between Buller and Wolseley were quite soured, though this did not reflect any plotting against Wolseley. The new organisation of the Army Board and the various departments now reported directly to the Secretary of State for War. This in many ways circumvented the Commander in Chief's power to command. Wolseley did not like this at all and endeavoured at every chance to get the departments to report through him. Wolseley also did not allow the various heads to overrule his decision as was originally intended. Wolseley observed the Salisbury manoeuvres in 1898 and made some very poignant commentary on the officers and their errors. As outlined by Wolseley, they employed formations that exposed the men to artillery fire, open order was adopted too early in an engagement and the use of ground was poor. Furthermore the use of machine-guns was lacking since they were employed en masse rather than defensively. Machine-guns were employed like artillery rather than infantry support weapon systems. These shortcomings were proved to be eerie predictions of problems that surfaced a year later in South Africa during the Second Anglo-Boer War (1899–1902).[50] The men suffered greatly from these errors by regimental officers on the battlefields of Magersfontein and Colenso. Some of the men appointed to command positions in South Africa by Wolseley were dismal failures, such as Sir George White and even Buller did not perform that admirably as commander of forces in South Africa.

The organisation of the War Office was not up to the task of ultimately supporting a force so large with many ancillary and support units, which had been paper units only. Some of this blame can be shouldered by Wolseley but overall it is more of the 'system' that was in place in the late Victorian army that limited the capability of the army more so than any one individual. Wolseley was responsible for some much-needed reform and his influence cannot be denied in this area as a reformer and innovator in army organisation.[51]

Wolseley did lay the framework for the birth of a modern British army and some of his reforms did pay dividends in 1914. However, he was faced by many challenges, with the Duke of Cambridge being one of the greatest obstacles to his reform ideas. Wolseley's 'ring' was one of three rings (Roberts, Cambridge and

Wolseley) that existed and the rivalry between the rings could be ascribed to the personal nature of the late Victorian army. The Wolseley 'ring' did produce some talented and determined officers who were promoted more on merit than social status. This in many ways was a major legacy of Wolseley. One of his boldest achievements was the organisation of the British army into corps ready for general mobilisation. Wolseley was motivated by his driving ambition to make the late Victorian army more efficient in the waging of modern warfare. In the environment of low-intensity conflict, Wolseley can be seen as an influential impetus for the adoption of modern strategic, tactical and most importantly logistic structural changes in the British military system. Where Roberts, 'Bobs', was considered the most-loved and congenial general of this period, Wolseley can be considered the more distant 'father' of the modern British army.

Bibliography

Garnet Wolseley was a prolific author. He wrote a memorable two-volume biography, *The Life of John, 1st Duke of Marlborough 1650–1702* (1894), and also a shorter biographical sketch, *The Decline and Fall of Napoleon* (1895). His contribution to British army service manuals is evidenced by five editions of *The Soldiers Pocket-Book for Field Services* (1868–89), and he also wrote *The Field Pocket Book for the Auxiliary Services* (1873). Wolseley is also known for some of his personal observations on the American Civil War, some of which were published in magazine articles and have been reproduced in James A Rawley, ed., *The American Civil War: An English View by Field Marshal Viscount Wolseley* (Charlottesville: University Press of Virginia, 1964). His contributions on the Franco-Prussian War are also noteworthy with articles in the *United Service Magazine* such as 'Field Marshal Count von Moltke' (1891) and 'Franco-Prussian War of 1870–71' (1891). He also wrote his own two-volume autobiography, *The Story of a Soldier's Life* (London: Archibald Constable & Co., 1903), though this only takes his career up to the end of the Asante campaign. Wolseley's *Narrative of the War with China in 1860* (London, 1862) was heavily edited by his sister, Matilda. The most recent standard single-volume biography of Wolseley is Halik Kochanski, *Sir Garnet Wolseley: Victorian Hero* (London: Hambledon, 1999), and this represents the most up-to-date scholarship. There are earlier more popular accounts by Joseph Lehmann, *All Sir Garnet: A Life of Field Marshal Lord Wolseley* (London: Jonathan Cape, 1964); Leigh Maxwell, *The Ashanti Ring: Sir Garnet Wolseley's Campaigns 1870–1882* (London: Leo Cooper, 1985); and a chapter on Wolseley in Byron Farwell, *Eminent Victorian Soldiers: Seekers of Glory* (New York: Viking Press, 1985). A still earlier work is R J Kentish, *Maxims of the Late Field Marshal Wolseley* (1916). There are also the hagiographical works of Sir Frederick Maurice and Sir George Arthur, *The Life of Lord Wolseley* (London: Heinemann, 1924) and Charles Rathbone Low, *General Lord Wolseley (of Cairo): A Memoir* (London: Richard Bentley & Son, 1883), which was based on interviews with Wolseley. Sir George Arthur, ed., *The Letters of Lord and Lady Wolseley, 1870–1911* (London: Heinemann, 1922) chronicles the correspondence between Wolseley and his wife throughout his life but in an often heavily bowdlerised form. However, four of Wolseley's campaign journals have been published in full: Adrian Preston, ed., *Sir Garnet Wolseley's South African Diaries (Natal) 1875* (Cape Town: A A Balkema, 1971); Anne Cavendish, ed., *Cyprus, 1878: The Journal of Sir Garnet Wolseley* (Nicosia: Cyprus Popular Bank Cultural Centre, 1991); Adrian Preston, ed., *Sir Garnet Wolseley's South African Journal, 1879–80* (Cape Town: A A Balkema, 1973); Adrian Preston, ed., *In Relief of Gordon: Lord Wolseley's Campaign Journal of the Khartoum Relief Expedition, 1884–85* (London: Hutchinson, 1967). Wolseley's remaining journal of the Asante campaign is to be published by the Army Records Society in an edition by Ian Beckett in 2009. Wolseley's version of events is also presented in those official or semi-official histories produced by his own staff: G L Huyshe, *The Red River Expedition* (London, 1871); Henry Brackenbury, *The Ashanti War: A Narrative* (Edinburgh: William Blackwood & Sons, 1874); Frederick Maurice, *The Campaign of 1882 in Egypt* (London: HMSO, 1887); and H E Colvile, *History of the Sudan Campaign* (London: War Office Intelligence Division, 1889).

Notes

1. Field Marshal Viscount Wolseley, *The Story of a Soldier's Life* (London: Archibald Constable & Co., 1903), I, p. 135.
2. Halik Kochanski, *Sir Garnet Wolseley: Victorian Hero* (London: Hambledon Press, 1999), pp. 1–5.
3. Wolseley, *Story of a Soldier's Life*, I, p. 55.
4. Byron Farwell, *Eminent Victorian Soldiers: Seekers of Glory* (New York: Viking, 1985), pp. 194–96.
5. Charles Rathbone Low, *General Lord Wolseley (of Cairo): A Memoir* (London: Richard Bentley & Son, 1883), p. 25.
6. Ibid., pp. 27–28.
7. Kochanski, *Wolseley*, pp. 20–24.
8. Low, *General Lord Wolseley*, pp. 119–24.
9. Ibid., pp. 140–46.
10. The *arme blanche* was the doctrinal belief in using mounted cavalry as an offensive weapon. The impetus of the mounted charge was believed to overcome modern breech-loading rifles and machine-guns. It was a derivative of offensive doctrine of European military institutions of the period 1870–1914.
11. Henry Havelock and George Denison wrote extensively on the use of cavalry on the modern battlefield and were proponents of the use of mounted infantry, which was the antithesis to the *arme blanche* school of this time (1870–1914). Mounted infantry doctrine determined that horses were best relegated to transportation of soldiers to the battlefield and not as offensive weapons themselves: essentially a means of transportation to the battlefield. Dension's book, *Modern Cavalry*, appeared in 1896.
12. Jay Luvaas, *The Military Legacy of the Civil War: The European Inheritance* (University Press of Kansas, 1959), pp. 110–12.
13. For a more comprehensive study of the 'Wolseley Ring' see Leigh Maxwell, *The Ashanti Ring: Sir Garnet Wolseley's Campaigns, 1870–1882* (London: Leo Cooper, 1985) and Ian F W Beckett, 'Wolseley and the Ring', *Soldiers of the Queen*, 69 (1992), 14–25.
14. Brian Bond, *The Victorian Army and the Staff College 1854–1914* (London: Eyre Methuen, 1972), pp. 117–19.
15. Edward M. Spiers, *The Late Victorian Army, 1868–902* (Manchester: Manchester University Press, 1992), pp. 153–54.
16. Major General Sir Garnet Wolseley, 'England as a Military Power in 1854 and in 1878' and 'Long and Short Service,' *Nineteenth Century* 111 (March 1878), 433–56 and IX (March 1881), 558–72, cited from, Spiers, *Late Victorian Army*, p. 154.
17. Spiers, *Late Victorian Army*, p. 157.
18. Shelford Bidwell and Dominick Graham, *Fire-Power: British Army Weapons and Theories of War 1904–1945* (London: Allen & Unwin, 1982), pp. 7–10.
19. National Library of Scotland, Blackwood Mss, MS 4315 and 4403, Brackenbury to Blackwood, 27 November 1874 and 11 October 1880, cited from, Spiers, *Late Victorian Army*, p. 158.

20. Low, *General Lord Wolseley*, p. 239.

21. Wolseley Journal, 'Memorandum by Wolseley' (printed extract), August 1872, cited from Henry Brackenbury, *The Ashanti War: A Narrative* (Edinburgh: William Blackwood & Sons, 1874), pp. 117–23.

22. Kochanski, *Wolseley*, p. 64.

23. The National Archives (TNA), WO 33/26; WO 106/285; WO 147/27.

24. Maxwell, *Ashanti Ring*, p. 72.

25. Low, *General Lord Wolseley*, p. 317.

26. Kochanski, *Wolseley*, pp. 77–81; Maxwell, *Ashanti Ring*, pp. 91–95.

27. Kochanski, *Wolseley*, pp. 98–102.

28. Low, *General Lord Wolseley*, pp. 397–400.

29. Hove, Wolseley Mss, W/PP SSL8, Notes for autobiography, cited in Kochanski, *Wolseley*, p. 111.

30. Wolseley to Childers, August 1881, Childers Mss 5/37, cited in Kochanski, *Wolseley*, p. 119.

31. Alan R Skelley, *The Victorian Army at Home: The Recruitment and Terms and Condition of the British Regular, 1859–1899* (Montreal: McGill University Press, 1977), pp. 62–63.

32. South Lanarkshire Council Museum, Hamilton (hereafter SLCM), Wolseley Diaries, 27 July 1882.

33. Kochanski, *Wolseley*, p. 135; Maxwell, *Ashanti Ring*, p. 177.

34. Kochanski, *Wolseley*, p. 136.

35. Maxwell, *Ashanti Ring*, p. 179.

36. SLCM, Wolseley Diaries, 9 May 1882.

37. Kochanski, *Wolseley*, pp. 141–42.

38. SLCM, Wolseley Diaries, 13 September 1882.

39. Wolseley to Childers, 16 September 1882; PRO, WO 32/6096.

40. Maxwell, *Ashanti Ring*, pp. 229–30.

41. Kochanski, *Wolseley*, pp. 147–48.

42. Ibid., p. 178.

43. Ian Hamilton, *Listening for the Drums* (London: Faber & Faber, 1945), pp. 129–30 and 170.

44. Arthur P. Ponsonby, *Henry Ponsonby: Queen Victoria's Secretary* (London: Macmillan, 1943), pp. 222–24.

45. Kochanski, *Wolseley*, p. 191.

46. Anthony Smith, *Machine Gun: The Story of the Men and the Weapon That Changed the Face of War* (London: Piatkus, 2002), p. 153.

47. Ibid., p. 159.

48. Spiers, *Late Victorian Army*, p. 244.

49. Kochanski, *Wolseley*, p. 226.

50. Ibid., p. 228.

51. Ibid., p. 244.

Chapter 2

Evelyn Wood

Stephen Manning

T he year 1906 saw the publication of Evelyn Wood's hugely successful autobiography entitled *From Midshipman to Field Marshal*. The book's title immediately identified that, quite unusually, Wood had begun his military career in the Royal Navy, seeing active service in the Crimean War, before transferring to the army. Here Wood was to enjoy a long and illustrious career, which saw his involvement in many of the great colonial campaigns of Victoria's reign, before he reached the pinnacle of his profession as a Field Marshal.

Evelyn Wood was arguably one of Victoria's most successful field commanders, as well as one of her closest friends. He was mentioned in dispatches on twenty-five occasions. He became the holder of medals from the Crimea, India, Asante, South Africa and Egypt, as well as the Victoria Cross, the Legion of Honour, the Medjidieh and the Khedive's Star. He was a Knight of the Grand Cross of the Bath and a Knight of the Grand Cross of the Order of St Michael and St George. After Wolseley's victory against the Egyptian army in 1882, Wood was given the responsibility of reforming and training the former enemy along British lines. He became the second most senior soldier in the British army when he was appointed to the position of Adjutant General in 1897. Wood was a survivor; his longevity meant that he outlived Victoria, as well as such contemporaries as Wolseley and Buller. He also had a talent for personal survival and he was able to ensure that his reputation was to remain largely intact following the debacle of 'Black Week' during the Boer War, when many of his colleagues suffered criticism at the hands of the press. Wood even managed to maintain the belief that he was the most successful field commander during the Zulu War, despite suffering a serious defeat at Hlobane on 28 March 1879.

There is no doubt that Wood's personality and character were somewhat flawed. His vanity was well known and became something of a trademark. It was even rumoured that he wore his decorations on his pyjamas![1] Although this last tale was no doubt fanciful, there is evidence that he did place a small black border around each of his many ribbons so that the contrast would make them stand out more, or perhaps add to the length of the rows on his chest. On one particular occasion Wolseley could not resist chaffing Wood over the use of the black border

Chronology

9 February 1838	Henry Evelyn Wood born at Cressing, Essex
	Educated at Marlborough
15 April 1852	Appointed Midshipman in Royal Navy
1 January 1855	Appointed ADC to Naval Brigade, Crimea
18 June 1855	Severely wounded in assault on the Redan, Sebastopol
7 September 1855	Commissioned Cornet, 13th Light Dragoons
1 February 1856	Promoted Lieutenant
9 October 1857	Exchanged into 17th Lancers
1858–60	Service in India
1 November 1858	Appointed Brigade Major, Central India Flying Column
19 October 1858	Won VC at Sindwaha
16 April 1861	Purchased Captaincy
19 August 1862	Promoted Brevet Major
21 October 1862	Exchanged into 73rd Foot
1862–64	Attended Staff College
10 January 1865	Exchanged into 17th Foot
31 July 1866	Appointed Brigade Major, Aldershot
1867	Married the Hon. Paulina Southwell
22 June 1870	Purchased Substantive Majority
28 October 1871	Exchanged into 90th Foot
19 January 1873	Promoted Brevet Lieutenant Colonel
1873–74	Service on Gold Coast
1 April 1874	Promoted Brevet Colonel
10 September 1874	Appointed Superintending Officer of Garrison Instruction
23 March 1876	Appointed AQMG, Aldershot
1878–79	Service in South Africa
3 November 1878	Promoted Substantive Lieutenant Colonel
3 April 1879	Appointed Brigadier General, South Africa
15 December 1879	Appointed Brigadier General, Belfast
1881	Service in South Africa
12 August 1881	Promoted Major General
14 February 1882	Appointed GOC, Chatham
1882	Service in Egypt
21 December 1882	Appointed Sirdar of Egyptian Army
1 April 1886	Appointed GOC, Eastern District
1 January 1889	Appointed GOC, Aldershot
1 April 1890	Promoted Lieutenant General
9 October 1893	Appointed Quartermaster General
26 March 1895	Promoted General
1 October 1897	Appointed Adjutant General
1 October 1901	Appointed GOC, I Corps
8 April 1903	Promoted Field Marshal
2 December 1919	Died at Harlow, Essex

Appointed CB, 1874; GCMG, 1879; GCB, 1901

and he shouted, 'Hullo! Evelyn you seem to have got some more medals lately. Where did you get them? From the Mahdi [his forces were then besieging Khartoum]?'

Wood conveniently used his renowned deafness to pretend not to hear Wolseley's comment and the moment passed.[2]

Wood also possessed a love of money, which was no doubt encouraged by his wife, Paulina, the daughter of a Viscount, who had somewhat expensive tastes. His passion for fox-hunting and horses saw him incur the expense of his own stables and his constant need for money made Wood sometimes behave in a rather mercenary manner. This was certainly the case when he contested the will of his Aunt 'Ben' and schemed during the divorce proceedings surrounding his youngest sister, Kitty O'Shea. Yet all who served under him thought him kind, considerate and possessed of the ability to smile and make a joke even in the most demanding of circumstances. On his death, General Sir Ian Hamilton, who had served under Wood in South Africa, Egypt and at home, wrote 'Sir Evelyn's vitality was so intense, his spirit so dauntless and so bright . . . I have never known Evelyn give expression to a selfish, vindictive, or jealous thought. His heart was young, and it was his constant endeavour to give youth a chance.'[3] This last characteristic was clearly seen in Wood's skill and ability as a trainer of troops. This was given free rein when he commanded at Aldershot and in the Southern Command. He had a foresight that many in the upper echelons of the army of the late nineteenth century did not possess, and with this he recognised the flaws in the army.

It must not be forgotten that Wood was attempting to reform a system that was highly suspicious of change. This was particularly true during the leadership of the Commander in Chief, the Duke of Cambridge, with whom Wood and Wolseley often clashed. Wood's reforms and innovations began from a very low base of knowledge and experience within the army. For example, until Wood introduced the concept of night-time manoeuvres in the Eastern Command, based at Colchester, the British army had never considered such exercises important or worthwhile.[4] His legacy was much more than his evident bravery and his ability to inspire and organise; he allowed those who served under him to consider deeply their profession and this, perhaps, alone ensured that these officers, such as Kitchener, French and Smith-Dorrien, were later to shine in their army careers.

Henry Evelyn Wood was born in Cressing, Essex on 9 February 1838, the youngest son of John Wood, a vicar, and one of thirteen children, of whom only seven would survive to reach adulthood. It was his mother, Emma, who was the major early influence on his life and they remained extremely close. Indeed it was to be Emma's intervention that saved Evelyn from the barbaric care he received from Florence Nightingale's nurses during the Crimean War. During the Victorian period two of his sisters would also gain some fame, or notoriety. His eccentric sister Anna Steele achieved success as a novelist, while his youngest sister, Katharine, better known as Kitty O'Shea, became notorious for her affair with, and subsequent marriage to, the Irish Nationalist Leader, Charles Stewart Parnell. The divorce case that centred on their affair caused a sensation in Victorian Britain.

After an unhappy time at Marlborough, Wood managed to persuade his mother that his career lay in the Navy. Through the influence of his uncle, Captain Frederick Michell, Evelyn joined the crew of HMS *Queen* in July 1852, aged just 14 years. Within two years Wood had been promoted to the rank of midshipman and had already displayed a willingness to accept responsibility and take risks. He was to first experience the sounds of battle when his ship was assigned to a flotilla, which had been ordered to bombard the Russian port of Odessa as part of the opening salvoes of the Crimean War. HMS *Queen* was later to support the British and French landings at Kalamita Bay and, from the high rigging of the ship, Wood was able to watch as a spectator as the Allies and the Russians fought at the battle of the Alma.[5] The subsequent retreat of Russian forces into Sebastopol was to lead to the Allied siege of that city.

The need for heavy siege guns to bombard the Russian defences resulted in the formation of the Naval Brigade, under the command of Captain Peel, and, with his uncle's encouragement, Wood became part of the initial deployment of men and guns. This was to be the beginning of eight months of continuous service, during which Wood struggled to survive not only the Russian guns, but also the appalling weather and living conditions that the Allies suffered over the winter of 1854–55. During this time he was to receive his first of two recommendations for the Victoria Cross when, under constant Russian fire, he put out a blaze that was threatening his guns' ammunition magazine. After the failed Russian attempts to break the siege at the battle of Inkerman, both sides focussed their aggressive activities on exchanges of shells, in which Wood's batteries were heavily engaged. By June 1855, the Allies planned a massed combined assault upon the Russian Redan, but the attacks of 18 June were ill-timed and both the British and the French forces were beaten back. The Naval Brigade joined the assault and Wood was the only officer to reach the base of the enemy defences. However, he was seriously wounded in the assault. Although Wood was successful in managing to persuade the army doctors not to amputate his injured arm, he was forced to return to England to recover. The bravery that the 17-year-old Wood had shown gained him much recognition in the Crimea, and the Allied Commander, Lord Raglan, wrote him a glowing testimonial, and even provided his own carriage and physician to convey Wood back to HMS *Queen*.[6]

Despite the notoriety he had gained while serving in the Navy, it is clear that Wood did not see a future in this service. It seems that he considered that there was not much fame left for him to earn there and that he yearned for something more active than keeping harbour watch or any of the daily duties on board a warship. Having obtained his parents consent to join the army, Wood wrote to the Commander in Chief, asking for a commission in any light cavalry regiment, and enclosed a copy of Lord Raglan's letter. It only took one week for Wood to receive the news that he had been accepted as a cornet in the 13th Light Dragoons, and the speed of the decision, together with the fact that Evelyn was not obliged, as others were at that time, to purchase his commission, suggests that his fame, and the support given by Raglan's letter, had allowed him an easy transfer. This move, however, does seem to have cost Evelyn his VC, for despite the support given to him by Raglan and others, and the fact that his name was third on the list of recommendations, he was turned down for the award.[7]

Wood returned to the Crimea as a cavalry officer in January 1856. He was soon struck down with a combination of typhoid and pneumonia and was delivered to Scutari hospital, and into the hands of Florence Nightingale and her team. He seems to have been particularly unfortunate in that much of his care was left to a sadistic nurse, who would deliberately inflict pain on the ailing dragoon. Wood lost so much weight that the bones of both hips had pierced his skin. When changing his bandages, the nurse, rather than wetting them first, would tear off the lint roughly, ripping off skin and drawing blood. She would also slap and hit Wood when left alone with him. Of course, this did nothing to aid his recovery and on more than one occasion the doctors considered him close to death and informed Wood's parents of the seriousness of the situation. His parents travelled to the Crimea, where Wood's mother soon established that her son was being mistreated and, in a confrontational meeting with the doctors, and Nightingale, she insisted that she be allowed to take her son back home. Despite protestations from the hospital staff, and claims that Wood would not survive the journey, Lady Wood safely extracted her beloved son, who made a slow return to health in England.[8] Her actions almost certainly saved Wood's life.

Wood's recovery coincided with news of the Indian Mutiny and, desperate for active service, he negotiated a transfer to the 17th Lancers, and in October 1857 sailed for India. During the voyage, he busied himself by learning Hindustani and his endeavours were rewarded when he was given the position of company interpreter. Although Wood arrived after the last of the large set-piece battles of the Mutiny, he was actively involved in the pursuit of many of the prominent leaders of the mutineers, including Tatya Tope. Thus, as part of the Central India Force, Wood spent many months in the saddle, in extremely trying conditions of oppressive heat, in, mostly, futile attempts to corner the rebels. This is not to say that he was not involved in a number of skirmishes. In September 1858, at a place called Rajghur, a troop of cavalry, commanded by Wood, made contact with the rearguard of Tatya Tope's army, and Wood successfully led his troopers against the fleeing rebel artillery. This action forced the rebels to abandon many of their artillery pieces. The following month Wood, leading a reconnaissance patrol, first engaged the rebels at Sindwaha. This was to be the largest engagement Wood was to witness while in India and he would receive much praise for his action in the pursuit of the fleeing rebels after the battle. With only his orderly by his side, Wood charged a party of sepoys, who had turned to make a stand. In the resulting clash, Wood killed one of the rebels with his sword, and, following his example, he was then joined by the remainder of his command, who quickly dispatched and dispersed the remaining mutineers.[9]

A brief rest in the pursuit saw Wood trying to ride a giraffe! He was staying with the Prince of Jaora, who possessed a menagerie of animals in his palace grounds. One of Wood's fellow officers waged with him that he could not ride a giraffe, which was being led around by a string through its nostrils. Never one to turn down a challenge, Wood gamely jumped on the animal's back and initially had some success riding the beast, until it, unfortunately, bolted for its stable door. Wood decided that he should lower himself off the giraffe's back, but, in doing so, he was hit by the animal's knee, which knocked Wood underneath its hind legs, where the hooves mangled Wood's face and nose. He regained consciousness three days later, but was able to rejoin the pursuit of the rebels the following week.[10]

Although Wood and his comrades were unsuccessful in their attempts to corner Tatya Tope, who was later captured as a result of the treachery of one of his followers, Wood received much praise from his commanding officers for his conduct throughout the lengthy pursuit. General Michel wrote to the Commander in Chief of the British army that Wood had, 'highly distinguished himself',[11] while Brigadier General Somerset commented on Wood's 'unwearied zeal'.[12] Such praise allowed Wood to assume the position of Brigade Major of Beatson's Horse, an irregular cavalry unit of native troops, which was headquartered at Arangabad. Wood was later to complain that his new command showed all the imperfections of a unit raised in haste to meet the threat of the Mutiny. Most of the native officers were illiterate, the majority of the men were poor riders, and little time had been given over to drill to improve this situation. Wood set about transforming the unit, although his direct, energetic approach upset several of his native officers, who were used to an easier pace of army life. Indeed, the situation became so severe that Wood faced a mutiny and feared for his life. It was only with the arrival of reinforcements, from a nearby army base, that the potential for rebellion diminished and he was able to restore his authority.

Within a month of taking command, Wood had transformed the regiment and he could at least put several squadrons into the field. This was timely, for Wood received intelligence from the town of Sindwaha that a band of rebels, under Madhoo Singh, were in the vicinity and that they had kidnapped an influential landowner called Chemmun Singh, who had offered active support to the government in the suppression of the Mutiny. Wood knew he had to act quickly if the man's life was to be saved and, with the help of a former mutineer, he set out to find the rebels. Still wary of some of his men's loyalty, Wood elected to take with him only fifteen troopers, unaware that his command was to face a band in excess of eighty men.[13]

A slow, cautious approach brought Wood's party to the edge of the sleeping rebels and it was then that he realised he faced overwhelming odds. Retreat was briefly considered, but aware that the kidnapped victim would surely be hung, Wood instead ordered a surprise attack. As Wood charged, he realised that only two of his men had joined him, but in the noise and confusion, the rebels assumed that they were being attacked by a large force and fled, leaving their victim alive, tied to a tree. The remainder of the detachment, who had held back, made up for their lack of activity by shouting to the fleeing rebels 'Bring up the artillery, bring up the Cavalry', and Evelyn later admitted that this action was perhaps more effective in dispersing the rebels than any bayonet charge might have been.[14] The final act was when Wood was forced to knock out a private who became 'idiotic' at the sight of blood. News of the daring rescue was conveyed to the Viceroy of India, who did not hesitate to recommend Evelyn's actions to the Queen for the award of the VC.

Wood was to receive reports that he had indeed been awarded the VC in September 1860. By the time of this news, Wood was back in England, his promising career in India cut short. It appears that, in pursuing his orders to arrest rebels who were known to be sheltering in the palace of the Prince of Naringhgarh, Wood overstepped the mark and insulted the elderly Prince, and even threatened to arrest him. When news of this reached the local political agent, Wood was severely reprimanded and he felt compelled to offer his resignation and return to England.[15]

Wood was now destined for a considerable period of home service and in this time he was to find love and marriage, to the Hon. Paulina Southwell, as well as to continue his increasingly successful army career. He passed through the Staff College at Camberley, his natural ability at languages ensuring that he passed out in the top 10 per cent of candidates. An unhappy period in Ireland followed, during which time the wet climate there severely affected his health. He was to much enjoy his next posting to Aldershot, which was to become his second home. Here, Wood experienced his first role as a staff officer, when he served under General Horsford, and he gained a real appreciation of what was required to enhance the training of the British soldier, as well as the need to expand upon the number and quality of army manoeuvres. This experience was to cement his future thinking on army reform.

Wood's continuing health problems, combined with ongoing financial concerns, led him to consider his long-term future in the army. In his position as Brigade Major, Wood had acquired some interest and knowledge in military law, and this seems to have made him consider becoming a barrister. Thus, while serving at Aldershot, he studied to pass his entrance examinations to the Middle Temple. He, somehow, managed to balance his responsibilities at Aldershot with study in London and an ever-growing family. After years of study, in which Wood would rise at 0400 and study until 0730, he passed his final exams in 1874 and became a Barrister-at-Law in that year.[16] However, sudden army advancement, from the middle of the 1870s, ensured that he would never be obliged to earn his living at the Bar.

Wood's return to active service came as a result of a supposedly chance encounter with Wolseley, who was to command an expedition to Ashanti (Asante) in 1873. The Asante, led by the aggressive King Kofi Karikari, had invaded the British Protectorate on the Gold Coast of West Africa, and had the affront to attack, unsuccessfully, the British coastal fort at Elmina. The British government clearly felt that the Asante needed to be taught a lesson and, if Wolseley's force was unable to secure adequate peace terms and assurances, it was then tasked with travelling from the coastal region into the very heart of Asante to destroy the capital at Kumase. Wolseley was able to obtain the services of a number of promising officers including Buller, Brackenbury and Wood, and these men, and others, were to be become central figures in what became known as the 'Ashanti Ring'. Wolseley later showered his patronage on these like-minded officers and they served alongside him throughout his career.

With around thirty officers, a West India Regiment and the assistance of a number of marines, Wolseley planned his campaign. Wood was tasked with moulding a number of separate friendly tribes, which included the Hausas and the local Fante, into a fighting force, to be known as 'Wood's Irregulars'. Yet the material he was forced to work with was not promising. The Fante were later described as the 'most cowardly of mankind'[17] and Wood described one tribe, the Bonny, as very clever at basket work, but with no aptitude for war![18]

Wolseley's first action was to plan a raid along the coast, to attack those villages that had been supplying the Asante army. Wood was given command of this mixed force, although in a crucial moment during a fire-fight, Wolseley stepped in and started giving orders, much to Wood's annoyance. Although the raid had been a success, it demonstrated to Wolseley that he would not be able to rely on the fighting abilities of the friendly tribes and he was forced to request that two battalions be sent from England. To pacify a somewhat disgruntled Wood, Wolseley wrote to him to state, 'I have to congratulate you upon the very able manner in which you did everything yesterday. I am very much obliged to you. The operations were well carried out, and all your previous arrangements were admirable.'[19]

Activity now centred on preparing for the arrival of the British troops. 'Wood's Irregulars' were used to clear a path through the dense jungle, to the banks of the River Pra, the boundary of Asante proper, and here build a camp large enough to accommodate 5,000 men. While engaged in this activity, Wood's men had a number of encounters with Asante picquets and, much to Wood's fury, they again did not distinguish themselves. Indeed, on one occasion Wolseley was to write of their actions that: 'Their duplicity and cowardice surpasses all description.'[20] While at the Pra River camp, Wood received a delegation of officials from the Asante King, who had come to seek peace terms. During the time it took for Wood to receive Wolseley's response to the terms, he showed the Asante the latest British weapon, the Gatling Gun. This demonstration so overwhelmed the chiefs that one of the party committed suicide. Wolseley was furious that Wood had behaved so childishly and he severely reprimanded his second in command.[21] Although this was the first campaign in which the British had the ability to use this new weapon of mass destruction, the Gatling Gun proved too unreliable for battlefield operations. It was be five years, during the Zulu War, before the Gatling was to overcome the initial technical problems. Here the weapon caused high numbers of casualties, particularly at the battle of Ulundi, and it was to serve effectively in many of the colonial campaigns of the later Victorian period.

With the British troops in place by the end of January 1874, Wolseley marched in force across the River Pra. The main Asante army was met in battle at Amoaful on 31 January and, in a hard-fought, 12-hour long engagement, a British victory was only secured by the use of an artillery piece, firing case shot at point-blank range into the Asante warriors. Wood was prominent throughout the battle, as he tried to encourage his reluctant force forward, in what Brackenbury was later to describe as a 'rare example of bravery and fortitude to his men'.[22] It was thus not surprising that Wood was finally shot, in the chest just above his heart, by a rusty nail fired from one of the Asante antique firearms. He was forced to withdraw from the battlefield and the location of the wound meant that the doctors were unable to extract all of the nail. When it became clear that his life was not in danger, all that Evelyn was prescribed was rest and Brand's essence of beef and brandy.[23]

When Wolseley was informed of Wood's injury, he joked that he expected to see Wood back leading the advance within a week, and indeed this was the case. Wood managed, somehow, to persuade his doctor that he was fit to return to service and Wolseley gave him the honour of leading his Irregulars against the Asante army, which had massed to make a last stand before Kumase, at Ordasu. Again, Wood was to experience frustration, as his men would simply not advance against the firepower of the Asante, and he was forced to retire, while British regulars achieved battlefield success against their formidable enemy. Wolseley was able to enter Kumase on 4 February, and the following day the capital was burnt to the ground. Although the King was never captured, peace terms were agreed and the expedition was considered a great success. Wolseley was to earn much praise, and his officers, including Wood, received much reflected glory. Wood had, perhaps, been unfortunate in that he had been given an impossible task, that of trying to turn the local tribes into an effective fighting force. However, the expedition gave him much valuable experience of handling troops in the field.

Back in England, Wood was promoted to full Colonel of the 90th and he again returned to Aldershot. Here he was able to continue to introduce new ideas in field exercises and manoeuvres and he began to acquire a reputation as a reformist and innovator. In 1877 he was offered the position of Commandant at the Royal Military College, Sandhurst, although he declined this, in the hope of active service.[24] His patience was finally rewarded when he received the news that he was to accompany General Thesiger, later Lord Chelmsford, to South Africa to quell a rising of the Gaika tribes, which was to become known as the Ninth Frontier War. The conflict was centred on the Amatola Mountains and the Perie Bush, outside of King William's Town in the Eastern Cape. Although of only a short duration, the conflict was particularly bitter and exhausting. The British played a 'cat and mouse' game with the rebels, who used the cover of the bush superbly and frustrated the British repeatedly. It took four months for Thesiger and Wood to perfect their tactics for such warfare and achieve the capture and surrender of the rebel tribes. Wood had, once more, gained useful experience of handling friendly natives, as well as an understanding of how to deal with colonial troops, which would be of much use in the future conflict with the Zulus. Thesiger was later to report to the War Office that 'I cannot speak too highly of the good service rendered by this officer [Wood]. He has exercised his command with marked ability and great tact. I am of opinion that his indefatigable exertions and personal influence have been mainly instrumental in bringing the war to a speedy close.'[25]

The two men now journeyed to Natal, where both planned the likely invasion of Zululand. Wood was heavily involved in the logistics of acquiring suitable and sufficient wagons to transport stores for three British columns as they advanced on the Zulu capital of Ulundi. After his success at Khambula in March 1879, Wood maintained his independent command and his Number 4 Column was renamed 'Wood's Flying Column', and was at the vanguard of the advance on Ulundi during the Second Invasion. Wolseley, who replaced Chelmsford after Ulundi, firmly believed that if it was not for Wood's drive and determination, Chelmsford would never have had the energy to advance on the Zulu capital. Throughout the final battle, Evelyn stayed by the side of Lord Chelmsford, as both mounted men exposed themselves to Zulu fire. Archibald Forbes, the special correspondent of the *Daily News*, was to write of Wood at Ulundi, 'Evelyn Wood's face was radiant with the rapture of the fray as he rode up and down behind his regiment exposed to a storm of missiles.'[26]

To express his thanks to Wood, Wolseley issued the following order: 'Sir Garnet Wolseley desires to place on record his high appreciation of the services they [Wood and Buller] have rendered during the war. . . . The success which has attended the operations of the Flying Column is largely due to General Wood's genius for war, to the admirable system he has established in his command, and to the zeal and energy with which his ably conceived plans have been carried out.'[27] Privately, Wolseley informed Evelyn that, 'you and Buller have been the bright spots in this miserable war, and all through I have felt proud that I numbered you among my friends and companions in arms'.[28]

Wood was to return to England as a 'conquering hero', with his reputation enhanced. Queen Victoria was very keen to meet the Empire's latest saviour, and Wood was invited to Balmoral. Here he clearly impressed the Queen, who wrote in her journal that, 'Sir Evelyn is wonderfully lively and hardly ceases talking, which no doubt comes from his deafness and inability to hear any general conversation. He is clever and amusing, and all he says is very interesting.'[29] The monarch also wrote to Disraeli, now Lord Beaconsfield, that she had found Wood a remarkable man and an admirable general with, 'plenty of dash as well as prudence', and a man of 'Imperial views, loyal and devoted to Sovereign and country'.[30] A real friendship developed between Wood and Victoria, which was to last to her death.

The Boers of the Transvaal region of South Africa had been recently annexed into the Confederation of South Africa. There was real discontent among the Boers over British rule and this was to spill over into open warfare in 1880. The Boers achieved three crushing victories against the British, commanded by Sir George

Colley. Gladstone's government decided to send reinforcements to bolster Colley, and Wood was chosen to accompany the troops. On his departure, Wood wrote to his doctor and physician, Norman Moore, and he displayed a complete ignorance of the difficulties he was to face when he stated, 'I scarcely expect to see a fight this time and anticipate the rebellion will collapse as soon as the British reinforcements arrive, if not sooner.'[31] His political naivety was to cost Wood dear.

On his arrival, Wood wasted no time in bringing up a column of reinforcements to support Colley and both men set about planning the next British action against the Boers, who had taken position on Laing's Nek, which transversed the border of Transvaal and Natal. Wood returned to Pietermaritzburg to encourage the remaining reinforcements forward, and he received a promise from Colley that no further military action would be taken until his return.[32] It appears that Colley wished for one last engagement to try to regain his battered reputation and he also believed that the Boers might soon accept British peace overtures, while still in possession of Natal territory. Colley seems to have considered that peace on such terms would have been disreputable and he thus wanted to clear the Boers from Laing's Nek before peace could be agreed. To this end, on the night of 26/27 February 1881, Colley led a force of 300 troops to occupy the extinct volcano of Majuba, which looked down upon the Boers at Laing's Nek. Once in place, Colley thought the British occupation of Majuba would make the Boer position untenable and force their retreat. Colley underestimated the resilience of the Boers, and their determination to throw the British off Majuba. The small British force was insufficient to hold the position against a determined attack. The Boers routed the British and in the resulting confusion Colley was killed.[33]

On hearing of the defeat, Wood immediately had himself sworn in as Acting Governor of Natal and Administrator of the Transvaal, and rode to Laing's Nek in an attempt to restore order and moral. While it is clear that Wood's first concern was for his troops, particularly those besieged in their Transvaal garrisons, he also began planning a fresh action against the Boers. He felt that he needed to buy some time to allow for the arrival of reinforcements and decided to again enter into negotiations with the Boers, with the apparent aim of reaching a settlement. On 5 March, the day before he met Joubert in peace talks, Evelyn telegraphed the Foreign Secretary, Lord Kimberley, and stated: 'My constant endeavour shall be to carry out the spirit of your orders but considering the disasters we have sustained I think the happiest result will be that after a successful action which I hope to fight in about 14 days, the Boers should disperse without any guarantees, and the many now undoubtedly coerced will readily settle down.'[34] Evelyn also confirmed to the Queen that his intention had been to fight before entering into peace negotiations.[35]

Wood, by agreeing to a truce, had entered the world of politics, and any freedom to negotiate with the Boers he might have possessed was taken out of his hands by the British government. He was even compelled to become one of the Special Commissioners tasked with agreeing peace terms with the Boers.

Although Wood was to express privately to the government his dissatisfaction at his position, he felt that he could not resign and carried out the government's instructions as to the peace negotiations. Many found his actions inexplicable, and one of his sternest critics was the Queen herself. She wrote, 'Oh! Why have you [Wood] made peace after them [the 3 British defeats] and a peace giving up the Transvaal? It is so unlike Sir E. Wood's character that the Queen looks for some explanation to what (she is bound to tell him) has produced a very painful impression here and we hear at the Cape too. To give up the Transvaal when the Government maintained they would retain it is very humiliating. The Queen has such faith in Sir E. Wood that she trusts he can explain that this is not so – but she feels anxious and unhappy about it all.'[36] Wood was stunned by this criticism and responded by stating, 'Sir Evelyn Wood is unfortunate in being the instrument of a policy which is condemned as he anticipated it would be by a great majority of the educated classes in England. He is unfortunate in that his proceedings have made his Sovereign anxious and unhappy but he would consider himself as still more unfortunate if the Queen should cease to trust him.'[37]

Although, after a series of exchanges, Wood was able to explain his actions to the Queen, and regained her trust to the extent that she asked him to name his latest daughter after her, he had little success in pacifying certain sections of the army. Officers in South Africa openly denounced the 'abject surrender', and even one of Wood's own colonels offered his resignation, so disgusted was he by the peace agreement. Even Wolseley bitterly claimed that, if Colley had had 10,000 men at his command, as Evelyn had, he would never have made such a peace, and he furiously declared that by signing the peace treaty Wood 'has injured our national renown most seriously abroad'.[38] Wolseley could not bring himself to forgive Wood for not driving the Boers out of Natal before agreeing a settlement, and his patronage lessened for a number of years, and as a consequence Wood's career suffered.

Wood was next to see active service in Egypt. Wolseley was given command of a British expedition that was designed to defeat the Egyptian forces commanded by Arabi Pasha, who had led a populist nationalist uprising against the government of Khedive Tewfik. It appears that, following his decision to agree peace terms with the Boers, Wood was a reluctant choice for a command on this expeditionary force, and he was thus forced to seek the support of the Queen to secure a position.[39] Despite this patronage, Wolseley appointed Wood to the rather unsatisfactory role of commander of the British forces guarding the lines of communication around Alexandria. Wood's force also acted in a diversionary manner, while Wolseley led the main British assault on the Egyptian entrenched position of Tel-el-Kebir. To add to Wood's dissatisfaction, Wolseley took with him Major General Gerald Graham, who was junior to Wood. Graham would later see action at the battles of Magfar, Kassassin and Tel-el-Kebir, which must have further angered the ambitious Wood and he wrote to Victoria to express to her how 'aggrieved' he was that he had been overlooked and that Graham had been favoured.[40]

With Wolseley's victory at Tel-el-Kebir, the war was effectively won, and Wood returned to England to resume his command at Chatham. Within a few months he was back in Egypt, following an approach from Lord Granville to accept the position of head, or Sirdar, of the re-commissioned Egyptian army. Granville played upon Wood's vanity and Wood accepted this new role, although he was to later tell Victoria that he had reluctantly taken the post.[41] The backbone of the training of the new 6,000-strong army fell upon 25 specially selected officers, who were recommended to Wood by the War Office. Wood was blessed with the quality of men he received; thirteen would later rise to the rank of at least Major General in the British army, and many, such as Lord Kitchener, Smith-Dorrien and Sir Archibald Hunter, would become the more enlightened leaders of men in future conflicts.

Wood and his officers made astonishing progress with the Egyptian troops and Wood was later to express his delight at their achievements to the Queen. He candidly stated, 'The soldiers marched past in a manner which astonished Everyone but none perhaps more than Sir Evelyn himself!'[42] Despite his delight, Wood was well aware of his men's limitations. In an openly frank letter to the Duke of Cambridge, in December 1883, Wood stated; 'these four battalions are as good as Egyptians can be made in ten months and I think will stand up well until their English officers are knocked down, when they would become sheep. I regard the other four battalions as practically useless for Field work.'[43]

It was thus no surprise to Wood that his Egyptian force was not sent to clear rebels from the Red Sea coast area around Suakin, but that British regulars, under Graham, were chosen. However, when the British government finally agreed to send a force to relieve Gordon in Khartoum, Wolseley was happy to use 2,000 of Wood's Egyptian army as porters along the lines of communication, with Wood as commander of this force. The futile attempts to rescue Gordon placed extreme stress upon all those involved, but perhaps no more so than Wolseley and his immediate subordinates. Wolseley's feelings towards Wood, in particular, became more virulent and he stated in his journal that,

> Wood's vanity and self seeking and belittlement of everyone but himself would be positively disgusting if one did not view it from the ridiculous side, and laugh at it and him instead of being angry over it. When I look back and remember my estimate of Wood's character as it was presented to me ten years ago . . . I begin to think I can be no judge of character, for Wood's cunning completely took me in. . . . All this ridiculous Egyptian Army has been worked by him for purposes of self-glorification.[44]

There is no doubt that Wood's Egyptian forces made a positive contribution to the efforts to reach Khartoum and although Wood did make mistakes as Director of Lines of Communication, for example, in his decision to purchase cheap, inferior camels, his usual drive carried the force forward and success was almost achieved. His last task, after resigning his position as Sirdar and resuming his rank in the

British forces, was to supervise the withdrawal of troops, from their advanced position at Gakdul back to Korti. This ten-day march, although superbly controlled and handled by Wood, was extremely testing, and Wood's health suffered to such an extent that on his return Wolseley ordered him to travel back to England to seek rest and medical treatment.[45]

This was to be Wood's last period of foreign service and, for the rest of his career, he was based in England, where he was at the forefront of army reform. Despite Wolseley's loathing of Wood's personality, he did recognise that Wood had an inherent ability as a trainer of men and the zeal of a reformer, and Wolseley thus secured for Wood a number of appointments in which he could demonstrate his skills. The first one of these was as commander of the Eastern District, based at Colchester, but Wood was also to gain command of Aldershot, the army's main training base, and here he at last had the open space to expand fully his ideas on field training. From 1891, Wood held regular manoeuvres, and he was the first to introduce large-scale manoeuvres, in which all branches of the armed forces were actively engaged. In his official report to the War Office on the lessons learnt from the various exercises, Evelyn clearly outlined that the services had demonstrated a clear lack of understanding of each other and how each unit worked and interacted. Continued exercises soon demonstrated to Evelyn how important it was to educate all men with an understanding of all branches, and he was, for example, keen to teach infantry and cavalry officers the importance of effective artillery fire on the battlefield. On his departure from Aldershot, *The Times* stated that Wood:

> struck a blow – a mortal blow, we may be allowed to hope – at that system of interminable parades, which disgusted the soldier, filled up his time and squandered his energies. In compensation, field-training, which is, after all, the best substitute and preparation we can give the soldiers for his ultimate business of fighting the enemy, has been invested with actuality, and brought to a pitch of excellence hitherto unknown in the British Army in time of peace. . . . Sir Evelyn Wood will be remembered as the originator of the cavalry manoeuvres. What is still more important, he has taught the three arms to work together as they have never worked before. . . . To sum up, the intelligence and interest of all ranks have been spurred, and troops quartered at Aldershot are far in advance of others in field training. Aldershot has become what it ought to be, the exemplar to which all other camps of exercise look for light and leading. Sir Evelyn Wood has breathed into it a new spirit. It would not be too much to say that he has founded a new system.[46]

Wood later rose to the rank of Quartermaster General and finally Adjutant General, the second most senior position in the army. Both were secured with the patronage of Wolseley, although the Queen had to take some persuading to support Wood's candidature for the position of Adjutant General, as she felt that he was a better commander than administrator.[47] Wood was greatly aided in his new role as Adjutant General by the passing of the Manoeuvres Act of 1898, which he had earlier advocated. This Act allowed greater access to land for exercises, which had always been a hindrance to Wood's plans for large-scale manoeuvres. His plans were further enhanced when the government purchased 41,000 acres of Salisbury Plain. Here the army was able to assemble two army corps for field manoeuvres. In the months before the mobilisation of forces for South Africa, Wood ensured that this land was utilised for both cavalry and artillery exercises. He was also able to develop and expand the School of Musketry at Hythe, in Kent, and Wood was able to persuade Ian Hamilton to be its new commandant. Both men worked well together and much credit should be given to them for the foresight that resulted in improvements in musketry skills in the British army, which would reap dividends on the fields of France in 1914.[48]

With the outbreak of war with the Boers in 1899, Wood was responsible for the mobilisation of British forces and for their dispatch to South Africa. The efficient manner in which this took place received much praise.[49] However, Wood was, to a lesser extent than many of his contemporaries such as Wolseley and Buller, criticised for the performance of the British army in its first engagements. Although he managed to avoid most of the criticism directed at the War Office at this time, any ambitions he may have had of active service were dashed. Furthermore, Wolseley bluntly informed Wood that, 'This Ministry will never employ you in South Africa with the remembrance of the Laing's Nek Treaty [1881 Peace Treaty].'[50] There is no doubt that, by signing this treaty, Wood's active field career was ruined.

Wood's last task for his friend and patron, Queen Victoria, was to co-ordinate the plans for her funeral. The Queen passed away on 22 January 1901 and, as Adjutant General, Wood worked alongside the Lord Chamberlain and Viscount Esher to ensure that the funeral of 2 February went well. Wood, displaying the same level of military precision he had displayed at army manoeuvres, came away from the day with credit for all his hard work. He had been one of Victoria's generals and a friend for over twenty years. He would continue to serve his country until his death in 1919. After the Boer War he commanded the Southern District where, with the encouragement of the Commander in Chief, Lord Roberts, Wood furthered his plans for army reform. It was left to the Queen's son, Edward, to appoint Wood to the rank of Field Marshal in 1903 and he retired from the army the following year. In his retirement he still served the cause of the army; he argued strongly for national conscription and, when this was not forthcoming, supported Haldane's attempts to raise a Territorial Force. During the First World War he served in an informal capacity and Wood was always ready to make a speech or present a medal if he felt he could benefit the war effort. He outlived all his senior contemporaries and lived to have the satisfaction of seeing British arms victorious against their German foe. On his death, *The Times* concluded its obituary by stating that Evelyn was a 'magnificent if not very great man, who lived a magnificent life and did his country service such as it has been given to few to do'.[51] A plaque was erected in St Paul's Cathedral, the words of which epitomised Wood's service to his Queen and Empire. It states 'INTREPID IN ACTION, UNTIRING IN DUTY FOR QUEEN AND COUNTRY.'

Hlobane and Khambula, 1879

Following the crushing Zulu victory at the battle of Isandlwana on 22 January 1879, the commander of British troops, Lord Chelmsford, was forced to withdraw his remaining forces back across the Thukela River, the physical boundary into Zululand. From his base in Natal, Chelmsford awaited reinforcements and planned the next stage of the campaign, which was centred on relieving the British troops, under Colonel Charles Pearson, who were besieged by the Zulus in the town of Eshowe. At the start of the campaign Colonel Evelyn Wood had been given independent command of Number 4 Column, which comprised approximately 1,500 men of the 1/13th Foot and Wood's own Regiment, the 90th. He also had a number of native and colonial troops, who were given the names of Wood's Irregulars and the Frontier Light Horse (FLH), with the latter under the command of Redvers Buller. With news of Isandlwana, Wood realised that any further advance into Zululand was now impractical and he decided to consolidate his forces in a strong defensive position on the slopes of the Khambula Hill.

Over the next few weeks, Wood did not remain idle, and the war now entered a much more brutal phase in which Wood's men focussed on the need to destroy the Zulus' homes and economy, in an effort to wear down their resistance. Wood ordered Buller to conduct a number of harrying raids and reconnaissances towards the Hlobane mountain. This activity led the Zulus to fortify further their sanctuary on this mountain by the construction of stone walls, and their vast herds of cattle were moved to graze on the plateau of the mountain. Also, Prince Mbilini, the local Zulu commander, who loyally supported the Zulu King, Cetshwayo, led a series of retaliatory, marauding parties into the neighbourhood of Luneberg and the next weeks were characterised by a series of brutal raids and exchanges between Wood's forces and the Zulus.

Wood soon earned the fear and respect of the Zulus. Indeed he learnt that they named him Lakuni, which was the native word for the particularly hard wood that was used to make the Zulu's smashing weapon, the knobkerrie.[52] Chelmsford was delighted by Wood's aggressive approach, as well as his coup in enticing a local chief, Prince Hamu, Cetshwayo's eldest brother, to come over to the British with all his followers. Chelmsford showed his appreciation by appointing Wood as Brigadier General and, when he planned his rescue of Pearson's men from Eshowe, he turned to Wood for assistance. Chelmsford requested that Wood use his forces to mount a diversionary attack so as to relieve some of the pressure from the British advance on Eshowe.[53]

The obvious target for Wood was the Zulu mountain stronghold of Hlobane, from which local Zulus had been staging their raids, yet Evelyn had no idea of the number of Zulus on the summit, or of the terrain. His desire to assist Chelmsford seems to have blinded him as to the difficulties of attempting such an operation without proper intelligence. Furthermore, his Zulu spies had already informed him that the main Zulu army had been directed to attack his command. Although correct that Evelyn was to face the main Zulu assault, his spies incorrectly reported that the army had left Ulundi on 27 March and would not be in the vicinity of Hlobane until 30 March at the earliest. In fact the Zulu army had left on 24 March and would reach the mountain on the same morning as Wood's men were attacking it, on 28 March.[54]

Wood devised a two-pronged assault on Hlobane, with mounted troops under the command of Buller and Cecil Russell. This plan soon met with difficulty as the terrain did not facilitate the easy passage of horses. Indeed Russell's men were unable even to reach the summit. To compound these difficulties, Wood had no idea that the main Zulu army was rapidly approaching his position. While at Khambula, Wood always insisted that mounted scouts were placed at least 6 miles out from the camp to learn of any impending Zulu attack, yet on the morning of 28 March he took no such precautions, despite the fact that he was aware that the Zulu army was on the move. This must be considered a serious failing on Wood's part.

When colonial forces, under the command of Colonel Weatherley, sighted the approaching Zulu impi of 20,000 men and reported the fact to Wood, he would not believe them, so sure was he of his own intelligence sources. One of Hamu's scouts finally convinced Wood that the Zulu impi was on a collision course with his escort party and he immediately dispatched a staff officer to Russell with the following order: 'There is a large army coming this way from the South. Get into position on the Zunguin [Zungwini] Nek.'[55] It was apparently Evelyn's intention that Russell's force assume a defensive position on the neck of land between the lower plateau of Hlobane and the Zungwini Mountain and from where he would be able to support Buller's retreat.

Russell had seen the approaching Zulu army, and his men had already withdrawn off the mountain to the position where Wood had intended them to be. However, when giving his order, Wood had confused the place names; he had actually wanted Russell to move to the Zunguin range, where he was now located, not the Zungwini Nek, which was to be found 6 miles to the north-west. Russell decided to accept Evelyn's instruction without question and moved his force to where it could be of no conceivable help to Buller and his men, whose retreat was soon to become a rout.[56]

Wood made no further contribution to the defeat at Hlobane. In his official report, written two days later, he stated that he and his escort had assumed a position on Zunguin Nek – that being his incorrect version of the nek's location. However, it is now considered that he occupied an elevated position at the south-eastern end of the range, about 2½ miles from the bottom of the plateau. From here he could view the dramatic life-and-death struggles of Buller and his men as they tried to make their escape down the slopes of Hlobane, via what was to become known as the 'Devil's Pass'. Wood claimed that he remained in his position until 1900 hours, when he then returned to Khambula.[57]

Hlobane was a disaster for Wood: 15 officers were dead and a further 80 men out of a total European force of 404 were killed. Further losses included well over 100 Hamu warriors and Wood's Irregulars. However, the fight had delayed the main Zulu army from their attack on Khambula, and Evelyn had thus been given vital time to prepare his defences for the imminent attack. Khambula allowed Wood the opportunity to redeem his failures at Hlobane, as well as conveniently to hide the true scale of the defeat.

The overwhelming threat from the 20,000-strong Zulu army to the entrenched position at Khambula certainly inspired Wood. The Zulus had spent the night just 10 miles from Khambula and in the morning they marched steadily, in five separate columns, towards the camp. Around midday, the Zulu commander, Chief Mnyamana, reminded his warriors of the King's instruction not to attack the British behind their entrenched position, but to seize the camp cattle, which, it was hoped, would lure the soldiers away from their defences. The attack began at around 1300, with the Zulu army in its customary 'horns of the buffalo' formation. The simple plan was for the right and left horns of the army to surround the camp and join forces to raid the cattle kraal. However, the left horn was stalled by the need to cross swampy ground and Wood made a brave and inspired tactical decision to provoke the right horn into an attack before the left horn could join them.

Wood ordered Buller, and 100 of his mounted men, to ride out from the protection of the camp to within 100yd of the right horn and pour volley fire into the mass of warriors, before retreating back to the safety of their laager. This action had the desired result, and the right horn lost its discipline and charged forward into a killing ground of rifle and artillery fire. Evelyn had earlier positioned range-markers, so this British fire was particularly effective.

The survivors of the right horn were in retreat before the left horn could muster its attack. Eventually the left horn managed to mass within 100yd of the cattle laager and Zulu snipers, using British rifles captured at Isandlwana, began to pour a persistent, if somewhat inaccurate, fire into the camp, which forced the British to seek cover. It was at this crucial moment that Private Banks of the 90th saw Evelyn among his men and he described Wood's actions,

> I do not think there are many like him in the army. He is as cool and collected in action as if he were in a drawing room. Walking down from the fort to the laager under a heavy fire, swinging a stick and whistling, then going past the wagons he has a pleasant look and a smile of encouragement for every one he meets, let him be private or officer, it matters not. The men here I am sure would follow him anywhere, they are so fond of him.[58]

Plan of the battle of Khambula, 1879. (From Sir Evelyn Wood, *British Battles on Land and Sea*, London: Cassell & Co., 1915)

Wood experienced several near misses as he exposed himself to enemy fire, 'I . . . lost all sense of danger, except momentarily, when, as on five occasions, a plank of the hoarding on which I leant was struck. This jarred my head.'[59] Wood ordered his young infantrymen to fire volley after volley into the warriors. His men responded and this attack was blunted.

Zulu riflemen now sought cover behind anthills, in ravines and in any 'dead' ground that would provide some degree of safety from the British fire. From their cover, the Zulus fired back into the laager. Under intensive fire, Evelyn was forced to withdraw a company of the 13th, and this encouraged a large body of warriors, who had sought refuge in a nearby ravine, to make the 100yd dash to occupy the laager. The remaining British troopers in the cattle kraal were forced to depart hastily and Wood rushed forward to try to save one British infantryman who had fallen in front of the advancing Zulus. He had to be physically restrained by three of his officers, including Lieutenant Lysons, who told his commanding officer, 'Really it isn't your place to pick up single men!'[60] The soldier was saved, although one of the rescuing officers was severally wounded during the sortie. This was the crucial moment of danger for the British during the battle and Wood could see that he could not let the Zulus maintain a hold on the cattle laager. Within a few moments, the number of Zulus there could have swelled to thousands, and it was only a 50yd rush to the main British redoubt.

Evelyn selected two companies of the 90th to charge the Zulus in the laager at bayonet point. In bitter fighting, the British drove the Zulus back to the ravine. Wood now became actively engaged in supporting his men. One Zulu chief, holding a red flag, was standing at the top of the ravine trying to encourage his warriors forward. Wood borrowed a rifle from a nearby trooper and, with his second shot, he hit the Zulu chief who fell back into the ravine. On three further occasions a Zulu warrior picked up the red flag and waved it in defiance and encouragement, only to be shot by Evelyn.[61] Despite this success, the Zulus continued their sniping from the ravine and soon casualties began to mount. Evelyn, realising their position was untenable, ordered the withdrawal of the 90th.

Wood knew that the Zulu snipers must be silenced and he directed his artillery to pour shells into the ravine. This action nullified the enemy riflemen at a vital moment in the battle, as the warriors of the head and centre of the Zulu attack had massed for a direct attack on the main laager. Without the hindrance of sniper fire, Wood was able to repeat the tactic of the bayonet charge, so as to break the Zulu advance before it had a chance to gain momentum. A company of the 13th was sent out to engage the enemy, only to be beaten back by the rushing warriors. However, this retreat brought the now-disorganised Zulus under the British artillery guns and, loaded with case shot, they carved swathes through the warriors, who fled back down the hill. The battle had been raging for nearly 4 hours and still the Zulus had strength and reserve for two more charges, both of which were stopped by rapid and accurate infantry fire.[62]

The day's slaughter was not yet over. At around 1730, the Zulu army seemed, individually, to decide to retreat and Evelyn used this opportunity to unleash his mounted troops under the revengeful command of Buller. This act ensured the retreat became a bloody rout. Buller's men gave no quarter as they pursued the

Zulus for over an hour, until darkness ended the mayhem. Over 800 dead Zulus were found within 800yd of the camp. However, the pursuit is estimated to have cost a further 1,500 lives. British casualties, killed and wounded, numbered 83.

Edited copies of Wood's official report of the events surrounding Khambula were to appear in the newspapers of Britain from around 17 April. Evelyn's report, as published in major and many provincial newspapers, read,

> DESPATCH FROM COLONEL WOOD. Kambula Camp. March 29th 9.00pm. We assaulted the Kholobana [Hlobane] successfully yesterday and took some thousands of cattle but while on top about 20,000 Zulus coming from Ulundi attacked us, and we suffered considerable losses, the enemy retaking the captured cattle. Our natives deserted. Our camp was attacked today from 1.30pm to 5.30pm in the most courageous manner by about 20,000 men. We have lost about seven officers and seventy killed and wounded, but we have entirely defeated the enemy who were pursued for a considerable distance.[63]

What Wood did not make clear in this initial report was that the casualty figures referred only to those that occurred at the battle of Hlobane. This ambiguity in the report continued in the press reporting of the events surrounding the two battles. For example, both *The Times* and the *Daily News* of 17 April listed Captain Ronald Campbell, Mr Lloyd and Piet Uys as among seven officers and seventy men killed at Khambula, although both men had been slain at Hlobane. Such losses could be accepted if they were linked with a crushing victory. Although the confusion as to casualty figures was finally resolved in May 1879, by then Wood was viewed as the hero of Khambula and his military reputation was assured.

It is clear that both Wood and Buller pursued a policy of 'total war' against the Zulus, in which Zulu civilians and property were targeted, and it is certain than many Zulus were killed in their flight from Khambula. Whether Wood could have stopped, or would have wanted to stop, this slaughter is open to doubt. Certainly, by today's standards, the actions taken by many of his men, including Wood's Irregulars, would be considered as war crimes, for which, if such events occurred today, he would be held ultimately responsible. On the field of battle Evelyn was a determined and clear-sighted professional soldier of his age, sure of what needed to be done to overwhelm and defeat the enemy. It is certain that he would have viewed the slaughter of fleeing Zulus as a necessary measure that would bring about the defeat of the enemy and the end of the war. There exists no concrete evidence that Evelyn knew of, or actively encouraged, the slaughter of wounded Zulus.

Bibliography

Stephen Manning, *Evelyn Wood VC: Pillar of Empire* (Barnsley: Pen & Sword, 2007) is the first modern re-assessment of Wood. Previously, the principal sources for Wood were his own autobiographical writings: Field Marshal Sir Evelyn Wood, *From Midshipman to Field Marshal*,

2 vols (London: Methuen & Co., 1906) and *Winnowed Memories* (London: Cassell & Co., 1918). He was also the subject of a chapter in Byron Farwell, *Eminent Victorian Soldiers* (London: Viking, 1985). Controversial aspects of his role in the Zulu War are covered in Ron Lock, *Blood on the Painted Mountain* (London: Greenhill, 1995) and in the Anglo-Transvaal War by Joseph Lehmann, *The First Boer War* (London: Jonathan Cape, 1972) and John Laband, *The Transvaal Rebellion – The First Boer War 1880–81* (London: Pearson/Longman, 2005).

Notes

1. Joseph Lehmann, *The First Boer War* (London: Jonathan Cape, 1972), p. 226.
2. J Paine, 'From Midshipman to Field-Marshal – The Centenary of Sir Evelyn Wood, V.C.', *The Cavalry Journal* Vol. XXVIII (1938), 231.
3. The *Daily Telegraph*, 3 December 1919.
4. Byron Farwell, *Eminent Victorian Soldiers* (London: Viking, 1985), p. 258.
5. Private Collection, Sir Norman Moore Mss, Case Box 18, 17 February 1895, p. 159.
6. Killie Campbell Africana Library (hereafter KCL), Wood Mss, KCM 89/9/16/8 (a) & (b), Michell to Raglan, 20 June 1855, and Raglan to Michell, 21 June 1855.
7. KCL, Wood Mss, KCM 89/9/16/25, Lushington to Wood, 28 February 1857.
8. E Bradhurst, *A Century of Letters 1820–1920: Letters from Literary Friends to Lady Wood and Mrs A C Steele* (London: Thomas & Newman, 1929), p. 77.
9. Evelyn Wood, *The Revolt in Hindustan 1857–59* (London: Methuen, 1908), p. 331.
10. Farwell, *Eminent Victorian Soldiers*, p. 245.
11. KCL, Wood Mss, KCM 89/9/17/3 (a), Michel to Chief of Staff, India, 14 April 1859.
12. Ibid., KCM 89/9/17/4, Somerset to Asst. Adjt General, 14 April 1859.
13. Evelyn Wood, *From Midshipman to Field Marshal* (London: Methuen & Co., 1906), I, p. 177.
14. Ibid., pp. 179–80.
15. KCL, Wood Mss, KCM 89/9/18/9, Wood to Mayne, 6 August 1860.
16. Wood, *Midshipman to Field Marshal*, I, p. 239.
17. Leigh Maxwell, *The Ashanti Ring – Sir Garnet Wolseley's Campaigns 1870–1882* (London: Leo Cooper, 1985), p. 38.
18. Wood, *Midshipman to Field Marshal*, I, p. 261.
19. C Williams, *The Life of Lieut-General Sir Henry Evelyn Wood* (London: Sampson Low & Marston, 1892) p. 55.
20. Wood, *Midshipman to Field Marshal*, I, p. 265.
21. Ibid., p. 273.
22. Henry Brackenbury, *The Ashanti War of 1873–4* (London: Frank Cass, New Impression, 1968), I, p. 181.
23. Wood, *Midshipman to Field Marshal*, I, p. 276.
24. Williams, *Life of Wood*, p. 64.
25. Ibid., p. 70.
26. Ibid, p. 107.
27. Ibid, p. 105.
28. Wood, *Midshipman to Field Marshal*, II, p. 82.
29. Royal Archives (hereafter RA), VIC/QVJ/1879, The Queen to Beaconsfield, 9 September 1879.
30. Farwell, *Eminent Victorian Soldiers*, p. 257.
31. Private Collection, Wood to Moore, 18 January 1881.
32. Melton Prior, *Campaigns of War Correspondents* (London: Edward Arnold, 1912), p. 128.
33. For a detailed explanation of the reason for the assault and the defeat at Majuba see John

Laband, *The Transvaal Rebellion – The First Boer War 1880–81* (London: Longman, 2005).
34. William Perkins Library, Duke University, Wood Mss, DUK III/6/3, Wood to Kimberley, 5 March 1881.
35. RA, VIC/QVJ/1881, Wood to the Queen, 3 May 1881.
36. RA, VIC/MAIN/039/207, Queen Victoria to Wood, 31 March 1881.
37. RA, VIC/MAIN/040/144, Wood to the Queen, 4 May 1881.
38. Halik Kochanski, *Sir Garnet Wolseley: Victorian Hero* (London: Hambledon Press, 1999), p. 111.
39. RA, VIC/QVJ/1882, Wood to the Queen, 4 July 1882.
40. RA, VIC/MAIN/018/24, Bigge to the Queen, 6 November 1882.
41. KCL, Wood Mss, KCM 89/9/38/9, Granville to Wood, 28 November 1882.
42. RA, VIC/MAIN/Z 209/3, Wood to the Queen, 1 April 1883.
43. RA, Cambridge Mss, VIC/MAIN/ADDE/1/10573, Wood to Cambridge, 18 December 1883.
44. Adrian Preston, ed., *In Relief of Gordon – Lord Wolseley's Campaign Journal of the Khartoum Relief Expedition 1884–1885* (London: Hutchinson, 1967), pp. 31–32.
45. Wood, *Midshipman to Field Marshal*, II, p. 177.
46. *The Times*, 7 October 1893.
47. RA, VIC/MAIN/E64/54, Davidson to the Queen, 7 April 1897.
48. John Lee, *A Soldier's Life – General Sir Ian Hamilton 1853–1947* (London: Macmillan, 2000), p. 44.
49. H O Arnold-Forster, *The War Office, The Army and The Empire* (London: Cassell, 1900), p. 40.
50. Evelyn Wood, *Winnowed Memories* (London: Cassell, 1918), p. 292.
51. *The Times*, 3 December 1919.
52. Paine, 'Midshipman to Field Marshal', 232.
53. Saul David, *Zulu* (London: Viking, 2004), p. 250.
54. Ibid., p. 251.
55. Ibid., p. 261.
56. Ron Lock, *Blood on the Painted Mountain* (London: Greenhill, 1995), p. 178.
57. Wood, *Midshipman to Field Marshal*, II, p. 53.
58. Frank Emery, *The Red Soldier: The Zulu War of 1879* (London: Hodder & Stoughton, 1977), p. 179.
59. Wood, *Midshipman to Field Marshal*, II, p. 53.
60. Maxwell, *Ashanti Ring*, p. 118.
61. Wood, *Midshipman to Field Marshal*, II, p .62.
62. Lock, *Blood on the Painted Mountain*, p. 197.
63. *The Times* and *Daily News*, 17 April 1879.

Chapter 3

Redvers Buller

Stephen M Miller

During a heated discussion on biblical military leadership at an evening dinner party, William Ewart Gladstone, the towering Liberal leader of the late nineteenth century, was reported to have exclaimed, 'Joshua! Joshua! Why, he couldn't hold a candle to Redvers Buller as a leader of men.'[1] And yet, Sir Redvers Buller, distinguished winner of the Victoria Cross, key figure in the 'Wolseley Ring', veteran of campaigns in China, Canada, the Gold Coast, South Africa, Egypt and the Sudan, Adjutant General, and one-time choice for Commander in Chief of the British army, would be forced to resign in great ignominy after his failure in the South African War (1899–1902) and his utterance of a few unwise comments at a Volunteer luncheon in 1901.

The second son of James Wentworth Buller, a distinguished Member of Parliament and wealthy landowner, and his wife Charlotte, Redvers Buller was born at the family seat of Downes, Crediton, on 7 December 1839. After graduating from Eton, he chose not to follow his father into politics but instead opted for a career in the military, something most Bullers had traditionally shunned. In May 1858, James Buller purchased for his son a commission in the 60th (King's Own Rifles) Regiment. In 1859, Ensign Buller joined the 2nd Battalion of his regiment for a brief stint in Benares where the Indian Mutiny was winding down. The following year he joined an Anglo-French expeditionary force sent to Hong Kong and took part in the actions at Taku (Peiho) Forts and Peking (Beijing). Some have described the young Buller during this period as an unlikable figure, known to argue with his fellow officers, whose speech and appearance were altered for the worse by an unfortunate run-in with a horse in China.[2] All agree, whether they liked him or not, that Buller, even as a young man, was full of conviction. After returning to England, he refused to wear his China medal because he viewed the campaign as unjust.

It was in Canada, where he had been posted as a lieutenant in the 4th Battalion, that the young Buller was transformed into a talented officer under the aegis of his commanding officer, Colonel R B Hawley. Hawley was a great believer in cultivating the qualities of junior officers; delegating responsibility, emphasising the importance of staff duties, making each take charge of the training and leading

Chronology

7 December 1839	Redvers Henry Buller born at Downes, Crediton, Devon
	Educated at Harrow and Eton
23 May 1858	Purchased commission as Ensign, 60th Rifles
1859–60	Service in India and China
9 December 1862	Purchased Lieutenancy
1862–70	Service in Canada including Red River Expedition (1870)
28 May 1870	Purchased Captaincy
1871–73	Attended Staff College without completing course
1873–74	Service on Gold Coast
1873	Appointed DAAQMG, Gold Coast
1 April 1874	Promoted Brevet Major
1 April 1874	Appointed DAAG, Horse Guards
30 January 1878	Appointed Special Service Officer, South Africa
22 April 1878	Took command of Frontier Light Horse
11 November 1878	Promoted Brevet Lieutenant Colonel
28 March 1879	Won VC at Hlobane
27 September 1879	Promoted Brevet Colonel
13 March 1880	Promoted Substantive Major
29 March 1880	Appointed Local Major General, South Africa
April 1880	Appointed AAQMG, Scotland
July 1880	Appointed AAQMG, Aldershot
10 August 1882	Married Lady Audrey Jane Charlotte Howard
1 September 1882	Appointed DAQMG, Intelligence Department, Egypt
22 July 1883	Appointed AAG, Horse Guards
1884	Service at Suakin as Chief of Staff
21 May 1884	Promoted Major General
26 August 1884	Appointed Chief of Staff, Gordon Relief Expedition
1 November 1885	Appointed DAG, Horse Guards
16 August 1886	Appointed Special Commissioner for Clare and Kerry, Ireland
15 October 1887	Appointed Quartermaster General
1 October 1890	Appointed Adjutant General
1 April 1891	Promoted Lieutenant General
24 June 1896	Promoted General
9 October 1898	Appointed GOC, Aldershot
9 October 1899	Formally appointed C in C, South Africa
14 October 1899	Sailed for South Africa
25 November 1899	Assumed personal command in Natal
18 December 1899	Superseded as C in C by Roberts
24 October 1900	Departed South Africa after requesting he be relieved
January 1901	Resumed as GOC, Aldershot
21 October 1901	Dismissed from Aldershot Command
2 June 1908	Died at Downes

Appointed CB, 1874; CMG, 1879; KCMG, 1882; KCB, 1885; GCB, 1894; GCMG, 1900

of his own men. It was also Hawley who gave Buller a great appreciation for the need to maintain the welfare of the rank and file. Buller thrived in this environment for seven years and Hawley's impact was lasting. To the end of his service, Buller continued Hawley's practices of always treating the men with respect and providing them with adequate food, shelter and rest. As a result, even in the most difficult times, Buller always retained the warm feelings of his troops. A young (later Lieutenant General) William Francis Butler, whose career for nearly forty years paralleled Buller's own, described Buller as 'the best type of regimental officer possible to be found. Young, active, daring, as keen for service as he was ready to take the fullest advantage of it, he stood even then in the front rank of those young and ardent spirits who might be described as the ruck of army life which is waiting to get through.'[3]

In 1870, Buller returned briefly to Canada to rejoin his regiment for what would be his last service with it. The 1st Battalion, 60th Regiment, along with militia raised in Quebec and Ontario, was assigned the daunting task of traversing some of North America's most difficult terrain to restore authority over Fort Garry, the former chief outpost of the Hudson Bay Company in Prince Rupert's Land, which had just been transferred over to the Canadian government. By rail, steamer, canoe and foot, the Red River Expedition would cover some 1,200 miles. Captain Buller quickly caught the eyes of his commander, Colonel Garnet Wolseley, who described him as 'full of resource, and personally fearless, those serving under him always trusted him fully'.[4] When the campaign was over, Wolseley put Buller in for a promotion. Although nothing came of it, Buller had won himself a powerful supporter.

Shortly after his return to England, Buller entered the Staff College. He opted out early, however, to tour the Franco-Prussian War battlefields and never returned to take his exams. While busy on the continent, trouble brewed in West Africa. The Ashanti (Asante) King had rejected the Dutch transfer of the fort at Elmina on the Gold Coast (Ghana) to British control. An Asante advance toward Cape Coast Castle led to a general panic among the Fante Confederation and a flood of refugees. Commander John Glover, RN, a former administrator in West Africa, proposed a counter-march on the Asante capital of Kumase and requested Buller's services. The British government accepted Glover's recommendations in part but supplemented his plan with an army operation commanded by Wolseley. Buller was appointed Deputy Assistant Quartermaster General and arrived at Cape Coast Castle in October 1873. During the Second Asante War 1873–74, he was primarily responsible for intelligence and 'from the beginning, show[ed] a skill and judgement worthy of a trained detective'.[5] He enlisted interpreters, met with local traders, examined prisoners and organised a corps of scouts. He also assisted Wolseley in choosing the path of advance into the interior. It was in this campaign that Buller honed his logistical skills and became a full member of Wolseley's 'Ring'.[6]

After convalescing from a fever that sent him home early from the expedition, Buller was promoted to major and took a position as Deputy Assistant Adjutant General at the War Office.[7] There he remained until 1878. In that year, Lieutenant General Frederic Thesiger, later Lord Chelmsford, was dispatched to the Cape

Colony as Commander in Chief, and took Buller with him. Buller participated in the Ninth Frontier War against the Ngqika-Gcaleka as a staff officer and also commanded the Frontier Light Horse, an amalgamation of locally recruited Britons, Boers and others. The Frontier Light Horse was his first independent command. Upon the conclusion of the war, Buller did not return to the Cape with his men but instead was ordered up country where trouble was brewing with the Mpondo. It was against the Zulu, however, that recently promoted Lieutenant Colonel Buller would next command his men in battle.

By late 1878, Sir Bartle Frere, the British High Commissioner in South Africa, had come to the conclusion that the Zulu needed to be eliminated as an independent people capable of threatening British influence in the region. Border violations provided Frere with the ammunition he needed, and despite resistance from London, he issued an ultimatum in December to Cetshwayo, the Zulu chief. Unable to meet the demands that would have disbanded the Zulu army and seriously curtailed his authority over his people, Cetshwayo had no choice but to allow the ultimatum to lapse and accept the inevitability of war. The Anglo–Zulu War began in January 1879.

Even before the start of the conflict, Buller and the Frontier Light Horse, as part of the more than 2,200-man column commanded by Brigadier General Evelyn Wood, had crossed the Ncome River and moved into north-west Zululand. Buller had developed a close relationship with Wood in the Asante campaign and the two would remain on good terms throughout their careers. Buller's primary responsibilities were patrolling and leading the irregular horse in reconnaissance operations. While Chelmsford's centre column was being surprised at Isandlwana, Wood's column operated without major obstacles through most of January. With Buller's able assistance, Wood was able to advance on the White Mfolozi gathering livestock, clearing the area and inducing lesser Zulu chiefs to surrender. Buller led the mounted forces in a number of successful skirmishes during this movement. After Isandlwana, however, Wood cautiously took his forces back across the Mfolozi River.

With the ruin of the centre column and the inability of another column to move forward from Eshowe, Wood provided the only offensive operations for the British in early February. Chelmsford relied on Wood and Buller to turn the war around. 'You two will have to pull me out of the mire,' he optimistically heliographed to Wood.[8] And, indeed, they did. Throughout February and into mid–March, Wood continued to press the Zulu by authorising Buller to conduct several successful punitive raids around Hlobane. Seizing cattle hurt Cetshwayo's ability to conduct operations and weakened his people's resolve, which led to a number of defections. Buller assisted in the movement and protection of these growing refugees.

In late March, Wood decided to strike at Hlobane, a site where the Qulusi chief had taken up a defensive position. If he could not directly engage the Qulusi, he would still satisfy himself by taking the hundreds of cattle grazing on Hlobane's two plateaux. Buller and Lieutenant Colonel J C Russell were put in charge of the two advancing parties. On 28 March, at 0330, under the cover of a thick mist, Buller began his ascent of the eastern slope of the mountain, while Russell, shortly afterwards, moved on the western slope.[9] The terrain, sheer cliffs, crevices and a narrow winding foot path, was difficult to traverse to say the least, but to make things worse for the British, it also allowed for as many as 3,000 Zulu to keep their positions well hidden.[10] Buller was able to reach the summit and, after a brief attack led by Piet Uys and Captain Robert Barton, the Zulu fled. Most of Buller's men immediately began gathering cattle on the higher plateau, while Barton was ordered to take a few men down the hill and bury the dead. Russell, likewise, was able to make it up the western slope, although with greater difficulty, and he too gave orders to seize the Zulu cattle. Neither Buller nor Russell had realised that they had walked into a trap.

Although the Zulu on the summit had been surprised by the timing of the British advance, they had expected that an eventual attack would come and had prepared for it. The terrain atop Hlobane provided perfect cover for them. Increasing pressure was put on Buller's party as the morning went on. To make matters worse, Cetshwayo had also prepared for a British attack and had ordered an army from Ulundi (oNdini) to move against Wood's column. He had expected to meet Wood at Khambula. Some of Wood's irregulars had seen Zulu campfires the night before but had not alerted their officers.[11] That army had now caught up with the British having been redirected to Hlobane. Wood spotted the advancing Zulu in force, perhaps as many as 20,000 strong, moving in from the south and sent runners up the mountain to warn Buller and Russell.[12] Buller and Russell did not need to read Wood's message. They both spotted the approaching Zulu and ordered their men to descend the mountain. The Qulusi had also seen the Zulu and more came out of their hiding places to engage the British, sometimes coming within a hundred yards.[13] Russell was ordered to position his men to cover Buller's retreat. He misinterpreted those orders, however, and moved westward toward Zungwini Nek.[14] Buller would eventually reach the same position but not until after coming close to utter disaster. He had gathered most of his men together and had retreated across the long plateau. As difficult as the ascent had been, the descent was much worse. The narrow cattle track that he and his men followed often had jumps downward of 5ft at a time. Barton, with his burial party, was ordered to retreat down the right side of the mountain.[15] He and most of his men were killed.

Buller was one of the last to come down Hlobane. Piet Uys was with him, but returned to the mountain when he learned his son had yet to make it. Uys was killed. Buller also returned at least twice and was credited for personally saving the lives of four of his men, acts of supreme bravery that earned him the VC. Wood learned of the details of the rescues only with great difficulty because Buller refused to discuss them.[16] The British retreat was only salvaged by the Zulu decision to regain their cattle and rest rather than pursue them. In all, 15 British officers and about 80 men were killed, in addition to as many as 100 auxiliaries.

As the bulk of the British force escaped to Khambula, Buller was put in charge of the evacuation of the wounded. Even after that was accomplished, he still could not rest. At 2100, he learned that there were still some soldiers trying to find their way to the camp. He and some volunteers from the Frontier Light Horse rode out at once to meet them and brought in the last survivors from Hlobane. It may be true, as Waller Ashe and E V Wyatt-Edgell wrote in their 1880 account of the Anglo-Zulu War, that Buller 'did all that a skilled general could effect to bring off his men with small loss', and, as Wood's report details, that because of Buller's 'grand courage and cool head that nearly all the dismounted men were saved'.[17] Yet, if it were not for the events of the next day Buller's actions would only be remembered as one bright spot in a dismal battle and Wood and Buller's decision to attack Hlobane would have met with serious scrutiny at the top levels.

Wood had anticipated that the Zulu would move on Khambula and had ordered his 2,000 men and 6 guns inside the camp's perimeter. With a fort already situated on the high ground, Wood took decisive defensive measures: a laager was thrown up and reinforced with bags of mealies, an earthwork redoubt was hastily built, the cattle were secured, ammunition boxes were distributed and opened and range-markers were placed all around the approaches to the camp. In his report on the battle of Khambula on 29 March, Buller wrote 'as we were sadly musing over the events of the day before, our scouts came in to say that the Zulu army we had left in the valley below were on the move, and about 10 they came in sight, moving in five very heavy columns. We at once commenced preparations for defence'.[18] For his part, Buller was happy to encourage the attack, riding out to meet the Zulu as they arrived, pulling them towards the British defences, and then retreating to the safety of the laager. Buller wrote,

> They stood our advance a little, but they could not stand our attack as I pressed home, and the advance of their right column, about 2000 strong, turned and charged us. I need not say that the eighty or ninety men I had got on their horses pretty quick, and we scampered back to camp . . . Our attack succeeded. It was evident it upset their plans.[19]

Khambula is a battle that should never have taken place; Cetshwayo had given clear directions to his commander, Chief Mnyamana, to avoid it. Why the Chief defied his King is not known for sure, but as John Laband has argued, it probably occurred as a result of the competition among young Zulu warriors who eagerly sought glory on the battlefield. They probably forced their general into making the change in plans.[20] Buller was also right in stating that his tactic had upset the Zulu plans. A traditional Zulu formation on the battlefield took the shape of a bull's horns. The bulk of the attacking warriors would walk in tight formation, several ranks deep. Once they came into contact with the enemy, smaller groups of men on both sides would extend around and gradually close in. At Khambula, Buller provoked the right horn into attacking prematurely. As it chased him back to camp across open ground, it was hit by overwhelming British firepower without any cover to seek. Within 45 minutes, before the Zulu centre and left horn could be brought into the fight, the right horn was annihilated.

Despite this setback, Zulu morale remained high and the remaining troops moved on the British right and centre. This attack was better co-ordinated and sustained. Armed with many Martini-Henrys, the Zulu unleashed a devastating firepower of their own. Although it required two sorties, the British managed to repulse the left horn's attack on their cattle laager and kept the Zulu centre from reaching their trenches. Canister fire was particularly effective against the densely packed advancing Zulu. Wave after wave of assaults was checked and after more than three hours, this attack ended in defeat as well.

As the sun was setting, Wood sensed victory and prepared Buller and his mounted troops for pursuit. What followed next was a massacre. Buller was 'like a tiger drunk with blood', wrote the commander of the Kaffrarian Rifles, F X Schermbrucker.[21] Commandant Cecil D'Arcy, Frontier Light Horse, one of the men Buller had saved at Hlobane, reputedly yelled to his men, 'No quarter, boys, and remember yesterday!'[22] The retreating Zulu were in no condition to offer any organised resistance. Many were too tired even to raise their rifles. Although a few prisoners were taken, true to D'Arcy's exclamation, most of the Zulu did not receive quarter. The pursuit continued all the way back to Hlobane. Nearly 800 bodies were found the next day, but perhaps as many as 2,000 Zulu were killed in the onslaught. The British lost just eighteen men and suffered sixty-five additional casualties at the battle of Khambula.

For the next two-and-a-half months, Wood's column remained in and around Khambula. Wood's success in late March, thanks in part to Buller's role, allowed Chelmsford to renew his offensive. However, it was not until mid-June that the reconstituted column began its advance toward the Zulu capital of Ulundi. During this period of relative inactivity, Buller's responsibilities included overseeing daily patrols, seizing Zulu cattle and keeping the Zulu occupied. He was also assigned, for a time, the task of keeping a celebrity visitor out of harm's way. Louis Napoleon, the Prince Imperial, had made his way to South Africa in a British uniform thanks to his family's connections. Chelmsford did what he could to keep him out of any real danger. Buller allowed the Prince Imperial to accompany him on several patrols. However, during one such reconnaissance mission with the Frontier Light Horse, he found him to be too reckless and refused to take responsibility for his safety again.[23] A few days later, on 1 June, while on patrol with Lieutenant J B Carey, the Prince Imperial was killed by the Zulu. Buller and Wood were riding ahead of the column when they were approached and told the news by Carey. Buller was furious with Carey and accused him of abandoning the Prince Imperial. Carey was later court-martialled and found guilty, but, thanks to the intervention of Empress Eugénie and Queen Victoria, the sentence was never ratified.

With his impending supercession by Wolseley, Chelmsford was determined to move quickly and finish the campaign. Upon receiving no reply from his 30 June ultimatum, he put Buller in charge of reconnaissance and ordered him to advance as far as he could toward Ulundi, selecting the best ground from which to attack, and determining the location and size of the Zulu force. Not only did Buller gather all the information requested but he wisely avoided a Zulu trap. Chelmsford later called Buller's operations, 'one of the finest episodes in this eventful war'.[24]

Confident from the day's activity and aware of the Zulu force, its position and the likely strategy that it would employ, Chelmsford ordered an attack the next morning, 3 July, at 0645. Buller's mounted troops would be the first to cross the White Mfolozi before holding up to take their place near the front of the forming square. As at Khambula, Buller provoked the Zulu to come within firing range by engaging them in two ranks and retiring alternately. Once his force had returned to the safety of the square, Chelmsford left it to the infantry's volley fire to finish off the Zulu. For most of the battle, the Zulu failed to come within 65m of the British force. And, as at Khambula, once the attack had faltered, orders were given for pursuit. 'Buller had posted the mounted infantry so as to fire within the flank of the retiring enemy, and the remainder of his mounted men, making for the country beyond, killed some 450 in the pursuit.'[25] All fleeing Zulu were hunted down and killed or left to die from their wounds. Only two prisoners were taken.[26] Ulundi was burned to the ground before noon.

It was left to Wolseley to hunt down Cetshwayo and to develop a strategy that would prevent future Zulu challenges to British authority. Wolseley wanted Buller to remain in South Africa, but he simply was too tired and veldt sores had crippled his hands.[27] He returned home with a CMG, was promoted to Colonel, and was appointed aide-de-camp to Queen Victoria. Buller refused to join the celebrations that followed the end of the war, even snubbing an invitation by Prime Minister Benjamin Disraeli because Chelmsford was not offered the same.

In 1880, his battalion was ordered to Afghanistan, but Buller was sent to Scotland as Assistant Adjutant and Quartermaster General of the Northern British District. After just a few months he was transferred to Aldershot to take up the same post. His stay there was also brief. The First Anglo–Boer War had erupted and Buller was ordered to return to South Africa. He arrived in Cape Town on 27 February 1881, the same day that British forces were defeated at Majuba Hill and the British commanding officer, George Colley, was killed. Reuniting with Wood, the new commanding officer, Buller pressed for an immediate offensive against the Boers. The British government, however, wanted peace not a prolonged war and Wood and Buller were made negotiators. Buller was furious: 'I like the Boers,' he wrote, 'and am glad to see them get their country back, but I do not think that either the time or manner of the settlement arrived at was fortunate.'[28] He remained in South Africa for much of the rest of the year, taking up an administrative position in Natal.

In 1882, after marrying Lady Audrey Howard, Buller had to cut his honeymoon short to take up an appointment as Chief of Intelligence in Wolseley's expedition to Egypt to put down the Arabi revolt. Buller was the 'brain of Wolseley's little army' and most notably carried out the reconnaissance of Tel-el-Kebir on the day before that decisive battle.[29] Although British artillery could not locate Buller's chosen point for the attack, Wolseley achieved victory nonetheless with little loss of British life.[30] Wolseley's expedition, thanks in part to his efficient staff, secured British objectives in Egypt. For his part in the campaign, Buller was given a KCMG and shortly after his return to Great Britain was made Assistant Adjutant General at the War Office.

Once again, however, Buller's administrative responsibilities at home were interrupted by conflict in Africa. The failure of an Anglo-Egyptian army under William Hicks (Hicks Pasha) to deal with Mahdist forces in the Sudan at the end of 1883 led to direct British army intervention. Buller was sent to Suakin as Chief of Staff and second in command to Major General Sir Gerald Graham. In addition to staff duties, Buller also commanded the 1st Infantry Brigade. After concentrating near the coast at Trinkitat, Graham led his forces into battle against Osman Digna's followers at El Teb on 29 February 1884. Buller employed his brigade in a traditional square, and although the enemy was able to penetrate it, the formation held fast. At Tamai, two weeks later, Buller repeated the tactic. Although his square held once again, a second square, commanded by Colonel Davis, fell apart. Buller was able to support Davis and to overcome desperate hand-to-hand combat. After this more difficult victory, Graham's force returned to Suakin where it was given instructions not to press further. In April, the force was withdrawn to Cairo and Buller was sent back to the War Office, where he was promoted Major General.

A little over a month after the withdrawal, Mahdist forces seized the town of Berber, cutting off Khartoum, the Egyptian administrative capital of the Sudan, from all British support. In August, Parliament authorised and provided funds for a relief expedition. Well before that, Wolseley had already mounted his campaign to lead it. He proposed an advance up the Nile River rather than a desert march along the Suakin–Berber route. This plan was highly contested by most of the officers who had genuine experience in the region. But Wolseley wanted to repeat the successful strategy of the Red River campaign, relying on small boats to carry his force some 600 miles. Buller loyally supported his chief and wrote letters to the War Office asserting the feasibility of the strategy. When Wolseley was chosen to lead the expedition, Buller was appointed his Chief of Staff.

Wolseley brought with him to Egypt almost his entire surviving ring. But these men were no longer eager junior officers willing to perform their tasks obediently. They were some of the leading minds and most ambitious men in the late Victorian army, and they clashed with one another and with their chief. Buller rarely saw Wolseley during the entire campaign and received messages from him that often alternated between support and scorn. Buller's failure to acquire enough coal for the Nile steamers that caused a delay in the advance, in particular, upset Wolseley. 'What an odd man is Buller,' Wolseley wrote in his diary, 'I should never again have him as Chief of Staff.'[31] Buller never seems to have been too interested in the campaign. Perhaps this was a result of his indifference to the fate of Charles Gordon, the popular Victorian 'hero' who commanded the post in Khartoum. Buller even questioned whether Gordon was 'worth the camels'.[32]

As preparations were being made for the advance up the river, a desert column under Sir Herbert Stewart had repulsed the enemy at Abu Klea on 17 January 1885, and was moving towards Metemmeh. At Abu Kru, a few days later, Stewart was mortally wounded in a brief skirmish. Command of the column devolved to Sir Charles Wilson, an officer who inspired little confidence in his men, and more importantly, was an outsider to Wolseley's Ring.[33] As soon as he learned the news, a dejected Wolseley dispatched Buller to take command. 'Above all,' Wolseley wrote caringly, 'don't get wounded; I can't afford to lose you.'[34]

'The minds of all now turned to Redvers Buller, the fighting Buller', the future Lord Dundonald wrote: 'Let us have Buller here, every one said, and then reinforced we will march to Khartoum and smash the Mahdi. Alas! It was not to be. Buller came, not to avenge as we hoped, but to lead our retirement, the first step in the abandonment of the Soudan.'[35] Dundonald was right. Buller could have pressed the enemy, but he doubted the capability of his troops to fend off further attacks from an enemy whose numbers were increasing daily and he worried about his sick and wounded and his growing lack of supplies. Wolseley sent Buller often contradictory orders, and Buller replied in kind. He considered attacking Metemma, then Berber, and then thought about a decisive strike at Abu Klea. But his actions were anything but decisive. Most likely, Buller had made his mind up after the fall of Khartoum. He complained to Wolseley that his troops were worn out both physically and morally and he was not going to risk an offensive. Wolseley was far from confident in his subordinate's appraisal of the desert column's situation, but the river column was experiencing troubles of its own.[36] The British advance ground to a halt. When Prime Minister Gladstone ordered the expedition's recall, Buller stayed behind to oversee the evacuation. He finally returned home in August with a KCB and was made Deputy Adjutant General of the forces, serving again under Wolseley. This appointment was followed in 1886 with a very controversial fourteen-month tenure spent in Ireland trying to restore order and ending up earning the wrath of both the government and the Irish landlords.

After the Gordon relief expedition, Buller did not see battle again until he was sent to South Africa in 1899, but he remained very busy for the next decade and a half working to reform the British army. In 1887, Buller returned to the War Office first as Quartermaster General and then, in 1890, as Adjutant General. These were very productive years and he thrived as an administrator. Buller can be credited with accomplishing four major tasks during these years. First, he improved the service conditions for the enlisted as regards to food, quarters and uniforms. Secondly, he revised the *Manual of Military Law*. Thirdly, he drafted a new Drill Book. And fourthly, and most significantly, he created the Army Service

Corps.[37] The creation of a special corps, like the Royal Engineers, to deal with issues related to supply and transport, brought a high level of professionalism to these neglected areas of staff service, raised the importance of logistics and, at the same time, provided flexibility to deal with local concerns. Since every unit would be given Army Service Corps officers and its own allotment of transport and supply, commanders would have more control over their movement, making them less dependent on any central command. This system, which proved effective during the first months of the South African War, was dismantled by Lord Roberts upon his arrival.

Buller developed a good working relationship with Henry Campbell-Bannerman, the Liberal Secretary of War from 1892–95, and when the 76- year-old Commander in Chief of the British army, the Duke of Cambridge, was forced to resign in 1895, Campbell-Bannerman pushed for Buller over Wolseley as his replacement. Buller was very uncomfortable with this decision.[38] He saw the move as an act of disloyalty to his old chief. But many Liberals were upset with Wolseley over his position on Home Rule, the Queen was pushing for her son, the Duke of Connaught, and Buller appeared to be a good compromise candidate. However, on the day of the appointment, 21 June 1895, the government fell over a vote on ammunition reserves. The new Conservative government appointed Wolseley as Cambridge's successor.

When Buller's appointment ended as Adjutant General he was placed on half pay for a year and then was promoted to full general, succeeding the Duke of Connaught in the command at Aldershot. There, in 1898, Buller conducted six days of manoeuvres. He did a poor job. 'I have been making a fool of myself all day,' he was overheard saying.[39] Buller had not handled men in many years and sitting behind a desk no doubt had taken away his edge. It was this older Buller, out of shape, with a strong penchant for good food and wine, who had come to doubt his abilities, who was appointed the Commander in Chief of the British army in South Africa a year later when hostilities broke out between the British and the Boers.

As early as April 1899, many in Lord Salisbury's Cabinet had come to accept that war with the Boers for the control of South Africa was likely. In that month, Lord Lansdowne, the Secretary of State for War, Lord Milner, the High Commissioner in South Africa and Governor of the Cape Colony, Lord Wolseley, Buller and others sat down to discuss strategy. The group was very divided and remained so into the summer. With the failure of direct negotiations between Milner and Paul Kruger, the President of the South African Republic, however, it became imperative to prepare for the inevitable. Despite reservations, Wolseley recommended the appointment of Buller as the commander of the expedition. Buller had his own reservations about accepting the offer. 'I said that I always considered that I was better as second in a complex military affair then as the officer in chief command,' Buller wrote.[40] Nevertheless, he accepted the most difficult challenge of his military career.

South Africa, 1899–1900

Planning for the war was haphazard because the government was still reluctant to commit itself. According to Buller, during the summer and into the autumn, he had very little influence on some of the most basic yet crucial decisions that shaped the direction of the war. For example, Buller later claimed that he had no control over the appointment of his commanders and senior staff officers, he was not invited to attend meetings of the Army Mobilisation Board, his recommendations regarding the size and composition of the Field Force were ignored, and perhaps, most stunningly, he had little control over strategy.[41] Buller had relied upon the advice and the information presented by his old friend, William Butler, who until July 1899 and his forced resignation had served as the Commander in Chief of British forces in South Africa. Butler had warned that the Cape Colony and Natal, in particular, were open to invasion and Britain did not have enough troops in South Africa to defend their frontiers adequately. Butler encouraged a defensive strategy until reinforcements could arrive, and this incorporated a retreat from any currently held forward positions, including the garrison town of Ladysmith.[42] This strategy, which Buller endorsed, was rejected by politicians and subverted by officers in the field. Also, for the actual route of the British advance into the Boer Republics, Buller favoured a concentration of forces in the Cape Colony followed by a movement through the Orange Free State, a plan Lord Roberts later implemented. Buller promoted this plan of action even before the Orange Free State's intentions were known. However, Lansdowne thought differently. Lansdowne did not want to do anything to upset the Free State and was also concerned about the political ramifications of a Boer occupation of the northern Natal, a sentiment that Natal politicians echoed.[43] In the end, Buller was pressured to comply with political needs and popular demands and altered his original intentions. That Buller felt frustrated with the sometimes indifferent planning and political obstruction can be seen clearly by his decision to go directly to Salisbury in early September.[44]

The Boer ultimatum and Britain's refusal to comply with its demands led to the declaration of war on 11 October 1899. Buller sailed for Cape Town a few days later and arrived on 30 October. Assessing the situation, he was filled with immediate anxiety and pessimism as he wrote to his brother, Tremayne, on 3 November: 'I am in the tightest place I have ever been in, and the worst of it is that it is I think none of my creating. I don't know if I can . . . get out of it alright, and I think if I fail that [it] is fair my family should know afterwards what at any rate I had to say in my own defence.'[45] There was certainly reason to despair. Despite Buller's opposition, British forces had gone on the offensive in Natal, had pushed their way to Dundee and Talana Hill, and were now forced to abandon these forward positions because of the enemy's advances. Similarly, Lieutenant General Sir George White had failed at Nicholson's Nek and, despite Buller's warnings, had allowed his troops to get entrapped in Ladysmith. Two other Boer sieges had been laid at Kimberley and Mafeking and there were not yet enough troops in the Cape Colony to stop a Boer advance at the frontier which only aggravated the general fear that a sizeable portion of the Cape's Dutch population would rise up and join their Free State and Transvaal brethren. Buller may have had good reasons to be concerned but his letter gives credence to the comments later made by Leo Amery, one of Buller's fiercest critics, that Buller was more than just concerned; he 'had completely lost heart'.[46]

Buller's actions, however, did not betray his doubts. His decision to head to Natal and personally lead the operations to relieve Ladysmith, something for which he came under much attack, was decisive as was his order to break up the Army Corps.[47] 'I therefore decided upon every ground that the deliverance of South Natal must be my first object,' Buller wrote, 'But at the same time I felt it impossible to ignore Kimberley. That town represented to the Native the symbol of British power and property in South Africa; and I feared the effect of its fall.'[48] If all went well, the Boers would be forced out of Natal, Ladysmith would be relieved, and Buller could then return to his original plan of moving on Bloemfontein via Kimberley. Things, however, did not go well.

On 7 December, Major General William Gatacre's force suffered a serious setback at Stormberg. Two days later, Lieutenant General Lord Methuen's 1st Division was stopped at Magersfontein. To relieve Ladysmith, Buller had originally selected a route that crossed the Tugela River at Potgeiter's Drift. From there, he hoped to move through open country across the enemy's flank. The two failures, however, made him choose a new plan, one that he had initially ruled out because of the great risks posed by a massed enemy force well entrenched in extremely difficult terrain. 'With an enemy disheartened by failure I thought myself justified, in the peculiar circumstance, in risking a flank march of fifty miles with an enormous wagon-train, even though it might involve the uncovering of my communications,' Buller wrote. 'With an enemy elated by success this was no longer justified. I therefore determined to try to force the direct road to Ladysmith.'[49] After a two-day bombardment, Buller ordered a general assault of the enemy's positions at Colenso.

Buller was not optimistic on the morning of 15 December. Lansdowne had notified him that no reinforcements were forthcoming. White felt that he could not risk any attempt to break out and offer support. The mounted force he had, Buller believed, was insufficient to threaten the enemy's flanks or its lines of communication. He had poor maps and little information on the Boer position. And, as many of his contemporaries have noted, Buller disliked losing life, and certainly a success at Colenso was going to require a heavy sacrifice of men.[50]

The Boer position at Colenso was indeed strong but not impossible to breach. The capture of Hlangwane Hill would have dangerously exposed their flank to British artillery and rifle fire. Whether Buller recognised this and thought that the risks were too great to attempt to capture the position – Dundonald was sent there but was eventually ordered to retreat – or whether he failed truly to appreciate Hlangwane's importance is contested.[51] The written orders of Clery, the general

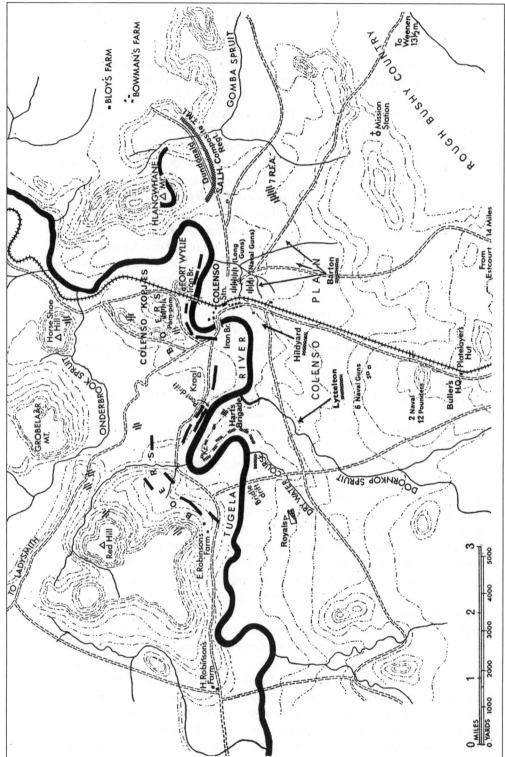

Plan of the battle of Colenso, 1899. (From W. Baring Pemberton, *Battles of the Boer War*, London: Batsford, 1964)

nominally in charge of the attack at Colenso, do suggest that Buller saw some importance in taking the position but his actions the day of the battle indicate that the movement against Hlangwane was nothing more than a sideshow.[52]

While Dundonald's mounted troops on the right moved on Hlangwane Hill, on the left, Hart's 5th Brigade was ordered to cross the Tugela at Bridle Drift. Buller hoped that if successful, the brigade could then support Hildyard's 2nd Brigade, which would attempt to force the river at Iron Bridge in the centre. Hart, however, could not locate the drift and got caught in the salient loop of the river. He pressed his men on forward but, without any place to go, his units got terribly entangled. With daybreak almost upon him, Hart still refused to give the orders to extend. Buller quickly identified the danger and a rider was sent to tell Hart to get out of the loop. A second rider told him that the drift was further west.[53] But it was too late. The Boers opened up a crossfire on the helpless, bunched up British soldiers. As one soldier recounted, 'General Hart had his Irish Brigade well out towards the banks of the river, and as soon as they began to rise and make an advance the most awful rifle fire ever witnessed broke out form the dark and silent trenches across the river. Men fell like sheep.'[54] Buller ordered Lyttelton's 4th Brigade, which had been held in reserve, to support a retreat, but the damage was already done. Hart's Brigade suffered the heaviest casualty rates of the day.

While Buller was trying to extricate Hart's men, a second disaster was unfolding. Colonel C J Long's 1st Brigade Division, RFA had been ordered to support Hildyard's crossing of Iron Bridge. Buller had given Long strict orders not to move his guns forward, a tactic that he had successfully utilised in the Sudan in 1898, and to remain under the cover of Barton's 6th Brigade. Long disregarded the command and pushed past his escort. Boer firepower quickly silenced the guns and all attempts to rescue them failed. Although Hildyard's brigade managed to advance coolly towards the river in extended formation and drive the Boers from their trenches on the other side, and most of Lyttelton's brigade had seen no action, without the guns and without Hart's support, Buller did not want to risk a river crossing. He ordered a retreat and British forces fell back to Chieveley and Frere.[55]

Some, like Amery, have suggested that Buller lost heart at Colenso. But if he had, his men still were not aware of it. Dundonald, who was deeply disappointed in the outcome of the battle, believing that he could have taken Hlangwane with support from Barton, wrote of his chief, 'He was here, there and everywhere, riding over the field. Buller's personal courage created a feeling of confidence amongst the men which they held throughout the whole Natal campaign.'[56]

Although the men may have still supported Buller, the Cabinet no longer did. Following this third loss of 'Black Week', Lansdowne wanted change. He wanted both Gatacre and Methuen sacked, the latter of whom he wanted replaced by Sir Charles Warren. Buller saw these 'proposals' as meddling, and he also thought that it was unfair to condemn these generals directly, and himself indirectly, for the limitations that the War Office and Treasury had placed upon them. If Buller's intransigence was not enough to earn Lansdowne's ire, his final undoing was an awkwardly worded message to White which was interpreted by Lansdowne as an invitation to surrender. There is no way to read Buller's 16 December heliogram to White as anything but despairing. He informed White of the Colenso defeat and his inability to relieve Ladysmith with his current forces. He told White that no help would be coming for at least a month. He encouraged him, if he could not hold out, to destroy his ammunition and to 'make the best terms you can'.[57] Although Buller could claim afterwards that he was not telling White to surrender, the pessimism of the message and other exchanges with both White and Lansdowne rang loudly. Lansdowne made it clear that the government did not consider surrender an option.[58] On 18 December, Buller was notified that although he would continue to command 'the prosecution of the campaign in Natal', Roberts had been appointed the Commander in Chief of British forces in South Africa.[59] Buller wrote to his wife that same day, 'Two days after I arrived here they ordered me to supersede Sir George White, and I would not, they then ordered me to supersede Gatacre and I would not, and then Methuen and I would not, so now they have superseded me.'[60]

White did not surrender and, as Buller had ordained, Warren's 5th Division was ordered to Natal rather than the Cape Colony. It arrived there on 2 January. Buller put Warren in command of the next advance. By 11 January, British forces had returned to the Tugela but Warren was not ready to try to cross it. With an entrenched Boer force at Potgeiter's Drift, what Buller wanted from his subordinate was a crossing near Trichardt's Drift, 5 miles up river, followed by a wide flanking movement towards either Acton Homes or Fair View, which would have opened up a clear path to Ladysmith. The plan was similar to the one he had conceived prior to Black Week. Especially after Colenso, he wanted to avoid another attempt to force the Boers from a difficult spot. But, after crossing the Tugela, seizing the hills that commanded the drift and sending the mounted brigade toward Acton Homes, Warren decided that his army did not have enough food to carry out the operation, a claim that Buller later vigorously denied.[61] Warren then vacillated and Buller grew frustrated. 'I debated with myself,' he wrote, 'whether or not I should relieve Warren of his command.'[62] But Buller chose not to dismiss Warren and pressed him to take action. Still concerned about his supplies, however, Warren gave up on the flank march and gravitated towards a more direct route to Ladysmith. He challenged the enemy's defences at Tabanyama, made some headway, but called off the attack. He then considered Spion Kop, a position that towered over the Tugela and commanded any movement towards Ladysmith. According to Warren, Buller gave him two choices: immediately attack Spion Kop or retreat. On 23 January, he attacked.[63]

The British had been threatening action for over a week and the Boers had plenty of opportunities to extend from Potgieter's Drift toward Spion Kop and Tabanyama. However, they only weakly reinforced their position atop Spion Kop. At 2100, Major General Edward Woodgate and 1,600 men of his 11th Brigade began their advance. They reached what appeared to be the summit, chased off the Boers with a bayonet charge and, in complete darkness and under the cover of a thick mist, began to entrench. Only when light began to pierce the mist at about 0800 did Woodgate realise that he had failed to position his men on the crest, and they were now subject to enfilading fire from nearby Aloe Knoll. Woodgate was one of the first casualties of this error. As Boer fire continued, now in support of their counter-attack, Warren gave orders to Major General J Talbot Coke to take two battalions of his 10th Brigade up Spion Kop. Lieutenant Colonel Alec Thorneycroft was appointed acting commander replacing Woodgate, although this order was not communicated to either Thorneycroft or Coke.[64] Thorneycroft was forced temporarily to evacuate the trenches due to a concerted Boer attack, but once companies of the 10th Brigade began to arrive, he was able to retake them. The British held the line till nightfall but then Thorneycroft, unbeknownst to Warren and Coke, made the decision to retire; the Boer guns were still pounding his trenches and they could not be silenced, he had no knowledge if any further support was forthcoming, and his men were running out of provisions.[65] As Thorneycroft descended to the foot of Spion Kop he was surprised finally to run into reinforcements.[66]

Buller found Warren's inactivity particularly disturbing. He did little to alter the course of events atop Spion Kop, giving no orders for most of the day. Away from Spion Kop, he also did little. Twin Peaks commanded Aloe Knoll. Had the British succeeded in taking that position they would have silenced most of the artillery fire directed at Spion Kop and removed a substantial threat to Thorneycroft's men. Lyttelton's 4th Brigade had been making good progress in taking Twin Peaks, but Warren called it back prematurely. So frustrated was Lieutenant Colonel Buchanan Riddell of the 60th Rifles that he refused to obey Lyttelton's orders and actually seized the heights. Riddell's untimely death led to the withdrawal of the Rifle Brigade.[67]

The day after the battle, Buller called Dundonald to his side. 'I blame myself for not controlling [Warren],' Buller told him, 'but he was sent out after Colenso under such auspices that I did not like to interfere with him.'[68] After Spion Kop, Buller would not feel any pressure again to give Warren any major role in his operations. Roberts also complained about Warren: 'That it failed may, in some measure, be due to the difficulties of the ground and the commanding positions held by the enemy – probably also to the errors of judgement and want of administrative capacity on the part of Sir Charles Warren.'[69] But in Roberts's opinion, the failure was ultimately Buller's. 'But whatever faults Sir Charles Warren may have committed, the failure must also be ascribed to the disinclination of the Officer in supreme command to assert his authority and see that what he thought best was done . . .'[70] So damning were Roberts words that the Cabinet decided not to publish them, although Lansdowne went ahead and did it anyway.[71]

After reassuming command, Buller was ready to try to relieve Ladysmith again. Roberts, however, was sceptical. He did not want to see another failed attempt and preferred inaction expecting that his own advance towards

Bloemfontein would help weaken Boer defences in Natal. Buller, finally showing the strength of will he demonstrated so often during his early career, was determined to break the siege. He pressed his case and convinced Roberts that he had a very good chance in striking the Boers a few miles east of Spion Kop at Vaal Krantz. Roberts gave his approval to the plan on 4 February. Buller attacked the next day.

Buller's basic plan involved a feint attack on the Boer position at Brakfontein. This was conducted by Major General A S Wynne and four battalions of infantry. Within two hours of this diversion starting, Lyttelton launched the main thrust at Vaal Krantz. Prior to the attack, Buller had his engineers construct a 1½-mile road up the steep Zwarts Kop and put his naval guns and mounted guns atop to support Lyttelton's advance. Under the cover of artillery fire, the British successfully laid pontoons and crossed the Tugela, and Lyttelton's force chased the Boers from their positions, sometimes at the point of the bayonet. By nightfall, Lyttelton had taken Vaal Krantz and had ordered his men to dig in, an extremely difficult job since the ground was so rocky. It was also impossible to bring up the guns. To make matters worse, Boer guns, which remained safely out of range of Zwarts Kop, were able to mark the British positions.[72] Lyttelton, however, remained on Vaal Krantz through the night and most of the next day, repelling a Boer counter-attack in the afternoon. He was relieved later on the 6 February by Hildyard. Having taken Vaal Krantz, Buller could not think of a way to utilise it and continue the advance. On 7 February, he called his generals to a council of war. He wanted to retire and try again another day at another spot. Lyttelton, Wynne and most of the other generals agreed.[73] Keeping a token force near Potgeiter's Drift, the British returned to Chieveley.

This third failure to relieve Ladysmith had very little impact on Buller's overall vision or upon his morale. British forces remained very active on the Tugela for the next ten days, seizing a number of key positions on the south side of the river and extending their lines to the east past Colenso. Buller had already picked where he would strike next and was only waiting for good weather. On 17 February, he ordered Lyttelton to follow up on the successful attack made on Cingolo Hill the day before by the 2nd Cavalry Brigade. Dundonald would co-operate on his right; Hildyard, on the left. Warren and Barton's men were held in reserve. Despite reinforcement, the Boers could not withstand the steady British bombardment and Lyttelton's advance. After occupying Cingolo Hill, the advance continued on 18 February with a move across the nek and a successful assault on Monte Cristo. The next day, the guns were brought up to Monte Cristo and Hart and two infantry divisions moved against Hlangwane. The Boers put up fierce resistance but were forced to pull back across the Tugela. Although they managed temporarily to stop the British at Colenso on 20 February, a renewed attack on the 21st by Coke's 10th Brigade led to its occupation. British successes continued for the next several days at Onderbrook Spruit, Pieter's Hill, Railway Hill and Hart's Hill. The Boers retreated and the route to Ladysmith was finally cleared. On

28 February, Dundonald entered the beleaguered city and Buller followed on 1 March.[74] The siege of Ladysmith was finally over.

Even Leo Amery could not find fault with Buller's operations between 10 February and 1 March, writing, 'The credit of it belongs, in the first place to Buller.'[75] But his overall judgement of Buller's performance remained severe. 'In every great war there have been unexpected failures, and always must be,' he wrote. 'Buller was one of these.'[76] Roberts likewise had already made his mind up about Buller. With the threat to Ladysmith now over, he rejected Buller's suggestions to reoccupy the northern Natal and attack the passes leading to the Orange Free State. Instead he ordered him on the defensive and began stripping him of his divisions, arguing that they were needed in the Cape Colony and for his advance on Bloemfontein. For the next two months, Buller's men saw little action.

In early May, Roberts allowed Buller to begin advancing through northern Natal, a task he completed in just a couple of weeks. With a sizeable enemy force secure in the mountains concentrating in and around Laing's Nek, Buller moved quickly to threaten their flanks, seizing Botha's Pass on 8 June and driving them away from Alleman's Nek on 11th. The Boers were forced to retire from Laing's Nek without a fight on the night of 12 June. Much of the credit for the success of this operation was given to Roberts for his single-minded advance through the Orange Free State.[77] Many critics argued that the Boers pulled out of the northern Natal in order to defend against that advance. But Buller's flanking movements were decisive. 'None of the [Boers] can see that Lord Roberts' advance in any way affected [their] movements,' one of Buller's defenders wrote.'[78]

Through June, July and into August, Buller's operations were very limited in scope with his force acting around Standerton. Roberts would not approve any offensive thrust and anyway Buller no longer had the manpower to carry one out. But Buller did still possess some fight left in him. After a council of war on 25 August, Roberts ordered Buller, in conjunction with Major Generals John French and Reginald Pole-Carew, to attack the Boers 3 miles south-east of Belfast at Bergendal. The battle of Bergendal on 27 August is arguably the last set-piece battle of the South African War.

Bergendal Farm lay on a high crest at the junction of the Carolina and Dalmanutha–Belfast roads. A few hundred yards to the west, a Boer force occupied a 'natural fortress' of immense stones and rocky crevices. Colonel J F Brocklehurst was ordered to take some cavalry, mounted infantry and artillery to the left and provide cover for an advance and, at the same time, prevent the Boers from receiving reinforcement. Colonel Walter Kitchener took a second force to the right, entrenched, and then brought the guns forward. From these two positions and with assistance from other guns, the British opened up a massive three-hour bombardment of the kopje. Taken prisoner after the battle, a Boer declared, 'We dared not leave the post. We dared not – it was certain death.'[79] At about 1400, with Roberts observing, Buller ordered Kitchener's 7th Brigade to advance.

Extended across open ground, the 1st Bn Inniskilling Fusiliers and 1st Bn Rifle Brigade assaulted the Boer position. As the British fought their way into the enemy's defences, the Boers fled, abandoning all of Dalmanutha. 'The capture of Bergendal,' Buller cheerfully reported, 'cleared the whole of the high veldt of the enemy.'[80]

Although Buller continued on the offensive driving the enemy from Machadodorp and Helvetia in late August and Lydenburg in September, Buller's time in South Africa was coming to an end. Confident of an impending victory, Roberts had elected to return to Great Britain and succeed Wolseley as the Commander in Chief of the British army. Lord Kitchener was to take over his responsibilities in South Africa. Buller, who outranked Kitchener, would have to return to England. On 6 October 1900, the Natal Field Force was broken up and Buller said his goodbyes. A soldier wrote, on the occasion,

> When he appeared on the road to mount his horse, the guard of honour came to the present and forgetting all discipline broke out into three loud cheers, poor old Buller held up his hand, and with a broken voice, he thanked them for their kind cheers, and made a short speech [to the] lines of cheering soldiers. His eyes were very wet.[81]

Back in London, Buller was reinstated at his former post at Aldershot. Despite some reservations by those who felt Buller had made serious mistakes in the war, it seemed almost pro forma to William St John Brodrick, the new Secretary of State for War, that Buller would quietly finish his term there. Those who had objected, however, were not so quiet. Leo Amery, *The Times* correspondent who had reported from South Africa and was currently editing the newspaper's history of the war, was furious. Amery had heard rumours about Buller's alleged 'surrender' telegram to White and, under the pseudonym of 'Reformer', launched a series of scathing personal attacks on Buller in September 1901, declaring, '[Buller] was so utterly shaken and unnerved by the unexpected and terrible reverse of Colenso that for the moment he abandoned all hope.'[82] The *Morning Post*, the *St James's Gazette*, and the *Spectator* all joined with *The Times* in calling for his removal. Buller was beside himself. At a speech on 10 October, he defended his actions to a group of soldiers. But impetuously, he went too far. He referred to the secret telegram he had sent White, and, in doing so, he broke the King's regulations. Roberts demanded Buller's resignation and told Brodrick if Buller did not step down then he would.[83] Despite letters of support from his fellow officers, including the Adjutant General, Thomas Kelly-Kenny, Roberts would not budge. When Buller refused to step down, Brodrick went directly to Edward VII and Buller was removed from his Aldershot command and put on half pay on 22 October 1901.[84] All of Buller's appeals for a court-martial to give him a chance to tell his side of the story were rejected. His military career had come to a humiliating end. Buller died on 2 June 1908 from gall-bladder cancer and was buried in Crediton.

Bibliography

Two contemporary biographies are Walter Jerrold, *Sir Redvers H Buller V.C.: The Story of his Life and Campaigns* (London: S W Partridge & Co., 1900) and Lewis Butler, *Sir Redvers Buller* (London: Smith, Elder, & Co., 1901). The standard biography is Colonel C H Melville, *The Life of General the Rt. Hon. Sir Redvers Buller*, 2 vols (London: Edward Arnold & Co., 1923). Geoffrey Powell, *Buller: A Scapegoat? A Life of General Sir Redvers Buller 1839–1908* (London: Leo Cooper, 1994) attempts a re-assessment but is not entirely satisfactory in assimilating the most recent research. A study of Buller at the War Office is James B Thomas, 'Sir Redvers Buller in the post-Cardwellian Army: A Study of the Rise and Fall of a Military Reputation', unpub. PhD thesis, Texas A&M University, 1993.

Inevitably, it is Buller's later career in the South African War that has attracted most interest. The case for the prosecution was put forward by Julian Symons, *Buller's Campaign* (London: Cresset Press, 1963), while there was the beginning of a rehabilitation in Thomas Pakenham, *The Boer War* (New York: Random House, 1979). The military politics surrounding Buller's appointment are summarised in Ian F W Beckett, 'Buller and the Politics of Command', in John Gooch, ed., *The Boer War: Direction, Experience and Image* (London: Frank Cass, 2000), pp. 41–55.

Notes

1. Edmund Gosse, 'Sir Redvers Buller: A Character Study', in James Bryce et al., *Briton and Boer: Both Sides of the South African Question* (New York: Harper and Brothers, 1900), p. 305.

2. Buller's teeth were kicked in. For early biographical information on Buller, see Walter Jerrold, *Sir Redvers H Buller V.C.: The Story of his Life and Campaigns* (London: S W Partridge & Co., 1900), Lewis Butler, *Sir Redvers Buller* (London: Smith, Elder, & Co., 1901), C H Melville, *The Life of General The Rt Hon. Sir Redvers Buller* (London: Edward Arnold & Co., 1923) and Geoffrey Powell, *Buller: A Scapegoat? A Life of General Sir Redvers Buller 1839–1908* (London: Leo Cooper, 1994).

3. William Francis Butler, *Sir William Butler: An Autobiography*, 2nd edn (Toronto: Bell and Cockburn, 1911), pp. 103–4.

4. Field Marshal Viscount Wolseley, *The Story of a Soldier's Life*, 2 vols (Westminster: Archibald Constable & Co., 1903; reprint, New York: Kraus Reprint Co., 1971), II, p. 178.

5. Henry Brackenbury, *The Ashanti War: A Narrative*, 2 vols (London and Edinburgh: William Blackwood and Sons, 1874; new imp., Frank Cass, 1968), I, p. 170.

6. The 'Ring' was a clique of officers who accompanied Wolseley on many of his campaigns and who became very influential in building the late Victorian army. It included Evelyn Wood, Baker Russell, John McNeill, Henry Brackenbury, Frederick Maurice, William Butler, Thomas Baker, Robert Home, George Greaves, Hugh McCalmont and George Colley.

7. In 1874, his older brother, James, died, and Buller inherited the family estates.

8. Chelmsford to Wood, 3 February 1879, cited in John Laband, ed., *Lord Chelmsford's Zululand Campaign 1878–1879* (Dover, NH: Alan Sutton, 1994), pp. 91–92.

9. The National Archives (hereafter TNA), Buller Mss, WO 132/1, Buller's report on the attack on Inhlobana Mountain, sub-enclosure of Colonel Bellairs's dispatch.

10. John Laband, *Kingdom in Crisis: The Zulu Response to the British Invasion of 1879* (Manchester: Manchester University Press, 1992), pp. 150–51.

11. Ibid., p. 150.

12. Jerrold, *Buller*, p. 120.

13. TNA, WO 32/7724, Staff Officer's report, 29 March 1879.

14. Ian Knight, *The National Army Book of the Zulu War* (London: Sidgwick and Jackson,

2003), pp. 158–61.

15. See note 9 above.

16. Henry Evelyn Wood, *From Midshipman to Field Marshal* (London: Methuen & Co., 1906), II, p. 68.

17. Waller Ashe and E V Wyatt-Edgell, *The Story of the Zulu Campaign* (London: Sampson Low, Marston, Searle and Rivington, 1880; new edn, Cape Town: N & S Press, 1989), p. 12; TNA, WO 32/7226, Wood's report, 30 March 1879.

18. Buller's report of Khambula, 29 March 1889, as cited in Melville, *Buller*, I, pp. 120–21.

19. Ibid., p. 121.

20. Laband, *Kingdom in Crisis*, pp. 156–57.

21. Letter from Schermbrucker dated 1 May 1879, in Frank Emery, ed., *Marching Over Africa, Letters from Victorian Soldiers* (London: Hodder & Stoughton, 1986), p. 65; as cited in Laband, *Kingdom in Crisis*, p. 163.

22. D'Arcy was the awarded the VC at Ulundi. See Knight, *National Army Book*, p. 170.

23. F W Grenfell, *Memoirs of Field Marshal Lord Grenfell* (London: Hodder & Stoughton, 1925), p. 54.

24. Jerrold, *Buller*, p. 150.

25. TNA, WO 32/7763, Chelmsford's Report on Ulundi, 6 July 1879.

26. John Laband, *The Battle of Ulundi* (Pietermaritzburg: Shuter & Shooter, 1988), p. 40.

27. Powell, *Buller*, p. 43.

28. Melville, *Buller*, I, p. 151.

29. Jerrold, *Buller*, p. 193.

30. J F Maurice, *Military History of the Campaign of 1882 in Egypt* (London: HMSO, 1887), p. 75.

31. Adrian Preston, ed., *In Relief of Gordon: Lord Wolseley's Campaign Journal of the Khartoum Relief Expedition, 1884–1885* (Rutherford, NJ: Rutgers University Press, 1970), pp. 112–13.

32. Powell, *Buller*, p. 72; Robin Neillands, *The Dervish Wars: Gordon and Kitchener in the Sudan 1880–1898* (London: John Murray, 1996), p. 145.

33. Douglas Dundonald, *My Army Life* (London: Edward Arnold & Co., 1926), p. 58.

34. TNA, Buller Mss, WO 132/2, Wolseley to Buller, 29 January 1885.

35. Dundonald, *My Army Life*, p. 58.

36. Preston, ed., *In Relief of Gordon*, p. 162.

37. For Buller's years at the War Office, see James B Thomas, 'Sir Redvers Buller in the post-Cardwellian Army: A Study of the Rise and Fall of a Military Reputation', unpub. PhD thesis, Texas A&M University, 1993.

38. Buller to Henry Campbell Bannerman, 18 June 1895, as cited in Halik Kochanski, *Sir Garnet Wolseley: Victorian Hero* (London: Hambledon Press, 1999), p. 213.

39. W St John Midleton, *Records & Reactions, 1856–1939* (New York: E P Dutton, 1939), pp. 132–33; as cited in Powell, *Buller*, p. 114.

40. Melville, *Buller*, II, p. 2.

41. The War Office vigorously denied all these charge. See TNA, CAB 37/52/37, Buller to Lansdowne, 6 January 1900. For Buller's response to the charges, see ibid., CAB 37/52/49, Buller to Lansdowne, 17 April 1900.

42. Butler, *Sir Redvers Buller*, p. 420.

43. For further discussion of the military decisions made prior to the outbreak of the war, see John Gooch, ed., *The Boer War: Direction, Experience and Image* (London: Frank Cass, 2000).

44. TNA, Buller Mss, WO 132/24, p. 3.

45. Ibid., WO 132/6, Buller to Tremayne Buller, 3 November 1899.

46. Leo S Amery, *My Political Life* (London: Hutchinson & Co., 1953), I, pp. 118–19.

47. Buller and Wolseley had lost faith in White, yet he remained the senior officer in Natal. His juniors, Major Generals C F Clery, Henry Hildyard and Neville Lyttelton, encouraged Buller to come.

48. TNA, Buller Mss, WO 132/24, p. 17.

49. Ibid., p. 29.

50. Dundonald, *My Army Life, pp. 109–10.*

51. See, for example, Thomas Pakenham, The Boer War (New York: Random House, 1979), p. 226; and, Leo S Amery, ed., *The Times History of The War in South Africa 1899–1902* (London: Sampson Low, Marston and Co., 1900–9), II, pp. 430–40.

52. TNA, WO 32/7887, Orders by Clery, 14 December 1899.

53. Pakenham, *Boer War*, p. 239.

54. National Army Museum (hereafter NAM), Greening Mss, 8307–121.

55. British casualties at Colenso were 1,130. The Boers lost forty men.

56. Dundonald, *My Army Life*, pp. 109–10.

57. TNA, Buller Mss, WO 132/24, p. 37b.

58. Ibid., WO108/399, p. 55, Lansdowne to Buller, 16 December 1899.

59. Neither the Queen nor Wolseley were notified of the decision. See TNA, WO 108/39, p. 57, Lansdowne to Buller, 18 December 1899.

60. Buller to Lady Audrey Buller, 18 December 1899; as cited in Powell, *Buller*, p. 155.

61. TNA, WO 105/5, copy of letter to Lansdowne, through Roberts forwarding Warren's report on the capture and evacuation of Spion Kop, 30 January 1900.

62. Ibid., Buller Mss, WO 132/24, p. 51.

63. Buller denied this claim as well. See ibid., WO 105/5.

64. Great Britain, *South Africa, The Spion Kop Despatches* (London: Harrison and Sons, 1902), pp. 4, 29.

65. Ibid. Amery erroneously claimed that Thorneycroft was ready to stay but Coke had made the decision to retire. See Amery, ed., *Times History of The War in South Africa*, III, pp. 260–75.

66. British casualties on 24 January 1900 were 1,044. See Great Britain, *The Spion Kop Despatches*, p. 21.

67. Pakenham, *Boer War*, p. 317.

68. Dundonald, *My Army Life*, p. 133.

69. Great Britain, *The Spion Kop Despatches*, pp. 4–5.

70. Ibid.

71. Keith Surridge, 'Lansdowne at the War Office', in Gooch, ed., *Boer War*, pp. 34–36.

72. TNA, WO 105/5, Buller's Vaal Krantz dispatch, 8 February 1900.

73. Ibid., WO 132/24, p. 65.

74. War Office: Correspondence and Papers, South African War, Secret Despatches, 1901, Cd 457, xlvii, 87, Roberts to Lansdowne, 28 February and 15 March 1900; TNA, WO 108/380.

75. Amery, ed., *Times History of The War in South Africa*, III, p. 543.

76. Ibid., p. 549.

77. See, for example, Herbert Wrigley Wilson, *After Pretoria: The Guerrilla War* (London: Amalgamated Press, 1902), p. 125.

78. (An Average Observer), *The Burden of Proof* (London: Grant Richards, 1902), p. 76.

79. Amery, ed., *Times History of The War in South Africa*, IV, p. 452.

80. TNA, WO 105/10, Buller to Roberts, 13 September 1900.

81. NAM, Greening Mss, 8307–121.

82. Amery, *My Political Life*, II, p. 156.

83. Maurice V Brett, ed., *Journals and Letters of Reginald Viscount Esher* (London: Nicholson and Watson, 1934), p. 308.

84. TNA, WO 138/16, Kelly-Kenny to Roberts, 16 October 1901; and Brodrick to the King, 22 October 1902.

Chapter 4

George Colley

Ian F W Beckett

Writing about the two minutes' silence on Armistice Day in 1928, General Sir Ian Hamilton's thoughts were not of Gallipoli or of the Western Front but of an incident forty-seven years previously when he had been a young subaltern in the 92nd Highlanders, soon to become 2nd Battalion, The Gordon Highlanders:

> I ought, no doubt, to think only of those who died in the Great War. Yet, when I consciously set myself thinking, one of the first I always think about is Sir George Colley, stretched out, exactly as the effigy of a Knight lies in a cathedral, upon the flattened summit of Majuba . . . There he lay upon a site which might have been selected by Valkyries for a hero's grave, midway between the Transvaal and Natal with an eagle's outlook over both.[1]

Widely recognised as one of the most brilliant soldiers of his generation, George Colley had the distinction of passing out first from the Staff College at Camberley in only ten months instead of the usual two years with the largest aggregate of marks (4,274) ever obtained to that point. Moreover, finding the teaching undemanding, he had worked entirely on his own. Acquiring the habit of studying all manner of subjects in the early hours, he was also an accomplished water-colourist, played the flautina and became an authority on South African birds. Subsequently, as Professor of Administration and Law at the Staff College, Camberley, he wrote an influential article, 'Army', for the 1875 edition of *Encyclopaedia Britannica*. An excellent administrator and a writer of persuasive policy memoranda, Colley was considered by Evelyn Wood, 'the best instructed soldier I met'. Colley's mentor, Garnet Wolseley, also frequently referred to him as the ablest man he ever knew.[2] Yet, Colley's intellectual pre-eminence was to serve him ill in the field, his controversial defeat at Majuba on 27 February 1881 during the Anglo-Transvaal War (1880–81), which cost him his life, betraying lack of military judgement in his first independent command.

The third son of the Hon. George Colley, a retired naval commander from an old established Anglo-Irish family, Colley was born in November 1835. After travelling with his parents in Europe, he was educated at Cheam and the Royal

Chronology

1 November 1835	George Pomeroy Colley born in Dublin
	Educated at Cheam School and Royal Military College, Sandhurst
28 May 1852	Gazetted Ensign, 2nd Foot
1854–59	Service on the Cape Frontier
11 August 1854	Promoted Lieutenant
1860	Service in China
12 June 1860	Purchased Captaincy
1861	Service on Cape Frontier
1862	Attended Staff College, Camberley
6 March 1863	Promoted Brevet Major
July 1864	Appointed Brigade Major, Devonport
July 1871	Appointed Professor of Military Administration and Law at Staff College
15 May 1873	Promoted Brevet Lieutenant Colonel
17 December 1873	Joined Wolseley's Asante Expedition
19 December 1873	Appointed Director of Transport in Ashanti
31 March 1874	Promoted Brevet Colonel
14 April 1875	Appointed Colonial Treasurer, Natal
12 May 1875	Promoted Substantive Major
4 February 1876	Appointed Military Secretary to the Viceroy
October 1877	Appointed Private Secretary to Viceroy
14 March 1878	Married Edith Althea Hamilton
26 May 1879	Appointed Chief of Staff to Wolseley in Zululand
24 April 1880	Promoted Major General and appointed Governor of Natal, High Commissioner for South-eastern Africa, and C in C of Natal and the Transvaal
8 May 1880	Assumed additional prefix surname, becoming Pomeroy-Colley
28 January 1881	Defeated at Laing's Nek
8 February 1881	Defeated at Ingogo
27 February 1881	Killed at Majuba

Appointed CB, 1874; CMG, 1878; KCSI, 1879

Military College at Sandhurst, passing out first and thereby receiving his first commission without purchase in The Queen's Own Royal Regiment, the 2nd Foot, in May 1852. Regimental service in Ireland was followed by active service on the Cape Frontier, where Colley helped build a settlement for military pensioners being settled on the Kaffraria Frontier, surveyed the Transkei, and, still only 26, acted as a magistrate (administrator) for over 5,000 square miles of newly annexed territory. Colley rejoined his regiment when it was ordered to China for the Third China War in February 1860, being promoted to Captain in June 1860 and witnessing the capture of the Taku (Dagu) forts and the occupation of Peking (Beijing). En route home, he was detained at the Cape by the Governor, Sir George Grey, to resume his former frontier duties. Colley, however, wished to present himself for the Staff College entrance examination and declined a more permanent appointment at the Cape.

Passing out of Camberley and having been promoted to a brevet majority in March 1863, Colley spent five years as Brigade Major at Devonport, though this was enlivened by his appointment in 1867 as an examiner in military history and art for Camberley, Sandhurst and the Royal Military Academy, Woolwich. In 1869 Colley was offered the post of head of garrison instruction in England but it was vetoed on the grounds that he was too junior, and he then turned down the offer of military secretary to the C in C, Bombay.[3] In July 1871 he was then appointed to the professorship at the Staff College, where he remained until summoned to join Wolseley's Ashanti (Asante) expedition on the Gold Coast in November 1873. It is not clear when Colley and Wolseley had met previously, but they had clearly done so. Wolseley's choice of staff and special-service officers was a mixture of men he knew – not least from his earlier Red River expedition in Canada in 1870 – recent graduates of the Staff College, and those who had established some kind of intellectual reputation, such as Frederick Maurice and Henry Brackenbury, respectively instructor in tactics at Sandhurst and professor of military history at Woolwich. Thus, Colley's position at the Staff College would have been an obvious recommendation. Initially, Wolseley requested Colley's services to command what might be termed a 'special-service' battalion but was compelled to take regular battalions off the normal service roster. Colley then came out as a special-service officer.[4]

Placed in charge of the expedition's faltering transport arrangements immediately after his arrival in December 1873, Colley's administrative skills helped salvage Wolseley's need to get his force to the Asante capital of Kumase and back to the coast before the onset of the rains and before disease began to take its toll on his white troops. The problems had largely arisen from difficulties in first recruiting native carriers and then preventing them from deserting. Colley estimated that he needed 8,000 carriers to get the expedition to Kumase when there were only about 6,000 currently available. Part of the shortfall was found by converting the two West India regiments already deployed and an irregular native regiment commanded by Evelyn Wood into carriers. Colley reorganised the carriers into tribal companies and into regimental transport to accompany the troops and local transport to work on the lines of communication. Wolseley implemented a measure passed through local Judicial Assessors' Court to permit the arrest of those refusing to be conscripted for labour, forcing them to work without pay and making them liable to flogging if they refused to work. Colley also began to raid and burn recalcitrant villages. The measures got the expedition to Kumase and back, though Colley believed it had been a near-run thing with only five days' supplies to spare.[5]

The many newspaper correspondents accompanying the expedition differed in their opinions as to who was responsible for the initially chaotic transport arrangements, but all testified to the transformation wrought by Colley. Frederick Boyle, of the *Daily Telegraph*, wrote of Colley's 'astonishing activity which conduced so much to the success of the expedition', while G A Henty, of the

Standard, himself a former commissariat officer, wrote that Colley, 'by his activity, energy, and untiring zeal, excited the admiration of all'. For Winwood Reade, of *The Times*, Colley was 'an extraordinary man'. Reade noted that Colley constantly travelled back and forth along the tracks 'infested by parties of the enemy' but seemingly bore a charmed life. According to Reade, 'To Colley it is due that Coomassie was taken when it was.'[6] Wolseley's own final dispatch recorded that Colley's 'great talent for organisation soon placed the transport upon a satisfactory footing'.[7]

Colley was one of a number of officers who Wolseley offered the governorship of the Gold Coast to at the end of the expedition. Few were keen to remain. Still only a substantive captain, Colley preferred 'returning to my regiment as a captain till there is more soldiering to do', though 'it is pleasant to find that one's work has been favourably judged by those over me'. He also declined to lecture on the expedition to the Royal United Service Institution on the grounds that he 'only came when the uphill work was all over', Evelyn Wood subsequently delivering the lecture instead. Colley wrote to his brother, Henry, that he would be 'well satisfied' with the complimentary notices he had received in the press 'for I went out for fun and had my fun and a pleasant three months trip in a new country and a warm climate at government expense!'.[8] In the event, Colley's reward was the CB and promotion to substantive colonel. He spent the summer of 1874 visiting US Civil War battlefield sites and meeting a number of, mostly Confederate, generals.

Colley was now a key figure in Wolseley's 'Ashanti Ring', accompanying Wolseley's mission to Natal in February 1875, which was intended to persuade the colonists to accept inclusion in the proposed South African federation. Wolseley made Colley his Colonial Treasurer. Unexpectedly, however, when required to make a major speech to the Legislative Assembly in support of the bill to alter the Natal constitution on 20 May 1875, Colley's nerves got the better of him and he lapsed into silence. Wolseley was astonished: 'It was a curious case of nervousness, attacking a man who has had great experience in lecturing and who is gifted with a thoroughly logical mind and a very clear perception.' Colley himself wrote that he had not been prepared for the courteous nature of the debate for 'if they would only have made me angry I think I could have spoken'.[9] The bill passed by a narrow margin, Colley then undertaking an extensive tour through the Transvaal, Swaziland and Mozambique.

Colley next took up an appointment as AQMG at Aldershot, but after barely a month there was offered the influential post of military secretary to the new Viceroy of India, Lord Lytton, in February 1876. He accompanied Lytton to India in March 1876, becoming a leading advocate of the so-called 'forward policy' within Lytton's circle in the period leading to the outbreak of the Second Afghan War in November 1878. By the time the war began, he had become Lytton's private secretary, having turned down the chance to return to Camberley as commandant. Sir Neville Chamberlain noted that Colley, always present at meetings with Lytton yet always silent, 'has given the Viceroy the key to the discourse, and is his real military mentor'. Similarly, Wilfred Blunt wrote that Colley's influence over Lytton was so strong that 'he had persuaded the Viceroy that between them they could direct the whole detail of the plan of campaign from Simla'. Indeed, Colley's 'Memorandum on the Military Aspects of the Central Asian Question', completed on 7 June 1876 while Colley was on the voyage out to Bombay, has been characterised as 'the charter of Lytton's defence policy'.[10]

In terms of the possibility of a wider war against Russia, Colley selected the route through Peshawar and Balkh to Tashkent as the best line of offensive operations since Tashkent seemed the real seat of Russian military power in central Asia. With regard to the defence of India, Colley regarded Kabul as the key since it controlled most of the main routes between Afghanistan and India and would also enable eventual offensive operations to be mounted into the Central Asian khanates. By contrast, the C in C in India, General Sir Frederick Haines, was no less an advocate of a 'forward policy' than Lytton or Colley, but regarded the route through Kandahar to Herat and Merv as the most suitable. Haines's judgement was shared by his Quartermaster General, the then Colonel (local Major General) Frederick Roberts, though Roberts also appreciated the military significance of Tashkent. Colley, however, always believed that Herat lay beyond the realistic sphere of operations on logistic grounds, writing to one friend, 'I am a firm believer in the old military maxim that the difficulty of an operation increases in the ratio of the square of the distance.' Subsequently, Colley saw little point in retaining Kandahar after the conclusion of the Second Afghan War when Pishin appeared far more useful as a military base.[11]

With the more immediate prospect of a war limited to Afghanistan in the autumn of 1878, Haines responded to a request to suggest appropriate measures to secure the Kurram Pass from Thal and to advance on Kandahar from Quetta by additionally recommending a demonstration of force in the Khyber from Peshawar. Winter, however, was approaching and Lytton only wished to exert pressure on the Afghan Amir, Sher Ali, to accept a British mission at Kabul. Consequently, Lytton declined to authorise creating any reserve for the forces being gathered at Quetta, Thal and Peshawar. Solid and steady, Haines never quite grasped that Lytton wished to avoid an occupation of Afghanistan and to make further political points in proving to London that India could sustain operations without recourse to reinforcements from home, and in proving to St Petersburg that no threat to India would draw British forces out of Europe. Colley was to describe one conference as 5 hours of 'dull, stolid obstinacy such as I think I never witnessed before,' as Haines continued to argue for what Colley subsequently suggested Haines envisaged as 'a great campaign on the Oxus and a peerage'.[12]

Colley undoubtedly fed Lytton's unfavourable perception of Haines. Haines's frequent description of Colley, as 'the finest theoretical soldier he had ever met', is capable of more than one interpretation, while Haines also recorded on another occasion that Colley was 'a greatly overrated man'.[13] Haines certainly strongly deprecated Colley being sent in a supposedly private capacity to consult commanders on the Punjab Frontier on ways of dealing with incursions by the Jowaki Afridis in September 1877, seeing this as intervening directly between him and his subordinates, but Lytton angrily responded that he had not appointed Colley simply to compile his 'household accounts' and would use his personal staff unreservedly as he saw fit.[14] For his services in India, Colley was rewarded with the CMG in 1878 and the KCSI in July 1879, having been judged initially not to have performed sufficient 'signal' service for a knighthood when first proposed by Lytton in 1877.[15]

Part of Colley's wider agenda in India had been a complete reorganisation of the Indian army with the abolition of the three existing presidential armies and the substitution of four corps, and also bringing the whole of the North-West Frontier under a single trans-Indus authority wielding military and political power.[16] Wolseley was the obvious candidate for the latter if not the supreme military command in India. Colley's efforts to create an opening for Wolseley, however, were frustrated through the opposition of the army's C in C, the Duke of Cambridge.[17] At least Colley was able to achieve another part of the reform agenda by overseeing the establishment of a military intelligence department in India, meeting Colonel Robert Home of the War Office Intelligence Department while in London in March 1878 to settle a division of geographical responsibilities between the two.[18]

As one of Wolseley's protégés, and in seemingly intriguing to get Wolseley the chief command in India, Colley had fallen foul of Cambridge. The Duke had rejected the notion of Colley for the command at the Cape in 1878 and was equally opposed to Wolseley securing Colley's services as chief of staff when Wolseley was sent to take over the direction of the Zulu War in May 1879. In the event, through appealing to the Secretary of State for War, Frederick Stanley, Wolseley did secure Colley's services but only in the rank of Brigadier General rather than Major General as Wolseley wanted. Colley proved invaluable, Wolseley recording that he was 'so clear-headed & hard-working: he is never idle for a moment & works unremittingly'. Indeed, it has been suggested that Colley was the real architect of the political settlement that Wolseley imposed upon Zululand in that dividing the territory between thirteen compliant chiefs answerable to a British Resident resembled Indian security concepts. The renewal of the Second Afghan War in September 1879, however, saw Colley recalled to India.[19] In April 1880, however, Wolseley succeeded in seeing Colley appointed his successor, Colley being promoted to Major General on 24 April and made Governor of Natal, High Commissioner for South-eastern Africa and C in C in Natal and the Transvaal. Though uncertain whether he should do so when matters remained uncertain in India, and being delayed in any case, Colley took up his appointment in June 1880. He hoped, as he wrote to Wolseley, that he could 'do my master credit'.[20] In theory, and for reasons that remain unknown, Colley had assumed an additional prefix surname on 8 May 1880, becoming Sir George Pomeroy Pomeroy-Colley. It would appear, however, that he preferred to remain known as Sir George Colley and no one seems to have referred to him in any other way.[21]

The new Governor often appeared shy and modest and was certainly prey to self-doubt. Slight in stature, Colley's receding hairline gave greater prominence to a strong brow, usually taken as a sign of his intellect, though the eyes were said to be soft. For the last three years of his life, he was bearded. His biographer, William Butler, wrote of Colley as having a face 'beautifully modelled, a strong countenance developed to the utmost and informed with thought'. Musing upon his own career in 1876, Colley remarked that, in his early years, he had 'worked for ambition' but, when professor at the Staff College, he had been stimulated by work for its own sake and 'the influence I felt one could exert upon others by keeping them up to the mark'. Indeed, he still believed work well done gave him greater satisfaction than perceived success. Interestingly, Colley reminded some of the manner of Robert E Lee, and, significantly, Lee was his own 'greatest military hero', Colley writing of Lee's 'mixture of gentleness and everything that was sweet and tender with the grandest military personal qualities'.[22]

In his later years, Colley appears to have been much influenced by his wife, Edith Hamilton, daughter of Major General Henry Meade 'Tiger' Hamilton and fifteen years younger than Colley. Edith's brother, the future Major General Bruce Hamilton, acted as Colley's aide-de-camp during the Anglo-Transvaal War. The marriage in March 1878, when Colley was 43, had taken many by surprise.[23] All recognised Edith's lively intelligence and Colley was to write from Natal that she 'seconds me splendidly, and rows or laughs at the people who come to her with long faces or absurd stories'.[24] Yet she was also highly ambitious. Evelyn Wood noting in a letter on the very day on which, unknown to him, Colley had been killed, that her ambition for her husband 'obliterates apparently every thought of the personal danger which he has undergone'. In fact, Edith Colley wrote letters to her husband on both 15 and 24 February 1881 that suggest she did not 'care a rush for any such rubbish as work or success' and wished only to see him safe home again.[25] Nevertheless, it was widely believed that she had written to Colley after Laing's Nek and Ingogo to urge him into further action, the letter mysteriously disappearing after his death.[26] It was certainly much remarked that when the first train arrived at Pietermaritzburg in October 1880 following completion of the line from Durban – no gold had yet been discovered on the Rand to speed the development of railways in southern Africa – Colley stood on the footplate, but, symbolically, Edith was at the engine's throttle.[27]

Colley was certainly devoted to Edith, writing a touching last letter on 26 February 1881 'in case I should not return'. He lamented that he did not believe in an afterlife but concluded, 'Think of our happiness together, and our love – not a common love I think – and let that be a source of comfort and light to your future life, my own loved one, and think lovingly and sadly, but not too sadly or hopelessly of your affectionate husband.'[28] Wolseley, however, subsequently believed that she had married Colley as a matter of convenience rather than love, a conclusion reached in the light of her second marriage, and swift and financially productive separation in 1891.[29]

When Colley arrived in South Africa in June 1880, the most pressing problem appeared to be implementing Wolseley's political settlement of Zululand. Moreover, the Administrator, another Wolseley protégé, Sir Owen Lanyon, misled Colley as to the deteriorating political situation in the Transvaal. British politicians had sought to improve security and commercial integration and progress in southern Africa by correcting the politically fragmented nature of the region through confederation of the white colonies and subjugation of the Zulu kingdom. Wolseley had secured the half-hearted support of the British colonists in Natal for federation in 1875 and a Transvaal bankrupted by a disastrous war with the baPedi had been annexed in April 1877. By assuming protection of the Transvaal, the British had inherited an existing frontier dispute between Boer and Zulu that provided a pretext for the Zulu War. The end of the Zulu threat, however, had not reconciled the Boers to confederation as had been anticipated. Boer resentment had been exacerbated by Lanyon's strenuous efforts to collect taxes and by the alleged indiscipline of the small British garrisons in the Transvaal. Lanyon simply never realised the extent of Boer dissatisfaction, though the Boers in turn seriously underestimated the willingness of Gladstone's new Liberal government to make concessions once it took office in April 1880. Indeed, the Cabinet was split between Whigs such as Lords Hartington and Kimberley, determined to retain the Transvaal within the empire, and radicals such as John Bright and Joseph Chamberlain, who wished to be rid of it.[30]

As late as 11 December 1880 Lanyon's assessment was that the Boers were 'incapable of any united action' and such 'mortal cowards' that 'anything they may do will be but a spark in the pan'.[31] Two days later, a Boer meeting at Paardekraal resolved to re-establish an independent republic, though the proclamation could not be printed for several days. On 16 December shots were fired at British troops in Potchefstroom and, on the following day, Lanyon received a copy of the proclamation: he declared a state of rebellion on 18 December. On 20 December, the Boers ambushed a column of the 94th Foot at Bronkhorstspruit when it was moving towards Pretoria as part of a consolidation there. Of 273 men in the column, 57 were killed, over 100 wounded and all survivors captured. Colley, therefore, found himself faced with a rebellion by over 7,000 armed Boers. Since the British military presence in South Africa had been rapidly reduced after the end of the Zulu War, Colley had only 1,772 men available in Natal. Some 2,839 men from 3 different battalions and a cavalry regiment had been divided between 9 different garrison posts in the Transvaal in August 1880 before Colley initiated a consolidation, abandoning 3 posts and withdrawing 5 companies to Natal prior to the outbreak of hostilities. The six remaining garrisons at Pretoria, Standerton, Lydenburg, Rustenburg, Marabastad and Wakkerstroom were all now besieged by the Boers, together with a small detachment at Potchefstroom.[32]

Colley's dilemma was whether to wait for reinforcements, or to try to relieve the garrisons with the resources he already had available. This in itself might enable him to secure a victory sufficiently decisive to deter the Orange Free State from joining in common cause with the Transvaalers, and also to discourage any native disturbances while British forces were distracted since there was continuing unrest among the Basutos (baSotho) at the time. As Colley wrote to Wolseley on 17 January 1881, 'I would much like to know whether you at home are blaming my slowness in not moving forward earlier & with a smaller force, or think me rash in attempting to move with so small a one & without waiting for the reinforcements now coming out.'[33] In particular, Colley was concerned by the weakness of the British position at Potchefstroom, which he believed could not hold out beyond mid-February.[34] Accordingly, he decided to act before the arrival of reinforcements despite wet summer weather that made all movement difficult. As it happened, the 200 or so defenders of Potchefstroom held out for 95 days until forced to surrender through starvation on 21 March. This in itself was a result of deceit on the part of the local Boer commander in not communicating the terms of the armistice following Colley's death, concluded on 6 March, which provided for re-supply of the besieged garrisons.[35]

Though Roberts had a high opinion of Colley's abilities, he did suggest after Majuba that Colley was 'one of those men who believes that one Englishman is equal to 3 of any country'. Colley had also once remarked that 'a British regiment, 1,000 strong, armed with Martini-Henry rifles, ought to be able to march at will through the length and breadth of Afghanistan, when once clear of the Khyber and Kurram Passes' and there is no doubt that Colley underestimated the Boers' military capacity.[36] Consequently, he believed that his improvised field force of twelve infantry companies drawn from four different battalions and a handful of seamen landed from HMS *Boadicea* – no more than six companies were engaged in any of the subsequent actions – would be sufficient. A small mounted force was improvised by mounting some of the infantry and drawing upon the Natal Mounted Police since, despite the lack of mounted troops, Colley declined to employ any volunteers against the Boers in the belief that to do so would lead to an unacceptable escalation of the conflict. Certainly, from his Indian experience he was well attuned to political considerations. Thus, he had counselled Roberts strongly against imposing severe reprisals for Louis Cavagnari's murder once Kabul was reoccupied in October 1879, his judgement that Roberts had no 'political head' being entirely justified by the controversial executions Roberts had instituted. Similarly, Colley urged his troops to recognise that the Boers were 'actuated by feelings that are entitled to our respect'.[37]

The only practical route into the Transvaal was through the pass over the Drakensbergs at Laing's Nek, which the Boers promptly blocked with 2,000 men. Establishing his forward base at Mount Prospect, Colley attempted to 'try the Boers mettle'.[38] However, a frontal assault on 28 January was repulsed with 197 casualties. In some respects, Colley was unlucky in that the planned advance by his improvised mounted force on the Boers' left flank was launched prematurely, veered in the wrong direction and was not supported by a second line. The infantry, principally the 58th Foot, was left exposed to Boer fire as it advanced up a steep slope and lost heavily: it was the last occasion on which regimental colours were carried into action. Colley also lost several members of his own staff whom he allowed to lead the troops into action.[39] When setting out for Majuba, indeed, Colley was to decline to wake his sleeping brother-in-law, Bruce Hamilton, on the grounds that there was 'a kind of fatality' about his staff.[40] Writing later to Wolseley, Colley admitted that the assault had been hazardous without an adequate mounted force but that anything was 'better than standing still', though he also suggested that, if faced with the same situation, he would conduct the battle in exactly the same way. He felt keenly the loss of 'good men & personal friends' and the effect that the delay would have on the besieged garrisons.[41]

Characteristically, though perhaps unadvisedly, Colley addressed his force, taking the blame for the losses and suggesting that he would now await reinforcements, one observer remarking that Colley 'was a great hand at making speeches'.[42] On 8 February, however, Colley was compelled to attempt to reopen his line of communications back to Newcastle when the Boers placed a force across it at Ingogo (Schuinshoogte). Colley found himself surrounded on a small plateau by a more mobile Boer force and suffered another 150 casualties before withdrawing under cover of a violent thunderstorm. It was a chastening experience with more of his staff killed, Colley writing to his sister that, 'I have to look cheerful and I dare say am thought callous, and to-day am presiding at some races and sports, but sometimes it is hard not to break down.'[43]

Evelyn Wood, who had agreed to serve as Colley's second in command, though senior in rank, disembarked at Durban on 12 February and arrived at Newcastle with a small column five days later. Colley, who rode back to meet Wood, made it clear that he wanted to take the Nek himself, but promised to wait until Wood brought up further troops. It was a decision he also conveyed to the Duke of Cambridge, indicating he felt no decisive success could now be obtained without cavalry.[44] Apparently believing that he must restore British prestige, however, Colley resolved upon seizing Majuba, a commanding height comprising a plateau some 2,000ft above Laing's Nek that seemed to dominate the Boer positions, though actually so high as not to threaten them directly.

Gladstone's government had begun negotiations with the Boers secretly and without informing Colley even before the action at Laing's Nek. The reverse there and at Ingogo strengthened the hands of the radicals, who favoured continuing negotiations even from a position of weakness, whereas the Whigs within the Cabinet would have preferred attempting to achieve further leverage through success. On 16 February, therefore, Colley was instructed to offer an armistice and an inquiry by a Royal Commission into Boer grievances, but given discretion to act as he felt fit, with the proviso that 'we are anxious for your making arrangements to avoid effusion of blood'.[45] Understandably, Colley enquired whether he was intended to leave Laing's Nek in the possession of the Boers and to abandon his garrisons, to which the government replied that the garrisons should be enabled to provision themselves but Colley should not march to their relief or occupy Laing's Nek. On 21 February Colley indicated to the Boers that hostilities would be suspended if they were prepared to accept an armistice and a Royal Commission, adding in effect a 48-hour ultimatum to the terms being offered on his own initiative. No reply was received as President Kruger was travelling within the Transvaal without having delegated authority to anyone else to act on his behalf: he was only to receive Colley's offer on 28 February. With no reply received, Colley felt free to initiate the decisive move that he believed would end the war with a minimum of bloodshed by seizing Majuba as a legitimate means of improving British leverage. Moreover, as he wrote to Wolseley, he wanted to reverse the 'deep & permanent injury' to British prestige stemming from Laing's Nek before the government could end the campaign.[46]

Majuba, 1881

Colley's interest in Majuba was first noticed on 26 February by Thomas Carter, the war correspondent of the *Natal Times*, who saw him and his new Chief of Staff, Herbert Stewart, observing it intently through their field glasses. It might be noted in passing that, compared to some other commanders, Colley had a relaxed view of the presence of the press in the field.[47] In fact, Colley had undertaken a mounted reconnaissance with Stewart two days earlier, in which they had rode well to the west into the Transvaal to observe the other side of the mountain. The Boers were further entrenching at Laing's Nek but Majuba was as yet unoccupied save for a picquet during the day that was withdrawn each evening.

Colley chose 2 companies of the 58th, 3 companies of the 3rd/60th Rifles, 2 companies of the 92nd and a naval contingent, the whole including staff totalling 30 officers and 568 men.[48] En route to the summit, Colley detached 2 companies of the 3/60th and 1 of the 92nd to guard his line of communication, reaching the top with 19 officers and 383 men. No artillery or machine-guns were taken due to the precipitous nature of the terrain and it is doubtful if rocket tubes would have proved any more useful. Presumably, Colley took a mixed force in order to allow all to share in the expected victory, though some suggested that it was also intended to give as much prominence to the short-service recruits of the 58th as to the long-service veterans of the 92nd, who had been landed in South Africa while on their way back home from India, where they had served for thirteen years. Lieutenant Ian Hamilton of the 92nd certainly thought so: 'Well then, let the tiny force be so thoroughly well shuffled and mixed up that the Devil himself would be unable to say what these victorious troops were – long-service or short-service, soldiers or sailors.'[49] Certainly, the impact of short service, introduced as part of the Cardwell reforms between 1868 and 1872, was still hotly contested between conservative elements such as Cambridge and reformers like Wolseley. The composition of the force meant, however, that it lacked cohesion.

After an 8-hour climb to the summit on the night of 26 February 1881, Colley felt his men too tired to entrench and, although the extent of their fatigue was

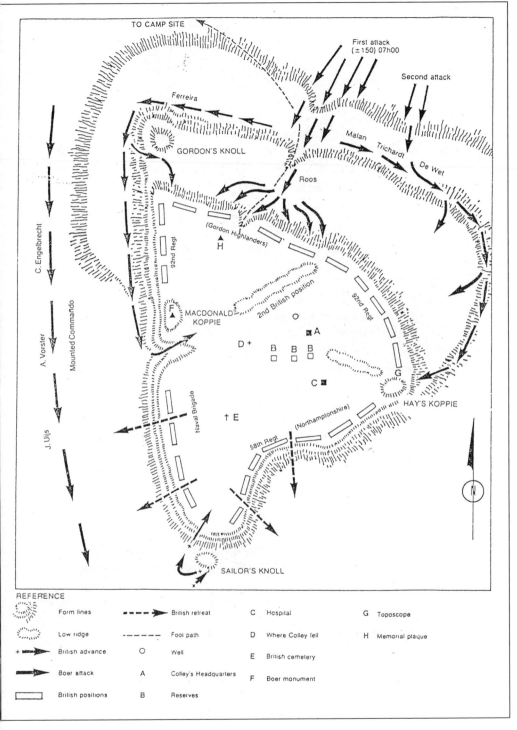

REFERENCE

Form lines	British retreat	C Hospital	G Toposcope
Low ridge	Foot path	D Where Colley fell	H Memorial plaque
British advance	O Well	E British cemetery	
Boer attack	A Colley's Headquarters	F Boer monument	
British positions	B Reserves		

Plan of the battle of Majuba, 27 February 1881.

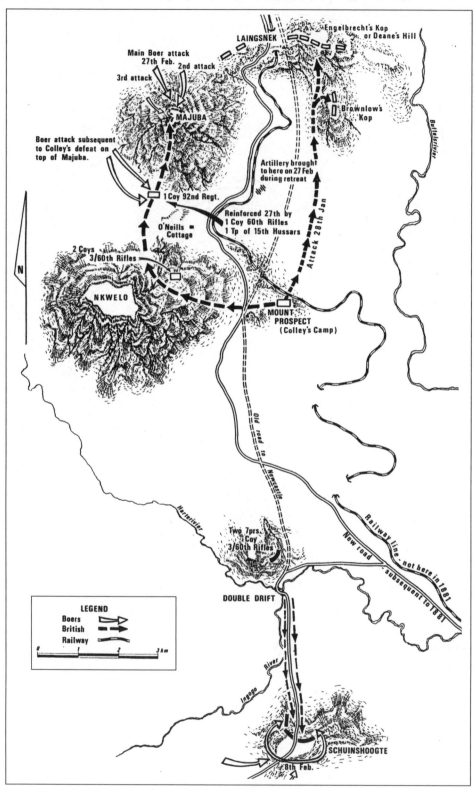

Plan of the battles of Laing's Nek, Schuinshoogte and Majuba, 1881.

questioned subsequently, in any case, he and Herbert Stewart believed the position impregnable. Colley is said to have remarked, 'We could stay here for ever.' Carter of the *Natal Times* asked one man why he was merely piling a few stones on top of each other, to be told, 'Oh, it's all right sir, it's good enough for what we shall want up here.'[50] As the light improved about 0500, several Highlanders stood on the edge, gesturing at the Boers below, and a few shots were fired to Colley's annoyance. Some Boers began to break camp but at about 0700 some 200 other Boers began to scale the heights. Eventually, some 450 Boers were involved in storming the British position, while 150 others rode round the bottom of Majuba to cut off the force on the summit, making skilful use of a considerable amount of dead ground.

Herbert Stewart was still unconcerned when sending a signal at 0930 to the effect that the Boers were wasting ammunition and Colley showed little interest when Ian Hamilton reported to him that the Boers were working their way up the hill, pinning down defenders who showed themselves with accurate musketry. Subsequently, Colley, Stewart and Commander Romilly of the Naval Detachment did go to look down the hill at about 1100, at which point Romilly was mortally wounded but, when Hamilton again went to report to Colley at about 1300, the latter was taking a short nap and could not be disturbed. By 1330, however, the Boers were reaching the edge of the rim of the plateau and, when Hamilton requested permission to charge, Colley responded that he would wait until the Boers were advancing before ordering a volley and charge. In reality, whether or not a charge would have worked, the moment had been lost and, with no defensive line prepared, some of the defenders began to fall back to the centre of the plateau. According to Carter, there was a 'sudden piercing cry of terror' and the British line broke.[51]

Colley was seen moving forward and firing his revolver while shouting encouragement to his men. There were some later suggestions that Colley committed suicide, was shot in the back while running or killed while waving a white handkerchief in surrender. The most reliable account suggests he was shot at close range above the right eye while still advancing on the Boers.[52] Evelyn Wood subsequently obtained Colley's helmet and wrote to Edith Colley that it showed clearly that Colley had been shot while facing the enemy, to which she replied tersely that the position of her late husband's head when he was shot was of no interest to her as she had 'never heard him charged with any fault in regard of personal courage except having it in excess'.[53] In all, Colley's force suffered 275 casualties, including 92 officers and men killed, 131 wounded, an additional 50 men captured and 2 missing; the Boers reputedly lost only 2 dead and 4 wounded. The prisoners from the 92nd included another future general, the then Lieutenant Hector MacDonald.

Colley's body was brought down from Majuba to be buried in the small cemetery at Mount Prospect on 1 March. One officer of the 92nd, the Hon. John Napier, suggested that Colley's defeat was 'the result of a series of inexcusable blunders in the art and practice of war'. The Duke of Cambridge concurred, being particularly critical of the mixed composition of the force. Redvers Buller, shocked by Colley's death, felt Colley had been 'lost to over confidence'. One young officer in the 83rd Foot, who reached the front only after Majuba, reported that 'the feeling amongst the troops here is very strong for the poor fellows who were murdered through the ambition and incompetence of our Colley – a politician but a theoretical and paper General' and that his memory was 'roundly' abused.[54] Certainly, be it carelessness bred of over-confidence, the failure to entrench, the lack of cohesion within the force, a failure of command on the summit or a combination of all, Colley had paid with his life.

With the Irish Land Bill a more pressing concern for many in the Cabinet, Wood was now directed by the government to obtain an armistice. This was concluded on 6 March with eventual agreement being reached on 21 March 1881 to restore self-government to the Transvaal under the vague formula of retaining the Queen's suzerainty. The agreement was signed on 23 March. On 24 March the latest reinforcements under the command of Roberts arrived at the Cape and were immediately ordered home: some 16,000 men were in or on their way to South Africa at the time the peace was signed. Wolseley was refused the command himself because the Secretary of State for War, Hugh Childers, said 'that he could not spare me, that he wanted me here to help him through his reforms etc., and that he had a high position in store for me'. Wolseley was never to forgive Wood for not avenging Colley's death, though he apparently persuaded Butler to remove 'two or three pages of vituperation' of Wood from his biography of Colley.[55] Roberts and his coterie were also lastingly critical because they had been equally frustrated in continuing the campaign.[56] Certainly, Majuba remained a stain on its honour that the army was determined to remove. Thus, in the first engagement of the South African War on 20 October 1899 British soldiers were urged to 'Remember Majuba'. A day later at Elandslaagte, with Ian Hamilton in command, Highlanders carried a Boer position with cries of 'Majuba'. It was then on Majuba Day, 27 February 1900, that Roberts took the surrender of the main Boer field army at Paardeburg.

As for 'Poor Colley', as most contemporary soldiers referred to him thereafter, a premature death had brought a highly promising career to a sudden close. The loss of Colley and later of Herbert Stewart, mortally wounded at Metemmeh in the Sudan in February 1885, were blows that Wolseley felt especially keenly. In a way, both men represented the advantages and the disadvantages of the 'Wolseley Ring' and its imitators. Wolseley himself was generally successful in co-ordinating the diverse talents of his chosen subordinates in way well suited to colonial campaigning. The problem was that improvisation was no substitute for a proper general staff. Wolseley's capacity to manage affairs decreased in proportion to the growth in the scale of operations, while the way he operated also militated against the development of initiative in his subordinates and, without him, they sometimes floundered.[57] Colley was an outstandingly able strategist and administrator and, while he may have been unlucky, such talents did not make him a great soldier.

Bibliography

Edith Colley first approached J A Froude to write her husband's biography but, on Wolseley's advice, he declined. In the event, the task was taken on by another of Wolseley's adherents, Lieutenant General Sir William Butler. Butler's *The Life of Sir George Pomeroy-Colley* (London: John Murray, 1899) remains the only biography and makes reference to Colley correspondence that has apparently not survived elsewhere. The Anglo-Transvaal War, however, has been the subject of a number of modern works. Brian Bond chose to cover the war himself in Brian Bond, ed., *Victorian Military Campaigns* (London: Hutchinson, 1967), while Joseph Lehmann, *The First Boer War* (London: Jonathan Cape, 1972) has now been substantially updated by John Laband, *The Transvaal Rebellion: The First Boer War, 1880–81* (London: Pearson/Longman, 2005). Majuba is covered in 'popular' accounts by Oliver Ransford, *The Battle of Majuba Hill: The First Boer War* (London: John Murray, 1967) and Ian Castle, *Majuba 1881: The Hill of Destiny* (London: Osprey, 1996), while there is a booklet from the Boer perspective, V E d'Assonville, *Majuba* (Weltevredenpark: Marnix, 1996), available in both English and Afrikaans.

Notes

1. General Sir Ian Hamilton, *Listening for the Drums* (London: Faber & Faber, 1944), p. 130.
2. Field Marshal Sir Evelyn Wood, *From Midshipman to Field Marshal* (London: Methuen & Co., 1906), II, p. 112; Liddell Hart Centre for Military Archives (hereafter LHCMA), Maurice Mss, 2/2/9, Wolseley to Maurice, n.d. (1881); South Lanarkshire Council Museum (hereafter SLCM), Wolseley Diaries, CAM.H.12, Diary, 31 December 1881; Hove Reference Library (hereafter Hove), Wolseley Mss, W/P 8/22 and 27, Wolseley to his wife, 26 August and 29 September–3 October 1879; Field Marshal Viscount Wolseley, *The Story of a Soldier's Life* (London: Archibald Constable & Co., 1903), II, p. 317.
3. Lieutenant General Sir William Butler, *The Life of Sir George Pomeroy-Colley* (London: John Murray, 1899), pp. 80–81.
4. The National Archives (hereafter TNA), WO 33/26, Wolseley to Cardwell, 24 October 1873; Royal Archives (hereafter RA), Cambridge Mss, VIC/ADDE/1/7217, Wolseley to Cambridge, 24 October 1873.
5. TNA, WO 147/3, Wolseley journal, 16 January 1874; ibid., CO 96/111, Report of Judicial Court, 14 November 1873; RA, Cambridge Mss, VIC/ADDE/1/7309, Wolseley to Cambridge, 25 January 1874; National Army Museum (hereafter NAM), Cooper Mss, 6112-596-8-5, Colley to Cooper, 26 February 1874; G Salis, 'Carrier Corps and Coolies on Active Service in China, India and Africa, 1860–79', *Journal of the Royal United Service Institution 24, 107 (1880)*, 815–46.
6. Frederick Boyle, *Through Fanteeland to Coomassie* (London: Chapman and Hall, 1874), p. 220; G A Henty, *The March to Coomassie* (London: Tinsley Brothers, 1874), p. 444; Winwood Reade, *The Story of the Ashantee Campaign* (London: Smith, Elder & Co., 1874), pp. 241–43.
7. Henry Brackenbury, *The Ashanti War: A Narrative* (Edinburgh: William Blackwood & Sons, 1874), II, p. 357.
8. NAM, Cooper Mss, 6112-596-8, Colley to Cooper, 26 February and 19 April 1874; Author's Collection, Colley to his brother, 'Wednesday morning' (March 1874).
9. Adrian Preston, ed., *Sir Garnet Wolseley's South African Diaries (Natal), 1875* (Cape Town: A A Balkema, 1971), p. 185; Butler, *Colley*, p. 123.
10. G W Forrest, *The Life of Field Marshal Sir Neville Chamberlain* (Edinburgh: William Blackwood & Sons, 1909), p. 153; Brian Robson, *The Road to Kabul: The Second Afghan War, 1878–81* (London: Arms and Armour Press, 1986), p. 70; Adrian Preston, 'Sir Charles

MacGregor and the Defence of India, 1857–87', *Historical Journal* 12, 1 (1969), 58–77.

11. British Library, Oriental and India Office Collection (hereafter OIOC), Burne Mss, Eur Mss. D951/8, Colley to Burne, 3 November 1878; NAM, Cooper Mss, 6112-596-14, Colley to Cooper, 24 February 1879; OIOC, Burne Mss, Eur Mss. D951/8, Colley to Burne, 15 November 1880; ibid., Lyall Mss, F.132/26, Colley to Stewart, 13 December 1878; Butler, *Colley*, pp. 217–18.

12. OIOC, Burne Mss, Eur MSS D951/11, Colley to Burne, 3 November 1878 and 20 January 1880.

13. Robert Rait, *The Life of Field Marshal Sir Frederick Paul Haines* (London: Constable & Co., 1911), pp. 213–14; RA, Cambridge Mss, VIC/ADD E/1/8794, Haines to Cambridge, 14 July 1879.

14. NAM, Haines Mss, 8108-9-5, Haines to Lytton, 7 October 1877 and Lytton to Haines, 9 October 1877; Ian F W Beckett, 'Cavagnari's Coup de Main: The Projected Attack on Ali Masjid, October 1878', *Soldiers of the Queen* 82 (1995), 24–28.

15. RA, VIC/MAIN6/47, Salisbury to Ponsonby, 12 February 1877.

16. Butler, *Colley*, pp. 192–93.

17. SLCM, Wolseley Diaries, CAM.H.9, Diary 3 October 1878; Hove, Wolseley Mss, W/P 7/26, Wolseley to wife, 2–4 April 1878.

18. W G Beaver, 'The Development of the Intelligence Division and its role in aspects of Imperial Policy-making, 1854–1901: The Military Mind of Imperialism', unpub. DPhil thesis, Oxford, 1976, pp. 41–45; A W Preston, 'British Military Policy and the Defence of India: A Study of British Military Policy, Plans and Preparations during the Russian Crisis, 1876-80', unpub. PhD thesis, London, 1966, pp. 96–102.

19. Giles St Aubyn, *The Royal George: The Life of HRH Prince George, Duke of Cambridge* (London: Constable, 1963), pp. 187–88; Hove, Wolseley Mss, LW/P, 5/11 Lady Wolseley to Wolseley, 30 October 1877; ibid., S.A.2. Wolseley to Stanley, 30 May 1879; ibid., W/P 8/26, Wolseley to wife, 24–25 September 1879; Preston, ed., *Wolseley's South African Journal*, pp. 2, 32–33, 35–36, 53, 122, 318; ibid., p. 106; Charles Ballard, 'Sir Garnet Wolseley and John Dunn: The Architects and Agents of the Ulundi Settlement', in Andrew Duminy and Charles Ballard, eds, *The Anglo-Zulu War: New Perspectives* (Pietermaritzburg: University of Natal Press, 1981), pp. 120–47.

20. OIOC, Burne Mss, Eur Mss. D951/11, Colley to Burne, 4 February 1880; Hove, Wolseley Autobiographical Collection, Colley to Wolseley, 15 April 1880.

21. NAM, Anstruther Mss, 5705-22, Anstruther to Gina Anstruther, 1 August 1880.

22. Butler, *Colley*, pp. 147–48.

23. OIOC, Burne Mss, Eur. Mss D951/8, Lytton to Burne, 7 March 1878; RA, VIC/MAIN35/45, Lady Lytton to the Queen, 7 September 1878.

24. Butler, *Colley*, p. 88.

25. RA/VIC/MAINO/38/276, Wood to the Queen, 27 February 1881; Butler, *Colley*, pp. 347–48; John Laband, *The Transvaal Rebellion: The First Boer War, 1880–81* (London: Pearson/Longman, 2005), p. 189.

26. Oliver Ransford, *The Battle of Majuba Hill: The First Boer War* (London: John Murray, 1967), p. 72.

27. Joseph Lehmann, *The First Boer War* (London: Jonathan Cape, 1972), pp. 88, 234.

28. Butler, *Colley*, pp. 367–8.

29. Hove, Wolseley Mss, W/P 20/23, 84 and 85, Wolseley to his wife, 8 February, 28 May and 31 May 1891; William Perkins Library (Durham, NC), Wolseley Mss, Wolseley to George Wolseley, 28 May 1891; Ian F W Beckett, 'Women and Patronage in the Late Victorian Army', *History* 85, 279 (2000), 463–80.

30. Brian Bond, 'The South African War, 1880–81', in Brian Bond, ed., *Victorian Military Campaigns* (London: Hutchinson, 1967), pp. 201–40.

31. Butler, *Colley*, p. 268.

32. Ian F W Beckett, 'Military High Command in South Africa, 1854–1914', in Peter Boyden, Alan Guy and Marion Harding, eds, *Ashes and Blood: The British Army in South Africa, 1795–1914* (London: National Army Museum, 1999), pp. 60–71.

33. RA, VIC/MAINO/38/141, Colley to Wolseley, 17 January 1881.

34. Butler, *Colley*, p. 283; Laband, *Transvaal Rebellion*, pp. 137–38.

35. Ian Bennett, *A Rain of Lead: The Siege and Surrender of the British at Potchefstroom* (London: Greenhill Books, 2001), pp. 212–18.

36. Killie Campbell Library, Wood Mss, KCM 89/9/35, Roberts to Wood, 6 January 1881; RA, Ponsonby Mss, VIC/ADDA36, Ponsonby to his wife, 3 March 1881; General Sir Luther Vaughan, *My Service in the Indian Army – and After* (London: Constable, 1904), p. 182.

37. RA, VIC/MAINO/38/6, Colley to Bigge, 1 January 1881; OIOC, Burne Mss, Eur Mss. D951/8, Colley to Burne, 20 January and 27 January 1880; ibid., Lyall Mss, F. 132/24, Roberts to Lyall, 29 January 1880; Butler, *Colley*, pp. 409–10.

38. RA, VIC/MAINO/38/141, Colley to Wolseley, 17 January 1881.

39. Laband, *Transvaal Rebellion*, pp. 146–57.

40. Butler, *Colley*, p. 369.

41. Hove, Wolseley Mss, Autobiographical Collection, Colley to Wolseley, 21 February 1881; RA, VIC/ADDMAINO/38/141, Colley to Wolseley, 30 January 1881.

42. Sir Percival Marling, *Rifleman and Hussar* (London: John Murray, 1931), p. 41.

43. Butler, *Colley*, pp. 311–12.

44. Ibid., pp. 293–96; RA, VIC/MAINO/40/27, Wood to the Queen, 13 April 1881; RA, Cambridge Mss, VIC/ADDE/1/9527, Colley to Cambridge, 18 February 1881.

45. Butler, *Colley*, p. 340.

46. Laband, *Transvaal Rebellion*, p. 190; Bond, 'South African War', in Bond, ed., *Victorian Military Campaigns*, p. 223; Hove, Wolseley Mss, Autobiographical Collection, Colley to Wolseley, 21 February 1881.

47. Thomas Carter, *A Narrative of the Boer War: Its Causes and Results* (Cape Town: Juta, 1896), p. 253; OIOC, Burne Mss, EUR Mss D951/11, Colley to Burne, 20 January 1880.

48. NAM, Essex Mss, 7505-49, Journal of the Natal Field Force, 26 February 1881 (reproduced in Paul Butterfield, ed., *War and Peace in South Africa, 1879–81: The Writings of Philip Anstruther and Edward Essex* (Melville: Scripta Africana, 1986), p. 213).

49. Hamilton, *Listening for the Drums*, p. 142.

50. Ransford, *Majuba*, pp. 82–83; Butler, *Colley*, pp. 383, 385.

51. Carter, *Narrative of the Boer War*, p. 276.

52. Ransford, *Majuba*, pp. 105–6; Lehmann, *First Boer War*, pp. 247–49, 252.

53. Natal Archives Depot, Wood Mss, III/2/6, Lady Colley to Wood, 26 October 1881; Laband, *Transvaal Rebellion*, p. 209.

54. Ransford, *Majuba*, pp. 120–21; Willoughby Verner, *The Military Life of HRH George, Duke of Cambridge* (London: John Murray, 1905), II, p. 195; Buller Family Mss, Box 1, Buller to Henrietta, 6 March 1881; ibid., Buller to Lucy, 7 June 1881; Sir Archibald Anson, *About Others and Myself* (London: John Murray, 1920), pp. 374–75.

55. LHCMA, Maurice Mss, 2/2/9, Wolseley to Maurice, n.d. (1881); Hove, Wolseley Mss, H.11, Memorandum, 3 March 1881; ibid., SSL. 10/1 Uncompleted Autobiography, xxxix, f. 33–38; Field Marshal Sir Evelyn Wood, *Winnowed Memories* (London: Cassell & Co., 1918), pp. 275–76.

56. National Library of Scotland, Minto Mss, MS 12380, Pretyman to Minto, 18 January 1892.

57. Ian F W Beckett, 'Command in the Late Victorian Army', in Gary Sheffield, ed., *Leadership and Command: The Anglo-American Military Experience since 1861* (London: Brassey's, 1997), pp. 37–56; idem, 'Wolseley and the Ring', *Soldiers of the Queen* 69 (1992), 14–25; idem, *The Victorians at War* (London: Hambledon, 2003), pp. 3–12.

Chapter 5

Lord Chelmsford

John Laband

highly charged debate took place in the House of Commons on 14 March 1879, during which the Conservative government's handling of the campaign in Zululand was vigorously challenged. Earlier, on 22 January 1879, the Zulu army had inflicted a comprehensive defeat on British forces encamped at Isandlwana. It had stunned a country grown complacent that victory was always to be anticipated in wars against 'savage' African foes. Blame for the unprecedented disaster had to be apportioned and scapegoats identified. When he rose in the Commons, Mr E Jenkins asked the Chancellor of the Exchequer whether the government proposed to replace the culpable General Officer Commanding in South Africa, Lieutenant General Lord Chelmsford. On being assured that the government did not, Jenkins retorted over continued cries and interruptions from the government benches:

> [W]hen any General suffers such a defeat as was suffered by General Lord Chelmsford at Isandula there is a prima facie case of incompetence against him . . . [S]ome explanation is required from the Government to justify their continuing in command a man who seems to have exhibited a great deal of want of discretion, if not of military misconduct and incapacity. ('Oh!')[1]

It is Chelmsford's singular misfortune to be remembered primarily for a military defeat at which he was not even present. But the troops the Zulu overran at Isandlwana were under his direct command; he had divided his forces in the face of an enemy whose massed presence he had failed to detect; and he was out of communication scouting while the battle was in progress. Despite his ultimate victory over the Zulu at Ulundi on 4 July 1879, his record as a commander has suffered accordingly in the eyes of his contemporaries and of posterity. Consequently, while it would be nothing short of quixotic to attempt to rehabilitate his bruised reputation, it is still worthwhile to consider why a conscientious, professional general officer of the late Victorian era failed so singularly in his command.

Chronology

31 May 1827	Hon. Frederic Augustus Thesiger born
	Educated at Eton
31 December 1844	Commissioned by purchase as Second Lieutenant Rifle Brigade
28 November 1845	Exchanged by purchase as Ensign and Lieutenant into Grenadier Guards
27 December 1850	Purchased promotion to Lieutenant and Captain
February 1852	Appointed ADC to Lord Lieutenant of Ireland
8 January 1853	Appointed ADC to C in C, Ireland
18 July 1855	Appointed ADC to GOC, 2nd Division, Crimea
2 November 1855	Promoted Brevet Major
8 November 1855	Appointed DAQMG on Headquarters Staff, Crimea
28 August 1857	Purchased promotion to Captain and Lieutenant Colonel
30 April 1858	Exchanged into 95th (Derbyshire) Regiment, stationed in India
13 July 1861	Appointed DAG British Forces, Bombay Presidency
30 April 1863	Promoted Brevet Colonel
1 January 1867	Married Adria Fanny Heath
21 January 1868	Appointed DAG, Abyssinian Field Force
15 August 1868	Appointed ADC to Queen Victoria
17 March 1869	Appointed AG in India
1 October 1874	Appointed Colonel on the Staff commanding Shorncliffe camp
1 January 1877	Promoted Brigadier General, commanding 1st Infantry Brigade, Aldershot
15 March 1877	Promoted Major General
4 March 1878	Appointed GOC, British forces in South Africa with local rank of Lieutenant General
5 October 1878	Succeeded father as Second Baron Chelmsford
9 July 1879	Resigned command in South Africa
1 April 1882	Promoted Substantive Lieutenant General
4 June 1884	Appointed Lieutenant of the Tower of London
16 December 1888	Promoted General
30 January 1889	Appointed Hon. Colonel of the Sherwood Foresters (Derbyshire Regiment)
7 June 1893	Placed on retired list
27 September 1900	Exchanged Colonelcy of Sherwood Foresters for 2nd Life Guards
9 April 1905	Died in United Service Club, London, and buried with military honours in Brompton Cemetery

Appointed CB, 1868; KCB, 1878; GCB, 1879; GCVO, 1902

Frederic Augustus Thesiger was born on 31 May 1827, the eldest of seven children, to Frederick Thesiger, first Baron Chelmsford (1794–1878), and Anna Maria Tinling (d. 1875).[2] The first Baron Chelmsford's father, Charles Thesiger (d. 1831), was Comptroller and Collector of Customs in St Vincent in the West Indies, where he purchased a large estate. As his only surviving son, Frederick Thesiger studied the law because it was the profession that carried the greatest social prestige and was the best training for administering the estate he expected to inherit. Unfortunately, a volcanic eruption on 30 April 1812 entirely destroyed the St Vincent estate, impoverishing the family, and Thesiger had to devote himself seriously to the law to earn a living. He pursued a distinguished and successful career at the Bar in England, which in turn provided entry into politics. He sat in the Commons as a hard-line Tory, and thereafter in the Lords once he was raised to the peerage on 1 March 1858 as Baron Chelmsford (hereafter Chelmsford Senior) shortly after becoming Lord Chancellor, an office he held again in 1866–67. Chelmsford Senior's antecedents were relatively humble but as a peer (albeit a landless one) he was fully assimilated socially into the ruling establishment. He died at the fashionable address of 7 Eaton Square, London.[3] He left £60,000 (equivalent to £4 million in 2006 using the retail price index),[4] which, though certainly a respectable fortune for a patrician professional, was not one on a truly aristocratic scale.[5]

In the mid-nineteenth century the majority of army officers were recruited from the aristocracy and gentry. Their claim to command was based on their high social position and on their traditional role as the knightly, fighting class but some scions of the ruling class, like Frederic Thesiger (hereafter Chelmsford), entered the army because their relatively impecunious circumstances required them to earn a living. The army was an ideal career because it was highly regarded and could confirm social recognition and status for relative newcomers like the Thesigers.[6] In any case, the socially ambitious Thesigers had already established a family tradition in the armed services. One of Chelmsford's uncles, Sir Frederic, had been a captain in the Royal Navy (not quite as aristocratic as the army, but a good life-long career) and had served as Lord Nelson's ADC at the battle of Copenhagen; another, George, had been a major in the army. His own father, Chelmsford Senior, had initially served as a midshipman; while his brother Charles would retire a lieutenant general.

On leaving Eton, Chelmsford started his military career in December 1844 as a second lieutenant in the Rifle Brigade. Commission was still largely by purchase. After the Cardwell reforms abolished purchase, competitive examination inevitably opened the army increasingly to the middles classes, and the aristocratic element dropped sharply away thereafter, except in the Household Division and among senior officers (like Chelmsford) who had gained their commissions before abolition.[7] Yet even before the Cardwell reforms the Foot Guards and Household Cavalry had been the most fashionable and prestigious regiments in the army.[8] Since membership of a fashionable regiment confirmed aspirant social status,[9] in November 1845 Chelmsford purchased an exchange into the Grenadier Guards as an ensign and lieutenant. (An officer in the Guards possessed a concurrent regimental and higher army rank up to lieutenant colonel.)[10] Purchase was no light financial undertaking, for a commission in the Foot Guards cost £1,260 (some £94,000 today), £810 (£60,000 today) more than a commission in a regiment of Foot, and equipment nearly as much again.[11] Later in life Chelmsford would bemoan the large sum invested,[12] but it was essential for advancement. The problem was that while a private income was the essential pre-condition of a military career, few regiments were as expensive as the Grenadiers with their extravagant uniforms and high mess bills for lavish entertaining. An officer in the Guards spent up to £900 (£67,000 today) a year above his pay, and failure to match the spending of brother officers offended against the etiquette of the mess.[13]

For a while Chelmsford sustained the life in London of a fashionable, aristocratic officer with high connections. Between 1849 and 1853 no promotions were filled in the Guards without purchase, so Chelmsford's promotion to lieutenant and captain in December 1850 cost him at least a further £525 (£36,000), which was the difference in price between his old and new commissions, though unspecified, over-regulation payments of up to double the regulated price were normally agreed upon.[14] He then proceeded to Ireland and Dublin Castle, where from February to November 1852 he served as aide-de-camp (ADC) to the lord lieutenant, and then from January 1853 to August 1854 to the GOC. The war with Russia provided Chelmsford with new opportunities. In May 1855 he joined his battalion in the Crimea, and his successful service opened the door to swift promotion. He served as ADC to the commander of the 2nd Division between July and September 1855, and then as Deputy Assistant Quartermaster General (DAQMG) at Headquarters from November 1855 until January 1856. He was present at the siege and fall of Sebastopol in September 1855, was mentioned in dispatches and awarded the Mejidieh (fifth class). He was made a brevet major in November 1855, the standard reward for distinguished service on the battlefield or in a staff appointment, and which conferred a rank in the army higher than in the regiment.

In August 1857 Chelmsford was promoted captain and lieutenant colonel in the Grenadier Guards, probably at well above the regulated difference of price in commissions of £1,150 (£109,000). A Foot Guards officer could exchange into a line regiment at his higher army rank, though to do so was unusual and generally deprecated.[15] Nevertheless, in April 1858 Chelmsford exchanged as its lieutenant colonel into the 95th (Derbyshire) Regiment of Foot, which after the army reorganisation of 1881 became the 2nd Battalion, Sherwood Foresters (Derbyshire Regiment).[16] He joined his new regiment in India in November 1858 where it formed part of the Central Indian Field Force under Sir Robert Napier that was extinguishing the dying ember of the Indian Mutiny, and was present at its final of fourteen actions. Chelmsford's motives for making his exchange into the 95th can only be inferred. It gave him command of a fighting regiment generally stationed abroad (it had been on its way to its next station at the Cape when diverted to India) and distinguished service in action was the surest way to accelerated promotion.

The Grenadier Guards, on the other hand, when not on active service were always stationed in London, and could Chelmsford afford that? Twice on his return to England after service abroad he declined offers of significant home commands: that of Deputy Adjutant General (DAG) at Horse Guards in 1877, and the command of the Western District in 1880. Both times he cited his preference for an Indian command because he believed he had acquired a special understanding of India's military requirements over sixteen years of service there. Revealingly, though, on the second occasion he gave the additional (and doubtless compelling) reason that the expense would be too great for his limited private income.[17] Chelmsford was then living at 50 Stanhope Gardens in South Kensington. Although a good address, Stanhope Gardens lacked the cachet of his father's house in aristocratic Belgravia.[18] On Chelmsford's death in 1905 his wealth would stand at just over £68,000 (£5 million today), which, although a very comfortable fortune, was not up to the lavish outlay expected of a general officer at a home command. More generous pay and allowances were to be gained by service in India. Officers like Chelmsford from marginally wealthy families habitually sought service there because they could better support the standard of living expected of their high status in British India's rigidly hierarchical society.[19]

Thus it was that Chelmsford spent the greater part of his active career in India, though it was one with a prosaic emphasis on the staff and administrative duties in which he excelled, rather than on practical experience in commanding forces in the field. From July 1861 to December 1862 he was DAG of the British troops in the Bombay Presidency. He was made brevet colonel in April 1863, as was the normal progression for those who had purchased the regimental rank of lieutenant colonel. In that year, on the amalgamation of the East India Company's European regiments with the British Army, and the reduction and reorganisation of the Indian Army, he was offered the post of DAG, but preferred to retain command of the 95th. In recognition of his administrative talents his old commander during the Mutiny, Sir Robert Napier, who had been appointed commander of the Abyssinian Field Force in August 1867 and who had drawn his force mainly from the Bombay Army, selected him to be his DAG. Chelmsford held the post from the beginning of the advance in January 1868 until the British withdrawal in June. He was present at the capture of Magdala in April 1868 and was mentioned in dispatches. In recognition of his efficient service in a campaign that had presented many administrative and logistical challenges, Chelmsford was made CB in August 1868 and was further rewarded by serving as an ADC to the Queen from August 1868 to March 1877. On Lord Napier of Magdala and Caryngton (Sir Robert had been raised to the peerage in July 1868) being appointed C in C in India, he insisted that Chelmsford be made Adjutant General (AG) in India, a post he held from March 1869 to March 1874.

It was also while in India that, in January 1867, the 40-year-old Chelmsford married Adria Fanny (1847–1926), the eldest daughter of Major General John Heath of the Bombay Army. She was twenty years his junior, but such discrepancy in ages was not at all unusual in a society where officers often postponed marriage until after 35 in order that family life should not interfere with their military duties.[20] They had four surviving sons who carried on the professional and service traditions of the family by pursuing careers in the army, law and diplomatic service. The eldest, Frederic John Napier Thesiger, who would succeed his father as the third Baron Chelmsford, followed the family tradition by entering the law, and then enjoyed a successful career as a senior colonial administrator. He consummated the Indian connection when he became Viceroy between 1916 and 1921. He was created the first Viscount Chelmsford on his retirement, though he remained, like his father, a landless peer.[21]

In 1874 Chelmsford returned to England as Colonel on the Staff, initially to command the camp at Shornecliffe between October 1874 and December 1876, and then as Brigadier General to command the 1st Infantry Brigade at Aldershot between January 1877 and February 1878 pending a suitable overseas posting. Through the operation of the seniority rule he was promoted to the rank of major general in March 1877. In terms of the Royal Warrant of 30 October 1871 Chelmsford might have chosen to be among the 888 officers who between November 1871 and November 1873 arranged that the Treasury reimburse them the purchase price of their commissions and then retired, but since he had decided to pursue his career and accept promotion, his substantial capital investment in purchase was lost.[22] However, with the acceptance of the recommendations of the Royal Commission of 1875, Chelmsford, as a major general, could expect on compulsory retirement at age 62 in 1889 a pension of £700. If he served until 67, and was promoted lieutenant general or general, his pension would be £850 or £1,000 respectively.[23]

On 1 February 1878 Chelmsford was selected as GOC in South Africa to replace Sir Arthur Cunynghame who (ironically considering Chelmsford's own future difficulties with the colonial administration in Natal) was superseded because of his inability to achieve a good working relationship with the civil officials of Cape Colony. Chelmsford's task was to terminate the Ninth Frontier War in Cape Colony against the Gceleka and Ngqika Xhosa, who for a century had been bitterly resisting the progressive seizure of their land by white colonists. When he took up his command in King William's Town on 4 March 1878 with the local rank of Lieutenant General (which he held from 25 February 1878 to 16 July 1879) only the Ngqika Xhosa were still in the field.

On 7 February 1878 Cunynghame had knocked the Gceleka out of the war at Centane. This was a time in the British army when tactical ideas were being transformed, relearning older lessons that fighting a mobile enemy over broken terrain required open deployment. Breech-loading rifles had a further revolutionary effect on the battlefield as it was now possible to fire more rapidly and to do so kneeling or lying down. The official War Office manual of 1877, *Field Exercise and Evolutions of Infantry*, stipulated that, when extending for the attack, an interval of three paces should be allowed for each file, and that, when skirmishing, the interval could be increased 'according to circumstances'.[24] Critically for Chelmsford's future tactics in South Africa, Centane seemed to validate the effectiveness of the extended infantry line in defeating an African mass attack in the open. At Centane Cunynghame had deployed units in advance of the main British position to draw the enemy into range of the infantry armed with the newly issued Martini-Henry rifles supported by light 7-pounder guns. The weight of disciplined firepower was such that, even in extended order, it was sufficient to halt and break up the enemy's charge. At that critical moment the mounted troops, supported by black auxiliaries, sallied out and turned the enemy's withdrawal into a rout.[25] This, it seemed certain, was the formula for winning battles against African armies.

Chelmsford had commanded a camp of exercise in India in 1874, but the Ninth Frontier War was his first independent command in the field. He at once found himself engaged in what would now be termed counter-insurgency. After Centane the Ngqika Xhosa (who as early as the 1830s had replaced spears with firearms) reverted to guerrilla warfare, skirmishing and ambushing British and colonial troops in the broken and forested country of their traditional stronghold in the Pirie bush. Before leaving for the Cape, Chelmsford had been advised by Sir John Mitchell, a veteran of two frontier wars, to anticipate irregular warfare.[26] But, as Jeff Mathews has shown, Chelmsford had already revealed in public lectures while in India that he favoured the conservative and stereotyped application of the military theory he had apparently begun studying with professional relish while still a junior officer.[27] So in the Cape, Chelmsford initiated the conventional strategy of sending in several strong columns with the intention of surrounding the Ngqika in a pincer movement and bringing them to the sort of pitched battle in which modern tactics had proved so successful at Centane. However, five offensives between March and May 1878 failed to trap the Ngqika, and by that stage Chelmsford's ineffective, but stubbornly pursued strategy was making him the 'laughing stock of the colony'.[28] At last persuaded to take the advice of colonials better versed in irregular warfare,[29] in late May he divided the area of operations up into eleven zones, each patrolled by a mobile mounted force. The Ngqika were thus broken up into small groups, harried and denied supplies. By August 1878 the war was over and Chelmsford received the formal thanks of both houses of the Cape legislature and was made KCB.[30]

Chelmsford had shown himself to be instinctively conservative strategically, although prepared from the outset to adopt more modern battle tactics. Nevertheless, as the later, irregular warfare stage of the campaign demonstrated, he was not entirely resistant to strategic innovation either. Furthermore, not only did he introduce flag-signalling the better to coordinate attacks and build paths to facilitate the movement of supplies, but he also recruited auxiliaries from the Mfengu (the traditional enemy of the Xhosa) to operate over the difficult terrain.[31] Chelmsford was also more solicitous of the colonial troops' welfare than Cunynghame, even if they were not much impressed by his performance as a commander.[32]

But then, whatever his shortcomings as a general – and they did not as yet seem critical – Chelmsford was always appreciated by his men for his unfailingly gentlemanly, courteous and modest behaviour, which he combined with a considerate yet firm manner to his subordinates. Although by nature somewhat withdrawn, he was able to adopt a genial manner in company and was an effective public speaker. He was a keen participant in amateur theatricals (so intrinsic to social life in India); nor did he hide his musical talent as a clarinet player. To balance these unmilitary accomplishments, and as befitted his class and upbringing, he remained fond of field sports and outdoor activities and always displayed considerable physical energy. Like many with his upbringing, he was compassionate towards animals, and soon after invading Zululand he 'even licked with his own hand a white-bullock-driver . . . for brutality to oxen'.[33] In conformity with the changing attitudes of the late Victorian army, that required a greater acceptance by officers of their paternalistic concern about their men's well-being, Chelmsford set an example of moderation and frugality. As a teetotaller, he attempted to stamp out drunkenness under his command and, to combat idleness among his young officers, encouraged them (as he had himself done) to study further. However, his inherent conservatism came out in his support for flogging as the most suitable punishment on active service since this did not take men out of the field as imprisonment would have.[34] For all that, his men recognised his essential decency and he earned their loyalty for his willingness to share their hardships on campaign and to set an example by his calm resolve under fire and readiness to expose himself fearlessly in battle. On the other hand, many also noted his reluctance to delegate successfully, which caused him to lose sight of the wider picture while he spent time and energy on routine duties more appropriately performed by his subordinates. As Major Cornelius Clery,[35] the Principal Staff Officer to No. 3 Column, wrote of him in the days preceding Isandlwana: 'his energetic, restless, anxious temperament led him into very minor matters for he used even to detail the patrols and constantly gave orders direct to commanders'.[36] This failing would have fatal consequences in Zululand. Furthermore, Chelmsford's diffident manner discouraged discussion with his staff, although he too easily allowed his habitually snap decisions to be swayed by contrary advice.[37]

Thus, although in one sense the pattern of the ideal officer of the time – brave, conscientious and industrious – Chelmsford exhibited important weaknesses as a commander. Though not closed to military innovation, he was (as operations in 1878 had demonstrated) a prosaic product of the system and remained inherently reluctant to adapt orthodox military practices to colonial conditions unless absolutely pressed. His relative lack of military flair and acumen would be ruthlessly exposed in the Zululand campaign of 1879.

The Anglo-Zulu War, 1879

On 9 August 1878 Chelmsford set up his headquarters in Pietermaritzburg, the capital of the Colony of Natal, to prepare for the invasion of the neighbouring kingdom of Zululand. The mission in South Africa of the High Commissioner, Sir Bartle Frere, with whom Chelmsford had earlier formed a bond of friendship while the former was Governor of Bombay from 1862 to 1867, was to create a confederation (along the lines of Canada) of the British colonies in the sub-continent. Abutting independent African polities were perceived as potential obstacles to this objective that had to be neutralised. The Ninth Frontier War had been fought to remove one such hindrance. Chelmsford's dash down the east coast to annex Port St John's on 31 August 1878, which overawed the Mpondo people between Natal and the Cape, overcame another.[38] The militarily powerful Zulu kingdom, able to field some 29,000 warriors, continued the greatest challenge, but Frere, misled by Chelmsford's recent operations where the Ngqika Xhosa had never constituted any substantial threat, fondly imagined that the Zulu could similarly be subdued at the price of a minor campaign.[39]

In planning and executing the Zululand campaign, Chelmsford faced many handicaps, not all of his own making. Colonial campaigns against irregulars, generally inferior in armaments, organisation and discipline to the British, though employing varied and unpredictable military styles, were in fact a highly specialised form of combat, requiring considerable adaptability in both strategy and tactics,[40] but Chelmsford had already shown that he lacked the requisite innovative flair. British regulars were the main striking force in any of Britain's nineteenth-century imperial expeditions, but the professional Victorian army was small, and its manpower and capabilities overstretched by a multiplicity of commitments across the globe.[41] The recent army reforms carried out by Cardwell, particularly the introduction of short service in 1870, and linked battalions in 1872, meant that the battalions serving abroad were often imperfectly trained and consisted of physically immature, untried soldiers and inexperienced NCOs. The army's C in C, the Duke of Cambridge, greatly resented civilian interference in military affairs and openly deprecated Cardwell's reforms. Chelmsford, as an Indian officer and therefore a believer in the merits of long-term recruitment that led to stable and experienced garrisons, aligned himself with the Duke and his conservative coterie. Nevertheless, he had no choice but to work in Zululand, as he had in the Ninth Frontier War, with young and inexperienced troops he increasingly found militarily unsatisfactory as the campaign developed.[42]

British regulars serving in South Africa might not have been up to standard, but they were still too valuable and scarce to dissipate on garrison and convoy duties, which were better undertaken by African auxiliaries. Moreover, as Chelmsford had found with his Mfengu levies in the Cape, they were also useful for scouting and pursuit. So Chelmsford raised African levies from the Natal native reserves and formed them under white officers and NCOs into the five battalions of the Natal Native Contingent (NNC). However, as with the Mfengu levies, they were poorly armed and trained and ultimately proved of doubtful morale and effectiveness.[43] Much more essential to the success of colonial campaigning than auxiliaries were mounted troops. They had proved pivotal in the latter stages of the Ninth Frontier War, and would be crucial in Zululand for reconnaissance and raiding purposes and vital in the pursuit of a broken enemy. Yet as Chelmsford was uncomfortably aware, he had not nearly enough for his purposes.[44] Regular cavalry would not be made available until the closing stages of the campaign, and he had to rely on small colonial units of irregular horse and some mounted infantry.

The dearth of horsemen for intelligence gathering was of particular concern, and would cost Chelmsford dear. The lack of accurate maps[45] meant that as field commander Chelmsford had no option but to rely as best he could upon mounted patrols, supplemented by the NNC, to relay him information about the terrain to be traversed, and to locate the enemy.[46] To make matters worse, Chelmsford was one with Cambridge in his gentlemanly amateurish disregard of the professional accumulation and analysis of intelligence, and in his positive hostility towards a Prussian-style General Staff and officers graduating from the Staff College established at Camberley in 1858. In this he differed sharply from that thrusting and very professional soldier, Sir Garnet Wolseley, with his advanced military ideas.[47]

Consequently, when he sailed for South Africa in 1878, Chelmsford was accompanied by a small staff selected not for outstanding talent (as would have been the case with Wolseley) but for easy compatibility. His ADCs, Brevet Major Matthew Gosset and Captain William Molyneux, had served with him at Aldershot. His Assistant Military Secretary, John North Crealock, had indeed passed the Staff College in 1868 and had held a series of staff appointments, but he possessed the additional recommendation of being an officer in Chelmsford's regiment, the 95th, and of having served in India with him. Made brevet lieutenant colonel in November 1878, Crealock continued on Chelmsford's personal staff in Zululand and was promoted to Military Secretary in May 1879, even though he was noted neither for his efficiency nor for the legibility of his dispatches.[48] Crealock was Chelmsford's constant companion in South Africa and was suspected of wielding undue influence over him. Privately he was critical of the general's military capabilities, but always staunchly defended him in public. His haughty and abrasive personality and facetious manner alienated many of his fellow officers and would play its part in exacerbating the ever more strained relations between the military and the government of Natal.[49] As Clery would later write of Chelmsford with Crealock obviously in mind: 'he wanted what he certainly had not – a man of solidity and ability at his elbow', and wondered that Chelmsford was not 'sharp enough to see through him'.[50]

Chelmsford did not appoint a chief of staff, being apparently confident in his own organisational abilities and reluctant to delegate. Not surprisingly, as the Zululand campaign unfolded, the deficiencies of Chelmsford's poorly trained and structured staff became increasingly apparent. As Crealock reported on 11 April 1879, 'We know Lord Chelmsford does not appreciate the importance of staff, and I can see in half an eye in 2 days, how chaotic all that part is.'[51] Chelmsford did not initially even appoint an intelligence officer to his staff, only doing so in May 1879 once the Isandlwana disaster (for which lack of proper intelligence was largely responsible) had made the need blindingly apparent. Even then, regular staff officers had to do their untrained best to help process intelligence as a normal part of their many other duties.

If Chelmsford seemed content to muddle along with an inefficient staff and inadequately processed intelligence, he did fully comprehend that it was essential for a commander to study and understand beforehand the military system of his prospective foe. To that end he had booklets prepared for his officers describing in detail the Zulu military system and way of war, and providing instructions on how British troops should be managed in the field.[52] Unfortunately, neither Chelmsford nor his officers seem to have believed what they read about the fighting qualities of the Zulu. In fact, it is clear that they wholly underrated them. The Zulu could be expected to be tougher adversaries than the Xhosa, but they were assumed nevertheless to be essentially in the same league. As Major Clery later put it, 'the easy promenade' in the Cape made 'all go into this business with light hearts'.[53] The consequence, he explained, was that,

> the general and his staff not only did not anticipate that the enemy would venture to attack him, but if they should do so that the only thing to be apprehended was that the fire of our people would frighten them so much that they would never come near enough to suffer any serious loss. So that to take any precautions against an attack, such as entrenching, etc., such a thing was never dreamt of.[54]

Most generals seem cursed to fight the current campaign based on the flawed assumption that it will be a repetition of the last. Chelmsford and his staff were no exceptions to the rule and set about framing a strategy based ultimately on a dangerous underestimation of the fighting qualities of the Zulu. More immediately, Chelmsford faced several strategic constraints.

When he advanced into Zululand he would leave the borders of Natal and the Transvaal vulnerable to the Zulu raids the colonists so dreaded. The broken terrain of the Natal frontier made that colony the more susceptible of the two to surprise attack, but the colonial authorities' contingency plans were limited to advising settlers to take refuge in the scattered government laagers. On 10 September 1878 Chelmsford persuaded the Natal government to raise a large field force of African levies and reserves to hold the countryside between the border posts garrisoned by imperial troops and colonial volunteers. In order to improve Natal's organisation for defence, on 10 November Chelmsford divided the colony into Defensive Districts, and on 11 January 1879 placed the entire border region under military control.[55]

Despite these arrangements, Chelmsford knew that the borders remained vulnerable and this affected the timing of his invasion. The rivers between Natal and Zululand were generally unfordable between January and March on account of the summer rains, and so formed a natural line of defence. Chelmsford confidently expected the campaign to be over before the rivers subsided if he invaded early in the year. Chelmsford calculated that late spring rains of 1878 and the delayed harvest meant that the Zulu would find it difficult to supply their army, while, conversely, the summer grazing was plentiful for the draft animals upon which the British advance depended. Frere therefore worked with Chelmsford on the political front to ensure that the invasion was launched on the ideal date of 11 January 1879.[56]

A swift, decisive campaign such as Chelmsford and Frere envisaged depended upon firm logistics. Unfortunately for Chelmsford, the Anglo-Zulu War exemplified one of the fundamentals of colonial war: it was a campaign against distance and natural obstacles as much as against an enemy, and problems of supply would overshadow its entire course. Since supplies could not be obtained from the theatre of war and had to be carried, Chelmsford's army was turned into an escort for its food, and garrisoned depots had to be established along its line of march.[57] For months before the invasion Chelmsford was engrossed in collecting and organising supplies and transport. If he had established better relations with the Natal government, and in particular with Sir Henry Bulwer, the Lieutenant Governor, their cooperation would have eased his logistical problems. Unfortunately, the Natal civil authorities, already wary of the coming war and its attendant costs and risk, were further alienated by the military's high-handed approach.[58] They consequently volunteered little in the way of help, forcing Chelmsford by the end of the campaign to have hired or bought the 27,125 oxen, 4,653 mules and 748 horses necessary to draw the 1,770 wagons and 796 carts he required at exorbitant rates from colonists eager to profit from the unexpected windfall.[59] He was also let down by the under-staffed Commissariat and Transport Department, the members of which were inexperienced in purchasing and in looking after its draft animals in South African conditions, which helped to drive up costs. The exasperated Chelmsford was only too aware of the Department's inadequacies, but came up against the jealously held prerogatives of the Victorian army. Consequently, despite repeated attempts, he failed to impose a remedy on the Department's unwilling personnel.[60]

Chelmsford's dependence on slow-moving and vulnerable supply trains that only averaged 10 miles a day over the broken terrain meant that his manoeuverability would be compromised. The larger the convoy, the slower it moved, so Chelmsford decided he must send in a number of smaller columns. This made each more vulnerable to attack, and colonists, harking back to their experience in war against the Zulu in 1838, urged him to make each column form a defensive wagon-laager every time it halted in Zulu territory. But laagering was a time-consuming and complicated procedure.[61] Chelmsford believed (until Isandlwana sharply taught him otherwise) that, for his well-armed columns, partial entrenchments would suffice instead.[62]

Chelmsford's deployment of several columns echoed his initial, unsuccessful deployment in the Ninth Frontier War. Nevertheless, he was sure that the strategy of converging columns was appropriate for Zululand. Not only would they move with greater speed, but he calculated that invasion by a number of supporting columns would discourage Zulu counter-thrusts against Natal and the Transvaal. Moreover, the widespread British presence would force the Zulu to keep fully mobilised and present them with difficult supply problems of their own. With Zulu raids in mind, Chelmsford selected invasion routes in sectors he believed vulnerable to Zulu attack: No. 1 Column of 4,750 men under Colonel Charles Pearson would protect the Natal coastal plain; No. 3 Column of 4,709 men under Colonel Richard Glyn (reinforced by the 3,871 African troops of No. 2 Column under Brevet Colonel Anthony Durnford) central Natal; No. 4 Column of 2,278 men under Brevet Colonel Evelyn Wood the Utrecht District of the Transvaal; and No. 5 Column of 1,565 men under Colonel Hugh Rowlands would protect the volatile eastern Transvaal that abutted the unpacified Pedi, Swazi and Zulu kingdoms. The invading columns were supposed to converge on oNdini, King Cetshwayo's capital.[63] Yet, as the day of invasion approached, the prospects for successful coordination, let alone mutual support, seemed ever less likely. With reason, Chelmsford began increasingly to obsess about deficient logistical arrangements, poor staff work, unreliable maps, difficult terrain and insufficient cavalry for effective reconnaissance, and daily exhorted his commanders to coordinate operations.[64]

When Chelmsford invaded Zululand on 11 January, he found that the rain-sodden ground rendered a rapid, coordinated advance impossible, and he was forced to consider an alternative strategy. He decided the slowly advancing columns should send out flying columns to occupy and devastate as much of Zululand as they could, and target in particular the *amakhanda* (military centres) that were the nodes of the King's authority, the rallying points for the *amabutho* (age-grade regiments) and the depots for Zulu supplies. Their systematic destruction was calculated to reduce Zulu ability to resist, and fatally damage the King's authority. The problem with this strategy was that mounted troops were essential for carrying it out, and the number of horsemen Chelmsford had available was limited.[65] Chelmsford forbade unauthorised excesses against the civilian population on pain of flogging,[66] but he hoped that by rendering the Zulu population hungry and shelterless that he would provoke Cetshwayo's desperate subjects into deposing him and surrendering. In this he was no different from other commanders in Queen Victoria's 'small wars' who accepted civilian suffering as an unfortunate necessity for victory, though he received some criticism regarding this at the time.[67] He was also heartened by intelligence of existing dissensions within the Zulu kingdom, and hoped to exploit these by encouraging disaffected chiefs to defect. He accordingly urged his commanders to enter into negotiations with Zulu notables, and to accommodate surrendered Zulu behind their lines.[68]

The unravelling of the Zulu kingdom, however, required prior military success that asserted British military ascendancy. At all cost Chelmsford hoped to avoid the desultory, protracted warfare he had experienced in the Eastern Cape, and intended to conclude the campaign expeditiously with a decisive battle.[69]

Fortunately, when fighting a people with aggressive military traditions such as the Zulu, it was very likely that they would be willing to risk all in pitched battle. Indeed, Chelmsford's operational gambit of dividing his army into several columns can thus be seen as conventional bait intended to entice the Zulu into attacking these small and thus deceptively vulnerable forces.[70] As experience in the Ninth Frontier War had apparently demonstrated, a disciplined force of British regulars, even when deployed in extended order, was invulnerable against a mass attack of traditionally armed warriors like the Zulu.[71] Isandlwana was still to administer the terrible lesson that a massed Zulu charge could break through an extended infantry line no matter how superior its armaments, and would confirm that the most effective way of concentrating fire and stemming the enemy's rush was to place troops in prepared all-round defensive positions such as fieldworks, wagon-laagers or infantry squares. After Isandlwana it became Chelmsford's overriding tactical concern to entice the Zulu into destroying themselves against such positions.

King Cetshwayo's strategy was to secure a rapid victory in the field that would force the British to withdraw and allow his armies to menace the borders of Natal before the British could bring in more reinforcements. He hoped that as a consequence the British would be pressured into concluding a peace favourable to the Zulu.[72] Able Zulu intelligence identified No. 3 Column that crossed into Zululand at Rorke's Drift on 11 January as the main British force because not only was it the strongest column, but Chelmsford himself was accompanying it. Indeed, Chelmsford quickly overshadowed Glyn and assumed active command. His forces scored an easy success in a skirmish at kwaSogekle (the stronghold of Chief Sihayo kaXongo) on 12 January in which the Zulu failed to make a determined stand, and which seemed to confirm that they would make no better a showing than had the Xhosa.[73] When during the skirmish Clery wished to send in some mounted men 'rather widely to flank', Crealock checked him in 'a remonstrating' way: 'Do not do that as it will cause what actually happened in the last war – the enemy to take flight and bolt before we can get at them.' Again, the general issued an order that the artillery was never to open fire until the enemy were within 600yd of them for fear of frightening them, and so deterring them from coming on, or making them bolt.[74]

Indeed, Clery was of the firm opinion that for both Chelmsford and his staff their misleading experience of warfare in the Eastern Cape would not let them admit that they were fighting with 'anything more than a superior [perhaps?] class of kafir, who had only to be hunted', and that 'the easy promenade' in the Cape made 'all go into this business with light hearts'.[75]

The difficult and muddy terrain held up Chelmsford's further advance, and on 20 January he set up camp at the eastern base of Isandlwana while he prepared to reconnoitre the way forward. The position was potentially difficult to defend because it was overlooked by a spur of the Nyoni hills to the north, and the layout of the camp was overly extended. But since Chelmsford regarded the camp as temporary, and considered no Zulu attack likely, no attempt was made to entrench it, nor to laager the wagons that were required to bring up supplies from Rorke's Drift. In any case, it had not been the practice to laager temporary camps when on the march against the Xhosa, and Chelmsford regarded a laager as protection for oxen, rather than to be used as a redoubt.[76] Two days later the Zulu overwhelmed the camp while Chelmsford and half his force were skirmishing away to the south-east.

Inevitably, the Isandlwana disaster has overshadowed all subsequent accounts of the Anglo–Zulu War and has formed the pivot for all discussions concerning Chelmsford's problematic generalship. Gosset, who classified and annotated Chelmsford's papers in 1906, wrote to Chelmsford's widow that he believed the General (whose foresight, consideration and zeal he commended) had been sadly misrepresented, and that he hoped 'justice' would eventually be done to the memory of that 'great & good man'.[77] Gosset would have been gravely disappointed, however, by the approach adopted by most future historians. The discussion that follows concerning Chelmsford's role in the Isandlwana disaster is based on the writer's own research and fieldwork.

The main Zulu army of 24,000 men had begun its march on 17 January, and on 20 January bivouacked by Siphezi Hill, only 12.5 miles east of Isandlwana. Chelmsford had no inkling of the enemy's close proximity, and believed that Chief Matshana kaMondisa was gathering a force in the broken country to the south-east of Isandlwana in order to interrupt his column's line of supply once it advanced further into Zululand. Accordingly, on 21 January, Chelmsford sent out a reconnaissance-in-force consisting of more than half his mounted men under Major John Dartnell (150 troopers) and the bulk of the NNC under Commandant Rupert Lonsdale (about 1,600 men) to scout the area. Some 2,000 Zulu under Matshana skilfully retired eastwards before the joint force, and by evening were massed on the Magogo heights. To forestall an advance by this force on Isandlwana, Dartnell and Lonsdale bivouacked for the night on the Hlazakazi heights, westwards across the valley from Magogo.

Meanwhile, the joint Zulu commanders of the main army, Ntshingwayo kaMahole and Mavumengwana kaNdlela, who had been considering a flank march to Chelmsford's east to cut him off from Natal, apparently decided instead to take advantage of his division of his forces. They detached men to reinforce Matshana, and on the evening of 21 January and during the next morning moved the main army to the Ngwebeni valley, concealed from Isandlwana by the Nyoni heights 9 miles to the south-west. The Zulu moved in small units, so that the British mounted patrols that sighted some of them had no idea that a whole army was on the move.

Around midnight on the night of 21/22 January there was a panic among the NNC encamped in a hollow square on Hlazakazi who groundlessly thought they were being attacked. Dartnell nevertheless sent Chelmsford a note, which the general received at 0130, urgently requesting support. Glyn, accompanied by

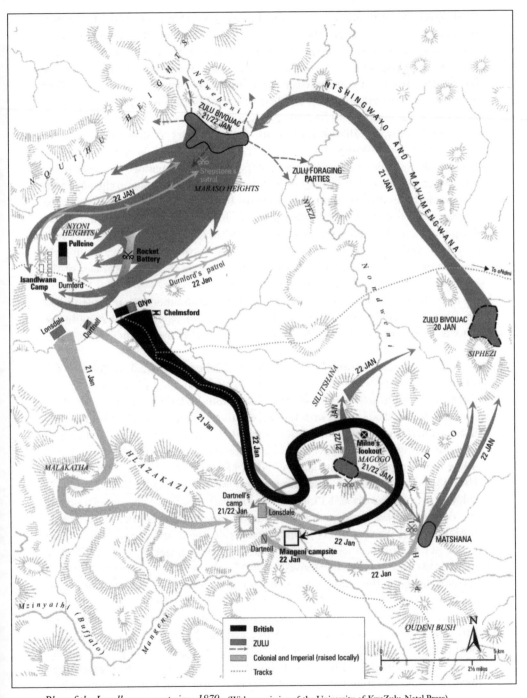

Plan of the Isandlwana campaign, 1879. (With permission of the University of KwaZulu-Natal Press)

Chelmsford, accordingly advanced at 0430 with 4 out of the 6 guns of the battery, 6 companies of the 2nd Battalion, 24th (2nd Warwickshire) Regiment, Mounted Infantry and Pioneers. Chelmsford left the camp with a garrison of 2 7-pounder guns, 5 companies of the 1/24th and one of the 2/24th, the remainder of the mounted troops and 4 companies of the 1/3rd NNC. Before he left, Chelmsford ordered up Durnford from Rorke's Drift with the available men of No. 2 Column to reinforce the camp. Until he arrived, when the troops in camp would amount to just over 1,700 men, Brevet Lieutenant Colonel Henry Pulleine would be the senior officer left in camp. As Clery later commented, 'nobody from the general downwards had the least suspicion that there was a chance of the camp being attacked'.[78] For those left in the camp, there was absolutely no apprehension that they might be in danger, and Captain Henry Harford (a regular officer seconded to the NNC) later noted in his journal that some officers 'were terribly disappointed at the thought of being left behind in Camp and lose [*sic*] the chance of a fight, and begged hard to be allowed to find substitutes'.[79] Even when early the next morning a thousand or more Zulu appeared on the hills to the east of the camp no officer was disconcerted for, as Lieutenant Henry Curling, RA (one of the few officers to survive the battle) later wrote to his mother: 'We none of us had the least idea that the Zulu contemplated attacking the camp and, having in the last war [Ninth Frontier War] often seen equally large bodies of the enemy, never dreamed they would come on.'[80]

When the badly strung out relief force reached Hlazakazi at about 0600, bringing the troops operating in the area to about 2,500, the Zulu on Magogo had broken away. Some had withdrawn south-east onto the Phindo heights and others north onto Silutshana, both with the intention of ultimately pulling back north-east to Siphezi and drawing the British after them, away from the camp. Dartnell took the bait, and became involved in a heavy skirmish on Phindo. Unaware of falling into a trap, Chelmsford decided to let Dartnell get on with taking Phindo, while the relief column cleared the area around Silutshana and the Nondweni valley between Magogo and Phindo. The General would use the opportunity to select a suitable new campsite for the column when it advanced, thereby adhering to his own precept that 'A commander must ride about and see the country for himself, or he will never be able to handle his troops properly.'[81] At 0930 while breakfasting near Magogo he received a message sent at 0805 by Pulleine that Zulu were advancing on the camp. No one suspected this could be the main Zulu army, and there seemed no sense of urgency in the message. Chelmsford himself, when Clery asked him what should be done, replied, 'There is nothing to be done on that.' His staff did not pursue the matter because he had become 'particularly touchy about suggestions being made to him'.[82] Chelmsford nevertheless sent Lieutenant A Berkeley Milne, RN of his staff to study the camp 12 miles away through a telescope from the slopes of Magogo. Milne kept watch for upwards to an hour, but saw nothing untoward. In fact, the shoulder of Silutshana cut off his view of the plain to the east of Isandlwana where the Zulu army was deploying.

Since all seemed in order, between 1000 and 1100 Chelmsford sent Captain Alan Gardner with orders to Pulleine to strike camp and move up. Chelmsford and a small escort rode off between 1030 and 1230 to scout the area. His movements were consequently unpredictable, and all subsequent messages concerning the unfolding battle at Isandlwana failed to find him or his staff. Having decided on a suitable campsite just east of Hlazakazi on the Mangeni River above its spectacular horseshoe falls, Chelmsford ordered the relief column under Glyn to concentrate there.

In the early afternoon sounds of firing were heard from the direction of the camp, and messages from the camp's garrison began to reach Chelmsford. Clery afterwards wrote that at that stage he heard Crealock exclaim: 'How very amusing! Actually attacking our camp! Most amusing!'[83] Shortly after 1315 Chelmsford went up Mdutshana hill just north of the new Mangeni campsite with some of his staff to examine the Isandlwana camp through their field glasses. The tents had not been struck as were the regulations during an engagement, and all seemed quiet. Chelmsford therefore came to the conclusion that if there had been a Zulu attack, it had been successfully repulsed. It was only at 1445 that Chelmsford decided to return to Isandlwana at a leisurely pace with a small escort to investigate. About 5 miles from Isandlwana he was met by Lonsdale, who had ridden back to Isandlwana to arrange for supplies to be brought up, and he reported that he had barely escaped the Zulu who were in possession of the camp. Chelmsford was appalled, purportedly exclaiming in disbelief: 'But I left over 1,000 men to guard the camp.' Chelmsford then acted decisively. He ordered the already exhausted forces concentrating at the Mangeni campsite 7 miles to the south-west of Isandlwana to retake the camp, though it was not until 1830 that Chelmsford had concentrated all his scattered forces within 3 miles of Isandlwana. Clery later described 'the look of gloom and pain' on Chelmsford's 'expressive' countenance, which clearly mirrored his inner turmoil.[84] Indeed, a soldier wrote home that he was 'very near crying'.[85] But Chelmsford never 'flunked' his duty and, anticipating Zulu resistance, addressed his dismayed troops with determination: 'Men, the enemy has taken our camp. Many of our friends must have lost their lives defending it. There is nothing left for us now but to fight our way through – and mind, we must fight hard, for we will have to fight for our lives. I know you, and I know I can depend on you.'[86]

The men cheered lustily in response. Chelmsford then advanced in darkness with his force in battle array, guns in the centre with British infantry on either flank, a battalion of NNC on each flank of the regulars with the mounted troops in advance of the NNC. Chelmsford halted half a mile from the camp to fire shrapnel. But the victorious Zulu had taken the camp at about 1400 and after looting it had withdrawn, so Chelmsford reoccupied it at about 2030 without resistance, though he remained on the alert for a night attack that never came. It was a horrific night spent bivouacked, as he laconically informed Frere, 'among the bodies from dead soldiers and of the enemy'.[87]

For the loss of about 1,000 men, the Zulu had killed 52 of the 67 British officers, 739 white troops, 67 white NCOs of the NNC and 471 recorded black troops out of a total of 1,707 men left to defend the camp. The defeat at Isandlwana comprehensively shattered Chelmsford's invasion plans. The heavy loss of life, weapons, ammunition and transport meant that he could make no further advance until his forces had regrouped and been reinforced and fresh transport assembled. Until then, he would have to stand on the defensive and do his best to rally the defences of Natal where panicking colonists were in daily expectation of a Zulu invasion. The stout defence of Rorke's Drift on the night of 22/23 January helped neutralise somewhat the shattering effects of Isandlwana, but it was now clear that if the British were to maintain their prestige in southern Africa they had to prosecute the war until the Zulu were utterly defeated in the field.

The Isandlwana disaster severely affected Chelmsford's health and morale, and for a time he seemed on the verge of a breakdown. Crealock reported several times to Alison in early February that the General was 'still not himself'.[88] Chelmsford unguardedly admitted in an official dispatch of 9 February to Colonel Frederick Stanley, the Secretary of State for War, that 'the strain of prolonged anxiety & exertion, physical & mental' was 'telling' on him.[89] This missive, along with others requesting a major general be sent out as second-in-command lest he break down under the strain, caused the Duke of Cambridge great embarrassment when he had to explain them away to his sceptical peers in the House of Lords. Chelmsford was later 'extremely annoyed' when he learned that what he considered confidential correspondence should have been made humiliatingly public.[90] To Evelyn Wood, the energetic commander of No. 4 Column, he wrote that he was 'fairly puzzled' when he contemplated future operations, and wished he saw his way 'with honour out of this beastly country'. He added that he was depending on Wood and his dashing commander of mounted troops, Lieutenant Colonel Redvers Buller, to pull him 'out of the mire'.[91] In reporting the 'sad disaster' to Cambridge he had, moreover, to explain why he had not remained long enough at the Isandlwana camp to bury the dead (as was expected of a commander), excusing himself primarily in terms of preserving the men's morale.[92] But the dead would continue to lie there, unburied until May, to haunt his reputation.

Chelmsford's first act after Isandlwana was to convene a Court of Inquiry on 24 January that sat from 27–29 January. Its instruction was to inquire very specifically into 'the loss of the camp', rather than into the surrounding circumstances that led to the Zulu taking it. Clearly, Chelmsford intended that the Court would not probe too deeply into his responsibility for the disaster. Much of the evidence heard was not recorded, since it was deemed irrelevant or repetitious. Conveniently for Chelmsford's reputation, the Court found that much of the blame for the disaster could be attributed to the imprudent actions of Durnford to whom, so Crealock claimed, he had sent written instruction on the morning of 22 January to take command of the camp. When Durnford (who had then purportedly inherited the superseded Pulleine's orders) moved out of the camp to support Chelmsford, whom he thought threatened to the rear by a Zulu movement, he allegedly overrode the written orders that Clery stated he had drawn up on his own initiative without consulting Chelmsford requiring Pulleine to stay strictly on the defensive.[93] Thus when Durnford encountered the Zulu advancing in force, Pulleine was forced against his instructions (so the argument went) to push troops forward in a haphazard manner to cover Durnford's retreat, thereby fatally over-extending the British line. Much emphasis was accorded the poor performance of the NNC, whose apparent collapse in the centre of the British line led (it was concluded) to the final Zulu breakthrough. In other words, the Court apportioned the blame for the disaster primarily to the conveniently dead Durnford, who was disliked by the military establishment for being too closely aligned with the colonial viewpoint after years in Natal; to a lesser extent to Pulleine, who was known to be a good administrator but short on combat experience; and to the NNC, who were equally conveniently neither white nor regular British infantry. With the honour of both Chelmsford and the regular British troops secured and the blame thrown on suspect officers, colonials and Africans, this is the version that passed into the official account.[94]

Eventually, the fatal holes in the official account would begin to reveal themselves. For one thing, when Crealock's instructions to Durnford were subsequently recovered from the battlefield, they showed that he had been merely ordered up to the camp without precise instructions either to reinforce it or take command. Earlier orders issued on 19 January had specified that he cooperate with No. 3 Column in clearing the country occupied by Matshana,[95] and it can be argued that is exactly what he was trying to do on 22 January. Clery later explained to Alison that when Chelmsford marched out of camp on the morning of 22 January he 'had not the smallest apprehension about the camp being attacked' and had thought to leave no special instructions for its defence. Thus when Clery told him he had left written orders, the General, who saw how this would save his reputation, exclaimed: 'I cannot tell you what a relief it is to me to hear this.'[96] Yet these written instructions, if they ever existed, were never found. Much was made of Pulleine's combat inexperience, but in fact his forward deployment was essentially in accordance with the instructions Chelmsford had issued column commanders in December 1878: guns forward with supporting flanking companies of British troops thrown back; the NNC clear of each flank and to their rear in echelon; mounted infantry covering the flanks; and a reserve of British infantry. Of course, whether an extended firing line was the most appropriate deployment may be questioned, though at the battle of Nyezane on the same day as Isandlwana, this was precisely the deployment used with great success by Pearson of No. 1 Column.[97] And, as a result of modern research, it is clear that the British line did not collapse because the NNC broke. Indeed, the extended skirmishing line falling back on the camp was holding its own well until its flanks were turned by the Zulu advance.

It is very clear that Chelmsford's staff and close associates were rallying around their chief to protect his reputation,[98] and not being too nice about how they did it. Perhaps the most unsavoury ploy was that initiated by Crealock who, some weeks after Isandlwana, tried to shift some of the blame for the disaster off Chelmsford's shoulders on to those of Glyn. The guileless but upright Glyn resolutely refused to take the fall, not least because it was well known that Chelmsford had entirely taken over effective command of the column, leaving him only with the discharge of routine duties. Distinctly embarrassed, Chelmsford hastened to disassociate himself from Crealock's dishonourable insinuations and, according to witnesses, hauled him over the coals for not behaving as a gentleman. As Captain J F Maurice later expressed it: 'Crealock certainly comes out in a very unpleasant light . . . The attempt to turn on Glyn . . . was as feeble as it was unfair.'[99]

The court's convenient finding was not sufficient to still criticism and angry public questioning in both Natal and Britain about Chelmsford's conduct of the war and his attempt to shift the blame for Isandlwana.[100] His own staff discreetly questioned his generalship.[101] Initially, though, the government stood by Chelmsford in harsh parliamentary debates that excoriated him for culpable incapacity as a commander, the Horse Guards for shielding his incompetence and the government for starting the unfortunate war in the first place.[102] On 16 February 1879 the government agreed to Chelmsford's urgent request for reinforcements and dispatched 6 battalions, 2 cavalry regiments, 2 artillery batteries and a company of engineers to Natal. By the end of March Chelmsford felt strong enough to march to the relief of Eshowe where the Zulu had been blockading No. 1 Column ever since Isandlwana. Chelmsford was determined to avoid his previous mistakes, and this time organised effective forward reconnaissance and while on the march painstakingly laagered every night. On the early morning of 1 April, the 5,670 men of the Eshowe Relief Column under Chelmsford's 'personal command' (as he could not resist reminding Stanley in his official dispatch that hums with a deep sense of personal vindication) routed the Zulu force of 10,000 men that attacked his laager at Gingindlovu. He then evacuated the Eshowe garrison.[103] Meanwhile, on 29 March at Khambula, far away in north-western Zululand, Wood had already routed the Zulu veterans of Isandlwana in a ferocious pitched battle. Khambula would prove the turning point of the war and the ruination of Zulu morale because it proved to the Zulu (a realisation confirmed at Gingindlovu) that they could not prevail against the British if they failed to catch them in the open as they had at Isandlwana, and that it was hopeless to attack them in prepared positions. Yet for once the usually punctiliously courteous Chelmsford could not bring himself to rise to the occasion, writing to his far too successful subordinate: 'One line to congratulate you upon your successful repulse of the attack made upon Kambula laager – I am up to my ears in work & cannot say as much as I could wish . . .'.[104]

The overwhelming victories at Khambula and Gingindlovu greatly buoyed up Chelmsford, who grasped that he had entirely regained the initiative. Yet it was not immediately clear to him what strategy he ought to follow in order to bring the war to an end. He seemed embarrassed by the large number of reinforcements rushed out to him by the anxious government, and was swamped by special-service officers anxious for action and promotion. He also had to allocate suitable commands for the four major generals Cambridge selected to accompany the troops, and whom he described with more regard to their proven loyalty to him (none being a Wolseley man) than to their abilities as 'excellent men, very intelligent, reliable and active'.[105] Moreover, the growing concentration of troops in Natal was putting intolerable strain on his Commissariat and Transport Department, which had already shown itself unequal to the demands placed upon it and now had to arrange for additional transport and supplies and establish depots. One thing, though, was clear to Chelmsford. This time he would exercise extreme caution to avoid a repetition of Isandlwana, and his second invasion of Zululand was characterised by his uninspiring motto: 'slow and steady wins the race'.[106]

Although his senior officers had advocated sending in a single column to place less strain on the Commissariat and Transport Department, Chelmsford eventually decided to send in two widely spaced columns to screen the Transvaal and Natal from a possible Zulu counter-blow.[107] The 1st Division of 7,500 men, under Major General Henry Crealock, was to advance on oNdini up the coast. The 2nd Division of 5,000 men, under Major General Edward Newdigate and accompanied by Chelmsford, was to march on oNdini from the north-west, on the way rendezvousing with Wood's 3,200 men, now renamed the Flying Column. The 2nd Division would not advance along the same route as the ill-fated No. 3 Column, but would take a longer and unfamiliar route that required much reconnaissance, but which avoided Isandlwana and the still unburied British dead. On 21 May, however, while the 2nd Division was concentrating at Landman's Drift and sending out patrols to clear the country ahead of it, a reconnaissance in force began the long-overdue interment at Isandlwana, stilling both public criticism and Chelmsford's own uneasy conscience.[108]

As a strong believer in the 'active defence', Chelmsford ordered diversionary raids by colonial troops across the Natal–Zululand border in support of his own advance. This brought him into sharp conflict with Bulwer and the Natal government, who correctly feared a damaging cycle of raid and counter-raid would be initiated. Much to the indignation of Chelmsford, who claimed command over all troops in the area of operations, Bulwer forbade the use of Natal troops in cross-border raids. Relations between General and Lieutenant Governor swiftly deteriorated, and both bombarded the home authorities with inordinately long and intemperate dispatches.[109]

This shrill dispute was one of the final straws for a British government that already perceived Chelmsford to be demoralised, uncertain of his strategy and unable to bring the increasingly expensive war to a speedy conclusion.[110] The public had heaped criticism upon Chelmsford after Isandlwana, but he had survived thus far in his command thanks to the increasingly grudging support of the Horse Guards and of the Prime Minister, Benjamin Disraeli, Earl of Beaconsfield. Disraeli had left Chelmsford Senior out of his Cabinet in 1868 because he thought him an incompetent Lord Chancellor, and it distressed him to have to supersede the son as an incompetent general.[111] Cambridge had initially stood staunchly behind Chelmsford, but was anxious to understand better what had gone wrong at Isandlwana, which had hit him like 'a clap of thunder'.[112]

On 6 March the AG, Major General Sir Charles Ellice, wrote to Chelmsford requesting satisfactory replies to seven searching questions on issues not covered adequately by the Court of Inquiry. Over the next months Chelmsford and his staff scrambled to come up with acceptable explanations, but their inadequacies left the Duke ever more perplexed and irritated.[113] At the same time that he started pressing for better answers about what had gone wrong at Isandlwana, the Duke was also becoming acutely conscious of Chelmsford's ineffectual logistical arrangements. In March the Duke sent out his ADC, Major General the Hon. Sir Henry Clifford, VC as Inspector General of Line of Communications and Base and to succeed to Chelmsford's command should he break down or die. Clifford resented that his command stopped at the Zulu border and was assiduous in denigrating Chelmsford's conduct of the second invasion to the home authorities. Chelmsford had initially welcomed Clifford's energetic efficiency in moving up supplies, but the latter's criticisms eventually stung him deeply.[114] Whatever the wrongs or rights of this fresh dispute, it did Chelmsford's reputation no good. Now even Cambridge began severely to question his conduct of the campaign.[115] The cabinet met three times between 19 and 23 May to discuss the South African situation. In a letter of 27 May Disraeli reported to the Queen (who was inclined to support Chelmsford): 'No one upheld Lord Chelmsford. Even the Secretary of War gave him up, and spoke as if the military authorities had done the same.'[116] The Cabinet's reverse judgement of Solomon was to create a single, unified command in South Africa that would subordinate both Chelmsford and Bulwer, and sideline Frere. Cambridge suggested Chelmsford's old commander, Napier, for the post but, to the fury of the Horse Guards, the cabinet selected Wolseley instead.[117] Chelmsford learned on 16 June of Wolseley's appointment, but was not appraised of the terms until 5 July, the day after his victory at the battle of Ulundi. In fact, it was only on 9 July that he at last received formal notice of his supersession.[118] Until then he continued to act as if he were still Officer Commanding in South Africa, although sure knowledge that Wolseley was on his way undoubtedly spurred him on to bring the war to a successful conclusion before his rival could rob him of the credit.[119] Although Chelmsford did his best to maintain an imperturbable front, back in England a bitter Lady Chelmsford understood well how 'insulting' her 'cruelly abused' husband found it to be 'thrown over by the Govt. without a word of thanks for all his hard work'.[120]

Yet further misfortunes and vexations continued to dog Chelmsford's path. On 1 June the Prince Imperial of France – who was accompanying his headquarters as an observer, and whose safety Chelmsford had assured Cambridge and the Empress Eugénie he would look after 'to the best of my ability'[121] – was killed while out on a patrol he had joined without Chelmsford's prior knowledge.[122] The Prince's death, the probing questions in Parliament,[123] the publicity surrounding the subsequent court martial of Lieutenant J B Carey (the officer in command of the patrol) and the popular impression that the latter was being made a scapegoat for the folly of his superiors, all occasioned as much consternation in Britain as the battle of Isandlwana, and further damned Chelmsford in the public eye.[124] Unfortunately for Chelmsford, he was very inept in his handling of the war correspondents that by 1879 were a standard presence with any British army on active service, and who were now joining his force in growing numbers. Determined self-publicists like Wolseley cultivated them to ensure a laudatory press, but Chelmsford, smarting deeply at press criticisms he considered ill-informed if not plainly malicious, could not bring himself to work positively with the war correspondents he so clearly despised and mistrusted.[125]

The slow, over-methodical advance of the 1st Division up the coast bore out the criticisms of those officers who had opposed the independent operations of a second column, but it was effective in securing the surrender of most of the coastal region even before the battle of Ulundi.[126] Cetshwayo made increasingly desperate efforts to negotiate with Chelmsford, but the General demanded crushing and impossible terms to ensure that Zulu resistance would have to continue until he had achieved the total victory in the field he was so determined upon to vindicate his reputation.[127] Bedevilled after 24 June by a stream of orders and suggestions from a frustrated Wolseley, who had arrived in Cape Town on 24 June but was not able to reach the front until 7 July,[128] Chelmsford cautiously advanced on Ulundi, his cavalry carefully reconnoitering the route ahead, while the troops laagered every night and regularly halted to establish fortified supply depots along the line of communications.[129]

On 4 July Chelmsford drew up his force in an infantry square in the Mahlabathini plain in the very heart of the Zulu kingdom where the *amakhanda* were clustered. The Zulu attack wilted before the concentrated British fire and the *amabutho* fled from a devastating mounted counter-attack. Decisively defeated in the open field, the Zulu knew further resistance was pointless, and the warriors immediately dispersed to their homes. With his army routed, his *amakhanda* burned and his chiefs hastily submitting, King Cetshwayo himself fled to the north.[130] Yet nothing Chelmsford ever did now went unquestioned. Immediately after the battle he withdrew his forces south to his base on Mthonjaneni instead of advancing north to consolidate his victory, as his critics later said he ought to have done. His decision was influenced by his shortage of supplies and the need to get his men under cover in bitter winter weather, as well as by his knowledge that organised Zulu resistance was no longer likely. Still, it cannot be ignored that a desire to leave South Africa as soon as possible was also playing its part now that Wolseley would imminently be in a position to assert his new authority. Chelmsford accordingly resigned his command on 5 July.[131] And four days later he wrote to Colonel Stanley informing him that he intended to make his way to England with 'as little delay as possible' in order (as he bitingly put it) to 'extricate myself from a false position'.[132] Cambridge subsequently considered the decision to return home only wise, because his position would have proven 'difficult, not to say embarrassing' if he had remained in South Africa.[133]

Nevertheless, as Clery wrote on 12 July: 'There is one universal feeling of extreme satisfaction that Lord C. fought the battle of Ulundi before his successor arrived. However one's opinion of him as a general may be shaken, everybody's regard and sympathy for him is as strong is it can be.'[134] Colonists in Pietermaritzburg and Durban received Chelmsford with rapturous acclaim, all previous criticism of his blunders erased by final victory over the Zulu. With their plaudits ringing in his ears, Chelmsford took ship at Cape Town on 27 July.[135] Wolseley, in a sly letter of farewell, assured Chelmsford that 'with the halo of success' he would be cordially received at the Horse Guards and the War Office, though he could not answer for those outside the Duke's circle.[136] But there Wolseley was wrong. On 11 August 1879 Ellice wrote to Chelmsford on behalf of the Duke making abundantly clear the latter's dissatisfaction with Chelmsford's responses to his enquiry of 6 March concerning Isandlwana, and spelling out the damning conclusions on his generalship. Chelmsford was found guilty of generally underestimating the Zulu, of adopting a poor invasion strategy that did not sufficiently concentrate his forces, of unwisely dividing the column on 22 January, of not reconnoitering sufficiently and of leaving the camp without proper defences.[137] Chelmsford could be left in no doubt where he now stood with his erstwhile patron.

His reception in England was otherwise mixed. Beaconsfield refused to accord the general who had brought such discredit upon his ministry anything but the coldest formal interview, and did not mince his words in itemising in damning detail to the Queen his reasons. But the Queen was determined to invite Chelmsford to Balmoral because she believed it showed 'a want of generosity' to condemn him unheard.[138] The Queen was favourably impressed when she received Chelmsford, and in August 1879 he was made GCB. As Wolseley snarled in his journal with perceptive paranoia: 'Because he is my Lord, society will back him up, the court included, & because all the Horse Guards clique, the Duke and all his old fashioned set included . . . hate me most bitterly, every endeavour will be made by them to cry him up hoping thereby to keep me down'.[139]

In the event, although Chelmsford maintained a dignified reticence in the face of his critics, and although Ulundi had gone some way to restoring his honour and reputation, he found rehabilitation difficult. Isandlwana in particular continued to haunt him. On 19 August and 2 September 1880 he was faced with the ordeal of having to defend his own conduct of the Zululand campaign in the House of

Lords before his peers. The opposition peer, Lord Strathnairn, led the extremely well-informed and acute assault on Chelmsford's generalship, focussing on his part in the Isandlwana disaster. Chelmsford replied with eloquence and at length, supported by government peers, but Strathnairn remained as unconvinced as Cambridge the previous year. His were the last and telling (if inelegant) words in the debate: 'Whatever might be said, there were not the necessary precautions taken to protect a camp in which most of our stores were.'[140]

In the course of his defence Chelmsford had again attempted to shift the blame to Durnford, blaming him for his impulsive disregard of orders. This provoked a determined response from Durnford's brother Edward and from Frances Colenso (the daughter of the controversially heretical and pro-Zulu Anglican Bishop of Natal), who had been romantically attached to Durnford. Their crusade took the form of letters to the newspapers, a pamphlet and two books,[141] and culminated in 1886 at a court of inquiry in Natal. To Chelmsford's relief, the court exonerated Captain Theophilus Shepstone from Frances Colenso's bizarre charge that he had removed papers from Durnford's body and suppressed them to protect Chelmsford's reputation.[142]

The Durnford issue caused Chelmsford much private vexation and embarrassment.[143] As far as his military career went, his reputation at the Horse Guards had been too badly tarnished for him ever again to be offered an active command, although the Queen conspicuously favoured him with honours. In April 1882 he was promoted to the permanent rank of lieutenant general. The Queen exerted her influence to have him appointed Lieutenant of the Tower, a position he held from June 1884 to March 1889. He became a full general in December 1888, evaded compulsory retirement in 1889 and was finally placed on the retired list only on 7 June 1893. In January 1898 he was appointed colonel of his old regiment, the Sherwood Foresters (Derbyshire Regiment), as the 95th was now called, and in September 1900 was transferred to the 2nd Life Guards. The Queen then appointed him Gold Stick, a ceremonial office open to Colonels of the Life Guards that required personal attendance on the sovereign at all state occasions. On his accession in January 1901, King Edward VII retained Chelmsford as Gold Stick and in 1902 made him GCVO. Gilded with honours, Chelmsford died in London on 9 April 1905 following a sudden seizure while playing billiards at the magnificent but ponderous United Service Club ('the Senior') in Pall Mall. Appropriately, the club stood across the road from the Crimean War memorial cast from the bronze of Russian guns captured at Sebastopol where Chelmsford had been present fifty years before.[144] Chelmsford was buried in a simple granite tomb carved with a plain cross behind his father's heraldically ornate resting place in London's Brompton Cemetery.[145]

In its accompanying commentary on 'Spy's' caricature of a gawky, ill-at-ease Chelmsford published a year after Chelmsford had been humiliatingly compelled to defend his generalship before his peers in the House of Lords, *Vanity Fair* condescendingly but not unfairly concluded: 'Lord Chelmsford is not a bad man; . . . But nature has refused to him the qualities of a great captain.'[146] The perceptive Clery had come to much the same opinion soon after the Isandlwana debacle when he wrote: 'I feel greatly for the poor general, for nothing could exceed his energy about everything, but I fear there have been some sad miscalculations about the whole business and that the enemy has been altogether underestimated.'[147]

Certainly, there is no doubting Chelmsford's professionalism, dedication to duty and care for the men under his command. Nor did he prove unwilling to learn from his mistakes, for he successfully adjusted his tactics during the latter stages of the Zululand campaign. His plodding, over-methodical strategy, on the other hand, distinctly lacked flair or dash. Inadequate staff support compounded his reluctance to delegate, and he consequently allowed himself to be overwhelmed by the pettifogging administrative work of managing a campaign. While Chelmsford would undoubtedly have found the routines of military administration comfortingly familiar, he was far less at home with the novel experience of an independent command in the field. Paradoxically, the relative ease of his ultimate success in the Ninth Frontier War (after an unpromising beginning) led directly to disaster in the Zululand campaign. He and his staff shared a perilous contempt for the military sophistication of the Zulu army, which was a product both of previous experience in the Eastern Cape and of an assured confidence in their decisive military edge based on their professional experience and on their ingrained sense of racial and class superiority. Thus, while Chelmsford was himself a captive of his aristocratic upbringing and its accompanying values, and of the culture of the army milieu in which he had spent his adult life, he shared his outlook and assumptions with his officers. Clery was surely right, therefore, when he reflected that Chelmsford had been singularly 'unlucky', for if the main Zulu army had gone against either of the two other columns invading Zululand in January 1879 instead of No. 3 Column, 'the same thing would have happened to them'.[148] Pearson or Wood, instead of Chelmsford, would have become the pilloried victim of the misplaced confidence that in early 1879 was initially common to all British officers in Zululand.

Bibliography

The only published biography of Chelmsford is Gerald French's *Lord Chelmsford and the Zulu War* (London: John Lane at the Bodley Head, 1939), a sustained refutation of the condemnation of Chelmsford's generalship in W H Clements's pioneering, if anecdotal, study, *The Glamour and Tragedy of the Zulu War* (London: Bodley Head, 1936). Both works are in the partisan tradition of contemporary commentary with the aggressive and spiteful *Daily News* war correspondent Archibald Forbes (whom Chelmsford had alienated by refusing his request for the Zulu War medal) and Lieutenant Colonel Edward Durnford (the aggrieved brother of the officer on whom Chelmsford attempted to pin the blame for Isandlwana) ranged against the able and informed defence of Chelmsford's generalship by Arthur Harness, who, as a lieutenant colonel in the Royal Artillery, had been away skirmishing with Chelmsford on the day of the battle. Recent years have seen the appearance of a number of annotated collections of

The Very Model of a Modern Major General: Garnet Wolseley, *c.* 1880.

Evelyn Wood in the full dress of a Field Marshal, the rank he attained in 1903.

Redvers Buller, *c.* 1895, in full dress uniform as Colonel of his regiment, the King's Royal Rifle Corps, in which he had been commissioned in 1858.

Charles Gordon in Egyptian uniform as Governor General of Sudan.

George Colley, in 1874, wearing the campaign dress Wolseley designed for the Asante campaign, complete with Elcho sword bayonet.

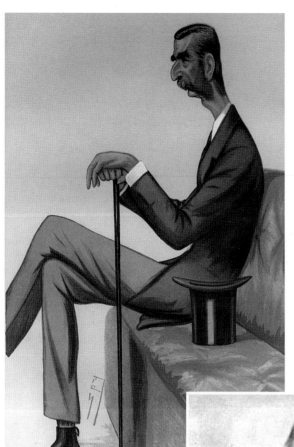

A caricature of Lord Chelmsford by 'Spy' for *Vanity Fair*, 3 September 1881.

Frederic Thesiger, Baron Chelmsford shortly after the Zulu War.

Frederick Roberts (centre) as C in C Madras, *c.* 1885, while at camp of exercise with General the Hon. Sir Arthur Hardinge, C in C Bombay (left) and General Sir Donald Stewart, C in C India (right).

Frederick Roberts outside his headquarters at Pretoria, 1900.

Herbert Kitchener as
Sirdar of the Egyptian
Army, *c.* 1898.

Kitchener as C in C in
South Africa, *c.* 1901.

contemporary letters, newspaper reports and diaries connected to the Anglo–Zulu War (though none has surpassed Frank Emery's pioneering *The Red Soldier* (London: Hodder & Stoughton, 1977) in verve or quality). Those that cast the most light on Chelmsford's day-to-day conduct of the campaign are the Harness Letters in Sonia Clarke's *Invasion of Zululand 1879: Anglo-Zulu War Experiences of Arthur Harness; John Jervis, 4th Viscount St Vincent; and Sir Henry Bulwer* (Houghton: Brenthurst Press, 1979) and the Alison Letters in her *Zululand at War, 1879: The Conduct of the Anglo–Zulu War* (Houghton: Brenthurst Press, 1984). The Alison Letters were solicited from various officers in the field by Major General Sir Archibald Alison, the DQMG for Intelligence at the War Office, in order to gain confidential and sensitive information on the conduct of the campaign. These letters are complemented by a selection from Chelmsford's own military correspondence and private papers in John Laband's *Lord Chelmsford's Zululand Campaign 1878–1879* (Stroud: Sutton Publishing for the Army Records Society, 1994).

As for the infamous battle of Isandlwana itself, conflicting interpretations continue to swirl about it. The starting point for any investigation is Major J S Rothwell of the Intelligence Branch of the War Office's compilation of reports from the field into an official history called the *Narrative of the Field Operations Connected with the Zulu War* (London: HMSO, 1881). Chapter IV is devoted to the battle of Isandlwana and sticks firmly to Chelmsford's view of events. The first modern critique of Isandlwana was Sir Reginald Coupland's carefully measured *Zulu Battle Piece: Isandhlwana* (London: Collins, 1949). Then in 1965 David Jackson brought out a series of articles in the *Journal of the Society for Army Historical Research*, in which he subjected the evidence to the most meticulous scrutiny. His revisionist interpretation has, as a consequence, become the orthodoxy followed by most subsequent historians. And these have not been lacking. Over two dozen books dealing wholly or in part with Isandlwana have been published since 1965. One of the most significant is R W F Drooglever's close examination in *The Road to Isandhlwana* (London: Greenhill Books, 1992) of the part played by Colonel Durnford (the official scapegoat) in the Isandlwana debacle. Of the many accounts aimed at a more popular market the best by far have been by Ian Knight, including *Zulu: Isandlwana and Rorke's Drift* (London: Windrow & Greene, 1992), which compare favourably with more lightweight treatments that revert to sensationalist derring-do typical of Donald Morris's classic *The Washing of the Spears* (London: Jonathan Cape, 1965). The most stimulating recent analysis of Isandlwana, *Zulu Victory* (London: Greenhill, 2002), is by Ron Lock and Peter Quantrill. Critics have been concerned by its questionable conclusions based upon unreliable evidence, but the book does have the merit of opening up debate afresh. Part Three that examines how the post-battle spin was managed is particularly revealing. The best short account available of the battle of Isandlwana, and one that presents a balanced synthesis of the various controversies that surround it, is Ian Beckett's *Isandlwana 1879* (London: Brassey's/Chrysalis, 2003). Chelmsford's role in the Isandlwana disaster is also analysed in the present author's own research and fieldwork published in three works in particular: John Laband and Jeff Mathews, *Isandlwana* (Pietermaritzburg: Centaur, 1992); John Laband and Paul Thompson, *The Illustrated Guide to the Anglo–Zulu War* (Pietermaritzburg: University of Natal Press, 2000) and John Laband, *Kingdom in Crisis: the Zulu Response to the British Invasion of 1879*, 2nd edn (Barnsley: Pen & Sword, 2007).

Notes

1. Hansard 3rd series, vol. 244 cc. 910–11, House of Commons: Questions, Mr E Jenkins, 14 March 1879.
2. Basic biographical information throughout this chapter concerning both the first and second

Barons Chelmsford is drawn from J A Hamilton, 'Thesiger, Frederick, first Baron Chelmsford (1794–1878)', rev. Sinéad Agnew; and J P C Laband 'Thesiger, Frederic Augustus, second Baron Chelmsford (1827–1905)', *Oxford Dictionary of National Biography* (Oxford: Oxford University Press, 2004); Chelmsford's obituary in *The Times*, 10 April 1905; and Adrian Greaves and Ian Knight, *Who's Who in the Zulu War, 1879: I, The British* (Barnsley: Pen & Sword Military, 2006), pp. 54–60.

3. In August 2007 the house was undergoing renovation.

4. Lawrence H Officer, 'Purchasing Power of British Pounds from 1264 to 2006', available at: http://www.MeasuringWorth.com (accessed March 2007). There are various other ways of computing the relative value of the pound sterling, such as employing the GDP deflator, average earnings or per capita GDP. Using the retail price index, as is done here, gives the lowest relative value, but is useful in suggesting contemporary buying power. All further calculations in this chapter of the current purchasing power of nineteenth-century pounds are derived from this same source.

5. David Cannadine, *The Decline and Fall of the British Aristocracy* (New York: Vintage Books, 1999), pp. 250–51.

6. Edward M Spiers, *The Army and Society 1815–1914* (London and New York: Longman, 1980), pp. 8–9; idem, *The Late Victorian Army 1868–1902* (Manchester: Manchester University Press, 1992), pp. 2, 94–95.

7. Spiers, *Victorian Army* pp. 93–94.

8. Between 1800 and 1849, sixty-nine peers and peers' sons served in the Grenadiers, and fifty-nine between 1850 and 1899. See Philip Mansel, *Pillars of Monarchy: An Outline of the Political and Social History of Royal Guards 1400–1984* (London: Quartet Books, 1984), p. 78: Table I.

9. G Harries-Jenkins, *The Army in Victorian Society* (London: Routledge and Kegan Paul, 1977), pp. 24–25.

10. Spiers, *Army and Society*, p. 18.

11. Ibid., pp. 11, 17: Table 1.6: Regulation of prices of commissions established by the Royal Warrant of 1821; Spiers, *Late Victorian Army*, p. 104.

12. National Army Museum (hereafter NAM) Chelmsford Papers (hereafter CP), 18/35, Chelmsford to Whitmore, draft of a letter sent for the consideration of the Duke of Cambridge, 2 January 1881.

13. Spiers, *Victorian Army*, pp. 105–6; Anthony Clayton, *The British Officer: Leading the Army from 1660 to the Present* (Harlow: Pearson Longman, 2006), p. 101.

14. Spiers, *Army and Society*, pp. 17: Table 1.6; 19.

15. Ibid., pp. 17: Table 1.6; 18.

16. When the Rifle Brigade was formed in 1816 its previous number of 95 was reassigned to the new foot regiment formed in 1823.

17. NAM, CP, 18/34, Chelmsford to Whitmore, 2 January 1881; ibid., statement of foreign, staff and active service of Major General Lord Chelmsford, 1 January 1881.

18. The houses in Stanhope Gardens were still largely in domestic use in 2007, though many in the surrounding area are being converted into hotels and businesses.

19. Richard Holmes, *Sahib: The British Soldier in India 1750–1914* (London: HarperCollins, 2005), pp. 146–77; Spiers, *Late Victorian Army*, p. 105.

20. Philip Mason, *A Matter of Honour. An Account of the Indian Army Its Officers and Men* (Harmondsworth: Peregrine Books, 1976), pp. 367–68.

21. P G Robb, 'Frederic John Napier Thesiger, first Viscount Chelmsford (1868–1933)', *Oxford Dictionary of National Biography*; Cannadine, *British Aristocracy*, p. 210.

22. Arvel B Erickson, 'Abolition of Purchase in the British Army', *Military Affairs* 23, 2 (Summer, 1959), 75; Spiers, *Army and Society*, p. 16.

23. Spiers, *Late Victorian Army*, pp. 90–93.

24. War Office, *Field Exercise and Evolutions of Infantry* (London: HMSO, 1877), pp. 53–54.

25. Philip Gon, *The Road to Isandlwana: The Years of an Imperial Battalion* (Johannesburg: Ad. Donker, 1979), pp. 134–40, 145–46.

26. NAM, CP, 2/13, Mitchell to Thesiger, 28 January 1878.

27. Jeffrey Mathews, 'Lord Chelmsford: British General in Southern Africa 1878–1879', unpub. DLitt et Phil thesis, University of South Africa, 1986, pp. 37, 40–1. See also *Vanity Fair*, 3 September 1881, for the sarcastic observation that although 'distinguished as an able player of Kriegspiel', he was 'outwitted, outmanoeuvered, and beaten in tactics by ignorant savages'.

28. Gon, *Road to Isandlwana*, p. 163.

29. *Cape Mercury*, 12 June 1878.

30. For Chelmsford and the Ninth Frontier War, see Gon, *Road to Isandlwana*, pp. 152–63; Mathews, 'Chelmsford', pp. 42–9; John Milton, *The Edges of War* (Cape Town: Juta, 1983), pp. 274–78.

31. NAM, CP, 2/12, Thesiger to Stanley, 10 April and 5 May 1878.

32. Gon, *Road to Isandlwana*, pp. 146–47, 156.

33. Crealock to Alison, 14 January 1879, cited in Sonia Clarke, *Zululand at War, 1879: The Conduct of the Anglo-Zulu War* (Houghton: Brenthurst Press, 1984), p. 74.

34. *British Parliamentary Papers* (hereafter *BPP*) XX of 1881 (C. 2719), *Report of the Committee of General and Other Officers of the Army on Army Reorganisation*, Q. 4699.

35. The ambitious Clery passed Staff College in 1870, was an instructor and then professor of tactics at the Royal Military College, Sandhurst (1871–75), and held various staff appointments before coming out to Zululand as a special-service officer.

36. Clery to Harman, 17 February 1878 (actually 1879), cited in Clarke, *Zululand at War*, p. 82.

37. Mathews, 'Chelmsford', pp. 26–7, 39–41, 341–42.

38. *BPP*, LI of 1878–9 (C. 2220), enc. 1 in no. 72, Thesiger to Frere, 2 September 1878.

39. Richard Cope, *Ploughshare of War. The Origins of the Anglo-Zulu War of 1879* (Pietermaritzburg: University of Natal Press, 1999), chapts 7–9; John Laband, *Kingdom in Crisis: the Zulu Response to the British Invasion of 1879*, 2nd edn (Barnsley: Pen & Sword, 2007), pp. 10–14.

40. Charles Callwell, *Small Wars: Their Principles and Practice*, 3rd edn (London: HMSO, 1906), pp. 21–23, 25–29; Spiers, *Late Victorian Army*, pp. 272–304; and G Harries-Jenkins, 'The Development of Professionalism in the Victorian Army', *Armed Forces and Society*, 1, 4 (1975), 484–85.

41. Peter Burroughs, 'Imperial Defence and the Victorian Army', *Journal of Imperial and Commonwealth History*, XV, 1 (1986), 58, 66, 72.

42. David French, *Military Identities. The Regimental System, the British Army, and the British People c. 1870–2000* (Oxford: Oxford University Press, 2005), pp. 10–20, 25–27; Spiers, *Late Victorian Army*, pp. 3, 5–8, 31–2; Mathews, 'Chelmsford', pp. 17–18, 22–26, 300–1, 313, 322, 324. See Chelmsford's comment in April 1879 that 'Drafts will not be of much use, as they are certain to be composed of boys' in KwaZulu-Natal Archives, Pietermaritzburg (hereafter KZNA), Wood Mss, II/2/2: Chelmsford to Wood, 22 April 1879.

43. The fullest treatment of the NNC is to be found in Paul Thompson, *Black Soldiers of the Queen: The Natal Native Contingent in the Anglo-Zulu War* (Tuscaloosa, AL: University of Alabama Press, 2006).

44. The National Archives (hereafter TNA), WO 32/7704, Chelmsford to Stanley, 25 November 1878.

45. While an improvement over earlier maps such as Lieutenant Colonel A W Durnford's *Sketch of Zululand &c. Compiled from Original Sources and from Personal Observation & Information* of September 1878, even the Intelligence Branch of the Quartermaster General's Department of the War Office's *Military Map of Zulu Land compiled from Most Recent Information*, and

published in March 1879, was still full of inaccuracies and empty spaces.

46. Major Ashe and Captain E V Wyatt-Edgell, *The Story of the Zulu Campaign* (London: Sampson Low, Marston, Searle, & Rivington, 1880), p. 189.

47. Spiers, *Late Victorian Army*, pp. 67–69, 109–11, 157.

48. Crealock excelled at water-colour paintings and sketches, and those executed on campaign in the Cape and Zululand in 1878–79 constitute an invaluable graphic record. The originals are in the Sherwood Foresters Museum in Nottingham, and a selection has been published in R A Brown, ed., *The Road to Ulundi. The Water Colour Drawings of John North Crealock (the Zulu War of 1879)* (Pietermaritzburg: University of Natal Press, 1969).

49. Gon, *Road to Isandlwana*, p. 147; J P C Laband, 'Crealock, John North (1836–1895)', *Oxford Dictionary of National Biography*, available at: http://www.oxforddnb.com/view/article/50002 (accessed 8 October 2008).

50. Clery to Alison, 1 February and 18 March 1879, cited in Clarke, *Zululand at War*, pp. 81, 124.

51. Crealock to Alison, 11 April 1879, cited in Clarke, *Zululand at War*, p. 205. See also Clery to Alison, 6 December 1878 and 18 March, cited in Clarke, *Zululand at War*, pp. 61, 124.

52. F Fynney, *The Zulu Army and Zulu Headmen. Compiled from Information Obtained from the Most Reliable Sources, and Published by Direction of the Lieut.-General Commanding for the Information of Those under His Command*, 2nd edn, revised (Pietermaritzburg: 1879); and Anon, *Regulations for Field Forces in South Africa 1878* (Pietermaritzburg: November 1878).

53. Clery to Alison, 13 April 1879, cited in Clarke, *Zululand at War*, p. 126.

54. Clery to Alison, 18 March 1879, cited in Clarke, *Zululand at War*, p. 122.

55. NAM, CP, 10/13, Memorandum by Chelmsford on the military requirements of the Natal Colony with regard to its N Eastern Border should offensive or defensive measures against Zululand be considered necessary, 23 October 1878; John Laband, 'Bulwer, Chelmsford and the Border Levies: The Dispute over the Defence of Natal, 1879', in John Laband and Paul Thompson, eds, *Kingdom and Colony at War: Sixteen Studies on the Anglo-Zulu War of 1879* (Pietermaritzburg and Cape Town: University of Natal Press and N & S Press, 1990), pp. 150–53.

56. J E Carlyle, 'The Zulu War', *British Quarterly Review* 69 (1879), 438–39; Captain H Hallam Parr, *A Sketch of the Kaffir and Zulu War: Guadana to Isandhlwana* (London: C Kegan Paul, 1880), pp. 170–71; Laband, *Kingdom in Crisis: the Zulu Response*, pp. 12–14.

57. Callwell, *Small Wars*, pp. 57–59, 64, 66; Howard Bailes, 'Technology and Imperialism: A Case Study of the Victorian Army in Africa', *Victorian Studies*, 24, 1 (1980), 89–103. Even cavalry chargers had to have their fodder transported since (unlike colonial horses) they could not live off the poor grazing.

58. H Bulwer to E Bulwer, 8 December 1878, cited in Sonia Clarke, *Invasion of Zululand 1879: Anglo-Zulu War Experiences of Arthur Harness; John Jervis, 4th Viscount St Vincent; and Sir Henry Bulwer* (Houghton: Brenthurst Press, 1979), pp. 212–14.

59. Intelligence Division of the War Office, *Précis of Information Concerning Zululand, Corrected to December, 1894* (London: HMSO, 1895), p. 58.

60. For an example of Chelmsford's abortive attempts to improve supply and transport, see NAM, CP, 5/20, Memorandum by Chelmsford for District Commissary General E Strickland, rough notes, undated (probably November 1878). For ox-drawn transport, see War Office, *Narrative of the Field Operations Connected with the Zulu War of 1879* (London: HMSO, 1881), p. 171; and Ian Bennett, ed., *Eyewitness in Zululand: The Campaign Reminiscences of Colonel Walter Dunne, CB, South Africa, 1877–1881* (London: Greenhill, 1989), pp. 43–45, 49–54. See also Jeffrey Mathews, 'Lord Chelmsford and Problems of Transport and Supply during the Anglo-Zulu War of 1879', unpub. MA thesis, University of Natal, 1979, pp. 1–9, 42–43; idem, 'Chelmsford', pp. 71–84, 111–12, 243–44, 344.

61. For laagering procedure as laid down by Chelmsford, see NAM, CP, 26/9, His Excellency the Lieutenant General Commanding, *Special Instructions Regarding the Management of Ox Transport on the Line of March, and for Conducting the Line of March when Troops March with Ox Wagon Transport, and for Forming Wagon Laagers* (Durban: 'Mercury' Press, n.d. [1879]), pp. 10–11, items 15–26.

62. Anon, *Regulations for Field Forces in South Africa 1878*, p. 3, item 19.

63. Arthur Harness, 'The Zulu Campaign from a Military Point of View', *Fraser's Magazine* new series XXI, 101, April 1880, 478–79.

64. For a selection of anxious letters addressed by Chelmsford to his commanders on the eve of invasion, see John Laband, ed., *Lord Chelmsford's Zululand Campaign 1878–1879* (Stroud: Sutton Publishing for the Army Records Society, 1994), documents 13, 23, 24, 26, 28.

65. NAM, CP, 27, Chelmsford to Wood, 11 January 1879, and Chelmsford to Frere, 16 January 1879; Ashe and Wyatt-Edgell, *Zulu Campaign*, pp. 306–7; Harness, 'Zulu Campaign', p. 478.

66. NAM, CP, Chelmsford to Col Bellairs, 31 December 1878.

67. John Laband, 'Zulu Civilians in the Rise and Fall of the Zulu Kingdom c. 1817–187', in John Laband, ed., *Daily Lives of Civilians in Wartime Africa from Slavery Days to Rwandan Genocide* (Westport, CT and London: Greenwood Press, 2007), pp. 64–76.

68. John Laband, 'The Cohesion of the Zulu Polity and the Impact of the Anglo-Zulu War: A Reassessment', in Laband and Thompson, eds, *Kingdom and Colony at War*, pp. 3–7.

69. KZNA, Sir Theophilus Shepstone Papers (hereafter TS) 35, Chelmsford to Shepstone, 28 November 1878.

70. Callwell, *Small Wars*, pp. 37–39, 90–91, 93, 103–4, 106.

71. Burroughs, 'Imperial Defence', p. 61; Hew Strachan, *European Armies and the Conduct of War* (London and New York: Routledge, 2001), p. 82.

72. Laband, *Kingdom in Crisis: the Zulu Response*, p. 60.

73. For a first-hand account of the fighting so reminiscent of the campaign against the Xhosa, see Daphne Child, ed., *The Zulu War Journal of Colonel Henry Harford, C.B.* (Pietermaritzburg: Shuter & Shooter, 1978), pp. 18–21.

74. Clery to Alison, 13 April 1879, cited in Clarke, *Zululand at War*, p. 126.

75. Clery to Alison, 18 March 1879, cited in Clarke, *Zululand at War*, pp. 121–22.

76. NAM, CP, 8/31, Notes by Chelmsford on the findings of the Court of Enquiry, n.d.

77. NAM, CP, 26/36, Gosset to Lady Chelmsford, 7 June 1906.

78. Clery to Harman, 17 February 1878 (actually 1879), cited in Clarke, *Zululand at War*, p. 84. See also Clery to Alison, 28 April 1879, cited in Clarke, *Zululand at War*, p. 129 for a reiteration of this statement.

79. Child, *Zulu War Journal of Colonel Henry Harford*, p. 23.

80. Henry Curling to his Mother, 2 February 1879, cited in Adrian Greaves and Brian Best, eds, *The Curling Letters of the Zulu War: 'There Was Awful Slaughter'* (Barnsley: Leo Cooper, 2001), pp. 91–92.

81. KZNA, TS, 35, Chelmsford to Shepstone, 7 December 1879.

82. Clery to Harman, 17 February 1878 (actually 1879), cited in Clarke, *Zululand at War*, p. 84.

83. Clery to Alison, 18 March 1879, cited in Clarke, *Zululand at War*, p. 122.

84. Clery to Harman, 17 February 1878 (actually 1879), cited in Clarke, *Zululand at War*, p. 85.

85. 'Letter from an Abergavenny Man', *Abergavenny Chronicle*, 29 March 1879, cited in Edward Spiers, *The Victorian Soldier in Africa* (Manchester and New York: Manchester University Press, 2004), p. 42.

86. Clery to Harman, 17 February 1878 (actually 1879), cited in Clarke, *Zululand at War*, p. 85.

87. NAM, CP, 8/15, Chelmsford to Frere, 23 January 1879.

88. Crealock to Alison, 2 and 9 February 1879, cited in Clarke, *Zululand at War*, p. 93.

89. TNA, WO 32/7709, Chelmsford to Stanley, 9 February 1879.

90. Hansard, 3rd Series, vol. 244, cc. 1494–7, House of Lords: Statement by the Duke of Cambridge, 24 March 1879; Chelmsford to Dillon, 14 May 1879, cited in Clarke, *Zululand at War*, p. 94.

91. KZNA, Wood Ms, II/2/2, Chelmsford to Wood, 29 January and 3 February 1879.

92. NAM, CP, 28, Chelmsford to Cambridge, 1 February 1879.

93. Clery to Harman, 17 February 1878 (actually 1879), cited in Clarke, *Zululand at War*, pp. 83–84.

94. The evidence is in TNA, WO 33/34, *Zulu War, Miscellaneous, 1878–9*, 234–42. It is conveniently reprinted in Ian F W Beckett, *Isandlwana 1879* (London: Brassey's/Chrysalis, 2003), pp. 105–21.

95. NAM, CP, 27, Chelmsford to Durnford, 19 January 1879.

96. Clery to Alison, 28 April 1879, cited in Clarke, *Zululand at War*, p. 129.

97. R W F Drooglever, *The Road to Isandhlwana* (London: Greenhill Books, 1992), pp. 181–82; Beckett, *Isandlwana*, p. 75.

98. See Ron Lock and Peter Quantrill, *Zulu Victory* (London: Greenhill, 2002), pp. 236–46, 251–57 for their careful assessment of the evidence.

99. Maurice to Alison, 23 June 1879, cited in Clarke, *Zululand at War*, p. 272. See also Clery to Alison, 11 and 18 March 1879, cited in Clarke, *Zululand at War*, pp. 100, 102, 125.

100. For typical, critical responses in the British press, see the *Daily Telegraph*, 3 March 1879 and the *Standard*, 3 and 8 March 1879. For the Natal press, see the *Colonist*, 15 February 1879 and the *Natal Witness*, 27 February 1879. See also Crealock to Alison, 24 February 1879, cited in Clarke, *Zululand at War*, p. 96 for comment on the stance taken by the colonial press.

101. Clarke, *Zululand at War*, pp. 26–29.

102. Hansard, 3rd Series, vol. 244 cc. 907–24; cc. 1865–1950; cc. 1991–2090; vol. 245, cc. 20–127, House of Commons: Questions and Debate, 14, 27, 28 and 30 March 1879; and vol. 244 cc. 1605–1697, House of Lords: Debate, 25 March 1879.

103. For Chelmsford's orders for procedures to be followed on the march, see NAM, CP, 3/37, Memorandum by Chelmsford, n.d. (c. 26 March 1879); for his long official report on the battle of Gingindlovu, see TNA, WO 32/7727, Chelmsford to Stanley, 10 April 1879.

104. KZNA, Wood Mss, II/2/2, Chelmsford to Wood (c. 15) April 1879.

105. Cambridge to Frere, 13 February 1879, cited in Clarke, *Zululand at War*, p. 110. See also Ian Beckett, *The Victorians at War* (London and New York: Hambledon and London, 2003), chapter 13: 'Chelmsford's Major-Generals'.

106. KZNA, Wood Mss, II/2/2, Chelmsford to Wood, 19 May 1879. Chelmsford quoted the proverb in Italian: 'Chi va piano, va sano e va lontano.'

107. NAM, CP, 28, Chelmsford to Cambridge, 11 April 1879; NAD, Wood Mss, II/2, Chelmsford to Wood, 25 April 1879.

108. See CP 13/19: Chelmsford to Stanley, 25 May 1879.

109. John Laband, 'Bulwer, Chelmsford and the Border Levies: The Dispute over the Defence of Natal, 1879', in Laband and Thompson, eds, *Kingdom and Colony at War*, pp. 150–65.

110. The cost of the war was eventually put at £5,230,328, considerably more than the government was willing to countenance for a colonial campaign.

111. W F Monypenny and G E Buckle, *The Life of Benjamin Disraeli, Earl of Beaconsfield*, new and revised edn (New York: Macmillan, 1929), II, p. 1297.

112. Cambridge to Frere, 13 February 1879, cited in Clarke, *Zululand at War*, p. 109.

113. TNA, WO 30/129, Ellice to Chelmsford, 6 March 1869; Lock and Quantrill, *Zulu Victory*, pp. 265–80.

114. NAM, CP, 17/34, Chelmsford to Clifford, 2 July 1879; Beckett, *Victorians at War*, pp. 123, 125–27.

115. Royal Archives, Cambridge Mss, VIC/ADD E/1/8658, Cambridge to Chelmsford, 8 May

1879. See also Cambridge to Frere, 20 March and 22 May 1879, cited in Clarke, *Zululand at War*, p. 114.

116. Lord Beaconsfield to Queen Victoria, 27 May 1879, cited in Monypenny and Buckle, *Disraeli*, II, p. 1304.

117. Beaconsfield to Queen Victoria, 27 May 1879 and Beaconsfield to Anne Lady Chesterfield, 28 May 1879, cited in Monypenny and Buckle, *Disraeli*, II, pp. 1303–4, 1305–6; Adrian Preston, ed., *Sir Garnet Wolseley's South African Journal, 1879–1880* (Cape Town: A A Balkema, 1973), pp. 6–7.

118. Crealock to Alison, 9 July 1879, cited in Clarke, *Zululand at War*, p. 245.

119. Mathews, 'Chelmsford', pp. 308–9.

120. Killie Campbell Africana Library, Wood Mss, 27/17, Adria Lady Chelmsford to Wood, 3 June 1879.

121. NAM, CP, 28, Chelmsford to Cambridge, 11 April 1879.

122. Ibid., 11/8, Chelmsford to Stanley, 2 June 1879.

123. Hansard, 3rd Series, vol. 247 cc. 401–3; 686–9: House of Commons: Questions, 19 and 26 June 1879.

124. For the authoritative account of the Prince Imperial in Zululand, his death and the aftermath, see Ian Knight, *With His Face to the Foe. The Life and Death of Louis Napoleon, the Prince Imperial: Zululand 1879* (Staplehurst: Spellmount, 2001). Carey's court martial and reception in England are discussed on pp. 229–32, 238–47, 256–64.

125. See John Laband and Ian Knight, *The War Correspondents: The Anglo-Zulu War* (Stroud: Sutton Publishing, 1996), pp. v–xix for a discussion on war reportage in the Anglo-Zulu War. For Chelmsford's querulous comments about hostile war correspondents, see NAM, CP, 28, Chelmsford to Stanley, 10 June 1879.

126. John Laband, 'Cohesion of the Zulu Polity', in John Laband and Paul Thompson, eds, *Kingdom and Colony at War*, pp. 12–14.

127. See John Laband, 'Humbugging the General? King Cetshwayo's Peace Overtures during the Anglo-Zulu War', in John Laband and Paul Thompson, eds, *Kingdom and Colony at War*, pp. 52–59.

128. Preston, *South African Journal*, pp. 43–52, journal entries 24 June to 7 July 1879.

129. Laband and Thompson, *Anglo-Zulu War*, pp. 60–61.

130. For Chelmsford's official report of the battle of Ulundi, see TNA, WO 32/7763, Chelmsford to Stanley, 6 July 1879. See Laband, *Kingdom in Crisis: the Zulu Response*, pp. 206–36 for a description of the battle and its decisive impact.

131. NAM, CP, 28, Chelmsford to Stanley, n.d. (5 July 1879).

132. TNA, WO 32/7770, Chelmsford to Stanley, 9 July 1879.

133. Cambridge to Frere, 26 August 1878, cited in Clarke, *Zululand at War*, p. 275.

134. Clery to Alison, 12 July 1879, cited in Clarke, *Zululand at War*, p. 248.

135. Mathews, 'Chelmsford', pp. 338–39.

136. NAM, CP, 21/9, Wolseley to Chelmsford, 12 July 1879.

137. TNA, WO 30/129, Ellice to Chelmsford, 11 August 1879.

138. Beaconsfield to Queen Victoria, 30 August 1879 and Queen Victoria to Beaconsfield, 1 September 1879, cited in Monypenny and Buckle, *Disraeli*, II, pp. 1331–32.

139. Preston, *South African Journal*, p. 107, journal entry, 4 September 1879.

140. Hansard, 3rd Series, vol. 256 c. 1035: House of Lords: Debate, 2 September 1880. For the full debates, see vol. 255 cc. 1543–67 and vol. 256 cc. 1025–35: House of Lords: Motion: 19 August and 2 September 1880.

141. See F E Colenso, assisted by Lieutenant Colonel E C L Durnford, *History of the Zulu War and its Origin* (London: Chapman Hall, 1881); and E C L Durnford, ed., *A Soldier's Life and Works in South Africa, 1872–1879: A Memory of the Late Colonel A W Durnford, Royal Engineers*

(London: Sampson Low, Marston, Searle & Rivington, 1882).

142. Gerald French, *Lord Chelmsford and the Zulu War* (London: John Lane at the Bodley Head, 1939), p. 316–23; Droogleever, *Isandhlwana*, pp. 243–46.

143. See NAM, CP, 22/5-7, 38-48, 52-3 for Chelmsford's extremely pained correspondence on this matter.

144. The United Service Club closed its doors in 1976 and the premises were taken over by the Institute of Directors. See Anthony Lejeune and Malcolm Lewis, *The Gentlemen's Clubs of London* (London: Bracken Books, 1984), pp. 276–83.

145. See French, *Chelmsford*, pp. 306–15, 324–67, 378–83. The inscription reads: 'Frederic Augustus, 2nd Baron Chelmsford, G.C.B., G.C.V.O., General. Colonel of the 2nd Life Guards. May 31st 1827 – April 9th 1905.' Twenty-one years later his widow joined him in his tomb (partially obscured in the summer of 2007 by ivy and uncut grass) surrounded by a cluster of other family members.

146. *Vanity Fair*, 3 September 1881.

147. Clery to Alison, 1 February 1879, cited in Clarke, *Zululand at War*, p. 81.

148. Clery to Alison, 28 April 1879, cited in Clarke, *Zululand at War*, p. 129.

Chapter 6

Charles Gordon

Gerald Herman

C harles George Gordon was born on 28 January 1833 near the Woolwich arsenal, where his father, Major (later Lieutenant General) Henry William Gordon served as Inspector of the Carriage Department. Gordon's mother, Elizabeth, was the evangelical and fundamentalist daughter of a prominent whaling-ship-owning family. He was one of their five sons and six daughters. Gordon himself gave up on church-going, later writing 'What husks the Evangelical religion is',[1] and committing himself to the Bible itself as the source of his faith. Because of a disciplinary proceeding in his senior year at Woolwich, Gordon's graduation was delayed by six months. He thus missed selection into the Royal Artillery and was instead commissioned into the Royal Engineers on 23 June 1852.

After training at Chatham, Gordon served at Pembroke Dock, where he experienced a spiritual awakening through the influence of a fellow officer, Captain Drew. Arriving at Balaclava in January 1855 and being assigned to the siege works before Sebastopol his first experience of being under (as it turned out, friendly) fire for the first time led him to embrace fully evangelical beliefs. There he also befriended the young Captain Garnet Wolseley, who, despite his superior rank, served under Gordon on engineering projects, and Lieutenant Colonel Sir Charles Staveley, under whom he would serve in China and who would become his brother Henry's father-in-law. After Sebastopol's capture in September 1855, Gordon was assigned to blow up its fortifications and docks. He also met for the first time the Piedmontese Bersaglieri, Captain Romolo Gessi, who would later play a significant role in his life.

Now an acting Captain, Gordon was assigned to the Rumanian principalities of Moldavia and Wallachia and the border territory of Bessarabia in May 1856 to help to draw their boundary line with Russia under the terms of the Treaty of Paris that ended the Crimean War. For the next year he trundled (often with Gessi acting as interpreter) back and forth between the Danube, the Ottoman Kurdish and Armenian provinces, and Constantinople, developing an idea to map the world of Judaism and Christianity. After a spell back in England, during which he was elected a member of the Royal Geographical Society, Gordon continued with

Chronology

28 January 1833	Charles George Gordon born at Woolwich
	Educated at Fullards School, Taunton, and Royal Military Academy, Woolwich
23 June 1852	Commissioned into Royal Engineers
17 February 1854	Promoted Lieutenant
1 January 1855	Arrived in Crimea
6 June 1855	Wounded before Sebastopol
18 May 1856	Posted to the Turco-Russian Boundary Commission
22 February 1858	Elected Fellow of Royal Geographical Society
1 April 1859	Promoted Captain
1860–62	Service in China
30 December 1862	Promoted Brevet Major
24 March 1863	Appointed Commander, 'Ever Victorious Army'
16 February 1864	Promoted Brevet Lieutenant Colonel
28 June 1864	Relinquished command of 'Ever Victorious Army' and awarded the Chinese rank of *ti-tu* (Provincial C in C or Field Marshal)
1 September 1865	Appointed CRE, Gravesend
15 November 1871	Appointed to Danubian Commission and as Vice Consul at Galatz
16 February 1872	Promoted Brevet Colonel
5 July 1872	Promoted Major
18 October 1873	Accepted offer to become Governor of Egypt's Equatoria provinces in southern Sudan
December 1876	Resigned as Governor of Equatoria
24 December 1876	Accepted appointment as Governor General of the Sudan
5 May 1877	Formally invested as Governor General in Khartoum
29 July 1879	Resigned as Governor General
2 March 1880	Declined command of Natal Colonial Forces
28 April 1880	Appointed Private Secretary to the Viceroy
2 June 1880	Resigned as Private Secretary
21 March 1881	Appointed CRE, Mauritius
24 March 1882	Promoted Major General
2 April 1882	Again offered command of Natal Colonial Forces
27 September 1882	Resigned as Commandant General of Natal Colonial Forces
15 October 1883	Offered appointment as Governor of (Belgian) Congo
18 January 1884	Accepted offer to become Governor General of the Sudan
21 January 1884	Formally appointed Governor General
18 February 1884	Arrived at Khartoum
26 January 1885	Killed at Khartoum

Appointed CB, 1864

to his duties as boundary commissioner and, in early December 1859 he returned to England to find he had been promoted to Captain and second Adjutant at Chatham.

Having volunteered for service in China, Gordon left England in July 1860, joining Lord Elgin's expeditionary force at Tientsin in September as a Brevet Major and second in command of an engineering unit.[2] Following the surrender of Peking (Beijing) on 13 October, Elgin ordered the destruction of the Emperor's Summer Palace as a reprisal for the torture and killing of British emissaries by three of the Emperor's generals and to encourage the Emperor to sign a peace treaty. Gordon later said that he regretted his participation in the place's destruction. Serving under the command of Staveley, now a Lieutenant General and C in C of the Madras army, Gordon stayed on for eighteen months, visiting the Great Wall, and then returning to Shanghai where he came under the influence of American Methodists and a Jewish Lithuanian merchant who introduced him to Jewish Hasidic fundamentalism.

On Staveley's recommendation, Gordon was appointed to command a multinational military force, the 2,100-man so-called 'Ever Victorious Army', at Sunkiang on 24 March 1863. This mercenary force had been created in June 1860 by Shanghai-based British, French, American and Chinese merchants to defend imperial and foreign interests against Taiping rebels.[3] The force was originally led by an American adventurer, Frederick Townsend Ward, who trained the force in western tactics and achieved several victories against the Taipings, but was killed in September 1862. Gordon became its fourth commander, replacing a British Marine Captain named Holland who had been defeated trying to capture Taitsan. The British Consul General characterised Gordon as the only British officer who had no enemies in the international community. He had few friends but he was much respected. He spoke French, which pleased the French, and French officers with whom he had served in the Crimean War thought well of him. Again he was respected in the American community and the influential Methodists spoke well of him. Of course, he had Staveley's support and Gordon's own father enjoyed the esteem of the War Office in London, which duly approved the appointment. It seemed there could be no better choice.[4] Gordon was made a Mandarin and General in the Chinese army subject to the authority of Li Hung-chang, *Kiangsu Futai* (provincial governor) and commander of the province's military forces.

In March 1863, another former commander of the 'Ever Victorious Army', an American called Henry Andrea Burgevine, who had succeeded Ward but had then been dismissed for striking a Chinese official, appealed to the American Minister, Anson Burlingame, to have him restored to his command. In turn, Burlingame appealed to the British minister, Frederick Bruce, who had already registered his objections to having a serving British officer in command of a Chinese force. Bruce referred the matter to the Chinese regent, who left the matter to Li. The latter rejected the appeal, recording in his diary: 'It is a direct blessing from Heaven, I believe, the coming of this British Gordon. . . . He is superior in manner and bearing to any of the foreigners I have come into contact with and does not show outwardly that conceit which makes most of them repugnant in my sight.'[5] Bruce ordered General W G Brown, who had replaced Staveley, to intervene, but he refused to do so and, to make his intentions perfectly clear, Li promoted Gordon to *tsung-ping* (Major General – the second highest rank in the Chinese army).

In April 1863 Gordon, carrying a short rattan cane – later referred to as 'the wand of victory' – captured Taitsan, avenging Holland's defeat, and suppressed a mutiny among his own men, who had not been paid and resented Gordon's prohibition of looting in the town: he received a commitment from the Chinese to establish a regular payment system for his soldiers. In May Gordon captured Quinsan and Chunyi, the keys to a complex canal system, and refurbished a small naval force to cut off the enemy's retreat to Soochow. Gordon's great tactical strengths – thorough planning, full reconnaissance and indirect tactics – appeared for the first time in these battles.

Without consulting Li, Gordon wrote to the rebel leadership in June 1863 offering to mediate peace. At the time, Bruce and the British director of Chinese customs were plotting to supplant provincial forces with a national Chinese military commanded by Europeans. The Chinese Imperial commander, General Ching, whose plan for an offensive against the rebels had been rejected by Li in favour of Gordon's, also coveted Quinsan as his headquarters. Consequently, Gordon offered Li Hung-chang his resignation, but it was refused.

On 1 August Burgevine, who had assembled a mercenary force at Shanghai, stole a gunboat and joined the rebels at Soochow. Gordon, who had vouched for Burgevine's good character when rumours about his intentions had surfaced in July, decided to stay on. In October, at the culmination of a complex series of plots and counterplots, Burgevine and other westerners were turned over to Gordon by the rebels in return for weapons and ammunition. After more twists and turns, which (along with rumours, spread by General Ching that Gordon was negotiating separately with the rebels) alienated Li from Gordon, Burgevine left China for Japan.

Gordon's first (night) attack on Soochow on 27/28 November was the first defeat suffered by the 'Ever Victorious Army' since Gordon had assumed command. The next day, however, a key fortification was captured. After much negotiation and intrigue, the Taiping leader in Soochow surrendered the city to Ching on 5 December. Gordon held the 'Ever Victorious Army' outside the city to enable the surrender to be a purely Chinese affair and to keep his force from participating in its looting. To offset the booty on which his troops counted, Gordon asked Li to award them with an extra month's pay. When Li offered only half that amount, Gordon submitted his resignation for a second time. Then, on 6 December, despite Li's promises of safe conduct, the Soochow rebel leaders were executed under mysterious circumstances on Li's barge. Gordon was enraged by the betrayal. Accordingly, he offered sanctuary to the rebel leader's son, withdrew to Quinsan, and resigned again.

In one of several attempts to heal the breach, Li sent Gordon a military medal and reward of 10,000 *taels* from the Emperor. Li also sent him two rebel battle flags, which Gordon rejected. In February 1864, however, Li accepted responsibility for the deaths and Gordon accepted the possibility that 'the *Futai* has some extenuating circumstances in favour of his action . . . I think we can scarcely expect the same discernment that we should from a European governor'.[6] Gordon resumed command of the 'Ever Victorious Army'. Bruce, who feared that Burgevine might return from Japan as a Confederate agent, now supported Gordon.[7] In the same month, Gordon received promotion to Brevet Lieutenant Colonel in the British army.

Attacking a heavily defended Kitang in March, Gordon was wounded in the leg and forced to withdraw after sustaining over 100 casualties. With Gordon thus sidelined by his wound, his army then failed to displace rebel forces outside the town of Waisso. Nonetheless, on 11 May 1864 the rebel fortress of Changzhou on the Grand Canal fell to the Imperial and 'Ever Victorious Army' forces. Gordon also helped plan the assault on the rebel capital of Nanking, though Chinese pride dictated that the 'foreign devils' not participate in the final victory on 19 July 1864. Hung Hsiu-ch'uan, the 'Heavenly King', committed suicide and some 100,000 rebels were killed or committed suicide in the attack and its aftermath.

Under public pressure following the newspaper reports of the Soochow 'massacre' the British government had withdrawn its Order-in-Council that permitted serving British officers to serve in the Chinese army and Gordon ended his service there. He refused any cash reward but accepted the rank of *ti-tu* (provincial C in C – the equivalent of a Field Marshal), the right (the first accorded to a 'foreign devil') to wear a Yellow Cape (the highest award in the Ch'in empire for military service) and a peacock feather in his hat.

Gordon left China in November 1864. Though he tried to slip away quietly, the banks of the canal were lined with Chinese soldiers setting off fireworks and artillery and playing martial music. In China he was known as 'The Great General Ko' and in Britain as 'Chinese' Gordon. About the publicity he was getting at home, he wrote to his sister, 'I do not care a jot about my promotion or what people may say, I know I shall leave China as poor as I entered it.'[8]

On returning to England, Gordon took up residence in Southampton with his parents and several of his brothers and sisters. He also welcomed his old friend turned recruiter for Garibaldi, Gessi. Gordon admired Garibaldi but Gessi failed to recruit Gordon to the cause of Italian Unification. Gordon's father, who died in September 1865, had requested that his son be appointed CRE at Gravesend and Gordon took up the post just a few weeks before his father's death. He was tasked with the erection of new fortifications on the Thames to protect London in the event of a possible French invasion.

Finding his official duties minimal, Gordon became concerned about the poor and destitute waifs and elderly in Gravesend. He made contact with various religious groups, all of whom believed that the poor should be morally regenerated and spiritually reclaimed from drink and prostitution, but did little to alleviate their poverty. He finally worked with a Nonconformist couple named Freese to write tracts of his own on the subject and he held garden parties at his official residence, with the leftovers being distributed to the poor. He also brought coal to the poor, ordered his gardens divided into allotments where they could grow vegetables, volunteered to teach at the local ragged school and invited some of the boys into his official residence at Fort House to sleep, giving them new clothes and boots when they left. In the autumn of 1867, he opened a ragged school of his own. For almost five years he devoted over 30 hours weekly to these endeavours. Based on Revelations 1:6 he called the boys 'Kings' and used the terms 'Lambs' (as Christ's followers were known) and the Chinese *wang* (princes of the Heavenly Kingdom of Great Peace) to their faces, but wrote privately of his efforts: 'How far better to be allowed to be kind to a little Scrub than to govern the greatest kingdoms.'[9]

Gordon volunteered for the Abyssinian expedition in 1868, but was refused on the grounds that its soldiers were all to be drawn from the Indian army. Then, in November 1871, in response to accumulated resentments at the War Office about Gordon's international fame and among his peers about his rapid promotions and Nonconformist attitudes, he was appointed the Foreign Office representative on the multinational Danubian Commission and Vice Consul at the Black Sea port of Galatz (Galati). At a plenary session of the Danubian Commission in May 1872, Gordon presented his idea of a Danube–Black Sea canal, which would speed commerce by shortening the distance by 250 miles and create a waterway wholly controlled by a single country (Rumania). The British government had little interest in the idea and, in his disappointment, and depressed that two of the boys that he had sponsored in England had died, Gordon was intrigued by a thinly veiled offer by the Egyptian chief minister, Nubar Pasha, to replace Sir Samuel Baker as Governor of Egypt's Equatoria Province with a salary of £10,000. Gordon responded that he would think about it if Nubar could suggest the canal project to the Ottoman Sultan, Abdul Aziz, to whom Egypt still owed nominal allegiance.

Frustrated by continued indifference to his canal idea and by the general inaction of the Danubian Commission, as well as his failure to gain a transfer to Wolseley's campaign against the Asante, Gordon accepted Nubar Pasha's renewed offer on 18 October 1873 and suggested that Gessi accompany him. In September, he received permission from the British government and was appointed a general of the Turkish army. His task was to solidify Egyptian control of the southern Sudan's ivory, foodstuffs, cotton and slave-trading wealth. Gordon formally accepted his appointment on condition that he could operate independently from his immediate superior, Ismail Ayub Pasha, the Governor General of the Sudan, though he would take care not to affront him. He accepted only £2,000 as his salary, showing the Egyptians 'that gold and silver are not worshipped all over the world'.[10]

Gordon believed that the Khedive's motives were honest,[11] but that Nubar and the Egyptian bureaucracy were not committed to the venture and had employed Gordon as a sop to public opinion in the country that now largely controlled Egypt's economy. After a difficult journey, Gordon arrived at Khartoum on 13 March 1874.[12] While there, he failed to detect the intimate relationships between government officials and the slave trade, but did issue decrees outlawing private armies, establishing ivory trading as a government monopoly, and banning the importation of gunpowder into Equatoria. This hampered the ability of slavers to maintain private armies and destroyed one of their chief covers, but also deprived the non-Muslim native tribes of a major source of income and drove many of them into uneasy alliance with the slavers.

On 16 April 1874 Gordon arrived at Gondokoro, where he found that military discipline had dissipated as the Egyptian garrison had not been paid in months and was compensating by taking bribes and engaging in the trading of African girls. The wily ruler of Buganda, Mutesa, who had participated in Egypt's slave trade since the 1840s, sent emissaries to Gondokoro to greet Gordon when he arrived there. Gordon responded by sending gifts and greetings. Gordon himself left Gessi in charge and returned to Khartoum, where he obtained chests full of Maria Theresa silver dollars (*thalers*) to pay his expenses in Equatoria. When he returned in May, he and his lieutenants decided to send the useless Egyptian garrison north to man a new fort – established by Gordon on his way back south – at a Shillook tribal village where the Sobat river joined the White Nile. At the northern boundary of Equatoria and therefore closer to Egypt, he hoped this would rebuild their morale: instead they soon developed a thriving trade in Somali slaves.

Frustrated by his lack of transport and by the need to deal with large numbers of freed blacks, Gordon concluded that the real evil was less slavery itself than the trade that brought the slaves north. He suggested, therefore, that instead of abolishing the slave trade, it should become a state monopoly under the control of a European director to rid it of its worst abuses. The proposal was rejected by the Khedive. In January 1875 a party of 500 ivory porters, led by Wad el-Mek, arrived at Gondokoro, adding to Gordon's available manpower and enabling him to send out three scouting expeditions. One, headed by a Union army veteran, Charles Chaille Long, moved westward into Makraka country to recruit porters and troops, but, ill, Long returned to brief Gordon in March and was sent back to Cairo.[13] A second expedition down the Nile to Lake Albert was led by a recently arrived Royal Engineer subaltern, Chippendall, who was prevented by a smallpox epidemic from reconnoitring all the way to the lake and rejoined Gordon at Kerri. He helped Gordon to construct the outpost there, and, having developed a huge growth on his neck, left for Cairo in late July. The third, to Mutesa of Buganda, was led by a French Arabist, Ernest Linant de Bellefond, who was surprised to find Henry Stanley there on a Christianising mission when he arrived at Mutesa's capital. Linant and Stanley joined forces to proselytise Mutesa and Stanley left convinced that he had converted him, making Mutesa a darling of British evangelists. The psychopathic ruler was now confronted, however, by new threats/opportunities from competing interests. Mutesa therefore sought to enlist the British in his war against the Bunyoro, and failing to do so, conscripted and detained Linant's men. They escaped and Linant reported back to Gordon in August.

Once Gordon's steamers finally arrived in July 1875 and having, he thought, secured the north, Gordon now undertook what he regarded as his chief logistical responsibility in Equatoria. This was to build a string of forts one day apart southward from Gondokoro to Baker's last surviving outposts at Foweira and Fatiko and thence, through Mrooli (deep in hostile Bunyoro country) to the northern end of the Great Lakes. His soldiers would then transport, in sections, metal steamers around Fola (Makada) Falls and their launch onto the lakes would open that region to Christianity and the 'legitimate trade' that were the harbingers of civilisation.[14]

On 25 August 1875 Linant was killed, falling victim to a Bari ambush as he and forty-three men crossed the river to burn their village in retaliation for earlier attacks: only one survived. Within three months, seven of Gordon's ten staff members – all alienated from him – died or returned to Khartoum and one of his captains committed suicide. Nonetheless, at the end of September, he established his first fort at Rejaf and by the year's end, he succeeded in setting up forts at Bedden, Kerri, Dufilé, Moogie and Patiko. He also had the 50-ton steamer *Nyanza* assembled at Dufilé, and pushed southward to Lake Albert. Wishing to avoid 'the inordinate praise which is given to an explorer',[15] Gordon gave Gessi the honour of sailing onto Lake Albert. Nuehr Agha, who had come with Gessi, was sent south in January to establish two new outposts at Urondogani (Murchison) Falls at Lake Albert and at Cositza (Ripon Falls) at Lake Victoria at the edge of Mutesa's domain. Mutesa forced him to build his fort at his capital at Rubega instead and 160 of his men were kept virtual captives there.

Nuehr got word back and himself reported to Gordon in mid-August. A German-Jewish doctor, Edouard Karl Oskar Theodor Schnitzer, who had entered Turkish service and converted (at least outwardly) to Islam, adopting the name Emin Pasha, had been invited by Gordon (in desperate need of a medical officer) to join him, despite his dislike of both Jews and apostates. Emin had arrived in May, and Gordon now sent him with Nuehr and ninety additional soldiers to Rubega to meet with the now thoroughly confused Mutesa, who had also received a British Christian mission sent by Stanley. Emin turned out to be a skilful negotiator, his mission ended successfully and they returned with the garrison stranded there earlier, but without a formal treaty. When, in 1878, Gordon concluded that the lakes region would never pay the costs of Egyptian control, he appointed Emin governor of Equatoria.

Gordon went home in October 1876, leaving an American, Colonel Prout, in charge. In Cairo Gordon claimed he had accomplished his mission to the extent possible and tendered his resignation to the Khedive. The Khedive offered him the Governorship of the Sudan and Gordon promised to think it over while in England. As Governor of Equatoria for three years, Gordon had not eradicated the slave trade, though he had limited, albeit less so than he thought, the slavers' access to riverine transport routes, and made the purchase of slaves less secure as an investment. The price of slaves declined in Khartoum during Gordon's tenure, because the purchaser could not be sure that he could keep his investment in captivity. Nor had he secured Egyptian control over the Lakes or over the Buganda or Bunyoro peoples of that region, or imposed administrative or legal control over any of the territory he charted. But he had extended southward Egyptian control of the Nile from Sobat to within 60 miles of Lake Victoria, increased the ivory trade to make his administration more economically self-sustaining and, in immediately imperceptible ways, roused both the expectations and fears of the peoples he encountered about the impacts that the northern conquerors might bring with them. While there, bouts of melancholia afflicted him periodically, his relations with his own small cadre of officers remained for the most part formal and distant – that with his men mostly indifferent and condescending – and his willingness to learn about or establish direct relations with the native peoples virtually non-existent, although he admitted that 'I cannot govern without knowing the language . . . I am quite like a blind man, I grope my way by instinct.' All agreed that as a leader he was 'incorruptible, conscientious, and even-handed'.[16] Given the meagre resources at his disposal, and the climatic and ecological obstacles he faced, and the complex politics of the region, these were considerable accomplishments. Financially, he was still not rich, but his Equatoria service did enable him to endow the annuity paid to his brother's widow and to buy his sister Victoria a small house.

Gordon arrived back in England in December 1876 as the Turks suppressed a rebellion in Bulgaria. As the Tsar threatened to come to their aid, there was some talk of the British government looking for a way to thwart Russian Balkan ambitions by recommending Gordon, already technically in Turkish service, as temporary Governor of Bulgaria. He discussed the possibility with the British Foreign Secretary, Lord Derby, but nothing came of it. Instead Disraeli, along with members of the royal family, supported the Khedive's plea for Gordon to return.

Gordon accepted his commission and sailed from England on 31 January. In Cairo, the Khedive informed him that he was now a Field Marshal of the Egyptian army, that Egypt was about to conclude an anti-slavery treaty with Britain and that he hoped that Gordon would assist in carrying out its terms. But the Khedive had a more urgent matter for Gordon. In 1874 the Swiss governor of Massawa, on the Red Sea across from Aden and technically part of the territory that Gordon was to administer, took advantage of a succession crisis in Abyssinia to seize one of its northern provinces, Bogos, and convinced the Khedive to seize the neighbouring Hamaçem province. The new Abyssinian *Negus* (King), Johannes, who also laid claim to Massawa, defeated the invading Egyptian force and sent an envoy to Cairo to negotiate the restoration of the antebellum boundary. The Egyptians imprisoned him until the British Consul secured his release, further angering Johannes. At the same time, a nominally Egyptian chieftain, Walid al-Michael, who controlled territory on both sides of the border, launched raids into Abyssinia, killing a district governor. Johannes demanded that the Egyptians turn him over for punishment. The Khedive made extricating Egypt from this quagmire Gordon's first assignment. Gordon thus travelled to meet with Walid, offering him, on Egypt's behalf, either an Abyssinian or an Egyptian governorship in return for his good behaviour. With nothing resolved, but with Johannes's attention turning to internal problems – chiefly an ongoing campaign against the Shoa – and Walid promising to stand down, Gordon left for Khartoum.

On 5 May 1877 Gordon was formally installed as Governor General. He initiated a series of proposals and reforms, promising, after he surveyed the deplorable state of the city's sewers, that pumps would be installed to bring river water into the city, abolishing flogging (though he retained the right to punish miscreants according to Islamic law), restoring privileges to the *ulema*, and making himself accessible to the public by placing a locked complaint box outside his office where anyone could anonymously make a complaint or report official misconduct. Despite these reforms, and much to Gordon's chagrin, administrative corruption continued, even within his own palace.

Gordon also wrote to Johannes offering to confirm the border and promising Egyptian neutrality in his war against the Shoa, but Johannes angrily rejected the offer, though the next year he accepted the terms. Gordon was immediately confronted with several pressing issues. There were 6,000 Bashi-Bazouk mercenary frontier guards who were out of control; and there was a threat of an uprising against them. Egyptian authority in general in Darfur and Bahr al-Ghazil, where Haroun al Rashid, the nephew of the slain Sultan of Darfur, was leading a Baggara rebellion in northern Darfur, was under pressure. In the south, Suleiman bin Zubeir, 22-year-old son of Zubeir Pasha, was threatening to join the rebellion with a *bazinger* slave army – they were also slave hunters – he had raised at his slaving capital of Shaka.

Faced with this rebellion and a complete lack of response by the Egyptian garrisons there, Gordon, his staff and his 300-man camel corps set out for Darfur. Arriving at the Egyptian border fort of Foggia, several hours in advance of his support force, on 7 June, he impressed its governor and garrison with his bearing, splendid uniform, and medals, and browbeat them into compliance. Gordon next led 150 men to relieve the siege at El Fasher. Learning of his advance, Haroun withdrew to Jebel Mara. Gordon had no wish to confront the rebel horsemen even with the whole of his 'rag-bag and bob-tail' force of 2,700 second-rate Egyptian soldiers, Bashi-Bazouks, and 'loyal' Sudanese tribesmen. With the siege lifted, Gordon moved to secure the road between Foggia and El Fasher and, between June and early October, secured most of the oases that slave caravans might frequent.

Desperate to find an effective administrator for Darfur, Gordon wrote to the explorer Richard Burton in June 1877. Burton, who was working in a British consular office in Trieste, refused, saying 'you and I are too much alike. I could not work under you, nor you under me'.[17] In September Gordon returned to Dara to

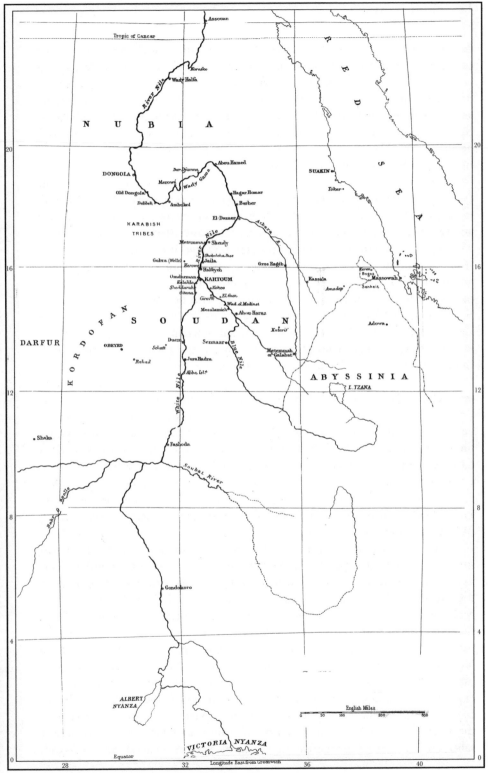

Map to illustrate General Gordon's Journals. (From A. Egmont Hake, *The Journals of Major-General C.G. Gordon CB, at Khartoum*, London: Kegan Paul, Trench, 1885)

confront Suleiman, who had pillaged his way there with his army. Again resplendent in his Egyptian uniform, Gordon used broken Arabic, body language and hand gestures to berate the chieftains. When they submitted to his authority, convinced that attacking an Englishman would unleash perpetual vengeance against them by the British, Suleiman had no choice but to do the same. Despite Suleiman's pleas for the position, Gordon made one of Zubeir's now 'reformed' officers, Idris Abtar, governor of Bahr al-Ghazil, with the disgraced and disgruntled Suleiman his second in command.

Uninterested in, and bored by, the tedium of day-to-day administration, Gordon embarked on a northern inspection tour in October 1877. He then received reports that trouble had again broken out along the Abyssinian border and set off for Suakin. Once there, he unsuccessfully attempted to communicate with Johannes and then, with a ten-man escort, visited Walid's camp. To keep him from marauding across the Abyssinian border, Gordon increased Walid's 'subvention' to £1,000 per year and suggested that he might seek Johannes' pardon for his prior bad acts so that Abyssinia might be available as a sanctuary if Sudanese forces attacked him later. On his return, Gordon was summoned to Cairo to help the Khedive sort out his financial problems.[18]

Gordon took up his new duties as Chairman of the Khedive's Commission of Inquiry in March 1878. He took an instant dislike to the young British Controller General, Evelyn Baring. Without experience in financial affairs, Gordon defended the Khedive's initial position, objecting to the presence of the Debt Commissioners on the Commission and insisting that current-year debt payments be suspended to permit the Egyptian government to continue functioning. When, under pressure from all of the European representatives in Cairo, the Khedive gave in, Gordon's position became untenable. Disillusioned, he resigned from the Commission and left Cairo, reducing his own salary from £6,000 to £3,000 in recognition of Egypt's financial crisis, and successfully protesting to the British Foreign Office about the Commission's proposal to double Sudan's annual tribute payment to Egypt.

In July, 1878 Romolo Gessi sailed from Khartoum with 2,800 dragooned, unwilling and long-unpaid men on the steamer *Bordein*, under orders from Gordon to suppress Suleiman Zubeir's revolt and to eject his 6,000 fighters from their strongholds at Dem Suleiman and Dem Idris, in Bahr al-Ghazal.[19] Gessi's orders were to recruit some 5,000 additional men en route and to offer £1,000 for Suleiman's capture. Privately, Gordon wrote, 'I hope he will hang him.'[20] Gordon had written to the Egyptian government for reinforcements, but to his horror was offered Zubeir Pasha instead. By a combination of deception and force, Gessi captured Dem Idris in December. Over the next three weeks, Suleiman's men engaged in unsuccessful and suicidal attacks to recapture the stockade, defended by Gessi's new artillery. Despite Gessi's reported victories, Gordon worried over the possibility that Suleiman and Haroun would join forces and that a third rebellion brewing in Kordofan might signal a more general Sudanese-wide rebellion. Gessi, however, routed Suleiman's forces, Suleiman barely escaping with his life. Gessi then began moving toward Shaka to rendezvous with Gordon.[21]

Based on what he saw of the slave trade and in order to tighten the noose around Bahr al-Ghazal, Gordon abandoned his policy of condoning small-scale trading by *Jalaba* families, operating on behalf of the riverine tribes, and ordered the Baggara to arrest all participants. This antagonised virtually all of the riverine tribes. On top of this, the slaves liberated by the Beggara were left without food or water wandering in the desert. Suleiman sent emissaries, including his chief secretary, to convince Gordon that he had never been disloyal to the Khedive. If Suleiman had not massacred Sudanese soldiers in the Bahr al-Ghazal as part of his take-over, Gordon 'might have pardoned [Suleiman's emissaries], but no, I shall not do so'.[22] Gordon had them court martialled and shot. In Cairo on the same day, Khedive Ismail moved to control simmering Egyptian nationalist unrest by dismissing Sir Rivers Wilson, the European controller, and appointing an all-Egyptian cabinet.[23] Britain and France then turned to the Ottoman Sultan for redress and the Sultan deposed Ismail on 25 June and appointed his son, Mohammed Tawfiq, in his place.

On 25 June 1879 Gordon and Gessi, now governor of Bahr el-Ghazal, rendezvoused north of Shaka. Gordon was informed that Ismail had been deposed and was ordered to proclaim Tawfiq's succession throughout the Sudan. On his way back to Khartoum, Gordon also met with Rudolph Slatin, an Austrian who had arrived in Khartoum in January 1879 as Finance Inspector and had been touring the provinces getting a first-hand education on Egyptian governmental corruption. Gordon appointed him *Mudir* of Darfur. The Darfur rebellion collapsed shortly thereafter and Haroun fled. Slatin caught up with him in March 1880, and shot him dead when he attempted to flee.

Gessi also eventually ran down Suleiman and he and his principal officers were summarily sentenced to death and shot. Gessi telegraphed the news to Gordon at Foggia and Gordon reported that 'Gessi only obeyed my orders in shooting him; I have no compunction about his death.'[24] Among papers captured, Gessi found a letter from Zubeir to his son which purported to confirm his instigating role in the rebellion. Based on this evidence, the Egyptian government tried Zubeir in absentia for treason, convicted him, and sentenced him to death. Gordon himself requested that the Khedive pardon Zubeir, and nothing was done about the verdict or the sentence. Later, Gordon modestly summed up his work in the Sudan: 'I do not profess to have been either a great ruler or a great financier; but I can say this – I have cut off the slave-dealers in their strongholds and I have made all my people love me.'[25] During his tenure, he had succeeded in cutting major slave-trading routes and making the trade much more difficult. He left, not loved, but respected by many as an honest man and resented by many others as an infidel, a tool of Egyptian imperialism or as a destroyer of what had by then become traditional ways of life.[26]

Having decided to resign his post, Gordon left Khartoum for Cairo in July. Arriving there, Tawfiq accepted his resignation, but asked him to undertake a last mission, to calm the renewed Abyssinian belligerency in Bogos province without ceding Egyptian claims or involving Egypt in a war. Gordon agreed and did a diplomatic dance with the King, who was at first aware neither of Tawfiq's accession nor of Gordon's appointment as his envoy. The King demanded territory, an indemnity, an Egyptian Coptic Bishop (to insure his own people's religious purity) and international guarantees as the price for peace, and Gordon agreed to carry a letter containing the demands back to Egypt.

Convinced that Johannes was 'rapidly going mad',[27] Gordon left Debra Tabor on 8 November 1879. His trip back to Massawa was difficult and frequently interrupted by tribesmen arresting, plundering and releasing him. Returning to Egypt, he was accused of failing to collect sufficient taxes in the Sudan, of using the succession crisis to detach the Sudan from Egyptian control, and of plotting to cede Egypt's Red Sea provinces to Abyssinia and Italy, since he had recommended both seek Italian diplomatic support and also some territorial concessions along the Red Sea coast as a possible path to maintaining peace with Abyssinia in a confidential ciphered telegram to the Khedive. He also confronted Baring, who had resigned from the Debt Commission to become British Comptroller General, over the relative importance of restoring Egyptian solvency and eradicating the Egyptian-controlled Sudanese slave trade. Gordon had recommended strongly that his predecessor, the Circassian officer, Ismail Ayúb, replace him and the appointment was actually recorded on 15 January, but his appointment was cancelled in favour of Ra'úf Pasha, a man he had twice fired for malfeasance. Gordon was enraged. He was in poor health and bad humour and was dissuaded by British Consul General, Edward Malet, from challenging the Egyptian Prime Minister, Nubar Pasha, to a duel over comments he made about Malet's predecessor. In early January 1880, he sailed for England. In Naples he visited the deposed Khedive, hoped in Rome to convince the Pope to preach a crusade against the influx of Jews into Jerusalem, and in Paris berated the British ambassador over Ra'úf's appointment, and shocked him by saying that perhaps a Frenchman ought to have been appointed. In accepting his resignation, Tawfiq publicly stated that: 'I have pleasure in once more acknowledging the loyalty with which you have always served the Government. . . . I should have liked to retain your service, but, in view of your persistent tender of resignation, I am obliged to accept it. I regret, my dear Pasha, losing your co-operation.'[28]

After a short stay in England, Gordon again travelled to the continent for a holiday in Switzerland, meeting with the Belgian King Leopold II in Brussels to discuss the Congo. While on holiday, Gordon was offered the command of the Cape Colony military forces to put down Boer and native unrest by force but declined the offer. In April 1880 Gladstone appointed the Marquis of Ripon as Viceroy of India and Ripon offered the post of Private Secretary to Gordon, for reasons that remain unclear.[29] Ripon asked Gordon to review the evidence concerning Afghan Emir Mohammed Yaqub Khan's complicity in the 1879 murder of Louis Cavagnari, the British Resident in Kabul. Gordon concluded that the Emir was not responsible and recommended that he be restored. Indian government officials disagreed and Ripon supported them so, on 2 June, Gordon resigned his post.

Gordon then received a letter from a friend, the Inspector General of Imperial Customs in China, Sir Robert Hart, inviting him to return to China, which was on the verge of war with Russia over disputed border territories in Chinese Turkestan. Concerned about the Russian reaction to Gordon's return to the scene of his greatest triumphs, the British Government refused permission, but Gordon boarded a ship bound for China anyway, wiring back: 'Arrange retirement, commutation or resignation of service. My counsel, if asked, would be peace, not war.'[30] By the time his ship reached Ceylon, the Government had changed its mind. Upon arrival, Gordon renewed old friendships, and plunged into court intrigues, counselling that, given the state of the Chinese army and Russia's need to further restore its prestige by imperial expansion, going to war would be 'idiocy': he proposed a five-point peace plan.[31] On 16 August, however, Gordon was ordered back to England. When he arrived home in October, he was sent on indefinite leave.

At a loose end and desperate for something to do in March 1881, Gordon chanced upon an old friend, Colonel Sir Howard Elphinstone, who complained that he had been posted as CRE on Mauritius, the Seychelles and Chagos Islands. Elphinstone considered it an exile to nowhere and offered £800 to anyone who would agree to go in his place. Since Gordon's biblical and geographical studies had convinced him that the exact site of the Garden of Eden lay somewhere in the Seychelles, Gordon jumped at the chance to replace Elphinstone, while refusing the cash. While in Le Havre awaiting a ship to take him to Mauritius, Gordon received a letter detailing the terrible death of Gessi.[32] By mid-May he had arrived at Port-Louis, Mauritius. He refused to become part of the social life of the island, swore off spirits, and vowed to reduce his smoking to only fifteen cigarettes a day. As quickly as possible, he turned his duties over to subordinates and set sail for the Seychelles, ostensibly to oversee repairs of the harbour facilities on Mahé, but really to fulfil his quest for Eden. He 'discovered' that the exact site was on the island of Praslin in the Vallée de Mai, and wrote an eight-page essay offering his proofs.

Meanwhile, in the Sudan, Muhammed Ahmed had publicly declared himself Mahdi in June 1881.[33] Sent by Ra'úf Pasha, Muhammed Abù-al-Su'ùd met with Muhammed Ahmed at Jazíra Aba on 7 August 1881. The mission failed, and three days later when Su'úd returned to capture the 'false prophet' with 200 men, a cannon, and a government theologian, he was ambushed and killed. Over the next two years – with one exception: on May 3, 1882, when acting Governor General Carl Geigler[34] defeated an Ansár[35] force at Abú-Haráz – Ansár forces won a series of victories over Egyptian forces and won or forced the loyalty of many of the country's clans, tribes and sheiks. Egyptian response was then hindered by growing nationalist pressure within the army led by Colonel Ahmed 'Arábi, which ultimately led to Wolseley's expedition to Egypt in August 1882. Wolseley destroyed 'Arábi's army at Tel el-Kebir. As a result, the Ottoman Sultan's power over Egypt was limited to receiving Egypt's annual tribute, France was frozen out completely and the British became the de facto rulers of the country. Major General Sir Evelyn Wood was appointed *Sirdar* (C in C) of the Egyptian army, and Sir Samuel Baker's younger brother Valentine was appointed to train and lead the Egyptian police.

In March 1882 Gordon had received his promotion to Major General, which made him too senior for the Mauritius posting. Therefore, having expressed an interest in the Cape Colony posting he had previously declined, Gordon was invited on 2 April 1882 to advise the Cape authorities on resolving its BaSotho (Basuto) problem.[36] Gordon was uncertain as to whether the Cape government wanted him to broker a peaceful solution to the Basuto problem or to lead a military expedition against them. He certainly tended to sympathise with the BaSotho. After receiving assurances from the Commissioner of Crown Lands and Public Works, John Merriman, that improving the quality and integration of the British, colonial, Boer and native forces would play an important role in resolving the Colony's tribal questions, Gordon travelled the 700 miles by rail and cart to King William Town. There he ruffled feathers by his attitudes toward military decorum and his oft-stated belief that local people, born to the saddle, made better soldiers than British regulars. He further strained his relationship with the Cape government and Basuto Agent Joseph Orpen by sending them a mass of lengthy and sometimes contradictory memoranda, most referring to matters outside his areas of responsibility and which were rejected accordingly. Increasingly frustrated, and having, in July, received a glowing report on the Congo from the Scottish East African merchant and ship owner, Sir William Mackinnon, Gordon considered resigning.

To forestall his resignation, Merriman, an advocate of the 'divide and conquer' approach to tribal relations, suggested in July that Gordon, along with the Cape's Secretary of Native Affairs, J W Sauer, go on a fact-finding mission to Basutoland. Sauer pressed Paramount Chief Lestie to organise an attack on the hostile chief Masupha, while Gordon claimed that he was there to find a peaceful resolution. Gordon offered to visit Masupha and Sauer agreed, but insisted that Gordon sign an agreement that this would be a private visit, with no authority to negotiate or reach agreements. Gordon informed Masupha of the personal nature of his visit, assured him that he would never wage war on him, warned him that divisions among the BaSotho would leave them vulnerable to the Boers, and, contrary to his instructions, offered, both orally and in writing, his suggestions for a peaceful resolution.

On 26 September 1882 Lestie unexpectedly launched an attack on Masupha led by his son, Lerothodi. Sauer, who did not believe that a negotiated settlement was possible and had pushed Lestie to take action, sent instructions to Gordon to leave Masupha's camp just before Lerothodi's attack, but Masupha received information during the night and accused Gordon of perfidy, claiming that he had been ready to accept Gordon's terms. Gordon convinced Masupha that he knew nothing about the raid and that he had not betrayed him and Masupha permitted him to leave. The attack petered out and Gordon returned to Cape Town and, convinced that he had been betrayed by Sauer, resigned his position.[37]

After returning to England, where businessmen who were Liberal Party supporters unhappy with Gordon's South African activities ensured that no new work was offered to him, and without a specific offer from Belgian King Leopold, Gordon left for Palestine in January 1883 to complete his biblical mapping project. From there – after weathering another bout of depression – he travelled to Haifa, where he visited with an old friend, Laurence Oliphant. He expressed his views that British policy in Egypt was sheer folly, and that the emerging problem with the Mahdi could be settled by the intervention of a British Commissioner who might negotiate some independence formula, using the threat of a rebellion by riverine sheikhs to force a compromise on him.[38] Moving on to Jerusalem, he lived in the house of an American missionary, and took communion in a nearby Greek-Russian Orthodox church. The result of his introspection, researches, travels and surveys was a series of letters to his friend, the Reverend R H Barnes, who turned them into a book, *Reflections in Palestine 1883*.[39] Encouraged by Mackinnon, King Leopold II telegraphed a firm offer to Gordon on 15 October 1883 to become Governor of the Congo. Upset by Gladstone's Liberal imperialism, and hopeful that the Congo might provide an alternative means for interdicting the slave trade, Gordon accepted.

Affairs in the Sudan, meanwhile, were causing concern with the outgoing British Consul, Sir Edward Malet, recommending on 4 November 1882 that Egypt should be encouraged to take all measures to repress the rebellion, but 'without aid or advice from Her Majesty's Government'.[40] Having decided to replace Ra'úf Pasha as Governor General in December, the British sent Lieutenant Colonel J D H Stewart of the 11th Hussars on a secret fact-finding mission to the Sudan. In January 1883 'Abd-al-Qádir Hilmi was formally replaced as Sudanese Governor General by 'Alá-al Dín Siddíq, a Circassian Major General who had been governor of the Sudan's eastern region. Shortly thereafter, another Circassian, 75-year-old Major General Suleimán Niyázi, was appointed to oversee military affairs. At the same time a new and even more motley and disaffected military force was assembled by the Egyptians to reclaim the Sudan from Ansár forces. A 53-year-old retired Bombay army officer, Colonel William Hicks, was suggested, almost by chance, by Valentine Baker and was appointed to lead this force, without in any way implying support by the British government for this effort. Upon accepting the appointment, Hicks was made a Major General in the Egyptian army and Chief of Staff to Niyázi.

Hicks soon found himself at odds with both 'Abd-al-Qádir and Niyázi, whose Chief of Staff he technically was, over his proposed Kordofan expedition. With respect to continued Egyptian control of the Sudan, Stewart's report to his superiors recommended that all of the provinces south and west of Khartoum be abandoned.[41] The Khedive refused to abandon any part of the Sudan. Accordingly, Hicks assembled a force of 3,200 Egyptian infantry, 300 Albanian cavalry and 2 artillery batteries and was relatively successful in a preliminary campaign on the east bank of the White Nile. In the eastern Sudan, however, the Mahdi's Emir, Osmán Digna, received support from the already converted Majdhúbia, converted the Hadendawa clan, the Erkowit, and, most importantly, Sheikh al-Táhir al-Tayyib at Suakin. By November, Ansár were besieging towns along the Red Sea coast. On 4 November, the British Consul in Suakin, Commander Lynedoch Moncrieff RN, was killed near Tokar, heightening British concerns over the security of the coast. With the Egyptian garrison near Suakin also badly mauled by Osman Digna, the Egyptian government assembled an expeditionary force of 3,715 Egyptian police recruits, led by Valentine Baker, and 6,000 black Sudanese, to be led by Zubeir Pasha, to reinforce Suakin and open a route from Suakin to Berber. When news of Zubeir's role became public, it caused public outrage and it was cancelled. Baker's troops, forced to board their Red Sea transport, arrived at Suakin on 27 December 1883 and received a change to their orders from Wood, giving them the smaller task of relieving the Sinkat and Tokar, and to do so only if Baker was convinced that his troops were reliable.

Meanwhile, urged on by the Egyptian Prime Minister, Sharíf Pasha, Hicks led some 10,000 men and an enormous baggage train from Khartoum in September. At around the same time as Hicks' departure, Sir Evelyn Baring (later Lord Cromer) arrived in Cairo as British Agent General, replacing Malet. On 19 November, he advised the British government that the Egyptians should 'fall back on any points on the Nile they can hold with confidence',[42] but was enjoined by his instructions from advising the Egyptians on matters pertaining to the Sudan. What Baring did not yet know was that on 5 November Hicks's force had been trapped in a densely clustered area of thorn bushes called Shaykan and destroyed, virtually to the last man. Lieutenant Colonel Henry de Coëtlogon, who had been left in charge at Khartoum by Hicks, reported to Cairo that, if the Mahdi continued to advance, Khartoum could not hold out for more than two months. Similarly, *The Times* correspondent (and honorary British consul) in Khartoum, Frank Power, whose dysentery had compelled him to return early from Hicks's campaign, reported that it was 'perfectly useless to attempt to hold this place, where the population is a slumbering volcano'.[43] Egyptian troops fleeing from southern garrisons soon began to arrive in Khartoum. After fighting off Ansár attacks for over a year, converting to Islam, experiencing rebellions and betrayals by his own troops and officers, and discovering that the Hicks's expedition had been destroyed, Rudolf Slatin, the Governor of Darfur, surrendered on 23 December.

Hoping to placate British public opinion and believing that his name carried weight in the Sudan, the British government asked Baring on 1 December if

Gordon would be 'of any use to you or to the Egyptian Government, and, if so, in what capacity?'[44] Concerned both about his eccentricities and his tendency to obey orders only if they suited him, Baring finessed by replying that the Egyptian government thought it unwise to send a Christian to suppress a Muslim revolt. Gladstone and Granville instructed Baring, who had been pleading for specific guidance for the last six weeks, to inform the Egyptians that Britain would not condone wasting Egyptian revenues on military expeditions 'of doubtful advantage to Egypt'.[45] While the British undertook to maintain internal order and safeguard her Red Sea ports, Egypt must withdraw its troops from the Sudan and 'abandon all territory south of Aswan, or at least of Wadi Halfa'.[46] Sharif Pasha proposed to return the eastern Sudan and Red Sea coast to direct Ottoman rule, but refused to order the withdrawal and, informed of Granville's conclusion that ministers 'must carry out this [British] advice or forfeit their offices', he resigned in protest on 4 January 1884.[47]

Three days earlier, Gordon arrived in Brussels. The next day, he met with King Leopold. He believed that there would be no problem with the British War Office, since he was no longer on the active list, but wanted to go back to England to wind up his affairs – arranging for the publication of his religious explorations and completing the transfer of the house in Southampton to his sister – before leaving for the Congo some time in February. On 6 January *The Times* reported that Gordon had accepted the Congo commission and Wolseley cabled him to 'come to London'. On the following day Gordon arrived at Southampton and discovered that the War Office refused him leave to go to the Congo. The next day he sent a letter of resignation – his nineteenth – to the War Office.

On 9 January, the *Pall Mall Gazette*, which opposed Gladstone's policy and had already run a story about the proposed evacuation, published a version of an interview that its editor, W T Stead, had had with Gordon when he saw him with or immediately after – the relationship between them remains controversial – a War Office delegation who visited him the day before. According to Stead, Gordon spoke out against the evacuation. Gordon regarded the rebellion as 'not really religious, but an outbreak of despair' that an uncorrupted government and amnesty could resolve: 'If this were done and the government entrusted to a man whose word was truth, all might yet be re-established.' Gordon suggested Sir Samuel Baker for the job, but Stead published under the headline: 'Chinese Gordon for the Sudan'.

Pressed by the Queen and by other Cabinet members, Granville again wired Baring about Gordon. After consulting Nubar, Baring again refused. Meanwhile, Sir Samuel Baker also urged Gordon to accept the assignment if it were to be offered and he and Gordon wrote coordinated letters to *The Times* attacking the government's proposed policy. On 15 January Gordon visited Wolseley at the War Office, ostensibly to discuss his resignation, and agreed to go to Suakin to 'inquire into the condition of affairs in the Sudan'.[48] Responding to the groundswell of both popular and influential support for Gordon, Granville wrote to Gladstone,

'If Gordon says he believes he could by his personal influence excite the tribes to escort the Khartoum garrison and inhabitants to Suakin, a little pressure on Baring might be advisable.'[49] Baring was then asked, for the third time, to accept Gordon. Now aware that Gordon was the only choice, Baring reluctantly agreed.

Baring's new choice for Prime Minister, Nubar Pasha, ordered all non-military residents of Khartoum to proceed northward by whatever means they could find. The order was received by garrisons south of Khartoum and, by 22 January some 6,100 troops defended the city and de Coëtlogon had begun digging a ditch between the Blue and White Niles. At the same time, Baring wired Granville that 'The Egyptian Government would feel obliged if Her Majesty's Government would send at once a qualified British officer to go to Khartoum with full power, civil and military, to conduct the retreat.'[50]

On 18 January 1884 Gordon was called to the War Office to meet with Cabinet members. There was no secretary available for this and subsequent meetings and the only record is a letter of 22 January by Gordon to Barnes. According to Gordon, while waiting to go in, Wolseley, who had been asked to obtain his answer in advance, asked Gordon to accept the principle on which the whole Cabinet had agreed: 'Her Majesty's Government want you to understand this Government are determined to evacuate the Sudan, for it will not guarantee future government . . . Will you go and do it?' Gordon replied 'Yes' and then met with Lords Granville, Secretary of State for War Hartington, First Lord of the Admiralty Northbrook, and the radical MP, Sir Charles Dilke, the President of the Local Government Board: 'Did Wolseley tell you our ideas?' 'Yes. He said you will not guarantee future government of the Sudan, and you wish me to go and evacuate it?'[51] The cabal of ministers then attached Colonel Stewart as Gordon's staff officer and hustled him off on his journey. At Charing Cross Station, Granville bought his ticket, Wolseley took charge of his bag and the Duke of Cambridge ushered him into his carriage for Dover. That night, Northbrook, who was Baring's cousin, cabled Gordon's agreement:

> The upshot of the meeting was that he leaves by tonight's mail for Suakim to report on the best way of withdrawing the garrisons, settling the country, and to perform such other duties as may be entrusted to him by the khedive's government through you. . . . does not believe in the great power of the Mahdi. Does not think the tribes will go much beyond their own confines, and does not see why the garrison should not get off. He did not seem at all anxious to retain the Sudan; and agreed heartily to accept the policy of withdrawal.[52]

Granville's more formal instruction to Baring reported that Gordon would advise on 'the best mode of evacuating the interior of the Sudan, and of securing the safety and good administration by the Egyptian Government of the ports of the Red Sea [and to counter] the possible stimulus to the slave trade which may be given by the revolution which has taken place'. Echoing Northbrook, he concluded that 'Gordon will be under the orders of H.M.'s Minister in Cairo [Baring], and will report through him to H.M.'s Government, and perform such other duties as may be entrusted to him by the Egyptian Government through Sir Evelyn Baring.'[53] Neither Granville nor Hartington advised Gladstone of the meeting until after Gordon's departure, and then only reported narrowly of his advisory role. Almost immediately thereafter Granville expressed his nervousness to Hartington: 'We were very proud of ourselves yesterday. Are you sure we did not commit a gigantic folly?'[54]

While travelling across France by rail, Gordon dispatched eight telegrams to Granville, two calling for a meeting of the eastern sheikhs at Berber to negotiate a withdrawal, two asking that the Khedive appoint him Governor General for the purpose of withdrawing Egyptian forces and restoring native rule, one calling for the restoration of the Darfur Sultanate and another calling on Egypt to recruit new Sudanese troops. While crossing the Mediterranean aboard the SS *Tanjore*, he sent another calling for the independence of a Sudan divided among local sultans who would collectively decide the country's future. Zubeir, he wrote, needed to be kept out of the process, perhaps by exiling him to Cyprus.

Gordon was met by Evelyn Wood at Port Said with a letter from Baring ordering him to proceed through Cairo and altering the terms of his mission from advising and reporting to one 'arranging for the withdrawal of the Egyptian garrison etc. as rapidly as is consistent with (1) the saving of life and so far as possible, property; (2) the establishment of some rough form of Government which will prevent, so far as possible, anarchy and confusion arising on the withdrawal of the Egyptian troops.'[55] In Cairo, Gordon paid his respects (and attempted to salve old grievances) to the Khedive and then returned to Wood's house, where he was staying, to meet with a committee made up of Wood, Baring, Graham, Nubar and Stewart to discuss the details of his mission. He was to proceed to Khartoum in a double role: as the Khedive's Governor General and as Her Majesty's High Commissioner; Gordon would have a credit of £100,000 made available to him; a gradual evacuation would be organised and carried out under his direction; he would be issued two *firmans* (Khedival proclamations), one publicly proclaiming him Governor General, and a second, to be kept confidential until the appropriate moment ordering evacuation and setting up a purely Sudanese government; he would be given resources to attempt to restore the Fur dynasty in Darfur; and he would meet with Zubeir the next day to seek his assistance.

On 26 January Gordon attended a meeting, arranged by Baring, with officers with experience in the Sudan. He was accompanied by Wood's ADC, Reginald Wingate, who was the only person present who could speak, read and write Arabic. Zubeir was present and he and Gordon fought about the death of Zubeir's son. The meeting ended badly with Wingate assigned to search Suleiman's courts-martial records for proof of Zubeir's involvement.[56] The meeting adjourned until the next day.

At the reconvened meeting, the difficulties involving the evacuation of 12–15,000 civilians – Christians, Egyptian government officials and their families

– as well as the garrisons arose. Baring stipulated that Gordon determine 'the most opportune time and the best method for effecting the retreat. It is neither necessary nor desirable that you should receive detailed instructions . . . You will bear in mind that the main end to be pursued is the evacuation of the Sudan . . . I also understand that you entirely agree on the desirability of adopting this policy.' Asked by Baring if he agreed, Gordon responded 'in the strongest terms', and Baring inserted into the written instructions the clause, 'and that you think it should on no account be changed'. Baring continued that the timing of the withdrawal was within Gordon's discretion, that the country should be left to those who ruled it before the Egyptian conquest, and that, while Egyptian troops should not be made responsible for imposing or maintaining this rule, Gordon was to have 'full discretionary powers to retain the troops for such reasonable period as you may think necessary in order that the abandonment of the country may be accomplished with the least possible risk to life and property'.[57]

Zubeir then came into the meeting and Gordon apologised to him. Zubeir then shook his hand (as he had refused to do the day before) and pledged him his services. Gordon announced that he wanted Zubeir to accompany him to install him in power once he and the Egyptians departed. Gordon said that he had a mystical feeling about his trustworthiness. Since many of the Mahdi's chiefs were Zubeir's, he would have little trouble 'end[ing] the Mahdi in a couple of months'.[58] A furious argument over Zubeir ensued and Gordon refused to attend a farewell dinner. Baring reassured Gordon that, once he reached Khartoum, if he still wanted Zubeir, he would support his request. After their departure, Baring wrote privately to Granville approving his selection, but characterising Gordon as 'half-cracked' and concluding, 'My only fear is that he is terribly flighty and changes his opinions very rapidly. I am glad that Stewart, who impressed me very favourably, is going with him, but I don't think that Gordon much likes it himself. He said to me, "they sent him with me to be my wet nurse".'[59]

On 4 February, Valentine Baker's force was slaughtered by Osman Digna at El Teb. When the Sinkat garrison heard the news, they spiked their guns and attempted to retreat to Suakin as well, but Digna's men ambushed them a mile from Sinkat and massacred all of the men and most of their women and children. Only a small party of Royal Marines now held Suakin. By 8 February the India Office, Hartington, Wolseley and the Queen had all called for action - demanding that the government reverse its policy of evacuation, leaving everything east of the Nile under British-supervised Egyptian control, that a British force under Gerald Graham be sent to Suakin to defeat Osman Digna and another sent to Wadi Halfa to support Gordon's efforts. Otherwise, Wolseley warned, sooner or later an expedition would have to be mounted to relieve Khartoum. Gladstone faced a five-day House of Commons debate and vote of confidence, which he survived while further confusing the government's Sudan policy, and Graham was ordered to Suakin.

Gordon and Stewart reached Abu Hamid on 7 February and received a positive welcome, especially when he announced tax reductions and a general amnesty. Emboldened, over the next two days, Gordon sent messages to Baring advising that the Egyptians should keep the Sudan and that the evacuation of Khartoum should be temporary. He still believed that Zubeir should lead the government there post-evacuation, and requested that Baring publish all of his cables to spur British public opinion. Three days later, Gordon sent a first message to the Mahdi at El Obeid, presenting him with Chinese silks and a Turkish tarbush – a hated symbol of the Turkiyya – offering him the Sultanate of Kordofan, and, contrary to Baring's instructions, requesting a meeting with him. He also offered to ransom Slatin and his men and asked the Mahdi to restore the Khartoum–El Obeid telegraph line to facilitate communication between them. At Berber on 11 February, 1884 Gordon was welcomed with great pomp and ceremony. Before arriving there, Gordon learned that the Khedive had replaced Hussein Pasha Khalifa as the *Murdir* of Berber with a Circassian. Gordon cancelled the replacement and announced that henceforth the Sudan would be ruled only by Sudanese. That night, Stewart informed him of Baker's defeat, of which the people of Berber had not yet heard. Reversing course again, the next morning Gordon announced the complete separation of the Sudan from Egypt (though still subordinate to Gordon's authority as Her Majesty's High Commissioner) and, to prove his sincerity, showed the secret *firman*, perhaps inadvertently – he couldn't read Arabic – to Hussein Pasha and Mohamad Tahir, a jurist thought to be an ally of the Mahdi. Hussein Pasha and the Berber leaders rejoiced at the announcements and at a proclamation that preserved the status quo with respect to slavery in the Sudan. Even Gordon soon recognised the mistake. Through Baring, Granville telegraphed Gordon soliciting his views on the implications of Baker's defeat and on whether Gordon himself should be recalled. Gordon answered no, calling on his superiors to do nothing precipitous that might interfere with a meeting of tribal chiefs that he was planning once he arrived at Khartoum, or that might drive them into the arms of the Mahdi.

On 12 February Gladstone finally gave in to the pressure and ordered British forces to protect the Egyptian Red Sea coast. The next day, Graham's brigade embarked for Suakin. By 5 March, the British had recaptured Tokar and fought and won the second battle of El Teb, forcing Digna's tribesmen temporarily back into the hills. Its effect on Gordon's mission would be to cast doubts on the latter's promises that Britain's objective was to return control of the Sudan to its native sheikhs. At around the same time, two British officers fluent in Arabic, Captain (and Egyptian Army Major) Horatio Herbert Kitchener and Leslie Rundle, were sent south to scout the shortest route between the Red Sea and the Nile.

Having survived a Mahdist ambush at the sixth cataract on board the steamer *Ismailia* (renamed *Tewfikieha*) escorted by the *Abbas*, Gordon arrived in Khartoum on 18 February. He received a warm reception from the city's notables in a formal ceremony at the Governor's Palace, and issued taxation remission and slavery continuation statements calculated to please the people. He then turned his attention to his mission, telegraphing Baring, again reversing his position on the Sudan's future, calling on Britain to assume direct control of the country and appoint a local ruler to whom Britain would offer moral support and a subsidy for good behaviour. 'As for the man H.M.G. (not the Khedive) should select one above all others, namely Zebeyr [*sic*].'⁶⁰ Baring, in accordance with his promise to Gordon, supported Gordon's recommendation to Granville, but suggested that Zubeir not be sent to Khartoum until Gordon completed his evacuation and left. Already feeling the outrage of anti-slavery supporters over Gordon's maintenance of the practice, Granville replied on 23 February that the government doubted the wisdom of appointing anyone and that 'public opinion here would not tolerate the appointment of Zebeyr'.⁶¹

Khartoum, 1884–85

Gordon sent the first party of Egyptian evacuees northward to safety on 26 February and by 11 March, when operations ceased, he had evacuated 2,140 Egyptians. At the same time, he sent a telegram to Granville stating his view that, to prevent chaos in the wake of the evacuation, the 'Mahdi must be smashed up'.⁶² However cogent this advice, the prospect of offensive action against the Mahdi diminished the Cabinet's confidence in Gordon. In the next few days, Gordon sent at least thirty telegrams to Baring, who took to reading them in batches in order to make sense of them, forwarding only the more lucid of them to Granville. On 29 February Baring wired Granville stating the options in stark terms: 'simply evacuate with no thought of consequence; or evacuate the country leaving some semblance of order behind'.⁶³ Gordon, he wrote, wanted to do the latter, but Zubeir was necessary to accomplish this, and Baring agreed with Gordon's analysis and conclusions. Graham's victory at El Teb convinced Gordon that the Suakin–Berber road would soon be open. On 13 March, however, Graham barely held off another attack at Tamai. Despite Wood's and Baring's advice, the Cabinet formally rejected sending Graham's troops further westward to Berber and ordered their withdrawal to Suakin. From there, the force was ordered back to Egypt on 3 April, leaving just two battalions to guard Suakin.

On 3 March Gordon wired Baring; 'Pray do not consider me in any way to advocate the retention of the Sudan. I am quite adverse to it, but you must see that you could not recall me, nor could I possibly obey, until the Cairo employees get out from all the places. How could I look the world in the face if I abandoned them and fled?'⁶⁴ A day later, however, Stewart sent a more sober evaluation pointing out that the weather and terrain would probably prevent such forays even if they were authorised. He supported Gordon's plea that Zubeir be sent. Baring made the plea to Granville but he flatly refused the request.

On 10 March *The Times* published Frank Power's account of an interview that Gordon had given (against Stewart's advice) dwelling at length on the necessity of sending Zubeir to Khartoum. The publication of Gordon's views ignited a firestorm of protest against empowering Zubeir 'the slaver'. On 13 March the telegraph line to Khartoum was cut. In response, Kitchener and Rundle were ordered to Berber to facilitate ongoing communications and to keep the Suakin–Berber road open, but they never got there.

The first Ansár forces, led by Sheikh al-'Ubeid occupied positions on the Blue Nile across from the city on 14 March, beginning a 319-day siege. On 15 March Sheikh el-Obeid led all the tribes between Berber and Shendi into revolt, and by 20 March some 30,000 Ansár tribesmen loosely surrounded Khartoum. On 22 March the Mahdi's response to Gordon's 10 February message arrived in Khartoum carried by three armed Ansár envoys under a white flag. He suggested Gordon renounce his faith and surrender.[65] Returning Gordon's compliment, the Mahdi sent Gordon a patched *jibba* – 'a filthy patched Dervish's coat'[66] Gordon called it – for Gordon to wear if he accepted the Mahdi's offer. Gordon responded that 'I cannot have any more communication with you'[67] – the Mahdi would send at least eight more letters to him by 18 January 1885 – and turned his attention to preparation for the defence of the city and its 34,000 inhabitants. Food continued to flow into the city, now supplemented by land and river raids organised by Gordon and Stewart. The city itself was mostly not fortified, bounded on three sides by the confluence of the Blue and White Niles. To the existing 8ft deep ditch and rampart, which ranged from 5,900 to 6,700ft long depending on the height of the rivers that bounded it, Gordon added barbed and telegraph-wire entanglements, studded the ditch and ramparts with spearheads, laced the first 100yd of open ground with triple-spiked iron 'crows feet' and the next 500ft with broken glass, and laid a mass of land-mines made up of tin biscuit boxes full of powder, nails and bullets electronically detonatable. When he ran out of electric triggers, he added somewhat less reliable match or pressure-detonated mines. The ditch was anchored by Fort Mogren at the Blue Nile end and by Fort Buri on the White. The town's two cross-river outposts, Omdurman across the White Nile and North Fort across the Blue Nile, connected to Gordon's headquarters in the Governor General's Palace by field telegraph, were also reinforced. With the summer high-water period approaching, Gordon felt confident of his defensive position.

Gordon could muster some 8,665 defenders comprising 2,316 black Sudanese regulars – many former slaves and Gordon's most reliable force – 1,421 Egyptian troops, 1,906 Bashi-Bazouk mercenaries from various tribes, 2,330 Shaigiya tribal irregulars and 692 volunteer townsmen. They would man the 15-mile parameter that enclosed both the town and grazing for the cavalry horses and the farm animals that helped to feed the city. He ensured their morale by paying them with money printed on his own presses and signed by him. Gordon also ordered the armouring and equipping of his small fleet of nine steamers with Krupp breech-loading artillery and Nordenfeld machine-guns.

On 9 April Gordon received the now month-old warning from Baring that the British had no intention of sending a force to Berber. Angered and blaming Baring, he responded that this left him 'free to act according to circumstances. I shall hold on here for as long as I can . . .'.[68] On 16 April, he sent a series of messages to Berber for transmission to Cairo, appointing Zubeir, who had already refused to go unless a series of impossible conditions were met, Deputy Governor General of the Sudan with orders to proceed southward. Heavy rains had raised the level of the river giving Khartoum better protection. Sorties into the countryside also brought in large quantities of grain and livestock. The Khartoum arsenal was producing large quantities of ammunition, and, at Gordon's request, Khartoum *ulema* denounced the Mahdi as a false prophet. Gordon also made frequent (and false) statements about rescue missions on the way.

The British Cabinet met on 23 April to consider memoranda penned by Wolseley and supported by Hartington, demanding that the government determine its policy with respect to the Sudan: Wolseley wanted an army sent. After four hours of debate, during which Gladstone expressed his fear that Gordon's rescue could be a cover for imperialist annexation, it was decided to ask Gordon about his intentions and what force it might take to bring him out. The inquiry would take three months to reach him. There were mass public meetings in Gordon's support and on 12 May Gladstone's government survived a vote of censure by just twenty-eight votes after Hartington assured the members that the government would spare no sacrifice to save Gordon.

Ansár forces overran Berber on 18 May, capturing two steamers, £60,000 and Gordon's medals, which had been sent there for safekeeping. With Berber now in the Mahdi's hands, Kitchener and Rundle organised an intelligence and courier network from Aswan. Indeed, on 20 July Gordon sent a message, via courier and telegram, through Kitchener in Dongola reporting that Khartoum and Sennar were still '*en bonne defence*' and asking for information about relief forces. Some of Gordon's messages were becoming garbled in transit and Kitchener had to interpret them before transmitting them to Cairo and London. On 2 September Kitchener reported that he thought Gordon was telling him that Khartoum could hold out until mid-November.

Gordon finally received Gladstone's questionnaire in July. He answered in a long letter dated 30/31 July, stating that he couldn't leave Khartoum because:

> the Arabs have shut us up, and will not let us out. . . . I will conclude by saying that we will defend ourselves to the last, that I will not leave Khartoum, that I will try to persuade all Europeans to escape, and that I am still sanguine that, by some means not yet clear, God will give us the issue.[69]

Gordon's letter did not reach Baring until early October. Meanwhile, on 5 August, in response to a threat from Hartington to resign unless an effort was made to rescue Gordon, Gladstone asked the Commons to authorise a sum 'not exceeding £300,000 to enable Her Majesty to undertake operations for the relief of General Gordon, should they become necessary'.[70] Though the sum was considered inadequate by military experts, the Commons did so and then began its summer adjournment.

Accordingly, on 8 August Gladstone authorised Lieutenant General Sir Frederick Stephenson, GOC in Egypt, to begin assembling transport and supplies, to concentrate a British force at Wadi Halfa and to begin contingency planning. Gladstone still hoped that Gordon might be induced to escape through Dongola, that the *Mudir* there might be induced to play the Zubeir role, that a small force might suffice to convince the Mahdi to withdraw and that the government would not become 'enslaved' to Gordon's views. He further insisted that no further decisions be taken until every Cabinet member had been consulted. Despite Gladstone's hesitancy, Hartington proceeded to spend £750,000 on military preparations. Again at Hartington's insistence and despite the Duke of Cambridge's strenuous objections, Wolseley was given command of the relief expedition on 26 August.

As the preparations began to be put in hand in Britain and Egypt, the Mahdi himself was moving towards Khartoum, arriving at Omdurman on 21 October. Slatin later estimated the force's strength as 200,000 spear-carrying men.[71] It was reported to Gordon that there were 40,000 riflemen but Gordon refused to believe it. Already, on 4 September, however, a force commanded by Mohammed Ali Pasha Husayn, who Gordon had ordered to break up an Ansár concentration at El Foun, 25 miles up the Blue Nile, went beyond the range of his steamer guns and was ambushed. He and over 1,000 of Gordon's best infantry were killed. As a result, the Ansár tightened their noose around the city, and the resupply of the city from the surrounding countryside virtually ceased.

Now more cut off than ever before and perhaps convinced that only direct information from Khartoum would finally move the British government to action, Gordon resolved on 9 September to send Stewart, Power and the French consul, Herbin, north on the specially refitted steamer *Abbas*, carrying letters, dispatches, Stewart's journal, Gordon's cipher books and a letter reproaching Baring for his inaction and silence. Gordon's exact reasons remain a mystery since, in various places in letters and in his journal, Gordon implied both that he had decided to send Stewart and also that he accepted Stewart's request to be sent. He sent the steamers *Mansurah* and *Safia* as well as two sailing boats loaded with nineteen heavily armed Greeks to escort them past Berber.

Wolseley arrived in Cairo on 9 September and, after three weeks' debate, vetoed Stephenson's plans to utilise the 480-mile Suakin–Berber route for the main force and to recruit 5,000 loyal tribesmen from Dongola to assemble native boats and drag them past the Nile Cataracts. Wolseley insisted that the falling Nile would not permit their use, choosing instead the 1,650-mile-long route up the Nile. Wolseley also determined to take some 1,600 men and 68 officers from crack mounted units to form a camel corps to race across the Bayuda desert shortcutting the Nile loop from Korti to Berber and El-Metemmeh, and then proceed upstream on Gordon's steamers to relieve the city.

Gordon did not initially believe word smuggled into Khartoum of the first British infantry arriving at Wadi Halfa but more definite news was received on

22 September. The day before, Gordon had received two smuggled-in telegrams which he couldn't read because he had sent his cipher books north with Stewart, some old photographed letters telling him that British senior officers were proceeding to Wadi Halfa and a message from Kitchener asking after Stewart's health that puzzled him. Gordon ordered a gun salute and pamphlets printed and distributed informing the populace of the news to raise their morale. On 29 September Gordon recorded his thoughts on the role the troops would play and about the Sudan's future:

> My idea is to induce Her Majesty's Government to undertake the extrication of all peoples or garrisons . . . and if that is not their programme, then resign my commission and do what I can to attain it. . . . Therefore, if her Majesty's forces are not prepared to [do this], the General should consider whether it is worth coming up – in his place I would not.[72]

On 3 October, he even drew up a detailed schedule for the progress of the relief force.

Anticipating the arrival of a relief force, Gordon sent Mohamad Nushi's steamers *Bordein* and *Tel el Hawein*, each with 300 soldiers, north to Shendi or Metemmeh to await its arrival. They would wait for 112 days. Wolseley, however, was moving deliberately, faced as he was with logistical failures from the lack of experience of the boat crews, the overloaded boats and dromedaries, and the lack of coal for the steamers. He also believed the messages from Gordon, who, unable to understand Arabic, selected the most optimistic bits from the rumours picked up by his staff and transmitted them through Kitchener at the El-Debbah terminus of the telegraph line. In turn, Kitchener emphasised Gordon's positive attitude to Cairo. In the messages transmitted the other way, Kitchener overestimated the speed and progress of the rescuing force. To staunch these overly optimistic reports, Wolseley himself sent ciphered messages to Gordon, reporting that the mission had fallen behind schedule, but without his cipher books, Gordon was unable to read them. Both Gordon and Wolseley felt that their opposites were not supplying them with sufficient or accurate intelligence, and the Nile was beginning to fall. In fact, Wolseley's mission was closely defined in the instructions Baring transmitted to him on 8 October: 'The primary object of the expedition up the valley of the Nile is to bring away General Gordon and Colonel Stewart from Khartoum. When that object has been secured, no further offensive operations of any kind are to be undertaken.'[73]

An inventory made by Gordon on 19 October now showed that he had 2,316 Sudanese regulars, 1,421 Egyptian regulars, 1,906 Bashi-Bazouks, 2,330 Shagiya tribesmen and 692 town militia, totalling 8,665 men at arms. For these, he had 2,165,000 rounds of Remington ammunition and his arsenal was producing 40,000 more each week. He had 12 artillery pieces on land and 11 in his remaining 7 steamers, and had 21,141 rounds of ammunition for them. But the food he needed for his soldiers and the 35,000 civilians in the city was running short. He estimated that he had nine weeks' supply. As hunger spread, looting broke out. Through spies and defectors, the Mahdi was kept well informed of the food situation and, given the leisurely pace of the rescue mission, believed the city could be reduced through starvation. Then on 22 October Gordon received a letter from the Mahdi politely requesting his surrender, and informing him of the deaths of Stewart, Power and Herbin and, as proof, providing a detailed list of the papers recovered from them. Though Gordon refused to believe the report, it was true. North of Berber, the *Abbas* had hit a rock at full speed and foundered. Its passengers and crew were forced to wade to an island, from which, after two days, Stewart sent a message asking for transport to a seemingly friendly local sheikh, who invited them to his house. Stewart, Power and Herbin went unarmed to confirm their intentions. While eating, armed men accosted them and they were massacred, followed by the crew and other passengers.[74]

On 12 November the Mahdi ordered his Nordenfelds and Krupp mountain guns, chronically short of ammunition and fired by locally recruited gunners, to disable or sink Gordon's remaining steamers. The *Ismailia* was hit numerous times as she steamed back and forth firing at Ansár forces. The next day, the *Husseinieh* was holed below the waterline, was grounded to prevent her sinking and, once her guns were removed, was abandoned. Shortly thereafter, as the falling of the Nile enabled the Ansár to move ever closer, the systematic shelling of the city began. Telegraphic communication between Khartoum and Omdurman was cut on 13 November. Gordon believed that this was a minor concern. Nonetheless, on 13 December, Gordon decided to close his journal and send it, along with some last letters, downstream to safety. The next day, after writing letters to his sister and to his friend Colonel Watson, Gordon made his last journal entry: 'Now MARK THIS, if the Expeditionary Force, and I ask for no more than 200 men, does not come in ten days, the town may fall; and I have done my best for the honour of my country. Good bye. C. G. Gordon. You send me no information, though you have lots of money.'[75] Two days later, he loaded them on to the *Bordein* and sent it through a gauntlet of fire to El-Metemmah. He also sent a small written message, 'Khartoum all right 14.12.84,'[76] and a longer verbal message by messenger to Wolseley, who received it on 31 December and interpreted it as advice to come quickly, but without leaving a hostile Berber behind. Wolseley reacted by strengthening his advance column and supply depots, causing further delays. At this point, there were about 14,000 civilians left in the city.

Recognising that his forces and supplies would not be at full strength until 22 January and conscious of Gordon's dire condition, Wolseley ordered Kitchener and his Arab scouts to lead the 1,100-man advance party of Herbert Stewart's Desert Column from their camp at Korti on 30 December to establish an intermediate supply depot at the wells at Gakdul 100 miles away and halfway to El-Metemmeh. They arrived on 2 January to establish British control. Leaving the Camel Regiment and Royal Engineers to prepare and defend the place, Stewart returned to Korti to lead on the rest of the force and their supplies. Stewart left Korti again with the remaining 2,000 men and supplies on 8 January and arrived back at Gakdul on 12 January. During this period, additional British forces arrived at Korti and Wolseley estimated that he would be ready for a full-scale assault in early March.

After several unsuccessful sorties to draw Ansár forces away from Omdurman, Gordon ordered the garrison, led by Faragh Pasha, to attempt a break-out on 4 January. But the Ansár forced them back into the fort. Shortly thereafter, completely out of food, Gordon authorised the fort's surrender. On the same day British units captured Hamdah and linked up with the River Column under General Earle. On 12 January the Mahdi again wrote to Gordon, pleading with him to surrender. Gordon did not reply.

After resting the exhausted animals for 60 hours, the Desert Column resumed its march toward the wells at Abu Klea, 20 miles north of the Nile at El-Metemmeh on 14 January. Colonel Sir Charles Wilson accompanied the column as its intelligence officer. He had warned, contrary to Wolseley's assumptions, that a considerable Ansár force blocked its way. Alerted by cavalry scouts that Abu Klea was occupied by a strong Ansár force, Stewart prepared a strong fortified position on 17 January and marched his column forward in a large battle square which absorbed attacks from the north and the east by some 10,000 onrushing Ansár warriors. Largely due to jamming problems in both the rapid-fire artillery and the soldiers' rifles, Ansár succeeded in penetrating the square, but the British emerged victorious. However, the man who Wolseley had selected to lead the advance from El-Metemmeh, Lieutenant Colonel Fred Burnaby, was killed. The next morning, the British began their march from the wells straight through to El-Metemmeh. They were confronted by another Ansár force near Abu Kru. Fire from the advancing Ansár mortally wounded Stewart, and Wilson, who had never commanded in combat before, took over. Fending off furious attacks, the force reached the river after nightfall and, succumbing to thirst and exhaustion, collapsed for the night. The next day, the Mahdi ordered a 101-gun salute to be fired outside Khartoum, signalling a great victory, but Gordon, watching the Ansár camps through his rooftop telescope, saw women wailing and recognised it as a ruse to convince him that the British advance had been halted. That evening the Mahdi held a war council where he determined to assault the city by way of a route suggested by a deserter, at the western end of the ditch and rampart where the river had lowered to dry land which the sun had dried into a soft bog. As the river receded, it took many of the protective mines with it.

On 21 January Wilson led an attack on El-Metemmeh, but finding a strong, well-entrenched Ansár force waiting there for him, ordered it halted. The British returned to Gubat. They were met by Gordon's armoured steamers: the *El Mansureh* had been sunk by Ansár guns, but the *Bordein* had by now joined the little fleet that also included *Tel el Hawein* and *Safia*. Wilson thus received Gordon's letters and journal but Abu Klea had convinced him that the Ansár were truly formidable, and his small force was exhausted and in disarray. Burnaby was dead, Stewart lay dying – he died on 28 February – and Lord Charles Beresford and he himself were wounded. Besides, a message from Gordon, perhaps intended to deceive the Mahdi and dated 29 December, stated 'Khartoum all right, could hold out for years.'[77] Wilson spent the next two days reorganising his forces, before deciding to load two of the steamers for a run to Khartoum on 24 January. Some 240 Egyptian and Sudanese soldiers and 20 men of the Royal Sussex Regiment in red tunics, led by Wilson, steamed upriver from Gubat toward Khartoum aboard the *Bordein* and the *Telahwiya*, which towed a grain-filled barge. With the river low, the boats moved slowly in daylight for three days, often running aground and engaging in fire-fights. Wilson approached the city under heavy fire on 28 January. When he observed the smouldering ruins of the Governor's Palace where he had expected to see an Egyptian flag flying, he ordered the steamers to turn northward. Under heavy fire, he retreated tortuously down the lowering Nile to Gubat. On 5 February Wolseley reported the fall of the city to the War Office.

On 25 January Gordon had observed the Ansár preparing to attack and called every able-bodied man to arms. The Mahdi ordered that Gordon not be killed in the attack and that night skirmishers crept through the city's southern defences. Before daybreak on 26 January, several thousand men overran the Egyptian defenders, while another attack was launched at the northern end of the rampart. By midday, most of the city's remaining male inhabitants had been killed along with Gordon himself. The varying accounts of his death, fighting to the last, attempting to detonate explosives in the Governor's Palace, serenely confronting his attackers (in the style of a Christian martyr), became the stuff of legend. Slatin reported that his severed head was presented to the Mahdi.

Gladstone's first response to the disaster – he barely survived another vote of censure on 27 February – was to call for a second, larger Sudan expedition to avenge Gordon. The Desert Column was reinforced and the River Column proceeded southward and successfully thwarted another attempt by the Ansár to delay it at Jebel Kirbekan on 10 February, though Earle was killed. Gerald Graham, who returned to Suakin on 12 March with a new expeditionary force, proceeded inland and won several hard-fought battles. Then, on 21 April, using Graham's securing of the Red Sea ports as his excuse, Hartington ordered Wolseley to withdraw, leaving all of the Sudan except for Suakin to the Mahdi. Gladstone's government resigned on 8 June, succumbing to its own internal rivalries. On 20 June, the Mahdi died, probably of typhus, and was succeeded by the Khalifa Abdullahi. Poor harvests, epidemics, tribal rebellions, Ansár misrule and enforced isolation combined to bring the Sudan to a sorry state, while the British compensated by idolising Gordon. Sensing the popular mood, the House of Commons awarded his family £20,000 and declared a national day of mourning. A final battle was fought at Ginnis on the Sudan-Egyptian border, where Ansár raids had been taking place: the British, under Stephenson, won, marking the end of the 1885 campaign.

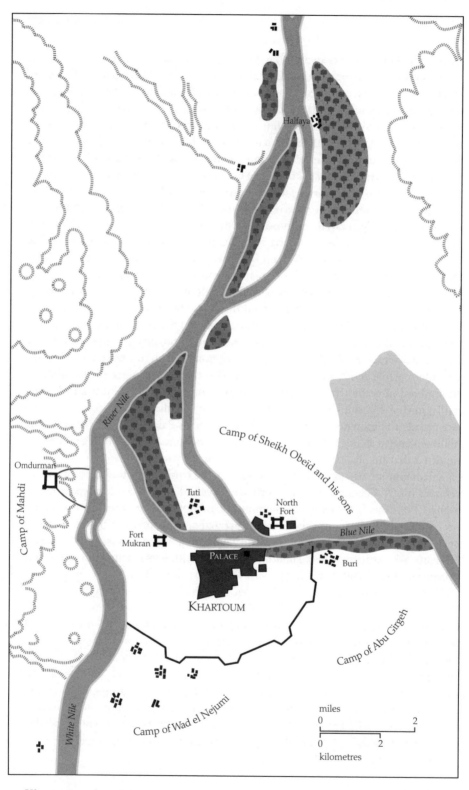

Khartoum and environs.

As for Gordon himself, he has remained a controversial and enigmatic character. His courage, his competence as a military engineer and his expertise in irregular warfare are unquestioned. His personal charisma and incorruptibility, which enabled him to win respect from the (often native) soldiers who fought under him and the civilians who supported him, his acts of charity and distain of material profit and his diplomatic skills, despite his sometimes foul temper and periodic bouts of depression, made him both an effective administrator and a popular hero during his own lifetime. Though not without Victorian prejudices, he was more open than many of his contemporaries to judge individuals on their abilities, rather than on their race or class, and was willing, within limits, to permit native peoples to govern themselves, rather than subject them to imperial control. However, his independence of mind and casual attitudes toward authority and instructions gave the military hierarchy, already jealous of his popularity, ample excuse to treat him badly.

On the other hand, his oft-proclaimed and highly eccentric religious certitude about the righteousness of his actions led him blithely to accept seemingly hopeless assignments, and his successes only fuelled his sense of divine direction – until his luck ran out. This sense of divine inspiration also justified his frequent policy reversals, his willingness to sacrifice principle to tactical advantage (both of which often angered or bewildered his supporters), his characteristically modern co-option and use of the press to build popular support for his private, if often noble, purposes and his belief that his character and policies would lead inevitably to a moral outcome, whatever the evidence to the contrary. His flexibility over the issue of slavery, his determination to reinstate the slaver Zubeir Pasha and his, it turned out, misplaced faith in the character of Leopold II to offset these compromises are the most visible examples of this. And his often capricious and scattershot flood of directives, proposals and information confused and exasperated both his friends and the military forces sent to rescue him at the end.

Ultimately he was a very Victorian religious reformer, who revelled in his perfectly acceptable eccentricities and cultivated outsider status, and who fervently believed that – with Bible and sword – the spread of Christian virtue and European ideals could enlighten the world.

Bibliography

Gordon was a prolific letter writer and, at times, an equally expansive keeper of journals. Four volumes of his letters, edited and 'corrected' to suit Victorian taste were published after his death, by, among others, his sister M Augusta Gordon, *Letters of General C G Gordon to his Sister* (London: Macmillan & Co., 1888); Demitrius C Boulger, *General Gordon's Letters from the Crimea, the Danube, and Armenia 1854–1858* (London: Chapman & Hall, 1884); and George Birbeck Hill, *Colonel Gordon in Central Africa 1874–1879, from Original Letters and Documents* (London: Thomas de La Rue, 1884, 4th edn, facsimile reprint by Kraus Reprints, 1969). His friend, the newspaper correspondent Samuel Mossman, published *General Gordon's Private Diary of His Exploits in China* (London: Sampson, Low, Marston, Searle & Rivington, 1885) and his colleague and acquaintance, A Egmont Hake, similarly published *The Journals of Major-General C G Gordon CB, at Khartoum* (London: Kegan Paul, Trench, 1885) and the *Private Diary of the Taiping Rebellion of C. G. Gordon* (London: W H Allen & Co., 1890).

Those involved with him also published, particularly Romolo Gessi, *Seven Years in the Sudan Being a Record of Explorations, Adventures, and Campaigns against the Arab Slave Hunters*, ed. Felix Gessi (London: Sampson Low, Marston & Co., 1892) and Sir Gerald Graham, *Last Words with Gordon* (London: Chapman & Hall, 1887). The British government prepared a post hoc report called *General Gordon's Mission to the Sudan, 1885: A Summary of Events Prepared for the Cabinet* (London, 1885). Hagiographies appeared shortly after his death as well. These include those of his brother, Sir Henry W Gordon, *Events in the life of Charles George Gordon* (London: Kegan Paul, 1885); Hake's *History of Chinese Gordon* (London: Remington & Co., 1885); the Reverend R H Barnes, *Charles Gordon: a Sketch with Facsimile Letters* (London: Macmillan & Co., 1885); W S Blunt, *Gordon at Khartoum* (London: Stephen Swift & Co., 1911); Annie Besant, *Gordon Judged Out Of His Own Mouth* (London: Freethought Publishing Co., 1885); and Eva Hope, *General Gordon the Christian Hero* (London: Walter Scott Publishing Co., 1885). Gordon's last mission and his interactions with the Mahdi are usually viewed through the eyes of European captives who lived to write their memoirs: Father Joseph Ohrwalder, *Ten Years Captivity in the Mahdi's Camp from the Original Manuscript of Father Joseph Ohrwalder, Late Priest of the Austrian Mission Station at Delen in Kordofan*, ed. and tr. Major R C Wingate (London: Sampson, Low, Marston & Co., 1892) and Rudolf C Slatin, *With Fire and Sword in the Sudan*, tr. Major F R Wingate (London: Edward Arnold, 1896). The British government's relations with him and its rescue mission were reported in the memoirs of their participants such as the Earl of Cromer, *Modern Egypt*, 2 vols (London: Macmillan, 1908).

More recent documents collections have been more comprehensive and penetrating such as M F Shurky, ed., *Equatoria Under Egyptian Rule: The Unpublished Correspondence of Col. C. G. Gordon with Ismail, Khedive of Egypt and the Sudan, 1874–1876* (Cairo: Cairo University Press, 1953) and Lord Elton, *General Gordon's Khartoum Journal* (London: William Kimber, 1961). Some more recent biographies have been less kind, notably, Giles Lytton Strachey, *Eminent Victorians* (London: Chatto & Windus, 1920) and Anthony Nutting, *Gordon of Khartoum: Martyr and Misfit* (London: Constable, 1966). From the literally hundreds of biographies and military histories related to Gordon, the following have been most valuable: Roy MacGregor-Hastie, *Never To Be Taken Alive: A Biography of General Gordon* (New York: St Martin's Press, 1985); Charles Chevenix Trench, *The Road to Khartoum: A Life of General Charles Gordon* (New York: W W Norton, 1978); John Pollock, *Gordon: The Man Behind the Legend* (Oxford: Lion, 1993); and John H Waller, *Gordon of Khartoum: The Saga of a Victorian Hero* (New York: Athenaeum, 1988).

Notes

1. John H Waller, *Gordon of Khartoum: The Saga of a Victorian Hero* (New York: Atheneum, 1988), p. 17.
2. Western Powers, led by Britain, had become increasingly frustrated with Chinese delays in carrying out the terms of the Treaty of Nanking and subsequent agreements. When ambassadorial missions were refused entry to the Chinese capital, the British and French resolved to end Manchu resistance.
3. The Taiping movement began with the preaching of Hong Xiuquan, a south China Hakka minority member who had several times failed the entrance examinations for the Chinese

bureaucracy, learned about Christianity from an American missionary and described himself as a brother of Jesus. In 1851, he proclaimed himself the Heavenly King of the Heavenly Kingdom of Great Peace. Feeding on long-festering anti-Manchu and anti-foreigner resentments, demands for tax relief and social reform, and religious fervour, tens of thousands joined his ranks and they soon occupied much of the Yangsi valley and central China.

4. Roy MacGregor-Hastie, *Never To Be Taken Alive: A Biography of General Gordon* (New York: St Martin's Press, 1985), pp. 67–68.

5. *Memoirs of Li Hung-chang*, quoted in Bernard Meredith Allen, *Gordon in China*, (London: Macmillan, 1933), p. 69.

6. Waller, *Gordon of Khartoum*, p. 104.

7. He did return early in 1865 to join remnants of the Taipings in Amoy. The Chinese government captured him in Changchow on 15 May, and his drowned body was found in Chekiang on 15 June.

8. Quoted in MacGregor-Hastie, *Never To Be Taken Alive*, pp. 76–77.

9. Octavia Freese, 'One Who Knew Him Well', in *More About Gordon* (London: Richard Bently & Sons, 1894), p. 44. These activities, combined with his awkward and, as far as is known, celibate relations with women, later led to allegations of latent homosexuality (or even paedophilia). The allegations were investigated by Frank M Richardson MD in a chapter of his *Mars Without Venus* (Edinburgh: William Blackwood, 1981). John Pollock's biography *Gordon: The Man Behind the Legend* (Oxford: Lion, 1993) suggests Asperger's Syndrome as an alternative explanation for Gordon's demeanour, behaviour and proclivities.

10. M. Augusta Gordon, ed., *Letters of General C G Gordon to his Sister* (London: Macmillan & Co., 1888), p. 91.

11. The Khedive, desperate for money and deeply in debt, was plotting with Zubeir to conquer Darfur, which they did in November, 1874, defeating one of Zubeir's major rivals, Sultan Ibrahim, and opening a whole new region to his slaving operations. Zubeir had massacred a 1,200-man Egyptian army sent to subdue him in 1869 and Ismail had made him Governor of the region to bring him to heal. From the growing slaving revenues, Zubeir paid an annual bribe to the Khedive, which he used to pay Sir Samuel Baker's salary. In November 1874, after Gordon complained to the British Consul in Cairo, he was given control over Bahr al-Ghazal and in August 1875, the Governor General ordered Zubeir back to Bahr al-Ghazal. The next June, Zubeir, wishing to rule Darfur as a direct vassal of the Khedive, travelled to Cairo to appeal the decision, leaving his son, Suleiman Zubeir, in control of his slaving operations. The Khedive detained Zubeir in Cairo. When bribes failed to gain his release, Zubeir appealed to Gordon to secure his freedom. When Gordon refused, Zubeir, it was widely believed, ordered his chieftains to organise a rebellion against him.

12. Khartoum was an Egyptian city, which began to be built in the wake of Ismail Pasha's expedition. The name 'Khartoum' means elephant trunk. Egyptians sent to the Sudan regarded service there as exile and it was quickly relegated to inferior or disgraced officers. As Egyptian control extended southward, the slave trade exploded. Romulo Gessi, in *Seven Years in the Sudan: Being a Record of Explorations, Adventures, and Campaigns against the Arab Slave Hunters*, ed. Felix Gessi (London: Sampson, Low, Marston & Co., 1892), p. 2, later reported that beginning in 1860, 'in the brief space of fourteen years more than four hundred thousand women and children were taken from their native country and sold in Egypt and Turkey, while thousands and thousands were massacred in the defence of their families'.

13. The two men discussed a plan to convince the Khedive to send a force to East Africa to push Mutesa into the Egyptian orbit. The Khedive obliged, sending Long to Zanzibar and thence to Juba. Fearful that this be seen as an effort to restore the slave trade, and eager to keep the friendly Sultan of Zanzibar free of Egyptian influence, the British government forced an end to the adventure.

14. George Birbeck Hill, ed., *Colonel Gordon in Central Africa, 1874–1879 from Original Letters and Documents* (London: Thomas de La Rue, 1884, 4th edn, facsimile reprint by Kraus Reprints, 1969), p. 67.

15. Quoted in MacGregor-Hastie, *Never to be Taken Alive*, p. 107.

16. Charles Chevenix Trench, *The Road to Khartoum: A Life of General Charles Gordon* (New York: W W Norton, 1978), p. 118.

17. W H Wilkins, *The Romance of Isabel, Lady Burton* (London: Hutchinson, 1897), II, p. 645.

18. In 1876, the British Paymaster General reported that the Khedive's debt had surpassed £81 million.

19. Though most Egyptians had little interest in altering either the customs or the lucrative slaving economy of the Sudan, they were interested in maintaining administrative and tax-collection control over the country, which involved not permitting the slavers to seize control of swathes of its territory.

20. British Library (hereafter BL) Add. MS 54495, 5 July, 1879, quoted in Trench, *The Road to Khartoum*, p. 144.

21. What to do in these instances was complicated by the conflicting instructions that Gordon possessed.

22. Quoted in Waller, *Gordon of Khartoum*, p. 232.

23. Earlier in the year an Egyptian officer mutiny had taken place over demotions and pay cuts, which they blamed on European control. A short-term loan from the Rothschild Bank had saved the day, but as a result, the Egyptian Prime Minister, Nubar Pasha, had resigned on 18 February.

24. Quoted in Waller, *Gordon of Khartoum*, p. 235.

25. *The Times*, 22 January 1880.

26. Waller, *Gordon of Khartoum*, p. 245.

27. George Birkbeck Hill, ed., *Colonel Gordon in Central Africa 1874–1879 from Original Letters and Documents* (London: Thomas de La Rue, 1884, 4th edn, facsimile reprint by Kraus Reprints, 1969), p. 426.

28. *The Times*, 9 January 1883, p. 3.

29. Some claimed that the offer was encouraged by their mutual friend, Florence Nightingale, while others attributed it to Ripon's hope that Gordon's earlier Danubian experience would help resolve the vexatious border issues between Britain and Russia. Still others claimed that Gordon's reputation for maintaining good relations with native populations would assist Ripon achieve his reform agenda.

30. Waller, *Gordon of Khartoum*, p. 261.

31. China eventually decided against war and China and Russia signed a treaty in 1881.

32. After numerous quarrels with Gordon's successor in the Sudan, Gessi had resigned as Governor of Bahr al-Ghazil. In September, while travelling on the steam ship *Saphia* with some 600 other passengers, it ran aground. For two months they struggled against starvation and disease, and some engaged in cannibalism to survive. Emaciated and mentally tortured by what he had witnessed, Gessi was brought to Khartoum, where the government continued to make life difficult for him. Resolved to return home, he embarked from Berber, but died at Suez. Gordon paid to have his body returned to Ravenna.

33. H Shaked, *The Life of the Sudanese Mahdi: A Historical Study of Kitáb sa'adat al-mustahdi bi-sírát al-imám al Mahdi by ismá-íl bin 'Abd-al-Gádir* (New Jersey: Transaction Press, 1978), pp. 75–76.

34. On 16 February 1882, Ra'úf Pasha had been replaced in that post by 'Abd-al-Qádir Hilmi, but he had not yet arrived to take up his duties and Geigler, a German telegraph engineer, who had been Ra'úf's deputy, took the post temporarily.

35. Ansár was the name connoting supporters of the Mahdi. It had been the name given to Muhammed's followers at Medina. The British preferred to call them 'dervishes', an Arab word

that literally means 'the poor' and was widely used to encompass a range of Muslim holy men.
36. Earlier in the century, the BaSotho had fought a thirty-year sporadic battle against the Boers, culminating in 1868 in the retention of their mountain territory and their capital at Thaba Bosiu. In 1869, caught between the Boer Orange Free State, Natal, the Zulus and the British, the BaSotho Paramount Chief, Mosheshwe, accepted a British offer to annex Basutoland. He welcomed the British administrators, but in 1871, for the sake of administrative convenience, the British turned it over to Cape Colony. When the king died in 1879, a rivalry emerged among his sons and the unrest caused the Cape government to impose direct rule through a system of Magistrates. The next year, the government passed the Peace Preservation Act, which included a formal demand for native disarmament. Of the four BaSotho chiefs, three (including the new Paramount Chief, Lestie) reluctantly accepted the demand, but the fourth, Masupha, rejected it. The Cape's new Governor, Sir Hercules Robinson, proposed maintaining disarmament in principle, but permitting guns to be held through licensing agreements. In August 1881, Robinson sent an Agent for the Basutos, Joseph Orpen, to present this to the chiefs. Orpen returned reporting that Masupha was still not convinced. In 1882, the new Cape Prime Minister, Thomas Scanlen, ignoring, to his political peril, the 'forward demands' of the businessmen, asked Robinson to ask the Colonial Office to seek Gordon's services.

37. BL Add MS 51296. Sauer was convicted in the court of public opinion of placing Gordon's life in danger.

38. Laurence Oliphant, *Haifa* (London: Blackwood, 1887), pp. 347–50.

39. Charles George Gordon, *Reflections in Palestine 1883* (London: Macmillan, 1884).

40. Dominic Green, *Three Empires on the Nile: The Victorian Jihad, 1869–1899* (New York: Free Press, 2007), p. 142.

41. Colonel John Donald Hamill Stewart, 'Report on the Soudan', *The Parliamentary Papers*, Egypt, No. 11, 1883, C-3670, p. 25.

42. Trench, *The Road to Khartoum*, p. 193.

43. Ibid., p. 194.

44. Ibid., p. 195.

45. Granville to Baring, 13 December 1883 (Public Records Office, London 30/29/199).

46. Ibid.

47. Earl of Cromer, *Modern Egypt* (London: Macmillan, 1908), vol. I, pp. 382, 429.

48. Lord Godfrey Elton, *Gordon of Khartoum* (New York: Knopf, 1955), p. 281.

49. John Morley, *The Life of William Ewart Gladstone* (London: Macmillan, 1903), Vol. III, p. 149.

50. The National Archives (hereafter TNA), FO 78/3665, Baring to Granville, No. 44, 16 January 1884.

51. BL, Add Mss 51298, Gordon to Barnes, 22 January 1884, cited with a slightly different wording in R H Barnes and C E Brown, *C G Gordon, A Sketch with Facsimile Letters* (London: Macmillan, 1885), pp. 102–3.

52. Earl of Cromer, *Modern Egypt*, vol. I, p. 429.

53. TNA, FO 78/3696, Granville to Baring, 18 January 1884.

54. Green, *Three Empires on the Nile*, p. 160.

55. Sudan Archive, University of Durham, Wingate Mss, 245/6; BL, Add Mss. 56451, Baring to Gordon, 22 January 1884.

56. Wingate found the file but not the incriminating letter. Some weeks later, a letter in Arabic, purporting to be the 'smoking gun' was provided to the Foreign Office by Gordon's brother and his biographer Egmont Hake. Wingate thought it a forgery.

57. Cromer, *Modern Egypt*, vol. I, pp. 390, 444–46.

58. Trench, *The Road to Khartoum*, p. 213

59. *Blue Book*, London, Public Records Office, No. 2, p. 6; TNA, PRO 30/29/162, Baring to

Granville, 28 January 1884.

60. Gordon to Baring, 18 February 1884, quoted in Trench, *The Road to Khartoum*, p. 230.

61. Granville to Baring, 23 February 1884, quoted in Trench, *The Road to Khartoum*, p. 230.

62. Gordon to Granville, 26 February 1884, quoted in Trench, *The Road to Khartoum*, p. 231.

63. Trench, *The Road to Khartoum*, p. 232.

64. Ibid., p. 234. After carefully considering all of the obstacles to evacuation, Trench, pp. 227–29, calculated that 'purely as an administrative exercise, provided there were no shipwrecks, or engine failures, the operation [of evacuating the 15–20,000 people from the city] could just be completed in about eleven lifts between March and the end of September'.

65. Father Joseph Ohrwalder, *Ten Years Captivity in the Mahdi's Camp, from the Original Manuscript of Father Joseph Ohrwalder, Late Priest of the Austrian Mission Station at Delen in Kordofan*, ed. and tr. Major R C Wingate (London: Sampson, Low, Marston & Co., 1892), p. 98.

66. Green, *Three Empires on the Nile*, p.176.

67. Ibid.

68. Waller, *Gordon of Khartoum*, p. 372.

69. Trench, *The Road to Khartoum*, p. 259.

70. Ibid., p. 257.

71. Rudolf C Slatin, *With Fire and Sword in the Sudan*, tr. Major F R Wingate (London: Edward Arnold, 1896), p. 17. The Mahdi used Slatin and Joseph Cuzzi, an Egyptian official captured at Berber, to communicate with Gordon. Appalled by their conversion to Islam (which saved their lives), Gordon refused to receive them.

72. A Egmont Hake, *The Journals of Major-General C G Gordon, CB, at Khartoum* (London: Kegan Paul, Trench, 1885), pp. 105–6.

73. Cromer, *Modern Egypt*, vol. I, p. 582.

74. Ohrwalder, *Captivity*, pp. 145–46.

75. Hake, *Journals*, p. 365.

76. Trench, *The Road to Khartoum*, p. 282.

77. Ibid., p. 288.

Chapter 7

Frederick Roberts

André Wessels

The military history of Queen Victoria's long reign is dominated by two renowned, albeit complex and controversial, commanders: Lord Roberts of Kandahar and Sir Garnet (later Viscount) Wolseley. Both of them, motivated in part by self-interest, worked tirelessly to promote the interests of the British Empire. Although they were rivals, they sometimes complemented one another. Each had his own 'ring' or 'circle' of very loyal and influential officers. The Wolseley (or 'Ashanti') ring included men like Redvers Buller; the Roberts (or 'Indian') ring included men like Ian Hamilton. Wolseley's ring hailed their leader as 'our only general', which led Roberts's followers to react by proclaiming him as 'our other general'.[1]

Frederick Sleigh Roberts (known as 'Fred' to his family, and affectionately known as 'Bobs' by his troops) was born on 30 September 1832 in Cawnpore, India. He had the good fortune to come from what can be regarded as typical Victorian officers' parentage. His father, Lieutenant Colonel (later General) Abraham Roberts, was a soldier of note and had fought in the First Anglo–Afghan War (1838–42). His mother, Isabella Bunbury, had previously been married to Major Hamilton Maxwell.

The Roberts family returned to England in 1834, where Fred was educated at Eton, the Royal Military College and the Honourable East India Company's school; but he was no great scholar. In December 1851, he was commissioned as second lieutenant in the artillery, and gazetted to the Bengal army. After some four months in India, he joined his father as ADC and battery officer at Peshawar. He took part in the suppression of the Indian Mutiny (1857–58). During the final successful attack on Delhi (14 July 1857), Roberts received the first (and last) wound of his career, albeit a slight one, and his first (of many) mention in dispatches. On 2 January 1858, near the village of Khudaganj, he saved a standard as well as the life of a loyal Indian trooper, and in doing so, won the VC.[2]

Roberts returned to England because his health was breaking down. In England, he met Nora Henrietta Bews, and they married in May 1859. Some three weeks later, they sailed for India, where he joined the QMG's department, which

Chronology

30 September 1832	Frederick Sleigh Roberts born at Cawnpore (Kanpur), India
	Educated at Eton, Sandhurst and Addiscombe
12 December 1851	Commissioned as Second Lieutenant, Bengal Artillery
31 May 1857	Promoted First Lieutenant
1857–58	Saw action in the suppression of the Indian Mutiny, wounded (14 July 1857), won the VC (2 January 1858) and earned seven mentions in dispatches
17 May 1859	Married Nora Henrietta Bews
12 November 1860	Promoted Captain
13 November 1860	Promoted Brevet Major
1863	Ambeyla Campaign, North-West Frontier, India
1868	Abyssinian Campaign
15 August 1868	Promoted Brevet Lieutenant Colonel
1871–72	Lushai Campaign
5 July 1872	Promoted Substantive Major
30 January 1875	Promoted Colonel, Acting Major General and QMG, India
1 April 1878	Commander, Punjab Frontier Force
22 October 1878	Commander, Kurram Frontier Force
31 December 1878	Promoted Substantive Major General
5 September 1879	Commander, Kabul Field Force as Local Lieutenant General
16 November 1880	Arrived back in England
6 March 1881	Sailed for Cape Town (arrived 29 March, departed 30 March)
14 June 1881	Created Baronet
28 November 1881	Arrived in India and took over as C in C of the Madras Army
26 July 1883	Promoted Substantive Lieutenant General
4 November 1885	Appointed C in C of the Indian Army as Acting General
28 November 1890	Promoted Substantive General
1 January 1892	Created Baron Roberts of Kandahar
8 April 1893	Left India for the last time
25 May 1895	Promoted Field Marshal
1 October 1895	Appointed C in C, Ireland
22 December 1899	Appointed C in C of the British forces in South Africa
28 November 1900	Relinquished South African command
11 December 1900	Departed from South Africa
2 January 1900	Created Earl Roberts of Kandahar, Waterford and Pretoria
3 January 1900	Took up position of C in C of the British army
8 February 1904	Retired as C in C of the British army
14 November 1914	Died at St Omer, France
19 November 1914	Buried in St Paul's Cathedral, London

Appointed CB, 1872; KCB, 1879; CIE, 1880; GCB, 1880; GCIE, 1887; GCSI, 1893; KP, 1897; KG, 1901; OM, 1902

brought him into contact with the leading military and civil service personnel in India. He served in the Ambeyla Campaign on the North-West Frontier (1863), but then ill health forced him to return to England. In Abyssinia (1868), Roberts served as AQMG on the staff of Lieutenant General Robert Napier. He then returned to India, and in the Lushai Campaign (1871–72) for the first time led troops in battle.

Roberts played a decisive role in the Second Anglo-Afghan War (1878–80). In the first phase of the war, he led the Kurram Field Force to victory at the Peiwar Kotal, and in the second phase, first led the Kabul Field Force to retake the Afghan capital, and later marched from Kabul to Kandahar. This seemingly epic (but overrated) march made him a household name throughout the British Empire, and ensured him enduring fame as military commander. Roberts returned to England, but when news was received that George Colley had been defeated and killed at Majuba in Natal, Roberts was sent to South Africa in March 1881 as Natal's new Governor and C in C. However, while he was still at sea, the British government decided to opt for a negotiated settlement. Roberts was furious, and within 24 hours of arriving in Cape Town, he was on his way back to England.

In November 1881, Roberts returned to India once more, to take up the post of C in C of the Madras army. He raised the standard of this army, improved the defence of the North-West Frontier and wrote on the defence of India and the threat that Russia posed to British interests. In November 1885, Roberts was appointed C in C of the Indian army. His primary concern was still the defence of the country against Russia, and consequently, he improved the fortifications and communications infrastructure on the frontiers. He also focussed his energy on several other tasks: he strengthened and reformed the Indian army; he re-equipped it with new weapons such as, for example, machine-guns; he improved training (especially with regard to musketry); and he recruited more of the so-called 'martial races' of northern India into its army. From November 1886 to February 1887, he commanded the British forces in the Third Anglo-Burmese War.

In April 1893, Roberts left Indian shores for the last time, and returned to England. As no suitable employment was immediately available, he wrote the autobiographical *Forty-one Years in India*, a best seller in its day. In May 1895, he was promoted Field Marshal, and in October 1895, appointed C in C, Ireland (as successor to Wolseley, who became C in C of the British army). When the Anglo-Boer War broke out on 11 October 1899, the Wolseley ring's General Buller was appointed C in C, South Africa.[3] Roberts was regarded as too old to take command in the field. Buller's offensive failed, and in what became known as 'Black Week' (10–15 December), he suffered three defeats at the hands of an untrained citizen army. (At Colenso, on 15 December, Roberts's son, Freddy, was mortally wounded.)

On more than one occasion, Roberts offered his services to the British government, and when the 'Black Week' defeats led to a public outcry in Britain and it became clear that Buller had not only lost the confidence of the British public and government, but also his nerve, the government approached Roberts to take over as C in C in South Africa. Roberts's appointment was a victory of his ring over that of Wolseley's. In practice, neither Wolseley (although he was the

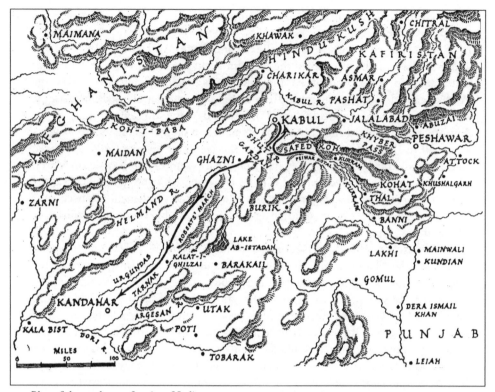

Plan of the north-west frontier of India. (From David James, *Lord Roberts*, London: Hollis & Carter, 1954)

C in C) nor the Queen (who still supported Buller) was consulted with regard to Roberts's appointment. Lord Kitchener was appointed as Roberts's chief of staff. In practice, these two distinguished soldiers complemented each other to a remarkable degree.

Roberts and his staff arrived in Cape Town on 10 January 1900, and he set about revitalising the British war effort in South Africa by reorganising the transport arrangements, raising more mounted troops (in the light of the British army's experience in South Africa thus far, but also drawing on his own experience in Afghanistan) and preparing for his advance. Roberts's campaign can be divided into six phases: (1) Preparations in Cape Town; (2) his advance from the Modder River via Paardeberg to Bloemfontein; (3) his forced halt in Bloemfontein; (4) his advance from Bloemfontein via Johannesburg to Pretoria; (5) his advance from Pretoria to Komatipoort; and (6) the guerrilla phase proper (until he handed over his command to Kitchener).

On 11 February 1900, Roberts implemented his elaborate flank march, based on a strategy of indirect approach. He first took his army of 49,500 men (out of some 120,000 deployed in South Africa at that stage) from the Modder River south to Enslin Station, then swerved eastwards via Ramdam to Watervalsdrif and

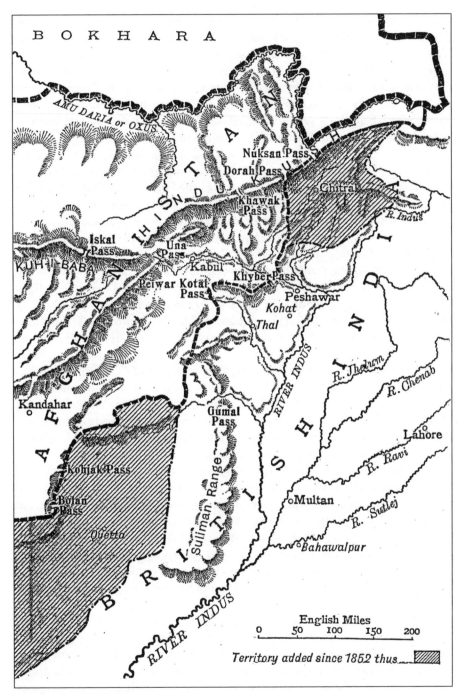

Plan of the north-west frontier and Afghanistan. (From G. Forrest, *The Life of Lord Roberts, KG, VC*, London: Cassell & Co., 1914)

De Kielsdrif on the Riet River, and then northwards to Rondawelsdrif and Klipdrif on the Modder River. From there his forces drove eastwards along the river, following on the heels of the Boers who had been forced to evacuate their positions at Magersfontein. While Major General J D P French rushed northwards to relieve Kimberley (15 February), the rest of Roberts's army cornered and then attacked and laid siege to General P A Cronjé's force near Paardeberg, where the Boers surrendered on 27 February 1900. From Paardeberg Roberts moved eastwards and occupied Bloemfontein on 13 March. After a forced halt of more than seven weeks, Roberts continued his advance northwards on 3 May, now all along the main railway line, occupying Johannesburg (31 May) and Pretoria (5 June). In the meantime, he annexed the Orange Free State (OFS), but he now also had to contend with Boer guerrilla activities, which started as early as 31 March when General Christiaan de Wet defeated a force at Sannaspos.

Roberts was convinced that 'our having gained possession of the capital of the South African Republic [i.e. Transvaal] will enable the war to be brought to a rapid conclusion'.[4] When he realised, however, that not even the fall of Pretoria would induce the Boers to surrender, he ordered an advance eastwards along the Delagoa Bay railway line, forcing the Boers to abandon their positions at Donkerhoek/Diamond Hill (11–12 June 1900) and Bergendal/Dalmanutha (21–27 August 1900) without really defeating them. On 1 September 1900 he annexed the Transvaal.

On 29 September 1900, Roberts was offered the post of C in C of the British army, and he accepted, convinced that all that was left to be done in South Africa was police work to get rid of the few isolated groups of Boers. At midnight, on 28/29 November 1900, Roberts handed over command to Kitchener and returned to England, where on 3 January he took up his new position. For his work in South Africa, he received many honours and awards.

Roberts's appointment as C in C was widely welcomed, but in practice, he performed no better than his predecessor. He did try to improve the professional education of the officer corps, placed more emphasis on realistic training, and introduced a new rifle (the magazine Lee-Enfield) and new motor vehicles. As a matter of fact, although Roberts was, strictly speaking, from the old school of thought (and really represented an older era), he modernised the army as far as possible in line with new technologies. To some extent, he also laid the foundation for the modern British army, and for what later became the General Staff of the Army. But otherwise, there was not much he could do to reform the army. After all, he had less scope in the War Office than he had when he was C in C in India.

Roberts's achievements as C in C were overshadowed by arguments concerning the exact role the C in C should play. In 1903, a Royal Commission recommended that the position of C in C of the British army be abolished, and consequently, in February 1904, Roberts left the War Office. Until November 1905, he remained a member of the newly formed Committee of Imperial Defence, but resigned because he disagreed with several of the government's defence policies, especially with regard to compulsory military training. He became president of the National Service League in November 1905, addressing many meetings on the issue of national service (and warning against a German threat), but the British press and public were averse to conscription. As an Anglo-Irishman, Roberts supported the Ulster Unionists, was against home rule for Ireland and was involved in the Curragh incident (March 1914).[5]

When Britain entered the First World War in August 1914, Roberts was appointed Colonel in Chief of the Empire (i.e. overseas) troops in France. In November, when he received word that men of the Indian Army Corps had arrived for service on the Western Front, Roberts was intent on going to France to meet 'his' troops. He crossed the English Channel and visited the headquarters of the Indian regiments. By the evening of 13 November it was clear that he had caught a chill; pneumonia of one lung and pleurisy rapidly developed, and he died at St Omer at 2000 on 14 November 1914. After a military funeral service in St Paul's Cathedral,[6] his mortal remains were interred in the cathedral's crypt, almost next to that of his old rival, Wolseley, and near the tombs of Nelson and Wellington.

Roberts was an unlikely soldier. He was a tiny man (only 5ft 3in tall), but sturdily built and very alert. As a 'delicate' child in India, he contracted 'brain fever', which left him blind in his right eye. Even by the end of the Victorian era, Roberts would not have physically qualified to be a soldier, but in mid-nineteenth-century Victorian Britain, someone with good military connections could get away with physical handicaps. He often suffered from digestive ailments and more than once, after concluding a campaign, ill health forced him to return to England.[7]

As most historical figures of note, Roberts had a complicated and even contradictory personality, and this had a bearing on his career. He was intelligent and a man of great charisma; he was friendly in his manners, courteous and renowned for his hospitality. He had many friends, had great influence on almost all who came into contact with him, was a team player and those who knew him well, in most instances, sincerely liked him.[8] He was a skilled organiser, a strict disciplinarian and had the reputation that he got things done. He led by example, especially on the battlefield. He also endeared himself to ordinary soldiers, because of his efforts to improve their social conditions.

Roberts liked parties, but was a teetotaller. Fred and Nora Roberts had a high social standing, and were regarded as charming hosts.[9] They and their children formed a close-knit family. They suffered the loss of four of their six children: three died in infancy and young Freddy after Colenso. Lady Roberts was in her own right a formidable and forceful woman, and it has been alleged that she had excessive influence over her husband, also with regard to military, personnel and other matters. Consequently, she was nicknamed 'Lady Jobs', and there were rumours of a 'petticoat government'.[10] Notwithstanding the fact that Queen Victoria disapproved of officers' wives going to the war zone with their husbands, and Roberts's reluctance to allow it, his own wife and daughters joined him in Bloemfontein in mid-April 1900, and later in Pretoria. They looked after the old field marshal, but the rumours persisted: some believed that Lady Roberts had something to do with the hardening policy towards the civilian Boer population, and also with regard to 'Endless stories, probably many of which are untrue, [that] reach the Queen respecting Lady Roberts' interference and her influence even exerted on the careers of officers in high command in South Africa.'[11] According to Roberts, his wife was a great help to him with regard to visits in hospitals: 'She can discover a great deal more than I can in my periodical visits of inspection.'[12]

Of course, there was also a less attractive side to Bobs's personality. Wolseley regarded him as a dreadful snob;[13] people like the Duke of Cambridge distrusted Roberts, and regarded him as an intriguer and an unscrupulous opportunist.[14] He was indeed shamelessly ambitious, and as a consequence could be manipulative, even devious, and did not shy away from self-advertisement or intrigue. Since the Jameson Raid of 1895–96, Roberts had been hoping that if war broke out in South Africa, he would be placed in command, but Buller was sent out. Roberts was undeterred. In the light of the fact that 'accidents happen', he wrote to Lansdowne, then Secretary of State for War, that if either Buller or Sir George White 'should be incapacitated, I hope you will send me to South Africa'.[15] He openly expressed his misgivings about Buller's ability to defeat the Boers, and in a rather arrogant letter to Lansdowne a week before the Colenso debacle, placed his 'services and . . . experience at the disposal of the Government'. But then he went further to make it clear that 'if it is accepted, I must necessarily be placed in supreme command' because 'the country cannot afford to run any unavoidable risk of failure. A serious reverse in South Africa would endanger the Empire.' The letter was ostensibly private, 'unless, after reading it, you [Lansdowne] think my proposal worthy of consideration, then you are welcome to show it to the Prime Minister, and if you wish, Mr. Chamberlain'.[16]

Having chosen soldiering as a career, Roberts loved war, although he would probably have admitted that essentially war was a terrible thing. He had compassion for the ordinary troops, but if necessary, he would drive his soldiers hard and ordered them to attack an enemy that (with the exception of his last campaign, in South Africa) was always numerically superior. He never suffered huge losses, but if need be, he would order his troops to attack under difficult circumstances. He could also be very harsh. An example to illustrate this is the way he dealt with those accused of being involved with the killing of Cavagnari's mission in Kabul. He would not allow his feelings (or questions relating to the ethics or morality of his orders) to interfere with what he regarded as his duty. Everything taken into account, he was indeed an inspirational leader, even though today one would not necessarily agree with all his decisions and actions. Roberts had many successes, but more often than not, also had luck on his side.

During the suppression of the Indian Mutiny, Roberts was lucky to see action in many clashes and very lucky to survive that brutal conflict with only a slight

Frederick Roberts 173

wound. How different it could have been. Roberts was furious when sent to Natal in 1881 to find that peace had been concluded, and must have thought himself extremely unlucky. But, perhaps, he was, instead, very fortunate, for the mountainous terrain of northern Natal afforded the Boers excellent cover from where they could beat back an advancing conventionally trained army. This happened to Colley in 1881, and again in 1899–1900, when Buller failed on several occasions to break through to Ladysmith; and once more, Roberts was sent as replacement C in C to South Africa – this time to experience relative success.

At the start of the Second Anglo-Afghan War in November 1878, it was Roberts's good fortune to be put in command of the Kurram Field Force, the smallest but best composed of the invading forces. In September 1879, Roberts was fortunate to be in command of the only force that at that stage could move out quickly to avenge Cavagnari's death. After taking Kabul, and as the Afghans prepared for an all-out onslaught against the besieged British cantonment, Roberts received the plan for the attack from a servant; consequently, he was able to take effective counter-measures, and the attack was beaten off.[17] He was also fortunate to have been put in command of the force to march from Kabul to Kandahar (August 1880), as Lieutenant General Donald Stewart could just as well have taken personal command of the relief force. The subsequent march provided Roberts with a unique opportunity to 'redeem' himself after the serious criticisms levelled against him for the way in which he had dealt with the alleged murderers of Cavagnari. And Roberts was lucky that towards the end of 1880, the British public was hungry for good news and for some 'heroic' exploits – his march from Kabul to Kandahar provided just that. The fact that he defeated an Afghan force the day after his arrival in Kandahar provided further reason to celebrate. Roberts realised the relative 'unheroic' nature of his Kabul–Kandahar march:

it surprised me very much to find that the kind people, by whom I was so greatly honoured, invariably appeared to think the march from Kabul to Kandahar was a much greater performance than the advance on Kabul the previous autumn, while, to my mind, the latter operation was in every particular more difficult, more dangerous, and placed upon me as the Commander infinitely more responsibility.[18]

But Roberts will forever be associated with the August 1880 march to Kandahar.

In South Africa, Roberts was very lucky that the Boers were almost obsessed with the siege of three garrisons, because this provided him with the opportunity to consolidate the British position and prepare unhindered for his flank march. Had the Boers exploited their mobility, invaded the British colonies at several places and destroyed the infrastructure, it would have put Roberts in a very difficult position. It was also to Roberts's advantage that he had not been sent out in October 1899. Given the British army's lack of preparedness for war in South Africa,[19] whoever went out first would encounter problems. By the time Roberts was appointed C in C, the British government had realised that more troops were needed. Roberts was also lucky to have had as his first opponent Piet Cronjé, who, although regarded as a great general by the Boers, was indeed in more ways than one not fit to lead an army in a modern war against a large European army. Had the Boers used the Orange River as a natural line of defence, it would have made Roberts's task that more difficult.[20]

After Magersfontein, Cronjé was not in favour of following up the Boer successes with an all-out assault on the British lines of communication, and when such operations did later take place, it was either too small (4–5 January 1900) or too late (February 1900).[21] When De Wet captured the British wagon train at Watervalsdrif on 15 February, Roberts took a calculated risk to continue with his advance. In this way, he didn't lose momentum, but forced his tired troops to go on half-rations until the end of the month.[22] This allowed Roberts to corner and in due course force Cronjé to surrender, but it also further undermined his troops' health and made them more susceptible to contracting typhoid – something that eventually forced a long halt in Bloemfontein.

This halt afforded the Boers the opportunity to consolidate their position and – after a crucial *krijgsraad* (council of war) meeting at Kroonstad on 17 March 1900 – implement a guerrilla type of warfare (thereby for the first time exploiting what was probably their greatest strength, namely mobility). Roberts was very lucky that the Boers did not immediately launch an all-out guerrilla offensive. For example, after his victories at Sannaspos and Mostertshoek, De Wet, strangely enough, opted for a conventional siege of a portion of the Colonial Division at Jammerbergdrif, near Wepener in the south-eastern Free State,[23] instead of destroying the British supply lines south of Bloemfontein, which would have left Roberts in a predicament. On the other hand, if Roberts had sent his cavalry in force to Sannaspos on 31 March, he might have been able to defeat the Boers and nip the guerrilla war in the bud. In due course, however, it became clear that the Boers had met their match in Roberts. They 'knew' Buller, because he had fought in the Anglo-Zulu War (1879), but the 'Indian' Roberts was an enigma to them.

Roberts is generally regarded as a good military leader, on and off the battlefield: he was a successful military administrator; he was a sound strategist in campaigns; and he was an excellent leader of men on the battlefield. However, he never had to take the field against an enemy that was really an equal (for example in Europe), and none of the battles he fought can really be regarded as great; as a matter of fact, his 'greatest' and most decisive battle, at Paardeberg, was more a siege than a battle (and on the first day, when there was an all-out British attack, Roberts was not even present). He is primarily remembered for his march from Kabul to Kandahar, although his march from Kushi to Kabul and from the Modder River via Bloemfontein to Pretoria were of greater military significance. Besides, his Kabul–Kandahar march was a test of endurance, rather than of strategy. However, as will be pointed out in the case study of the Second Anglo-Afghan War, Roberts was very successful in Afghanistan, and was regarded as the saviour of British prestige in the country.

Roberts was basically a Jominian in terms of his military thinking; he believed that the choice of the line of operations was the key to manoeuvring, and wanted to secure strategic objectives as quickly as possible.[24] After arriving in South Africa, Roberts also divided his force, in the sense that he did not abandon Natal to concentrate *all* his troops for a flank march. Interestingly enough, Buller originally also thought of invading the OFS from the west. Roberts had toyed with such an idea as early as 1897, but when he left British shores in December 1899, he still thought in terms of an advance from the south, all along the main railway line to Bloemfontein (i.e. Buller's planned line of advance, after discarding the idea of an advance from the west): 'I have no doubt in my own mind that we should adhere to the original intention of concentrating, South of the Orange River, and working thence by the principal route to Bloemfontein.'[25] But, en route to South Africa, Roberts reverted back to his 1897 strategy, and in due course refined it. He believed (correctly) that an elaborate flank march, based on the strategy of indirect approach, would be the surest way to position his force in such a way that the Boers would have to fight at a disadvantage. He wanted to throw the Boers off balance, relieve Kimberley, dislodge Cronjé from his Magersfontein positions (without a fight), hopefully defeat his force and capture Bloemfontein, and at the same time draw back the republican forces from the Cape Colony and even weaken their defences in Natal.[26]

In all this, Roberts was to a large extent successful, but Boer short-sightedness made his achievements look better than they really were. Roberts took a calculated risk in marching his army some 75 miles across the veldt, but on the eve of the march, he was in an excellent position: he had a huge army at his disposal; his strategy was sound (and had not leaked out); and the Boers were either demoralised after weeks of waiting or, in the case of the Colesberg front, confused, thanks to French's deception manoeuvres, which created the impression that the main British advance would start from there. The eventual successful implementation of Roberts's flank march is a classic example of how the strategy of an indirect approach can be applied. This 'Blitzkrieg' altered the course of the war, and Roberts showed that he could be a daring commander. His forced march from the Modder River to Bloemfontein can be superficially compared to his march from Kushi to Kabul in 1879, or from Kabul to Kandahar in 1880. In all instances, Roberts marched without a line of communication, but in South Africa the idea was to outflank a relatively large Boer army, to capture (not re-take) the enemy's capital and to draw the republican forces back from colonial territory. In South Africa, Roberts proved that he was a good strategist, although he outmanoeuvred the Boers, rather than defeated them. Paardeberg was a turning point, but it was still no Waterloo or Omdurman. It must also be kept in mind that Roberts's advance in South Africa took place in areas with not as much natural cover (for the Boers) as in Natal.

Roberts should only receive partial credit for the ultimate British victory in South Africa. It is true that at Paardeberg he ensured that the Boers could no longer win the war; that he laid the foundation for victory by capturing some 7 per cent of the Boer forces and dislocating them psychologically. But he underestimated the Boers' determination to continue the fight, even with the odds stacked high against them. By not defeating the Boers in the field and allowing them to regroup and successfully make the transition to guerrilla warfare, Roberts was also responsible for laying the foundation for a protracted and costly war.

Poplar Grove (7 March 1900) was supposed to have been a second Paardeberg, perhaps even on a larger scale, with French ordered to cut off the retreat of the 5,000 Boers who had taken up positions in the low-lying hills, while two divisions of infantry would attack from the south and south-west. But French moved too late, and when the Boers saw what was happening, they hastily evacuated their positions and fled eastwards. They had learnt their lesson at Paardeberg. If Presidents Paul Kruger (Transvaal) and Marthinus Steyn (OFS), who were both present, had been captured together with a large force of Boers, it could indeed have meant the end of the war. Roberts's military thinking was sound, but he was let down by his military instruments (i.e. cavalry and infantry).[27] At Abrahamskraal-Driefontein (10 March), Roberts was once again unable to defeat the Boers decisively, and they were able to escape and fight another day. So, Roberts succeeded in driving off the Boers, but did not destroy them, and they could regroup. Yet, after the capture of Bloemfontein, he was probably at the height of his whole military career, having dramatically changed the course of the war in the five weeks since he commenced his advance.

After driving the Boers from their positions at Doornkop and Klipriviersberg, south of Johannesburg (28–29 May 1900), Roberts allowed them to withdraw from the city before he entered it on 31 May. He wanted to avoid street fighting and the destruction of the gold mines, and also believed (with characteristic over-optimism) that the war was all but won. By allowing the Boers to escape, however, he probably added nearly two years to the duration of the conflict.[28] Pretoria was also captured without a fight; but again the commandos were allowed to escape. At Donkerhoek/Diamond Hill (11–12 June 1900), just east of Pretoria, General Louis Botha tried to stop the British advance. This was to have been a decisive British victory. Although the Boers evacuated their positions after heavy British bombardments and attacks, Roberts failed to destroy them, and they were able to fight another day.[29] And so, with characteristic impatience, Roberts kept on advancing, without (after Paardeberg) defeating the Boers in the field, and allowing them to regroup and operate behind the British line of advance, whereas in Afghanistan, after reaching Kandahar, he defeated the Afghans decisively on 1 September 1880. Through common sense and the intelligent application of the principles of war, Roberts indeed changed British fortunes in Afghanistan and South Africa, but was only able to defeat the Afghans and the Boers, not to conquer them.

When Roberts arrived in South Africa, there was a stalemate; by the time he left, both republics were officially in British hands, although in practice, they were only in control as far as their guns could shoot. Roberts indeed outmanoeuvred the Boers strategically, but did not defeat them tactically. The war against space was still far from over. Eventually, it was Kitchener who was ruthlessly successful in South Africa – but only after laying waste to large areas of the war zone, building some 8,000 blockhouses (a process started by Roberts), and expanding the scorched earth policy (once again, a policy that was started by Roberts). How long would Roberts have taken to do his own police work? Would the conditions in the internment camps (a term preferred to the controversial term 'concentration camps') in 1901 have been better under Roberts than under Kitchener? How would Roberts have dealt with local politicians? What kind of peace would Roberts have brought about – and when? What we do know is that '[h]e left behind him a campaign of uncertain duration, but of certain issue'.[30]

Roberts took Colonel George Henderson with him to South Africa as his Chief of Military Intelligence. They discussed the planned tactics in depth, and Roberts's strategy, as implemented, mirrored Henderson's ideas.[31] Although Henderson emphasised the importance of defeating the enemy in the field, he also focussed on the strategic value of threatening the opponent's capital, and that helps to explain why Roberts attached so much value to the rapid capturing of both republican capitals[32] ('I am a firm believer in the maxim that the surest way to disconnect and discourage an enemy is to go straight for their Head Quarters.'[33]) With hindsight, of course, this was a mistake because the Boers did not attach much value to their capitals, could quickly move their headquarters and continued their struggle long after the capitals had been captured. Consequently, after the fall of Pretoria, Roberts's strategy, in a sense, lost its momentum.

Roberts had many troops at his disposal, and yet he was still not able to force his will onto the Boers. After the capture of the Boer capitals and the annexation of both republics, Roberts was convinced that the Boer forces had been reduced to 'a few marauding bands',[34] and that the war 'is degenerating, and has degenerated, into operations carried on in an irregular and irresponsible manner by small, and in many cases, insignificant bodies of men'.[35] Roberts's lack of understanding of the prevailing military situation, is underscored by the fact that he allowed a considerable number of his officers and men to terminate their voluntary engagements, sending a regular unit home and asking soldiers to join the constabulary – in line with the misconception that only police work still remained to be done. These decisions fuelled the (wrong) perception that by the end of 1900 the war was 'practically over'.[36] In practice, the war was about to escalate geographically.

When purely military actions alone did not produce the desired results, Roberts resorted to unconventional methods. In Afghanistan, as was done on the North-West Frontier in India, the British Army from time to time burnt dwellings to pacify the country – in line with the unwritten rule of imperial warfare (against 'non-white' people). The almost summary execution of Cavagnari's alleged killers was most certainly also geared towards having a particular psychological effect on the local population. In South Africa, Roberts was adamant that it should be a white man's war. Initially, he also treated the Boers (the first white people he ever fought against) very leniently, hoping that a policy of conciliation would lead to the pacification of the country. For example, upon entering the OFS in the second week of February 1900, he made it clear that he would ensure the safety of ordinary citizens and their possessions, and in his proclamation of 15 March 1900 he invited the Free Staters to surrender and to take an oath of neutrality, so that they could return to their homes. On 31 May 1900, shortly after entering the Transvaal, a similar type of proclamation was issued.[37] Roberts hoped that, by treating the Boers leniently, they would surrender and the war would end. These and the following proclamations can, with hindsight, be regarded as a form of psychological warfare, and initially proved to be quite successful; for example, from March to July 1900, some 13,900 Free State and Transvaal burghers voluntarily surrendered.[38]

But Roberts underestimated the power of Afrikaner nationalism, because several Boers who surrendered, took up arms again. Where Boers who voluntarily surrendered previously could settle on their farms, they were now taken into custody, and in a proclamation dated 1 June 1900, Roberts said that those Boers who did not surrender would henceforth be regarded as rebels.[39] However, these threats did not intimidate those Boers who believed in their cause; they referred to Roberts's proclamations as 'paper bombs', and guerrilla activities increased. Consequently, Roberts gradually changed his attitude and strategy, and according to the proclamations of 16 and 19 June 1900, if a railway line was attacked or damaged, Boer houses in the vicinity would be burnt.[40] Roberts, in due course, became convinced that only 'severe measures' would subdue the Boers and that there had to be 'no mercy'.[41] He also made it clear that if burghers did not surrender, 'they and their families will be starved'.[42] What Roberts did in fact admit by issuing these ill-conceived proclamations was that he was unable to find a military solution to the problems his army faced. Soon, the destruction of Boer property became part and parcel of the British military strategy, with its concomitant internment camps, where those Boer (and black) civilians who had been left destitute by the scorched earth policy were kept – and where by war's end some 28,000 white (and at least 23,000, but probably many more black) civilians had died, leaving a trail of trauma and bitterness. The first official 'refugee camp' for whites was established at Mafeking in July 1900, primarily to house Boers who had surrendered voluntarily, plus their families. Before the end of 1900, eight other camps for whites were established.[43] So, Roberts's strategy in South Africa evolved from sporadic farm-burning to a fully fledged scorched earth policy, which Kitchener would later on expand even further.

Roberts's assessment of the situation in South Africa when he left in December 1900, also with regard to what remained to be done to end the war, was over-optimistic and did not tally with the situation at grassroots level. By burning farms, Roberts had – ironically – also removed an important reason why many

Boers drifted away from commandos; i.e. to look after their property and loved ones. As the guerrilla war intensified, and when the proclamations, and even the resulting destruction of property, did not have the desired effect, Roberts resorted to other forms of 'psychological warfare'. Boer women and children were sent to the Boer lines in the eastern Transvaal to put pressure on the republican forces to surrender, but to no avail. Roberts sent several letters to Louis Botha (Commandant General of the Transvaal forces), trying to convince him that further resistance was futile. He also offered Boer generals salaries, should they surrender; for example, £10,000 a year to Botha and Koos de la Rey, which was rejected with contempt, and strengthened the Boers' resolve to continue the struggle.[44]

Even Roberts had to admit that 'the guerrilla aspect that the war has assumed is an infinitely more troublesome phase of war than which has gone before'.[45] Eventually it was the British forces that were caught physically and psychologically unprepared for the new kind of warfare that the Boers waged from the end of March 1900 onwards. Roberts underestimated the Boers' resolve and ability to continue their resistance. But, everything taken into account, it is unlikely that any other general would have fared better.

On one terrain Roberts had full control. Through the years, he cultivated good relationships with politicians and had the support of his political masters. Writing to the Secretary in the Foreign Department, A C Lyall, from Kabul on 6 August 1880 (i.e. on of the eve of the start of his famous march, but referring to his march to Kabul the previous year), Roberts wrote: 'When I accepted the command of the Kabul Field Force last September [1879] it was on the understanding that I was to be supreme in political, as well as military, matters.'[46] With regard to the war in South Africa, Lansdowne gave Roberts a free hand and protected him from interference by other politicians. When Roberts's initial moderate policy with regard to the Boers did not produce the envisaged results, Lansdowne assured him that if he adapted a tougher stance, he (Lansdowne) would support and defend him.[47]

Roberts's participation in many battles in India (1857–58), his numerous mentions in dispatches and VC is the material on which a patriotic press and popular magazines feed and from which legends are made. His storybook career in India focussed press attention on him, and when he was a commanding officer, afforded him the opportunity to manipulate the media to suit his own interests. In Afghanistan, Roberts expelled a reporter who was critical of his actions,[48] while keeping and rewarding those reporters who were positively inclined towards his work. Roberts's reputation to a large extent derived from his Kabul–Kandahar march, and was created by the pro-Roberts media. By 1878, the electric telegraph and cable had been in use for some years, which meant that the dispatches of commanders and war correspondents could be transmitted quickly. Roberts used this technology to his own advantage, for example, to ensure that his own dispatches were transmitted before those of anyone else.[49] At the end of 1899, a number of reporters accompanied Roberts to South Africa. He was, once again, determined to control and 'manage' the press, and was successful, because most of the reports that were published about his campaign by 'the brilliant band of War Correspondents who accompany this Army',[50] were favourable. Rudyard Kipling's famous music–hall ballad 'Bobs',[51] of course, also ensured Roberts public exposure, fame and concomitant endearment and hero–worship – hero–worship that went back all the way to the war of 1878–80 in Afghanistan.

The Second Anglo–Afghan War, 1878–80[52]

On 12 April 1876, Lord Lytton became Viceroy of India. By this time there was growing concern in Britain about the possibility of Russian expansion in Central Asia, especially in the light of the fact that Sher Ali (the Amir of Afghanistan) was (mistakenly) suspected of being an ally of the Russians. While some officials in India believed in a policy of 'masterly inactivity' (i.e. non–interference), Roberts and others believed that a 'forward policy' (i.e. more militant, pre–emptive action) was the correct approach.[53] Lytton bought into the latter; he and Roberts became close friends, and in April 1878 he appointed Roberts as the commander of the Punjab Frontier Force. On 11 August 1878, a Russian mission arrived in Kabul, capital of Afghanistan, but was withdrawn soon after. When in September 1878, Sher Ali refused to allow a similar British mission to take up position in Kabul, an apology was demanded. When no answer was received, Britain declared war on Afghanistan on 21 November 1878.

During the first phase of the war, three British columns invaded Afghanistan. The smallest column, composed of excellent troops and known as the Kurram Field Force (116 officers and 6,549 men, with 18 guns), was commanded by Roberts. He left Kohat on the Indus River, quickly occupied the Kurram Valley and moved up to the Shutargardan Pass. On 2 December 1878, after a daring night march, Roberts (3,200 men with 13 guns) defeated an Afghan force (about 4,000 men with 11 guns) at the Peiwar Kotal, at the northern exit of the Kurram Valley. The Afghans were in excellent positions on the Kotal heights. Roberts broke the traditional military rules by dividing his small force, and with an excellent flanking movement took the Peiwar Kotal with 2,300 men, while the rest of his force attacked the enemy front. Roberts was successful because he did careful reconnaissance, correctly evaluated the terrain and situation from a tactical point of view, was prepared to take a risk in order to achieve surprise and attacked from an unexpected quarter (as he later did in South Africa, albeit on a much larger strategic scale). This was a dramatic and decisive victory, the first major British victory of the war, and it ensured the success of the British invasion. Sher Ali fled, leaving his son, Yakub Khan, on the throne. After Peiwar Kotal, Roberts started his expedition into the Kost Valley on 2 January 1879 and occupied it. If and when his camp or soldiers were attacked, he had the nearby villages looted and burnt, as was the custom in colonial warfare; a precursor to what happened in South Africa more than two decades later.

The first phase of the war ended on 26 May 1879, when the Treaty of Gandamak was signed. Roberts returned to Simla, having fought brilliantly against superior forces – his reputation as a national hero firmly established. In the meantime, Major Sir Louis Cavagnari, a friend of Roberts, was sent to Kabul as Britain's envoy, where he and his entourage were murdered by a mob in the British Residency on 3 September 1879. By that time only Roberts's Kurram Field Force was still available to be re-activated, and henceforth it was known as the Kabul Field Force (about 6,600 men with 18 guns). Roberts led his force from Ali Khel into central Afghanistan. He planned to concentrate his force at Kushi, some 40 miles from Kabul, from where he would march on the city. Roberts's military operations during the second phase of the war can be divided into four sub phases:[54] (1) The march from Kushi (which started on 30 September 1879) to occupy Kabul (9 October); (2) the attempts to quell the Afghan opposition, which culminated in him being besieged in Kabul; (3) the preparations for a spring campaign; and (4) the march from Kabul to Kandahar (8–31 August 1880) and the battle outside the city (1 September).

Roberts's force marched through unsurveyed, mountainous and hostile country. Just before reaching Kabul, Roberts met in battle, on 6 October, a large Afghan force under the command of Nek Mohammed Khan, on the Charasiab heights. Roberts had at least 3,800 British and Indian troops with 16 guns (plus 2 Gatlings) under his command, against probably about 12,000 Afghans with 20 guns. Roberts reached Charasiab village on the evening of 5 October. The next day, he skilfully dislodged the entrenched Afghan force by means of a flank movement, and followed it up with a cavalry pursuit. It was the first time that the British army used the relatively speaking new-technology Gatling guns in action. The road to Kabul was now open, thanks to Roberts's willingness to take a risk in an effort to ensure surprise. On 9 October 1879, a triumphant Roberts entered Kabul, and Yakub Khan was removed from the throne. This campaign was indeed a turning point in Roberts's career.

Roberts made a tactically wise decision not to use the formidable Bala Hissar Fortress overlooking Kabul as his base, but rather the as yet unfinished rectangular military cantonment at Sherpur, a mile north of the city centre. His first task now was to avenge the death of his friend Cavagnari. This he did swiftly and brutally, which led to much controversy, especially because the testimonies were not always very reliable, and since it was clear that a spirit of vengeance influenced the judgements. At least eighty-seven Afghans were executed (others were shot when they resisted being taken into custody), which soon led to an outcry in the British media and caused a political storm back home, raising doubts about Roberts's political judgement. Lytton, however, had made it clear to him that 'it is not justice in the ordinary sense, but retribution that you have to administer on reaching Kabul . . . . What is required is a prompt and impressive example . . . Your object should be to strike terror, and to strike it swiftly and deeply.'[55]

In the meantime, the Afghan forces opposed to British rule, reorganised, and 'jihad' was proclaimed. Some 100,000 Afghans answered the call. When Roberts realised that large numbers of Afghan tribesmen were gathering to the north of Kabul, he sent a force to catch those Afghans in a pincer movement. However, due to a lack of effective intelligence, Roberts did not realise how strong the Afghans were. His soldiers fought several days in and around the Chardeh Plain, without any real success; as a matter of fact, on 11 December, the British were nearly defeated and were lucky to be able to fall back to the Sherpur cantonment. The Afghans then re-occupied Kabul. This led to Roberts being besieged in Sherpur (15–23 December 1879). On 21 December, he ordered Brigadier General Charles Gough to speed up his march from Jagdalak to Kabul. This provoked a huge onslaught against Roberts's force. On 23 December 1879, just before dawn, the Afghan forces (about 50,000) under Mohammed Jan launched an all-out attack. The Afghans stormed the west, south and east walls of the cantonment but were driven back, and Roberts then ordered a counter-attack. The Afghans were thoroughly defeated in the ensuing battle. British and Indian casualties amounted to 33; the Afghans left about 3,000 dead on the battlefield. Roberts used Gatling guns and the new breech-loading Martini and Snider rifles with great effect. After Roberts repulsed the onslaught, he reoccupied the city of Kabul.

At the beginning of May 1880, Lieutenant General Donald Stewart took overall command in Kabul. While negotiations were underway to find a peaceful solution to the 'Afghan problem', a British force was severely defeated at Maiwand by Ayub Khan on 27 July 1880, some 35 miles west of Kandahar, and the garrison in the latter city (5,000 men, commanded by Major General J M Primrose) was then besieged. Roberts was ordered to relieve Kandahar, while another force under Major General R Phayre was ordered to march from Quetta to Kandahar. Of course, Roberts would try his best to get there first, in what was also referred to as the 'Race for the Peerage'. Consequently, his troops would march with as little kit as possible and only light mountain guns were taken with the force. On 7 August 1880, Roberts moved his hand-picked task force (basically a flying column) of 273 British officers, 2,562 British and 7,151 Indian troops, plus 18 guns, out of the Bala Hissar Fortress to Sherpur, and the next day the march proper began. Instead of taking the direct road via Maidan, the longer route via the Logar Valley was chosen, because it was deemed to be safer. Conditions were difficult: Roberts pushed his men as hard as possible; they marched without a line of communication; days were extremely hot, and nights very cold; there were dust storms, and a scarcity of water; many soldiers fell ill, including Roberts, who suffered from fever, headaches and constant nausea (and had to be carried in a doolie). On 27 August, news was received that Ayub Khan had abandoned the siege, when he heard of Roberts's approaching force. Kandahar was reached on 31 August. The march proper took place from 8–31 August; i.e. twenty-four days, during which time only two full days were used to rest the troops. A distance of 324 miles was covered; i.e. on each of the twenty-two marching days, an average of 14.7 miles were covered. There was no fighting during the march, but many casualties due to illness.[56]

After Roberts entered Kandahar on 31 August 1880, he resolved, notwithstanding his ill health, to attack Ayub Khan's force as soon as possible. The next day, 1 September 1880, Roberts moved out with approximately 11,000 men and 32 guns. Ayub Khan had about 13,000 men, also with 32 guns, under his command. The battle of Kandahar commenced at about 0930 at Baba Wali, some 2 miles north-west of the city, where the Afghans had their camp. The British charged the Afghan positions, drove them off and captured their camp and all their artillery. This was the most decisive victory of the Second Anglo–Afghan War. Roberts's force suffered 35 killed and 213 wounded; the Afghans lost at least 600 killed, but their total casualties were perhaps as high as 3,500. After the battle, Roberts collapsed, and on 8 September 1880, a medical board decided that he needed to go home.

Of all the British officers involved in the Second Anglo–Afghan War, Roberts did most of the fighting. As indicated earlier, he correctly pointed out that his march with the Kurram Field Force to Kabul in October 1879 was in more than one way a more important (and much more difficult and risky) military feat (as was Stewart's march from Kandahar to Kabul in April–May 1880). However, his renowned march 'from Kabul to Kandahar', with its alliterative ring, captured the imagination of the British public. The British army's defeat at Maiwand had refocussed the attention of the British public on Afghanistan, and Roberts's march (re-)attracted the attention of the British press and public like nothing else in the war had done.[57] The effect of his march can be likened to the way in which the defence of Rorke's Drift in the Anglo–Zulu War of 1879 counterbalanced the defeat suffered by the British at Isandlwana. Almost overnight, Roberts became a popular public hero, but also a rival (and logical successor) to Wolseley, who at that stage was QMG of the British army.

To defeat the Afghans militarily was one thing; to control them was something else. Fearing that they could once again become victims of Afghan retaliation (as was the case towards the end of the First Anglo–Afghan War), the Liberal Party that came to power in Britain in March 1881 decided to withdraw from Afghanistan. So the Second Anglo–Afghan War was indeed a Pyrrhic victory for Britain, and somewhat of an embarrassment – and it destroyed or tarnished several military and political careers. For 'Bobs Bahadur' (Bobs the Hero/the Brave), however, it was a triumph. He was fêted as the saviour of British prestige in Afghanistan, and was showered with honours and rewards. The Kabul–Kandahar march was the defining event of the Second Anglo–Afghan War and Roberts's career. It set him up for the important role he was to play in India and elsewhere in the years to follow; more than twenty years later, another of his marches would catch the British public's imagination and world media's attention, when he outmanoeuvred the Boer citizen armies in South Africa.

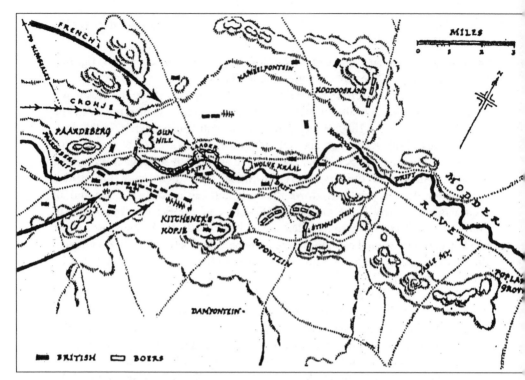

Plan of the battle of Paardeberg, 1900. (From David James, *Lord Roberts*, London: Hollis & Carter, 1954)

Paardeberg, 1900[58]

In the course of the twenty years that separated Roberts's role at Kandahar and Paardeberg, the infantryman's bayonet had been superseded by a modern rifle's bullet, the invention of smokeless gunpowder had made it more difficult to pinpoint the enemy's position and there had been an enormous increase in the range of guns and rifles – all the result of new technologies, with concomitant tactical implications for command and control in the battle space. As Roberts wrote to Lansdowne from Paardeberg: 'Another point which affects military operations nowadays is the long range of modern weapons . . .'.[59] In South Africa, Roberts for the first time faced a white foe, armed with modern rifles and artillery.

Paardeberg (the Dutch for 'Horses('s) Mountain'; in Afrikaans 'Perdeberg') lies just north of the Modder River, some 25 miles south-east of Kimberley and 70 miles west of Bloemfontein. The battle with and siege of General Pieter (Piet) Arnoldus Cronjé's force that took place during 18–27 February 1900, centred around the Boer laager at and near Vandisiedrif, which is some 5 miles north-east upstream from Paardeberg, although the latter mountain, or rather hill, gave its name to this turning point in the Anglo–Boer War. Here forces led by two completely dissimilar men clashed. On the one hand was the huge professional and conventionally trained army of Roberts, a man who had made a name for himself internationally. And then there was Cronjé, a man with little formal education, who led a citizen army made up of ordinary burghers (citizens) with no formal military training. His 'fame' as a military commander rested on the fact that in 1896 he defeated Dr L S Jameson and his raiders.

At 2000, on 15 February 1900, at last realising that the British forces were outflanking him, Cronjé gave the order for his army (more than 4,000 men, many on foot, and 400 heavily laden wagons) to start moving away from Bossiespan, and to trek in the direction of Bloemfontein. His idea was to take up new defensive positions somewhere along the way, in an effort to stop Roberts's advance. In the meantime, French, after relieving Kimberley on 15 February,[60] was ordered by Roberts to take his cavalry to Koedoesrand in an effort to cut off Cronjé's line of retreat. When Cronjé received notice of French's movements, and with mounted infantry attacking the Boer rearguard, he decided to cross the Modder River at Vandisiedrif; but as the first wagons were about to move, the twelve guns that French had positioned north of the drift opened fire, and the Boers were forced to take cover. The Boer convoy was trapped, and Cronjé decided to try and stave off British attacks at Vandisiedrif as effectively as possible until relief arrived.

In the night of 17/18 February, the Boers dug in as best they could on the northern banks of the Modder River. In the meantime, Roberts had contracted influenza and stayed in bed at his headquarters in the town of Jacobsdal, some 30 miles from Paardeberg. In South Africa, Thomas Kelly-Kenny held the local rank of lieutenant general, while Kitchener was only a substantive major general.[61] To clear up the command issue, a message was sent to Roberts at Jacobsdal, who sent a message back indicating that Kitchener's orders were to be regarded as his (Roberts's) orders.[62] So, Kitchener was placed in command of the forces at Paardeberg. (By not giving Kitchener precise orders, Roberts has to take some of the blame for what happened in the next 24 hours.) Kitchener had at his disposal at least 15,000 soldiers with more than 50 guns. Fearing a Cronjé break-out and/or attacks by other Boer forces, he wanted to defeat the trapped Boers as soon as possible – and, of course, be honoured as the man who defeated Cronjé. For the first time in his career, Kitchener led troops in a battle against a white foe. He nevertheless threw caution to the wind, as well as the lessons learnt until that time in the war.

At 0300, on Sunday 18 February 1900, Kitchener ordered an attack from the east. At 0630, the British troops started frontal attacks northwards from Oskoppies (later referred to as Kitchener's Kopje) under cover of a heavy artillery bombardment. With only four guns and a pom-pom,[63] the Boer artillery was unable to neutralise the British guns, and soon many Boer wagons were on fire. Most of the burghers were unharmed in their shallow trenches and dug-outs, and when the attacking British troops were within range, they were stopped. Kitchener's attacks from the south and west were unsuccessful. He then ordered another attack from the east, but that also failed. By mid-afternoon, with the British force's poorly co-ordinated attacks having been beaten back, it seemed as if Kitchener (who was galloping up and down in a frenzied way) had lost control over the situation, shouting orders that led to more confusion.

At 1530, Colonel O C Hannay, following orders from Kitchener, led a final charge from the north-east against the Boer positions, taking only about fifty men with him on what he quite rightly regarded as a suicidal mission. They got to about 250yd from the laager, when they were cut down, Hannay being among those who were killed. In the light of the 'Black Week' defeats, no responsible commanding officer would have ordered frontal attacks across the open veldt against well dug-in Boers. But Kitchener did ensure that Cronjé's force became immobile: many oxen and horses were killed, and all the other oxen and many horses were captured by the British. In a sense, 18 February sealed Cronjé's fate. Total British casualties amounted to 303 killed, 906 wounded and 61 captured; i.e. more were lost than on any other single day of the war, making 18 February 1900 the bloodiest day of the conflict. In the laager, no more than seventy Boers became casualties. It was the first and last time that Kitchener lost a battle. He was not necessarily wrong in deciding to attack the Boers on 18 February, but he failed to prepare properly for the battle.[64]

Several Boer commandos made every possible effort to relieve the Boer laager. On the afternoon of 18 February, Generals Christiaan de Wet and Philip Botha arrived from the south and drove the British from Oskoppies, adding to Kitchener's woes. So, an escape corridor had indeed been opened for the trapped Boer force, but the indecisive Cronjé refused to move. When news of the 18 February debacle reached Roberts at Jacobsdal, and when he heard that Kitchener planned to renew his attacks the next day, he found it necessary to get out of his sickbed at 0400 on 19 February and go to Paardeberg as quickly as possible in an effort to save the situation. Roberts arrived at the battlefield at about 1000, just in time to stop another frontal attack, which Kitchener was (against the advice of his fellow officers) about to launch. Roberts took stock of the situation, and – always fearful of incurring high losses – decided to settle for a siege, and concomitant bombardment. And on 22 February, Roberts sent Kitchener away to Naauwpoort, and from there to De Aar, to ensure that the main railway lines northwards from the Cape would be secure; and never again put him in charge of a pitched battle situation.

Roberts demanded unconditional surrender, which an indignant Cronjé rejected at 1300, on 19 February. Soon afterwards, Roberts ordered a heavy bombardment of the laager with the approximately eighty guns he now had at his disposal. The bombardment continued intermittently throughout the night of 19/20 February, and by the afternoon of 20 February the last Boer gun was put out of action. However, even if Roberts wanted to renew his attacks, it was not possible, because his troops were exhausted and hungry (they had to make do with half-rations, a result of the loss of Roberts's transport at Watervalsdrif), field hospitals were overflowing and many officers were dead or wounded. The British bombardment continued on 21 February. The besieged Boers had to contend with the danger and terrible noise of incessant bombardment (which left them without sleep), the stench of the rotting carcasses of animals, the lack of sanitation in the confined space of the laager, thirst due to the lack of clean water and hunger because there was no time to prepare meals safely. And then there was the plight of the wounded. Many started to doubt whether there was any purpose in continued resistance.

On 22 February, Cronjé repeated a request for medical assistance, but Roberts denied it – his own army was beginning to suffer from a lack of adequate medical support. By 23 February, morale was not only low in the laager, but also in the ranks of those Boers who were outside and who were supposed to create a breakthrough to enable Cronjé to escape. Even De Wet had problems in rallying his burghers for another attack, which, when it eventually took place, failed (23 February). On the night of 24/25 February, De Wet sent his champion scout, Danie Theron, to Cronjé on a mission that took him through the British lines. Theron explained to Cronjé that De Wet was prepared to risk one last attack against the besieging forces, on condition that Cronjé attacked from the inside and tried to break out. Everything taken into consideration, it was probably asking too much from the exhausted trapped burghers (who were also, in most instances, left without horses). Among the ordinary burghers there was in any case little will left to continue resistance. Roberts's tactics were having the envisaged effect.

The British artillery, guided by information supplied by an officer sent up in a (relatively new technology) balloon used for aerial observation, destroyed a 'chain-bridge' before anyone could cross. During the night of 25/26 February, a disappointed Theron slipped back through the British lines. The British bombardment continued on 26 February. Later that night, the British launched renewed attacks, and by sunrise on 27 February, some soldiers were only about 40yd away from the Boer perimeter. Even before the British artillery resumed their bombardment, a number of white flags were displayed along the Boer lines. By 0600, Cronjé had no other choice but to hoist a white flag above his headquarters. He then sent a note to Roberts, indicating that he surrendered unconditionally. At 0700, on 27 February 1900, the nineteenth anniversary of the Boer victory at Majuba (which had briefly brought Roberts to South Africa as a replacement for the killed Major General Colley), Cronjé met Roberts (girded with his Kandahar sword) at the latter's headquarters, and formally surrendered.

Over and above the casualties sustained on 18 February during Kitchener's abortive attempts to take the Boer laager Omdurman-style, Roberts's force had lost 239 killed, 1,095 wounded, 67 missing and 2 captured. Cronjé's total casualties (i.e. in the laager, including those suffered on 18 February) were at least 74 killed and 187 wounded, while 2,592 Transvaalers and 1,327 Orange Free Staters surrendered on 27 February and were sent to camps abroad. (The sixty-two captured women and children were soon set free.)

Paardeberg was in more ways than one Roberts's greatest battle. Here he commanded more troops than in any of the battles he fought; for the first time he faced a white army armed with modern weapons; the battlefield was larger than any of those on which he had fought previously; the tactical challenges were huge (a famous Boer general was well dug in, which made conventional infantry and cavalry attacks costly; a famous upcoming Boer general was present outside the battlefield, trying to force open an escape route); and he won after a ten-day siege, inflicting the largest defeat ever on the Boer armies, proving that his indirect strategy was indeed successful, and (with hindsight) ensuring that although the Boers could still prolong the war, they could probably no longer win it. But, interestingly enough, Roberts was not present when Cronjé was trapped (17 February) or when the heaviest fighting took place (18 February). Had Roberts been there, the battle of 18 February might not have taken place. Nearly 300 miles away from the battlefield, news of Cronjé's surrender inspired Buller's troops, and late on that same day (27 February) a breakthrough was at long last effectuated at Pietershoogte. The next day, Ladysmith was relieved. So, the psychological effect of Roberts's victory was far-reaching; and strategically the initiative was securely back in British hands (that is, until the guerrilla war gained momentum). One can argue that Roberts ensured the ultimate British victory by defeating Cronjé, and yet Paardeberg also set the scene for a prolonged conflict, because by drinking contaminated water from the Modder River at or in the vicinity of the battlefield, Roberts's soldiers were infected with typhoid. Many of them died after the capture of Bloemfontein, and this disease, together with other factors, forced Roberts to halt for seven weeks before he could continue his advance, allowing the Boers to regroup and launch the guerrilla war. It is therefore an open question whether Roberts's success should indeed be measured in terms of his military achievements at Paardeberg, or rather in terms of the enforced halt in Bloemfontein – at least partially the consequence of the 'Paardeberg virus'.

If Cronjé had surrendered earlier, Kitchener would probably still have received some of the credit, having rendered Cronjé's force immobile on 18 February. However, the fact that the siege continued for another nine days created expectations in the war zone and abroad, focussed attention on Paardeberg, and in a sense made Roberts's eventual success all the greater, more dramatic and more important. And with Cronjé's surrender, the Boer southern front collapsed, and soon the Boers also withdrew from around Ladysmith. Roberts had indeed, through the brilliant application of the strategy of indirect approach, brought about a turning point in the war, cementing his popular image as an outstanding field commander, although – as pointed out earlier – that is probably an oversimplification of his true value as a commander.

The man, whose physique made him an unlikely career soldier, indeed became one of the most famous men of his time and was regarded by many as the best general of the Victorian era. Roberts was a good administrator, a serious student of his profession, a hard worker and he led the British Army and soldiers from many British colonies with zeal. He was quite modern in his approach to military problems, a good tactician and at times a sound strategist, especially when he was inspired to do the unexpected (implementing an indirect strategy, for example).

He had a genuine concern for the welfare of the ordinary troops, but did not shirk from driving them hard and relentlessly when circumstances demanded it. He firmly believed in the British Empire and all that it stood for, to a large extent embodied that empire, did not question imperial ideals (though it often had serious detrimental effects on the victims of imperialism, be it Afghan, Boer or other civilians) and went out of his way to further the goals and prestige of his empire, and of his Queen and Empress; in the process, of course, he also furthered his own career and fulfilled his consuming personal ambitions. He was a popular imperial hero, and widely admired in Britain, India and elsewhere: the British press and public were convinced he was a successful commanding officer, and they sung his praises; and the government, most of the time, agreed or played along. But Roberts knew how to manipulate the media and public opinion, and had the right political connections at the right time. A critical analysis of his campaigns and battles makes it clear that essentially he was not always that effective – sometimes he was just lucky, very lucky. But how many military leaders are not?

In the low-intensity conflict environment that characterised most of Queen Victoria's 'small wars', Roberts was relatively speaking a good commander, and probably the most popular and best-loved of his Queen's many generals. He was devoted to his profession, an admired and gallant soldier, a bold leader and a role model for many. But his fame was primarily based on three marches: Kushi to Kabul, Kabul to Kandahar and from the Modder River via Paardeberg and Bloemfontein to Pretoria. These marches were typical of the 'small campaigns' in which Queen Victoria's generals fought.

Bibliography

The standard biography is still David James, *Lord Roberts* (London: Hollis & Carter, 1954). Earlier, shortly after Roberts died, the biography by Sir George Forrest, *The Life of Lord Roberts, KG, VC* (London: Cassell, 1914) appeared. At the height of his success in South Africa, 1900, the work by Violet Brooke-Hunt, *Lord Roberts: A Biography* (London: James Nisbet, n.d.) was published. Other biographies include Charles Rathbone Low, *Major-General Sir Frederick S Roberts* (London: W H Allen, 1883); Horace G Groser, *Field-Marshal Lord Roberts, VC, KP, GCB, GCSI, GCIE* (London: Andrew Melrose, 1900); the richly illustrated biography by J Maclaren Cobban, *The Life and Deeds of Earl Roberts*, 4 vols (Edinburgh: T C & E Jack, 1901); Harold F B Wheeler, *The Story of Lord Roberts* (London: George G Harrap, 1915); H de Watteville, *Lord Roberts* (London and Glasgow: Blackie, 1938) and W H Hannah, *Bobs: Kipling's General. The Life of Field-Marshal Earl Roberts of Kandahar, VC* (London: Leo Cooper, 1972). As far as Roberts's role in India is concerned, a basic source will always be his autobiography, *Forty-one Years in India: From Subaltern to Commander-in-Chief*, 2 vols (London: Richard Bentley, 1897), which was reprinted thirty-four times, translated into German, Italian and Urdu and transcribed into Braille. As far as his correspondence in India is concerned, see Brian Robson, ed., *Roberts in India: The Military Papers of Field Marshal Lord Roberts 1876–1893* (Stroud: Alan Sutton Publishing for Army Records Society, 1993), and for his correspondence with regard to the Anglo-Boer War, see André Wessels, ed., *Lord Roberts and the War in South Africa 1899–1902* (Stroud: Sutton Publishing for Army Records Society, 2000). The best recent study of the Second Anglo-Afghan War, in which Roberts's role is discussed in detail, is Brian Robson, *The Road to Kabul: The Second Afghan War 1878–81* (London: Arms and Armour Press, 1986). Other sources on that war that discuss Roberts's role in detail include J A S Colquhoun, *With the Kurram Field Force, 1878–79* (London: W H Allen, 1881); Howard Hensman, *The Afghan War of 1879–80*, 2nd edn (London: W H Allen, 1882); Archibald Forbes, *The Afghan Wars 1839–42 and 1878–80* (London: Seeley, 1892); C M MacGregor (compiler), *The Second Afghan War*, vols 1–3 (Simla: Government Central Branch Press, 1885), vols 4–6 (Calcutta: Superintendent of Government Printing, 1886); H B Hanna, *The Second Afghan War 1878–79–80: Its Causes, its Conduct and its Consequences*, 3 vols (Westminster: Constable, 1899–1910) and T A Heathcote, *The Afghan Wars 1839–1919* (London: Osprey, 1980). His role during the Anglo-Boer War is discussed in detail in, inter alia, J H Breytenbach, *Die Geskiedenis van die Tweede Vryheidsoorlog in Suid-Afrika, 1899–1902* (Pretoria: Die Staatsdrukker), the official (uncompleted) Afrikaner history of the war – see especially vols 4 (1977), 5 (1983) and 6 (1996); L S Amery, ed., *The Times History of the War in South Africa 1899–1902* (London: Sampson Low, Marston), especially vols 3 (1905) and 4 (1906); and Frederick Maurice (compiler), *History of the War in South Africa 1899–1902* (London: Hurst and Blackett) – also known as the 'Official History' – vols 1 (1906), 2 (1907) and 3 (1908); Keith Surridge, *Managing the South African War, 1899–1902: Politicians v. Generals* (Woodbridge: The Boydell Press, 1998) and Denis Judd and Keith Surridge, *The Boer War* (London: John Murray, 2002). Chapters on Roberts as military commander have been written by Byron Farwell in his *Eminent Victorian Soldiers: Seekers of Glory* (New York and London: W W Norton, 1985), pp. 147–91 and Peter Trew, *The Boer War Generals* (Johannesburg: Jonathan Ball, 1999), pp. 45–87, while there is a recent assessment by Rodney Atwood, 'So Single-minded a Man and So Noble-hearted a Soldier: Field Marshal Earl Roberts of Kandahar, Waterford and Pretoria', in Ian F W Beckett, ed., *Victorians at War: New Perspectives* (Society for Army Historical Research Special Publication No. 16, 2007), pp. 59–74.

Notes

1. David James, *Lord Roberts* (London: Hollis & Carter, 1954), p. 176; Byron Farwell, *Eminent Victorian Soldiers: Seekers of Glory* (New York and London: W W Norton, 1985), pp. 178–79.
2. Unless otherwise indicated, the biographical sketch on this and the following pages is based, inter alia, on James, *Roberts*; the article on Roberts by Brian Robson in H C G Matthews and Brian Harrison, eds, *Oxford Dictionary of National Biography: From the Earliest Times to the Year 2000*, vol. 47 (Oxford: Oxford University Press, 2004) (hereafter DNB), pp. 156–61; George Forrest, *The Life of Lord Roberts, KG, VC* (London: Cassell, 1914), as well as the other biographies mentioned in the bibliography.
3. The brief review of the war, and Roberts's role, is based on, inter alia, L S Amery, ed., *The Times History of the War in South Africa 1899–1902*, vols 3–4 (London: Sampson Low, Marston, 1905–6); Frederick Maurice, compiler, *History of the War in South Africa 1899–1902*, vols 1–3 (London: Hurst and Blackett, 1906–8); J H Breytenbach, *Die Geskiedenis van die Tweede Vryheidsoorlog in Suid-Afrika, 1899–1902*, vols 1–6 (Pretoria: Die Staatsdrukker, 1969–96); *The War in South Africa* (also known as the *German Official Account of the War in South Africa* (vol. 1 translated by W H H Waters, vol. 2 translated by Herbert du Cane; London: John Murray, 1904 and 1906); Thomas Pakenham, *The Boer War* (London: Weidenfeld & Nicolson, 1979); Bill Nasson, *The South African War 1899–1902* (London: Arnold, 1999) and Denis Judd and Keith Surridge, *The Boer War* (London: John Murray, 2002).
4. British Library (hereafter BL), Lansdowne Mss, L(5)48, Roberts to Lansdowne, 7 June 1900 – published in André Wessels, ed., *Lord Roberts and the War in South Africa 1899–1902* (Stroud: Sutton Publishing for Army Records Society, 2000), pp. 97–100.

5. For more on the Curragh incident and Roberts's role see, for example, Ian F W Beckett, ed., *The Army and the Curragh Incident, 1914* (London: The Bodley Head for Army Records Society, 1986).

6. Imperial War Museum, L A E Rice-Davies Mss, 77/78/3, programme of Lord Roberts's funeral.

7. James, *Roberts*, pp. 6, 53, 163–64; Farwell, *Eminent Victorian Soldiers*, pp. 148–49; Lord Roberts, *Forty-one Years in India: From Subaltern to Commander-in-Chief*, 2 vols (London: Richard Bentley, 1897), I, p. 411 and II, p. 373.

8. Farwell, *Eminent Victorian Soldiers*, pp. 156–57, 179.

9. Ibid., pp. 159, 182.

10. DNB, 47, p. 157; Ian F W Beckett, 'Women and Patronage in the Late Victorian Army', *History* 85, 279 (2000), 478–79.

11. BL, Lansdowne Mss, L(5)44, Bigge to Roberts, 18 August 1900 – published in Wessels, ed., *Roberts*, pp. 123–24.

12. Royal Archives, VIC/P12/58, Roberts to the Queen, 21 August 1900 – published in Wessels, ed., *Roberts*, pp. 124–26.

13. Farwell, *Eminent Victorian Soldiers*, p. 182.

14. DNB, 47, p. 158.

15. BL, Lansdowne Mss, L(5)47, Roberts to Lansdowne, 22 October 1899 – published in Wessels, ed., *Roberts*, pp. 13–14.

16. BL, Lansdowne Mss, L(5)47, Roberts to Lansdowne, 8 December 1899 – published in Wessels, ed., *Roberts*, pp. 14–16.

17. Brian Robson, *The Road to Kabul: The Second Afghan War 1878–1881* (London: Arms and Armour Press, 1986), pp. 169–72.

18. Roberts, *Forty-one Years in India*, II, p. 377.

19. André Wessels, 'The British View of a War in South Africa (1899)' and 'The British Army in 1899: Problems that Hampered Preparations for War in South Africa', (South African) *Journal for Contemporary History*, 28, 2 (2003), 153–67 and 168–89.

20. Leopold Scholtz, *Waarom die Boere die Oorlog Verloor het* (Pretoria: Protea Boekhuis, 1999), pp. 58, 62.

21. Breytenbach, *Tweede Vryheidsoorlog*, IV, pp. 89–100, 127–42; V, pp. 319–26, 337–49.

22. Ibid., IV, pp. 232–39; Amery, ed., *Times History*, III, pp. 397–400.

23. C R de Wet, *Three Years War (October 1899 – June 1902)* (London: Archibald Constable, 1902), pp. 101–9.

24. Jay Stone and Erwin A Schmidl, *The Boer War and Military Reforms* (Lanham and London: University Press of America, 1988), p. 56.

25. BL, Lansdowne Mss, L(5)47, Roberts to Lansdowne, 27 December 1899 – published in Wessels, ed., *Roberts*, pp. 21–24.

26. Scholtz, *Waarom die Boere die Oorlog Verloor het*, pp. 87–90.

27. Ibid., p. 120.

28. According to Pakenham, *Boer War*, p. 428, it was the most serious strategic mistake of the war.

29. A E Breytenbach, 'Die slag by Donkerhoek, 11–12 Junie 1900', unpub. MA dissertation (University of South Africa, 1980), passim; *History of the War in South Africa 1899–1902* (London: Hurst and Blackett, 1908), III, pp. 204–25.

30. *History of the War in South Africa 1899–1902*, III, p. 519.

31. Scholtz, *Waarom die Boere die Oorlog Verloor het*, p. 85; Jay Luvaas, *The Education of an Army: British Military Thought, 1815–1940* (London: Cassell, 1965), p. 237.

32. Amery, ed., *Times History*, III, p. 342; James, *Roberts*, p. 279; G F R Henderson, *Stonewell Jackson and the American Civil War* (London: Longmans, Green, 1905), I, pp. 306–7.

33. BL, Lansdowne Mss, L(5)4, Roberts to Lansdowne, 17 May 1900 – published in Wessels, ed., *Roberts*, pp. 80–83. See also Roberts's foreword in G F R Henderson, *The Science of War: A Collection of Essays and Lectures 1891–1903*, ed. Neill Malcolm (London: Longmans, Green, 1908), pp. xxxiv–xxxv.

34. *The Times*, 21 September 1900, p. 4.

35. See Proclamation 17 of 1900, 14 September 1900, as published in *Army. Proclamations issued by Field-Marshal Lord Roberts in South Africa* (London: HMSO, 1900) (hereafter Cd. 426), p. 17.

36. National Army Museum (hereafter NAM), Roberts Mss, 1971-01-23-126-3, Speech by Roberts, Cape Town, 10 December 1900 – published in Wessels, ed., *Roberts*, pp. 144–48.

37. Cd. 426, pp. 1–2, 7; Scholtz, *Waarom die Boere die Oorlog Verloor het*, p. 110.

38. Albert Grundlingh, *The Dynamics of Treason: Boer Collaboration in the South African War of 1899–1902* (Pretoria: Protea Book House, 2006), pp. 38–40; Idem, 'Collaboration in Boer Society', in Peter Warwick, ed., *The South African War: The Anglo-Boer War 1899–1902* (Harlow: Longman, 1980), p. 58.

39. Cd. 426, p. 8.

40. Cd. 426, pp. 10–11. As early as the second week of January 1900, when a British force briefly invaded the OFS, a number of Boer farms were burnt and cattle looted. See Breytenbach, *Tweede Vryheidsoorlog*, IV, p. 85.

41. Instructions to Major General R A P Clements, as quoted in S B Spies, *Methods of Barbarism? Roberts and Kitchener and Civilians in the Boer Republics January 1900–May 1902* (Cape Town: Human & Rousseau, 1977), p. 122.

42. Amery, ed., *Times History*, V, p. 8.

43. Fransjohan Pretorius, ed., *Scorched Earth* (Cape Town: Human & Rousseau, 2001), pp. 36–59, 242–63.

44. Scholtz, *Waarom die Boere die Oorlog Verloor het*, p. 114; Breytenbach, *Tweede Vryheidsoorlog*, VI, pp. 168–69.

45. Roberts to Milner, 18 August 1900, as quoted by Scholtz, *Waarom die Boere die Oorlog Verloor het*, p. 131.

46. NAM, Roberts Mss, 1971-01-23-101-1, Afghanistan Series. Correspondence with India and England while Commanding Troops in Afghanistan, by General Sir Frederick Roberts, vol. 13, 1878–80 (Simla: Government Central Printing Office, 1891), pp. 523–24, Document CCCCXXII, Roberts to A C Lyall, 6 August 1880 – also published in Brian Robson, ed., *Roberts in India: The Military Papers of Field Marshal Lord Roberts 1876–1893* (Stroud: Alan Sutton Publishing for Army Records Society, 1993), p. 208.

47. Keith Surridge, 'Lansdowne at the War Office', in John Gooch, ed., *The Boer War: Direction, Experience and Image* (London: Frank Cass, 2000), pp. 32, 34–39. See also NAM, Roberts Mss, 1971-01-23-34-373, Lansdowne to Roberts, 19 May 1900.

48. Farwell, *Eminent Victorian Soldiers*, p. 166.

49. Stephen Badsey, 'War Correspondents in the Boer War', in Gooch, ed., *The Boer War*, p. 196; Robson, *Road to Kabul*, pp. 93–94, 273.

50. NAM, Roberts Mss, 1971-01-23-126-3, Speech by Roberts, Bloemfontein, 28 March 1900 – published in Wessels, ed., *Roberts*, pp. 65–67.

51. *Rudyard Kipling's Verse: Inclusive Edition 1885–1918* (London: Hodder & Stoughton, 1920), vol. 2, pp. 200–2.

52. For general histories of the war see, for example, Roberts, *Forty-one Years in India*, vol. 2 and Robson, *Road to Kabul*, as well as the other Anglo-Afghan War books referred to in the bibliography. For Roberts's diaries, 1878–79 (the 1880 diary could not be traced), see NAM, Roberts Mss, 1971-01-23-92-18 and -19. Unless otherwise indicated, these sources were, inter alia, used in writing this case study of the war.

53. For the background to the war see, for example, *Causes of the Afghan War being a Selection of Papers laid before Parliament with a Connecting Narrative and Comment* (London: Chatto & Windus, 1879), passim, and Michael Edwardes, *Playing the Great Game: A Victorian Cold War* (London: Harmish Hamilton, 1975), pp. 1–99.

54. Robson, ed., *Roberts*, p. 111.

55. NAM, Roberts Papers, 1971-01-23-37-21, Lytton to Roberts, 9 September 1879 – published in Robson, *Road to Kabul*, p. 140 and in Robson, ed., *Roberts*, pp. 119–22. The letter is marked 'Very Confidential'.

56. James, *Roberts*, pp. 151–59; Roberts, *Forty-one Years in India*, II, pp. 341–61; E F Chapman. 'The March from Kabul to Kandahar and the Battle of the 1st September, 1880', *Journal of the Royal United Service Institution* 25 (1882), 282–302, 307–15.

57. Farwell, *Eminent Victorian Soldiers*, p. 174.

58. For general reviews of the battle see, for example, Breytenbach, *Tweede Vryheidsoorlog*, IV, pp. 232–430; Amery, ed., *Times History*, III, pp. 401–58, 473–87; Maurice, compiler, *History of the War*, II, pp. 73–179; J L Basson, 'Die Slag van Paardeberg', unpub. MA thesis, Pretoria University, 1972, passim; *The German Official Account of the War in South Africa*, I, pp. 154–230. The case study that follows is primarily based on these sources.

59. BL, Lansdowne Mss, L(5)48, Roberts to Lansdowne, 22 February 1900 – published in Wessels, ed., *Roberts*, pp. 54–57.

60. Charles Sydney Goldmann, *With General French and the Cavalry in South Africa* (London: MacMillan, 1902), pp. 74–86; J G Maydon, *French's Cavalry Campaign* (London: C Arthur Pearson, 1902), pp. 140–49.

61. The view is generally held that Kitchener was only a major general and thus junior to Kelly-Kenny, but according to the *Army List* of 1901 and onwards, Kitchener was promoted to lieutenant general on 23 December 1899; i.e. on the day when he was officially appointed as Roberts's Chief of Staff. If, for whatever reason, Kitchener was secretly (?) promoted, it explains why he was convinced that he was indeed the senior officer at Paardeberg. See André Wessels, ed., *Lord Kitchener and the War in South Africa 1899–1902* (Stroud: Sutton Publishing for Army Records Society, 2006), p. 13 and note 6 on p. 254.

62. Amery, ed., *Times History*, III, p. 419; Farwell, *Eminent Victorian Soldiers*, p. 332.

63. The Transvaal State Artillery had twenty-five 37-mm Maxim-Nordenfeld quick-firing guns; nicknamed 'pom-poms' due to the sound they made when in action. In the light of the success of these guns, and especially the demoralising effect they had on an enemy, Roberts acquired at least fifty-seven such new-technology guns for use in South Africa, where they were first used at Paardeberg (26 February 1900). See Breytenbach, *Tweede Vryheidsoorlog*, I, p. 87; Amery, ed., *Times History*, III, p. 482; IV, p. 17; V, p. 248.

64. For an evaluation of Kitchener's conduct of the battle see, for example, George Arthur, *Life of Lord Kitchener* (London: Macmillan, 1920), I, pp. 822–91; Amery, ed., *Times History*, III, pp. 446–53; James, *Roberts*, pp. 291–92; Philip Magnus, *Kitchener: Portrait of an Imperialist* (London: John Murray, 1958), pp. 164–69; C R Ballard, *Kitchener* (London: Faber & Faber, n.d.), pp. 124–31; E S Grew et al., *Field-Marshal Lord Kitchener: His Life and Work for the Empire* (London: The Gresham Publishing Company, n.d.), II, pp. 91–95.

Chapter 8

Herbert Kitchener

Keith Surridge

Horatio Herbert Kitchener was the last of Queen Victoria's most notable generals. By the time of her death on 22 January 1901 Kitchener, her Commander in Chief in South Africa since November 1900, in succession to Lord Roberts, faced the daunting task of ending the guerrilla war launched by the Boers months earlier. In her last letter to Kitchener she expressed her 'entire confidence' in him to finish the conflict, a view shared by many Britons at the time. Kitchener, of course, would conclude successfully the South African War and reap further acclaim. Indeed, his reputation would be such that, when war broke out in 1914, his presence in the government would be considered vital to the well-being of both nation and empire.[1]

The two wars that made Kitchener's reputation were very different in character and required contrasting methods of leadership. Kitchener's conquest of the Sudan between 1896 and 1898 was decided, ultimately, by an open battle, where British technological superiority proved decisive. In South Africa between 1900 and 1902, Kitchener spent two years formulating various schemes to defeat an elusive foe. This war was not only about fighting: it also meant making war on the Boer civilian population, most of whom supported the guerrillas with inspiration, food and intelligence. To some in Britain this amounted to using 'methods of barbarism' and constituted a stain on the character and nature of British imperialism. Nevertheless, with victory achieved Kitchener became the personification of the ruthlessness needed to sustain the empire at a time of growing international crisis and national decline. Kitchener's determination, his supposed machine-like efficiency and ability to get the job done, would provide anxious Britons, wondering what the post-Victorian era would bring, with a degree of certainty that few others could supply.[2]

Kitchener was born in Ireland on 24 June 1850, his father an eccentric retired lieutenant colonel. In 1864, owing to his mother's tuberculosis, the family moved to Switzerland for the air, but she died soon after arriving, a blow that shook the young Kitchener and saw him retreat into shyness and introspection. Although his education was mostly informal, his stay in Switzerland helped him acquire fluency

Chronology

24 June 1850	Horatio Herbert Kitchener born at Gunsborough Villa, Co. Kerry
	Educated privately and at Chateau du Grand Clos, Renaz
	(Switzerland), and at the Royal Military Academy, Woolwich
4 January 1871	Commissioned Lieutenant, Royal Engineers
Easter 1873	Appointed ADC to Brigadier General Greaves
2 November 1874	Seconded to Palestine Exploration Fund
3 September 1878	Seconded to Foreign Office and appointed to survey Cyprus
26 June 1879	Military Vice Consul in Kastamonu, Anatolia
15 March 1880	Returned to Cyprus
2 July 1882	Joined British fleet that bombarded Alexandria and went ashore to gather intelligence
4 January 1883	Promoted Captain
21 February 1883	Appointed to Egyptian cavalry
March 1884–April 1885	Provided intelligence for Gordon Relief Expedition
8 October 1884	Promoted Brevet Major
15 June 1885	Promoted Brevet Lieutenant Colonel
June 1885	Resigned from Egyptian service
6 November 1885	Seconded to Foreign Office and appointed to Zanzibar Boundary Commission
September 1886	Appointed Governor General of Eastern Sudan and the Red Sea Littoral
11 April 1888	Promoted Brevet Colonel and appointed ADC to Queen Victoria
September 1888	Appointed Adjutant General of the Egyptian army
Early 1890	Appointed Inspector General of the Egyptian police
13 April 1892	Appointed Sirdar of the Egyptian army
1896–98	Sudan campaign
25 September 1896	Promoted Brevet Major General
2 September 1898	Battle of Omdurman
November 1898	Created Baron Kitchener of Khartoum and Aspall in the County of Suffolk
19 January 1899	Appointed Governor General of Sudan
18 December 1899	Appointed Chief of Staff to Lord Roberts in South Africa
23 December 1899	Promoted Substantive Lieutenant General
29 November 1900	Appointed C in C, South Africa
31 May 1902	Treaty of Vereeniging
1 June 1902	Promoted Brevet General
12 July 1902	Created Viscount Kitchener of Khartoum, and of Vaal in the Colony of the Transvaal, and of Aspall in the County of Suffolk
28 November 1902	Appointed C in C, India
10 September 1909	Promoted Field Marshal
20 June 1911	Appointed British Agent and Consul General in Egypt
17 June 1914	Created Earl Kitchener of Khartoum, and of Broome
5 August 1914	Appointed Secretary of State for War
5 June 1916	Drowned at sea with loss of HMS *Hampshire*

Appointed CMG, 1886; CB, 1889; KCMG, 1894; KCB, 1896; GCMG, 1901; OM, 1902; GCIE, 1908; GCSI, 1909; KP, 1911; KG, 1915 in French and revealed an aptitude for languages. He later added Arabic to his repertoire. By the time Kitchener joined the Royal Military Academy, Woolwich in February 1868, he was a tall (6ft 2in or 1.85m), taciturn individual, not given to making friends easily. He was commissioned as lieutenant in the Royal Engineers on 4 January 1871, having already served in a French ambulance unit during the Franco-Prussian War. In 1874, after spells at Aldershot and Chatham, Kitchener was seconded to the Palestine Exploration Fund as a surveyor and in 1878 worked in Cyprus following its annexation by Britain.

When trouble broke out in Egypt in 1882, Kitchener flouted official regulations by leaving the island and joining the force sent to bombard Alexandria. After Egypt's conquest by Sir Garnet Wolseley, Kitchener transferred to the new, British-reformed Egyptian army in 1883 as captain. However, his knowledge of Arabic and his desire for action saw him appointed as Wolseley's chief intelligence officer during the abortive Gordon relief expedition in 1884–85, during which he led a band of Arab irregulars in the Sudanese desert. This gave Kitchener valuable knowledge of the peoples and area, and he would also learn from Wolseley's mistakes. Kitchener quickly resigned from the Egyptian service, but was soon appointed to the Zanzibar Boundary Commission in December 1885. The Governor Generalship of the Red Sea Littoral, the territory around the port of Suakin that Britain retained in the Sudan, soon followed and here Kitchener exercised military command for the first time. This, alongside the wound he received, enhanced Kitchener's reputation further, particularly as he came to the attention of the Queen.

Not long after, in September 1888, Kitchener was made Adjutant General of the Egyptian army, a force now fully reformed and commanded by British officers. In 1889, it fought and routed the Sudanese Dervishes, the followers of the Mahdi – whose forces had captured Khartoum and killed Gordon four years earlier – at the battle of Toski, with Kitchener successfully commanding the cavalry. After a spell reforming the Egyptian police he was made Sirdar, or Commander in Chief, of the Egyptian army in April 1892 and began to prepare the army for the reconquest of the Sudan. In a campaign lasting two years that culminated in the victory at Omdurman in September 1898, his finest battlefield achievement, Kitchener avenged Gordon. Afterwards, he proceeded south along the Nile to confront a small French expedition under Captain Marchand that had trespassed onto Sudanese territory at Fashoda. There the French-speaking Kitchener avoided confrontation and revealed deft diplomatic skills by persuading Marchand to leave the matter to the politicians. His role in the subsequent diplomatic defeat of France added to the laurels won at Omdurman.[3]

Promoted to Governor General of the Sudan in early 1899 he began the process of reconstruction and development. He was not destined to see it completed because in December he was ordered to accompany Lord Roberts to South Africa, where war had broken out with the Boer republics of the Transvaal and Orange Free State in October.

Once the Boer republics had apparently been conquered, Roberts left in November 1900 to be succeeded by Kitchener as Commander in Chief. He successfully brought the war to an end following the signing of the Treaty of Vereeniging on 31 May 1902, and then took over the Indian army. During his tenure he reformed the army and its administration, clashing with the viceroy, Lord Curzon, who resigned when he failed to stop Kitchener. Once he left India in 1909, Kitchener was made a field marshal but was at a loose end. Eventually, in 1911, he gained the post of British Agent and Consul General of Egypt and was on leave in Britain when war broke out in August 1914. Considered to be a figure too important to leave in an imperial backwater, Kitchener was persuaded to accept the vacant job of Secretary of State for War. By the time of his death in 1916, when he drowned after his ship was sunk by a mine on his way to Russia, Kitchener had achieved mixed results. He had, nevertheless, embodied Britain's determination to win and remained popular with the British public.

Kitchener's reputation as a commander was forged in the Sudan, but he was never a confident general, and being an engineer meant that he had not studied strategy and tactics fully. He owed his chance to Lord Cromer, who since 1883 had been the British Agent and Consul General, which meant, effectively, that he ruled Egypt. Cromer had followed Kitchener's career with interest and when the Sirdar, Sir Francis Grenfell, was recalled by the British government Cromer immediately gave Kitchener his job. According to Cromer, Kitchener's virtues were manifold but he particularly liked the fact 'that he left as little as possible to chance' and 'did not think that extravagance was the necessary handmaid of efficiency'. Furthermore, Kitchener 'suppressed with a firm hand any tendency towards waste and extravagance'.[4] Indeed, when the campaign began Kitchener's cheese-paring caused comment among his officers. Even so, the need for economies sometimes stretched Kitchener's abilities and on one occasion, when he felt he was spreading his budget too thinly, he offered his resignation: 'I must protest', he wrote to Cromer, 'against the manner in which I am being asked to make financial impossibilities possible and called for responsible estimates that cannot be more than approximate.' The resignation was, of course, rescinded, but it revealed the sort of pressure Kitchener worked under in the Sudan.[5]

This was not the only anxiety that undermined Kitchener's confidence. His appointment as Sirdar was not popular with the British army establishment in Egypt: their favourite was Colonel Josceline Wodehouse, with whom Kitchener had served at Toski in 1889. Kitchener was not liked because he shunned the mess and rarely mixed with wider British society, gaining him a reputation as aloof, gruff and boorish. Indeed, in 1890, Grenfell had reported that while Kitchener was 'very capable' and 'clear-headed', he was also 'very ambitious' and that 'his rapid promotion had placed him in a somewhat difficult position. He is not popular, but has of late greatly improved in tact and manner and any defects in his character will in my opinion disappear as he gets on in the service.'[6] Kitchener's friendship with aristocratic patrons, particularly Lord Salisbury and his daughter-in-law Lady Cranborne, seemed to confirm that he was an officer on the make. Kitchener certainly needed high-ranking friends because he had few contacts within the British army's hierarchy. The Egyptian army was not the responsibility of the War Office, but came within the remit of the Foreign Office, therefore within the purview of Salisbury, who was both Prime Minister and Foreign Secretary.

Consequently, when the Sudan campaign was launched in 1896, Wolseley, then Commander in Chief of the British army, thought Kitchener too reckless, and wanted an officer from the British army to take command. Thankfully for Kitchener, Cromer and Salisbury vetoed this, but when Grenfell was appointed to command the British garrison in Egypt in 1897, Kitchener's anxiety about being replaced grew immensely. His mood was not helped by his need for substantial British reinforcements in 1898 for the final leg of the advance. Already, Kitchener had been writing to Grenfell in obsequious tones in an attempt to soothe the latter's apparent disappointment at not taking overall command of the expedition:

> I should like to know if everything is going quite to your satisfaction and if there is anything I can do. Do we keep you sufficiently informed of the position and number of the troops? . . . I hope you will never imagine that I desire to work off my own bat and not loyally to serve under you, but in some things I do not see my way clearly. If you will place yourself in my position and tell me what you think I should do I will do my best to follow it. I feel the responsibility of my position to all officers and men under me [and] should be glad of advice from you.[7]

Following his victory at the battle of Atbara on 8 April 1898, the late arrival of congratulations from Wolseley and General Sir Evelyn Wood, the Adjutant General, only added to Kitchener's gnawing fear about his place in the military hierarchy and his desire for acceptance.[8]

In certain respects he was right to be concerned. Some British officers had been told to report directly to the War Office. Major (later Lieutenant Colonel) Charles à Court (later Repington) recalled that he had been ordered to keep Wolseley informed through his military secretary, Lord Erroll, or through his former colleagues at the Intelligence Department. Douglas Haig, who joined the Egyptian cavalry, was asked by Wood to keep him informed. Consequently, when British units arrived in the Sudan in early 1898, Kitchener's suspicions grew exponentially: Brigadier General the Hon. Neville Lyttelton felt at first that Kitchener regarded him as 'an emissary from the War Office sent to keep an eye on him', although he was friendly enough later.[9]

Nevertheless, Kitchener need not have worried. In early 1898 Cromer made sure the War Office knew his views on the matter. In a letter sent to Salisbury that found its way into the papers of the Secretary of State for War, Lord Lansdowne, Cromer stated bluntly that 'you will sooner or later hear some military mutterings due to jealousy of Kitchener . . . I have not a shadow of a doubt that the decision to keep Kitchener in command is wise'. And so he remained in command.[10]

All this anxiety, particularly during the early days of the campaign, took its toll on Kitchener's highly strung personality. Lieutenant Edward Cecil, Lord Salisbury's son and one of Kitchener's ADCs, remembered how loathsome his chief could be: 'He was more uncouth and uncivilised at that time [*c.* 1896] than he was later.' Quite often Kitchener could act the bully, with Cecil often on the receiving end. Even Major Reginald Wingate, Kitchener's invaluable and loyal intelligence officer, could be maddened by his 'boorish insults'.[11] Thus, any discussion of Kitchener's leadership must include his insecurities. All the worst traits in his character flowed from these.

His officers were not the only ones to suffer. Kitchener was also accused of being cavalier with the lives of his men and for being cruel. During the campaign's early stages he ordered Colonel Archibald Hunter, his second in command, to force march his men across the desert during which time they were caught in a sandstorm. Hunter raged in a letter to his brother:

> I have plumbed the bottom of Kitchener now – he is inhuman, heartless, with eccentric and freakish bursts of generosity specially when he is defeated: he is a vain, egotistical mass of pride and ambition, expecting and usurping all and giving nothing; he is a mixture of the fox, Jew and snake and like all bullies is a dove when tackled.[12]

The reputation for cruelty reached a height following the battle of Omdurman and threatened his career temporarily. This was about the killing of the wounded Dervishes and Winston Churchill, who was there, was particularly scathing on this point: 'The stern and unpitying spirit of the commander was communicated to his troops and the victories which marked the progression of the River War were accompanied by acts of barbarity not always justified even by the harsh customs of savage conflicts or the fierce and treacherous nature of the Dervish.' To his mother, Churchill was even more forthright: 'I shall merely say that the victory at Omdurman was disgraced by the inhuman slaughter of the wounded and that Kitchener was responsible for this.'[13] Ernest Bennet, Oxford academic and correspondent for the *Westminster Gazette*, pursued the matter after the war and complained about the killing of the severely wounded, who could offer no resistance, unlike some of those lightly injured. He failed to get the matter investigated and it never became a major issue. The British public liked their new hero and were not interested, while the attempt by the writer, Wilfred Scawen Blunt, to stop Kitchener receiving his £30,000 reward was an embarrassing failure. Nevertheless, wounded Dervishes were killed and some soldiers explained why it was done. Lieutenant Ronald Meiklejohn, in his personal account of the campaign, told how 'several dervishes, whom we passed as dead, or beyond harm, slashed at our legs with their swords, or rose and charged'. On an earlier page he had explained that before the battle of the Atbara specific orders had been given to spare those who put up their hands and to be aware of those feigning death or still capable of bearing arms. While it seems no such order was given before the battle of Omdurman presumably the same rules applied.[14] In the end very few complained about the killing of the wounded and it was soon forgotten.

As an army commander, especially during the quiet phases, Kitchener's methods often caused a great deal of scorn and bafflement to those expected to carry out his orders without question. The most common complaint was about his almost pathological secrecy, and the haphazard manner in which he operated. Captain Sir Henry Rawlinson, who joined the staff in the Sudan as an ADC in early 1898, was informed by Wingate 'that K is very sketchy in the way he fires off telegrams without letting anyone know sometimes and always without keeping a copy'. His fellow ADC, à Court, was equally exasperated by Kitchener's rectitude: 'He scarcely ever issued a written order, and confined himself to curt telegrams, the forms for which he carried in his helmet . . . He had particularly no staff, and did everything himself.' This was in spite of appointing his old comrade Colonel Leslie Rundle to be his Chief of Staff. Lieutenant Colonel John Maxwell, commander of the Egyptian 2nd Brigade, told his wife that when Rundle arrived about mid-July 1898 to take up his post, 'the Sirdar told him he did not want him to do anything except stay quiet and not fuss'. Evidently, Rundle saw the funny side of it and amused his dining companions with tales 'of the Sirdar's arbitrary way of doing things'. Brevet Lieutenant Colonel Horace Smith-Dorrien, who returned to the Sudan in July 1898 without knowing what he was to do, fortuitously bumped into Kitchener who told him to take command of his old unit the 13th Sudanese Battalion and then rode off: 'I found the 13th and announced I had come to take command and, as no one objected, I did.'[15]

Rawlinson complained that the Sudan campaign was 'too much of a one-man show. If anything were to happen to the Sirdar there would be chaos, as no one but he knows the state of preparedness in which various departments are'. Of course, Kitchener's luck held and nothing did happen to him. Consequently, the vices pointed out by Rawlinson and others were turned into virtues at the end. Grenfell, in his memoirs, wrote of Kitchener's 'powers of organisation, his clear head, and the remarkable way he managed a very difficult campaign'. Virtually all those willing to eulogise over Kitchener focused on his apparent ability to run the war single-handedly. Even knowing Kitchener's aversion to paperwork, Captain Alfred Hubbard could still praise him as a man 'gifted with tireless energy, unflinching determination, an inflexible purpose, combined with a marvellous memory'. Furthermore, one 'hot-off-the-press' account of the campaign helped give rise to an image of Kitchener that would last until his death and told how: 'The masterly grasp of detail and faculty of organisation possessed by the Sirdar, Sir Herbert Kitchener, showed itself clearly from the day he took command of the Nile Expeditionary Force, in 1896, to the day he finally destroyed the Khalifa's army. With machine-like precision he carried out his plans; never in a hurry, but never wasting a moment.' Machine-like was a term that certainly caught on thanks especially to the journalist George W Steevens of the *Daily Mail*, whose subsequent book lauded Kitchener's achievement. Steevens wrote of the robotic Sirdar, whose 'precision is so inhumanly unerring, he is more like a machine than a man'. Yet, hyperbole aside, Steevens also identified the most fundamental aspect of Kitchener's ability – his skills as an engineer, which were arguably far superior to those of Kitchener the warrior. His master stroke was the building of the Sudan Military Railway (SMR), which Steevens described as 'the deadliest weapon that Britain used against Mahdism', and this time he was not exaggerating.[16]

The historian of the SMR, Lieutenant Colonel E W C Sandes, writing in 1937, was unequivocal in his praise of Kitchener's forethought: 'It cannot be too clearly emphasized that the success of the Desert Railway should be attributed to Kitchener himself.' It was Kitchener's zeal for the enterprise and his determination to see it through that ensured the project's success. He had seen how Wolseley's expedition had struggled with boats and camels and decided that another way of moving troops and supplies was necessary. And he did this without really knowing whether a railway could be laid across the desert, and in the hope that water could be found along the route. Kitchener's appointment of Lieutenant E P C Girouard was masterly, not only because Girouard knew his business thoroughly, but because he knew how to handle Kitchener, who had the good sense to let him get on with his work and would often defer to his superior expertise. But what really demonstrated Kitchener's luck was the discovery of water at two points, 77 and 126 miles from the railhead at Wadi Halfa. To Steevens, this was 'the luck that goes with genius'.[17]

Omdurman, 1898

This was the biggest battle of Kitchener's career and the event that cemented his reputation as one of the era's great generals. In many respects it was a battle typical of its age in that the main problem had been to get the troops to the battlefield in reasonable shape across extremely hostile terrain. Once there British and Egyptian technical superiority would be decisive and would not require subtle or imaginative generalship. Omdurman, though, was not a foregone conclusion because the Dervishes were capable of defeating the allied force. Their mistakes gave Kitchener his chance and a good general, if perhaps not a great one, exploits his opponent's errors. This he did.

Previously, Kitchener's battlefield experience had been limited. He had only ever fought in the Sudan and had commanded small units before becoming Sirdar. His handling of that force in the early stages of the campaign, between 1896 and 1897, had been exemplary, but the army was not large enough to bring the reconquest to a successful conclusion. Consequently, in January 1898, British troops, under Major General William Gatacre, arrived to help deliver the final blow, and would be joined by more British regiments before the final march on Omdurman in August 1898.

The arrival of British forces was both a boon and a curse for Kitchener. On one hand, their arrival brought much-needed fresh men, who were well disciplined

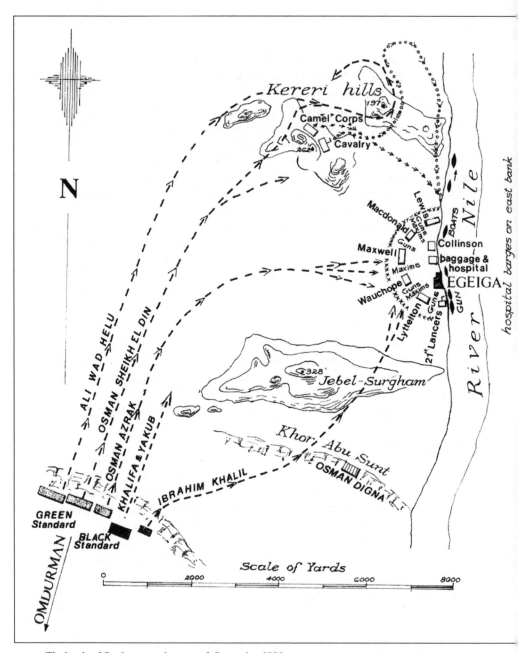

The battle of Omdurman, phase one, 2 September 1898.

and well armed. On the other hand, their arrival awoke Kitchener's latent anxieties about being superseded. Before the first major engagement of the combined British and Egyptian army, at the River Atbara on 8 April 1898, Kitchener completely lost confidence in his own ability when he received conflicting advice from his subordinates. The enemy commander, the Emir Mahmoud, had placed

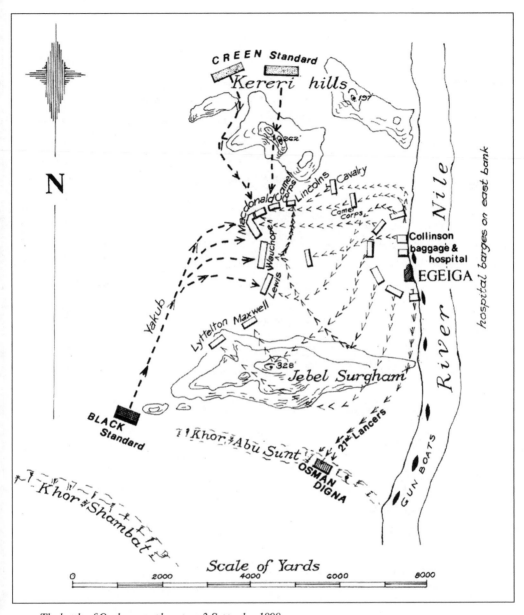

The battle of Omdurman, phase two, 2 September 1898.

his army in a strong defensive position and Kitchener became uncertain how to act. On 1 April 1898, he telegraphed Cromer asking for advice: Hunter, his fighting general, had advised caution, in the hope that Mahmoud would come out to fight; Gatacre, wanted to assault the Dervish position head on. Cromer consulted Grenfell, who then referred to the War Office. Eventually, Cromer too advised caution, but left the matter to Kitchener who was told that whatever he did he had the full support of the British government.[18] Buoyed by the government's faith in his ability Kitchener ordered a frontal assault, although he

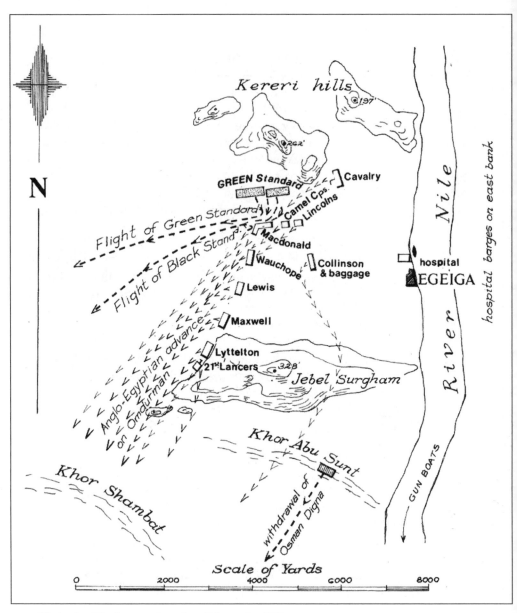

The battle of Omdurman, phase three, 2 September 1898.

left the handling of the respective armies to Hunter and Gatacre. The battle of the Atbara was a complete success, if somewhat costly, and Mahmoud himself was captured.

After this victory there was a sense among the army that the final phase of the campaign was imminent. For the last advance Kitchener was reinforced by more British troops and equipment. It was well appreciated that firepower was the key to success, but Kitchener was out of touch with some developments as he had hardly been in Britain recently. While the allied army would muster 20 Maxim machine-guns and 44 guns, Wolseley, it seems, drew Kitchener's attention to a new type of cannon available – the 5.5in howitzer that fired the new high-explosive (lyddite) shell – of which a battery (6 guns) was eventually sent.[19] Supplementing the army's artillery and machine-guns were those on board the gunboats that accompanied the army on its advance. There were 10 at Omdurman and together these massed 36 guns and 24 Maxims and would help protect the flanks of the allies during the battle. The gunboats had been with Kitchener from the start and were weapons in which he had taken a great interest.[20] The infantry were armed with two types of rifle: the Egyptian forces had the older, single-shot Martini-Henry, while the British had the recent Lee-Metford II, a magazine rifle that used bullets propelled by smokeless cordite and had a range of 2,500yd. This was similar to that of the Maxims, although it was more effective at shorter ranges. Gatacre, to increase the 'stopping' power of the bullets, had had his men turn them into 'dum dum' bullets, which would enter cleanly but leave a massive hole at the back. The artillery, mostly modern rifled breech-loaders, had a range of over 5,000yd. In all, Kitchener's forces numbered 25,000 men, 8,000 of whom were British.[21]

Against this powerful force the Khalifa 'Abdullahi, who had succeeded the Mahdi in 1885, could deploy some 50,000 men, although the numbers have been disputed. The only modern Sudanese account, that by 'Ismat Hasan Zulfo, does not suggest a figure but questions the numbers above, which was a British estimate. The captured Dervish musters were apparently out of date and there were large desertions the night before the battle, while years of warfare since the creation of the Mahdist state in 1885, against the British, the Abyssinians and among themselves, had weakened the Dervish cause considerably. Zulfo adds that Hunter and the journalist Bennet Burleigh both thought the Dervish army numbered between 30,000 and 35,000, but gives no references. According to his recent biographer, Hunter told a correspondent that 50,000 Dervishes attacked, while Burleigh's book of the campaign also gives that figure. Smith-Dorrien wrote later that the British cavalry estimated the Dervishes at 30,000, but 'it subsequently proved to be double that number'. À Court stated that Lieutenant Colonel Hector MacDonald, commander of the Egyptian 1st Brigade and Lieutenant Colonel G R Broadwood, commander of the Egyptian Cavalry, 'who are both sober people', thought the enemy numbered 60,000; while Rawlinson gave figures of between 40,000 and 50,000. Whether Zulfo is correct in assuming that the Dervish numbers were exaggerated to add lustre to the victory is a point that cannot be resolved. It was Wingate who used the figures from the captured Dervish books (upwards of 52,000) and this remains the only reliable source.[22]

What is not beyond doubt is the inferiority of the Dervish weapons compared to those of the allied army. While the Dervishes were not simply armed with swords and spears – although most were – the quality of their firearms was poor.

Their rifles, Remingtons and Martini-Henrys captured from the British and Egyptians ten years earlier, were obsolete or badly kept. Their ammunition, while plentiful, was hampered by poor-quality, homemade gunpowder. The Dervishes could field 35 guns, but 27 of these were antiquated: the 8 modern Krupp breech-loaders were good enough but had hardly been fired since their capture and were, like the rifles, hindered by inferior gunpowder. As it happened, only five would be used on the battlefield, the rest were placed in forts meant to defend the river against the gunboats.[23]

Kitchener's advance to the outskirts of Omdurman, the Dervish capital opposite the abandoned city of Khartoum, was trouble-free. The Dervishes might have made a stand at the Shabluka gorge which contained the Nile's sixth cataract (rapids). If forced to fight there the gunboats would have had little impact and the ground offered good defensive positions. The Dervishes did make an attempt to fortify the area but this was abandoned by the Khalifa who could not have provisioned his army there. Moreover, he preferred to lead the army himself and fight on familiar ground. Thus on 1 September 1898, Kitchener's army encamped on the plain of Kereri (Karari) outside Omdurman, in a semicircle around the village of el-Egeiga.[24]

Now they were so close Kitchener and his officers became anxious lest the Dervishes not come out and fight. There was some expectation that the Khalifa would make a stand in and around Omdurman itself and engage the allies in street fighting, where their technological superiority might be negated. What the allied army feared most, however, was a night attack and precautions were taken against such an eventuality: the gunboats' searchlights swept the plain and spies helped make the Khalifa think he would be attacked instead. After passing a peaceful night, Kitchener, who knew the Dervishes had come out of Omdurman, ordered the army to leave their defences and make ready to march on the enemy's capital because as dawn broke there was no sign of them. However, the 21st Lancers, having been sent out to find the enemy, found them very close indeed and on the move towards the allied forces. Lieutenant Meiklejohn summed up the army's mood on hearing this: 'I think everybody gave a sigh of relief, since it was much better that they should attack.'[25]

The allied army returned to its positions. Kitchener had disposed of his army in a defensive semicircle and had left the manner of its deployment to the two main commanders. Hunter, on the right, had positioned the Egyptians in shallow trenches, while Gatacre placed the British behind a zariba, or thorn-bush fence. The 21st Lancers came into the position, but the Egyptian cavalry and camel corps remained on the Kereri hills, which were slightly towards the north-west of the allied army. To the south-west lay the ridge known as Jebel Surgham and to the south of that lay a dried river bed, the Khor Abu Sunt, in which were eventually concealed about 2,000 Dervish warriors. Of these, 700 were Beja Hadendowa tribesmen under their wily chief Osman Digna, whom Kitchener had fought when governor of the eastern Sudan.

The Khalifa did not simply launch his army against the allies in the hope of overwhelming the enemy by numbers alone. The frontal assault under Osman Azrak, assisted by a smaller force under Ibrahim al Khalil that came over the Jebel Surgham, was meant to pin the allied forces, while a force of around 15,000, under the Green Standard and commanded by Osman Shaykh al-Din and Abu Siwar, moved into the Kereri hills in order to attack the right flank of the allied army. Meanwhile, the Khalifa, with his brother Ya'qub and senior officer Ali Wad Hilu, waited with the Black Standard (some 12,000 to 15,000 men) ready to charge the enemy at the right moment.[26]

The attack by the forces of Osman Azrak began at about 0630. The sight of these men on the move impressed all those who witnessed it. Lieutenant Colonel D F Lewis, commander of the 3rd Egyptian Brigade wrote: 'The order and pace with which they moved struck us so particularly. This was no horde of savages but a well-ordered army.' Rawlinson, agreed: 'It was a magnificent sight these thousands of wild, brave uneducated savages advancing to their destruction.'[27]

The allied artillery and gunboats fired first at about 0645 and then, as the survivors came closer, the Maxims and rifles of the infantry followed. There was little cover for the Dervishes and thousands fell. Ibrahim al Khalil's smaller force soon engaged the allied left flank from the Jebel Surgham but they had mistimed their attack and engaged the British forces too early, before Osman Azrak's assault had made any impact. They too were repulsed with heavy losses.

On the allied right, where stood the Egyptian army, the Green Standard had climbed the Kereri hills and driven off the Egyptian cavalry and camel corps with a sustained and unwavering charge. The Egyptians, heavily outnumbered, beat a hasty retreat: the camel corps, being slower, fled towards the allied main position covered by the timely fire of five gunboats. Broadwood, meanwhile, took the cavalry north, luring the Dervishes away from the main battlefield for some 4 or 5 miles before they realised they were needed elsewhere and headed back.

By 0800, the Dervishes' attacks had been beaten off with heavy losses. The bravery of these men earned high praise from the British officers and soldiers who had shot them down. Corporal Skinner believed that: 'Nothing could possibly stand against such a store of lead, in fact no European would ever think of facing it in the daring way these fanatics did.'[28] After a break of about an hour, Kitchener began the second phase of the battle by ordering the army out of its position and on to the plain. The brigades were meant to move southwards towards Omdurman in echelon in the hope of meeting all eventualities and to be mutually supporting. Thus the British Brigades were in the front and the Egyptians on the right and rear. Meanwhile, the 21st Lancers had been sent 'to clear the ground on our left front and head off any retreating Dervishes from the direction of Omdurman'. The Dervish survivors were apparently fleeing into the desert and Kitchener wanted to encourage the rest to do so.[29] The subsequent charge of the 21st Lancers, during which they were effectively ambushed by the forces of Osman Digna concealed in the dried river bed, the Khor Abu Sunt, has been well recounted, not least by its famous participant, Winston Churchill. Kitchener did not order the charge and though successful it ended the usefulness of the 21st Lancers for the rest of the day. They might have informed Kitchener that there was still a large body of Dervishes – the Black Standard – in the vicinity.

The second phase of the battle, for it was far from over, in spite of 2,000 to 3,000 Dervish dead, was the most controversial part and called into question Kitchener's tactical judgement. As the army moved towards the Jebel Surgham ridge the various brigades became separated and the cohesion of the army lost. The brigade of Lieutenant Colonel Hector MacDonald was out on the right flank when a serious gap emerged between it and the forward brigades so that it became isolated on the plain. This was far too tempting for the men of the Black Standard who surged from around the western end of the Jebel Surgham and headed straight for MacDonald. The Khalifa did not lead the attack himself, having already moved off towards Omdurman. Although heavily outnumbered, MacDonald's force was supported by eighteen guns and eight Maxims and held its own against the Dervish onslaught. MacDonald was not in great danger as he had seen the enemy early and was prepared. Nevertheless, when Kitchener received word of MacDonald's predicament he acted decisively by ordering one British brigade to support him. However, what might seem a decisive act also revealed one of Kitchener's shortcomings because he gave the orders to the brigade commander directly, without having consulted Gatacre. Thankfully for the allied cause the Dervish attack was repulsed with heavy losses, but MacDonald's travails were not over. No sooner had the Black Standard begun to waver then the Green Standard, the force that had chased off Broadwood's cavalry, returned to the battlefield right behind MacDonald's embattled brigade. With quick thinking, MacDonald demonstrated his brigade's superb training and discipline and turned them round in parade-ground fashion to face the new enemy. With Kitchener alert enough to send a British battalion to help, MacDonald's brigade fought off this new adversary with the same coolness and determination that it had shown earlier. In his dispatch after the battle, Kitchener readily praised MacDonald's brilliant handling of his troops.[30]

With the destruction of the Black and Green Standards the Dervish army was annihilated. The enormity of the victory and the huge losses sustained by the Dervishes were soon appreciated by the British. Captain Cameron admitted to his father that: 'It seems to me that as far as the British Division was concerned it was mostly a question of superiority of weapons for the Dervishes showed splendid courage.'[31] Dervish losses were huge: Wingate stated that 10,800 were killed, while the number of wounded was estimated at 16,000. British and Egyptian losses amounted to 48 dead and 434 wounded.[32]

The British victory was certainly helped by the Khalifa smashing his army against the shells and bullets of the allied forces, revealing his ignorance of modern weapons. Of the Dervish commanders only Osman Digna had real experience of what British firepower could do, having experienced it in 1884–85.

Osman Digna, however, was from the north-east and was of the Beja people, who were better known to the British as the 'fuzzy-wuzzies'. As an outsider his opinions did not carry much weight in the Dervish council because it was dominated by the Khalifa's family and tribe, the Ta'aisha of the Baqqara. The Khalifa was determined to fight the battle his way and paid the price.[33]

A succinct summary of the battle was provided later by à Court and he certainly identified the fact the Khalifa played a major part in his own downfall:

> We were a very fortunate army. The Dervishes had many chances and availed themselves of none. Had they held Shabluka, they would have forced us to fight in a difficult and waterless country where our gunboats were useless. Had they given battle in the thick scrub, they would have placed themselves almost on equal terms with us, and the weight of their 60,000 fighting men would have told. Had they attacked our widely extended line on the night of September 1–2, it is almost certain, considering their reckless gallantry, that their masses must have broken in somewhere. Had they held the mud houses, forts, and walls of Omdurman, we should hardly have turned them out with a loss of less than 3,000 men.[34]

Thus the old adage that victories are won because of the mistakes of the enemy was certainly applicable to the Khalifa and his generals.

Kitchener, then, did not need to exert direct control of the allied army during the battle. The placement of the troops and the actual conduct of the fighting he left to the more experienced men – Hunter and Gatacre. Nevertheless, the incident involving MacDonald's brigade showed Kitchener's judgement to be at fault. Hunter said he was too impatient, which was true; but the Dervishes could be handled out in the open. À Court criticised Kitchener for not having stated the required distances between the brigades as they moved off, but added 'What K needed was a good infantry drill man, and he did not have one.' Moreover, it seems the 1st British Brigade was too eager to get to Omdurman and marched far too quickly. 'They marched upon our heels [the 2nd British Brigade detailed to lead the advance] in spite of my protests.'[35] Consequently, the army moved off far too rapidly, which left MacDonald's brigade, as the last to deploy, isolated out on the right rear of the formation. Furthermore, if the 21st Lancers had done their job properly they might have given early warning of the Black Standard and enabled Kitchener to alter his movements and deployment.

Thus Kitchener's control of the Sudan expedition revealed his command of logistics; the key to the objective – Omdurman. In this respect the campaign was a triumph: the army was well fed and watered and the building of the desert railway a brilliant piece of engineering. The need to defeat the desert was foremost in Kitchener's planning. Yet, Kitchener revealed some alarming faults for a commander who would have to fight battles: particularly, his desire to control every aspect of the campaign and his failure to take his officers into his confidence. Had he been incapacitated things might have turned out differently. Or would they? Arguably, the Sudan campaign and its objectives were straightforward enough for any commander of proven ability. Even so, Kitchener's personal style of command, which was in keeping with Victorian practice, can also be explained by the two severe restraints under which he laboured. First, his fear of the generals and politicians of the War Office, who might have replaced him at any moment; and secondly, the financial constraints imposed by Cromer. Together, these, certainly in 1898, caused Kitchener acute anxiety relieved only by total victory. Kitchener was not a great battlefield tactician, but he handled the 'early Victorian formations' needed to combat a known enemy well enough.[36]

South Africa, 1900–2

On 11 October 1899, the South African War broke out following an ultimatum presented to the British by the president of the semi-independent Boer republic of the Transvaal. On 18 December 1899, Kitchener, along with Field Marshal Lord Roberts, was sent to the war zone to eradicate the mess created by the British military authorities.

Kitchener was made Roberts's Chief of Staff, a rather ambiguous post that lacked definition and for which, in the ordinary sense, he did not have the necessary training. Consequently, Kitchener was obliged to perform many different tasks: first, he reorganised the transport system in a way that suited his experience but not that of the British forces. Secondly, he took control of the army when Roberts was ill and fought a major engagement against the Boers at the battle of Paardeberg on 18 February 1900. Here his old faults resurfaced: he took complete control and bypassed the various British generals present by issuing orders directly to individual units – as he had done at Omdurman. This time there was no brilliant victory, and although the Boers were surrounded and pinned down, they had inflicted what for the British amounted to huge losses. It was the most controversial battle he ever fought and while he was lauded later for injecting an energy that few commanders had shown beforehand, the results appalled the other generals, including possibly Roberts who was too polite to say.[37]

Kitchener's credibility as a battlefield commander was questioned and he never fought a battle on this scale again. Roberts sent him away to tidy up other areas but Kitchener was back with him for the march into the Boer republics. From May 1900, the Boers, who would not face the British in open battle, opted for guerrilla warfare. While Roberts occupied their towns and cut them off from the outside world the Boer commandos hit at his precarious supply line, a single railway. Eventually, a tired Roberts, having declared the war to be at an end, left South Africa, leaving Kitchener to mop up and bring the guerrilla war to an end.

On 29 November 1900, Kitchener was appointed Commander in Chief in South Africa. Many felt that he would now provide the necessary leadership that Roberts lacked. Captain R J Marker believed that once Kitchener was in charge and given a free hand 'it [the war] will be over in a very short time'. However, not all were impressed by the change in regime: Captain Colin Ballard wrote,

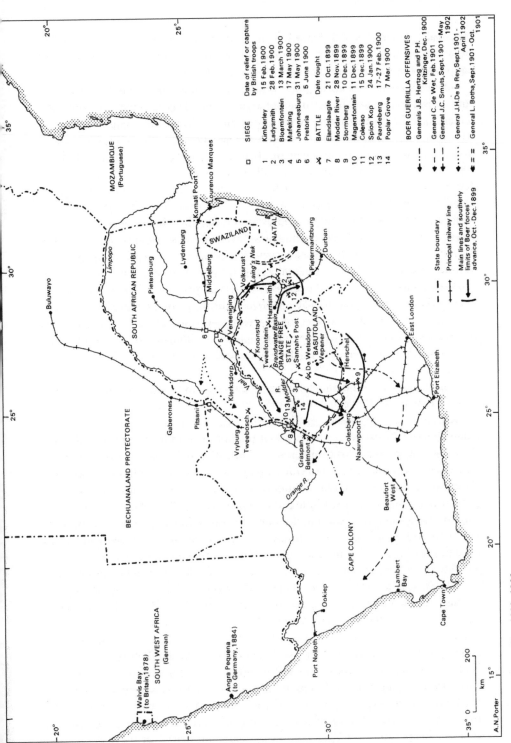

SIEGE		Date of relief or capture by British troops
□		
1	Kimberley	15 Feb. 1900
2	Ladysmith	28 Feb. 1900
3	Bloemfontein	13 March 1900
4	Mafeking	17 May 1900
5	Johannesburg	31 May 1900
6	Pretoria	5 June 1900

BATTLE		Date fought
✗		
7	Elandslaagte	21 Oct. 1899
8	Modder River	28 Nov. 1899
9	Stormberg	10 Dec. 1899
10	Magersfontein	11 Dec. 1899
11	Colenso	15 Dec. 1899
12	Spion Kop	24 Jan. 1900
13	Paardeberg	17–27 Feb. 1900
14	Poplar Grove	7 Mar. 1900

BOER GUERRILLA OFFENSIVES

Generals J.B. Hertzog and P.H. Kritzinger, Dec. 1900

General C. de Wet, Feb. 1901

General J.C. Smuts, Sept. 1901 – May 1902

General J.H. De la Rey, Sept. 1901 – April 1902

General L. Botha, Sept. 1901 – Oct. 1901

State boundary

Principal railway line

Main lines and southerly limits of Boer forces' advance, Oct. – Dec. 1899

A.N. Porter

The South African War, 1899–1902.

'Personally, I don't expect that Kitchener will do any better. Of course, I don't know him personally, but he is said to be very harsh and unfeeling – and all his old Egyptian lot expect him to take very stern measures.'[38]

The task before Kitchener, however, was becoming more complicated by the hour. The guerrilla war, hitherto confined to the former Boer republics, eventually spread into the British territory of Cape Colony, where the majority of white inhabitants were Boers themselves and many had already risen up in revolt before fading into the background when the British appeared to be winning. Indeed, some 10,000 had rebelled between 1899 and 1900 and the Boer high command decided that another rebellion, hopefully on a larger scale, would tip the balance in their favour. A further complication for Kitchener was the British government's desire for cuts in troop numbers and expenditure. Their hopes, however, proved illusory once several Boer commandos invaded Cape Colony in late 1900. Although the great uprising never occurred, with only a few rebelling again, these commandos, particularly those under the most implacable Boer commander, Christiaan De Wet, caused the British numerous problems. Kitchener made it clear to the new Secretary of State for War, William St John Brodrick, that it was premature to speak of cuts when more troops and resources were needed. Thus began a battle between Kitchener and the political authorities over control of the war, which provided a major backdrop to the military events.[39]

Kitchener would eventually employ several methods to defeat the commandos. First he launched numerous columns to chase them down. Initially, the main effort was against De Wet, who was subjected to three 'hunts'. The third was led by Kitchener himself who, in February 1901, tried to coordinate seventeen columns in what turned out to be a vain pursuit. The military aspect of the war thus saw Boer commandos being chased all over South Africa by British columns. The Boers occasionally inflicted embarrassing defeats on their pursuers and while these did not affect the overall situation, they increased the pressure on Kitchener, particularly from the press, leading him to complain to Roberts, 'I only wish the English papers would take a sounder line, they do all in their power to encourage the Boers and to dishearten our troops.' The strain told on Kitchener and his old anxieties resurfaced. For instance, when Lord Methuen's column was ambushed and Methuen himself captured on 7 March 1902, Kitchener sulked in his room for two days, something he had done in the Sudan when a new gunboat went wrong.[40] At one point he even urged Brodrick to sack him: 'If you think someone else could do better out here, I hope you will not hesitate for a moment in replacing me. I try all I can but it is not like the Soudan [*sic*] and disappointments are frequent.'[41] Moreover, when a major 'hunt' was underway Kitchener could not help interfering and would send orders direct to columns thus upsetting the cohesion of the operation. As one promising officer Brevet Lieutenant Colonel Edmund Allenby explained to his wife, Kitchener 'tries to run the whole show from Pretoria – a quite impossible job – and fails'. Douglas Haig, promoted a local colonel and operating in Cape Colony, confided in his diary that 'Lord K seems to meddle rather, and does not give French [Lieutenant General John French, who was appointed on 1 June 1901 to oversee operations in Cape Colony] quite a free hand'. And although Haig never suffered interference from Kitchener, 'Periodically he used to get a fit of the funks and think De Wet was going to invade the Colony.'[42]

Only when Lieutenant General Ian Hamilton returned to South Africa in late 1901, having been appointed by London to be Kitchener's Chief of Staff, was the burden lifted somewhat from Kitchener's shoulders. Hamilton was also meant to report on Kitchener's mental health, but he proved to be a loyal subordinate and worked well with his chief. Kitchener was pleased with the appointment having already tried Neville Lyttelton and told the War Office. 'Hamilton will I am sure do the work extremely well and relieve me of a good deal of worry'. When Hamilton arrived he was impressed by the measures Kitchener had taken to combat the commandos. Indeed, Kitchener had complemented his mobile columns by dividing the former Boer republics into zones with barbed wire and blockhouses of stone and corrugated iron. The commandos, consequently, were being squeezed into smaller areas already devoid of supplies:

> I never could have imagined, [wrote Hamilton] such a gigantic system of fortifications, barriers, traps and garrisons as actually exists. This forms the principal character of operations, supplying them with a solid backbone and involving permanent loss of territory to the enemy, which former operations did not. Thus, certain treacherous areas are now permanently under our control. Subsidiary areas are consequently now giving less and less trouble.[43]

To man the blockhouse line Kitchener used mainly local Africans who were armed for the purpose. Moreover, Africans were also being used as scouts for the columns and made a great contribution to the intelligence gathered. It is estimated that 50,000 black Africans and those of mixed race were armed by the British, while a further 100,000 served in British transport units. For these men, especially when uniformed and armed, capture by the Boers often meant certain death. On learning that De Wet and his government had ordered this fate for those captured, Kitchener indignantly informed him, 'I am very much astonished at the barbarous instructions you have given as regards the murder of natives, who, although placed in a very difficult position, have . . . behaved, in my opinion, in an exemplary manner during the war.' Any captured Boer commander found guilty of murdering non-whites faced the death penalty and some were executed, most famously Commandant Gideon Scheepers.[44]

The second method Kitchener used to defeat the commandos was the most controversial. This was the war against the Boer civilians that culminated in the concentration camps. Under Roberts, the British had retaliated against raids on the railway line by destroying local farms. The 'displaced people', alongside those who wished to surrender, were placed in encampments that were poorly protected from marauding commandos. Under Kitchener, the process of retaliation became systematic. At first, in response to government enquiries, Kitchener issued orders that farm-burning should be undertaken only as a punishment, as Roberts had earlier stated, but this proved difficult to enforce and soon it became policy to remove civilians anyway as the destruction of farms became part of an unfolding strategy. Kitchener had quickly identified Boer women as the heart of the resistance: 'There is no doubt the women are keeping up the war and are far more bitter than the men.' And later, 'The women left on the farms give complete intelligence to the Boers of all our movements and feed the commandos in their neighbourhood.'[45] To deny the commandos civilian help Kitchener issued Circular Memorandum No. 29 on 21 December 1900, which began '[I am] desirous that all possible means should be taken to stop the present guerrilla warfare.'[46] Thus troops were ordered to remove all civilians from their homes in areas where Boer commandos were prevalent. They were to be housed in camps near the railway line and separated according to whether their men remained on commando or not: surrendered men joined their wives and children. Any Africans living on Boer farms were to be sent to their own camps. The Memorandum made clear that this procedure was recommended by surrendered Boers as a way of forcing those on commando to capitulate.

The numbers of civilians brought in steadily grew until the camp authorities were overwhelmed. Disease killed thousands, particularly children, and the reaction of the officers in charge was generally slow so that by October 1901 the overall death rate reached 344 per 1,000. Although conditions improved thereafter about 10 per cent of the pre-war Boer population died. The figure for Africans who died in their camps is still a matter of speculation. Once the situation became known in Britain, thanks largely to Emily Hobhouse, outrage grew and led to the Liberal party leader, Sir Henry Campbell-Bannerman, describing this policy as 'methods of barbarism'. Kitchener appeared indifferent to all this, although his two most recent biographers disagree about his attitudes: Trevor Royle says he 'paid little heed to the proper provision of the camps'; while John Pollock notes that he did visit some camps, and that not all of them were death traps. Nevertheless, Kitchener cannot escape blame. The system lacked proper organisation: camp commandants could not make adequate arrangements as civilians kept being brought in without notice. Kitchener's main problem was that his mind was elsewhere – on the war. He expected subordinates to get on with things and it seems many were fearful of bothering him. Only when the civilian authorities, under the High Commissioner, Lord Milner, took control towards the end of 1901 did conditions improve. But by then Kitchener had reversed his policy of bringing in civilians. The farms were still being destroyed but now it was up to the commandos to look after their families.[47]

A third means of defeating the commandos was the use of surrendered Boers against their former comrades. Kitchener promoted the creation of two units, the National Scouts and the Orange River Colony Volunteers, whose knowledge of the country and Boer fighting methods proved invaluable to the British. Their impact upon the morale of those still fighting was vital, as Bill Nasson has noted:

'If by no means a principal factor in bringing about a Boer defeat, the plague of collaboration was there in the final losing equation between actual hardship and loss of faith.'[48]

For Kitchener commanding armies was not the only task he had to perform. The nature of the conflict required him to exercise total control over the war effort and this brought him into collision with the local civilian authorities. In 1901, especially, Kitchener demanded and got martial law extended to Cape Colony in the teeth of opposition from the colony's government, led by Sir Gordon Sprigg. This meant that military courts would exercise supreme authority in the colony, especially in trying rebels. This also led to problems with the British government, particularly when Lieutenant General French ordered public executions. Kitchener, however, actually proved quite lenient and from 500 capital cases only 33 were deemed severe enough to warrant execution. An important factor here was that because of the fear of rebellion, all agreed that the war in Cape Colony had to be ended promptly. Thus the British government found itself supporting Kitchener against the Cape politicians and against its own inclinations.[49]

Kitchener's civilian counterpart, Milner, High Commissioner since 1897 and one of the architects of the war, had his own views about how the war should be run, and was as strong-willed as Kitchener himself. For Milner, the war was secondary to the establishment of civilian government in the occupied areas, within which the British would dominate their Boer collaborators. His ultimate aim was to turn South Africa British, especially the Transvaal, by eventually settling British colonists in the countryside. Once the Boers were outnumbered in the richest part of South Africa then the 'weakest link in the imperial chain'[50] would be strong again. For Milner, the concentration camps were symbolic of Kitchener's slapdash approach and simply exacerbated Boer hostility; moreover, Kitchener seemed to be a man in a hurry, desperate to end the war quickly without thought for the future. As Kitchener showed no sign of agreeing with Milner's assessment of the situation in 1901, he took leave and lobbied the government in London. When Milner came back he had apparently won: he had obtained Cabinet backing for his plans; the mining industry was to be restarted; the British refugees from Johannesburg were to return, and the occupied areas were to be developed according to his ideas. In return, Milner had promised a reduction in troop numbers and cuts in expenditure. However, Milner then went too far and recommended restructuring the command in South Africa, but as the military situation was far from rosy, Kitchener hit back making Milner's optimism look rather ridiculous. Kitchener had refused to comply with Milner's demands and as Milner acknowledged Kitchener had 'probably more than the ordinary soldier's contempt for the opinions of a civilian . . . It is impossible to *guide* a military dictator of very strong views & strong character'.[51] However, Lord Salisbury refused to sack Kitchener on Milner's urging and wanted to know if a new commander would do any better. Indeed, Kitchener had virtually dared the government to sack him in the full knowledge that there was no one else who could replace him.

Kitchener's rivalry with Milner would come to a head during the peace negotiations between April and May 1902. Kitchener has often been condemned as thinking more of his next job – Commander in Chief in India – than the proper political settlement of South Africa. Such a view ignores his diplomatic skills first seen at Fashoda in 1898. Kitchener well understood that for Britain to retain South Africa the collaboration of the Boer leadership was vital and he was willing to talk to them if necessary. He had come close to a deal with Louis Botha, the leader of the Transvaal commandos, at Middelburg in March 1901, and although he and Kitchener had got on, Milner had done his best to sabotage the talks. Botha anyway had not wanted a settlement, and had simply tested the water, but by 1902 the situation had changed. The Boer cause was disintegrating: Kitchener's methods were working; the commandos were short of all supplies; their society was divided and in a state of civil war; their countryside was destroyed; their families were dying in the camps or roaming the countryside, and, to cap it all, Africans were inflicting defeats on Boer commandos. Kitchener believed that a moderate settlement was required once the Boers acknowledged their defeat; Milner, however, thought otherwise. If the Boer generals became popular leaders in peace he knew his plans would not work. He wanted the Boer collaborators installed, but Kitchener well knew this would cause trouble in the future. The Boer generals were the only ones who could deliver peace and reconcile their people to the new order. And it was Kitchener who got his way, making promises that the Boers found acceptable: they would be compensated for the destruction of their farms and the fate of the non-white population was to be a matter for post-war South Africa to decide. Consequently, Boer independence was ended when the Treaty of Vereeniging was signed on 31 May 1902, and Kitchener could leave as the most pre-eminent soldier in the British Empire.[52] Unfortunately, Queen Victoria had not lived to see one of her favourite generals bring, for Britain, a satisfactory end to the war.

As a military commander, Kitchener's faults had been outweighed by the nature of the campaigns fought. In the Sudan his command style, while erratic at times, had been sufficient to defeat the Dervishes because the campaign had called for other qualities beyond simply fighting battles. The same could be said for the war in South Africa. This required a strong will that could endure short-term defeats to ensure long-term victory. Kitchener had come close to cracking but his willpower, and foresight, had seen him through. He realised that victory required more than military operations and that a protracted guerrilla war meant that civilians too were on the front line. This type of warfare meant that he demanded, and received, power beyond that of guiding mobile columns. Kitchener, in effect, did become a 'military dictator' in South Africa, having demonstrated his political skills in obtaining the backing of those at the highest level in Britain. Those skills were shown further when he negotiated the peace treaty that secured a South Africa loyal to the British Empire for the next forty years or so. Thus warfare in the British empire often called for abilities beyond the battlefield and Kitchener had those. That is what made him the empire's most famous soldier because for him those qualities would be called on again in a far greater struggle.

Bibliography

Kitchener has been well served by biographers and many accounts appeared before his death. His campaigns in the Sudan and South Africa have also been well covered over the years and only a flavour of those can be given here. The standard biographies are those by Sir George Arthur, *Life of Lord Kitchener*, 3 vols (London: Macmillan, 1920); Philip Magnus, *Kitchener: Portrait of an Imperialist* (London: John Murray, 1958); Trevor Royle, *The Kitchener Enigma* (London: Michael Joseph, 1985); and John Pollock, *Kitchener* (London: Constable & Robinson, 2002). There are useful essays on Kitchener in Byron Farwell, *Eminent Victorian Soldiers* (London: Viking, 1986) and Mark Urban, *Generals* (London: Faber & Faber, 2005). Kitchener's public image is discussed in Keith Surridge, 'More than a great poster: Lord Kitchener and the image of the military hero', *Historical Research*, 74, 185 (2001), 298–313. For the Sudan campaign see Winston S. Churchill, *The River War*, 2 vols (London: Longmans, 1899); Henry Keown-Boyd, *A Good Dusting: a Centenary Review of the Sudan Campaigns 1883–1899* (London: Guild Publishing, 1986); Edward Spiers, ed., *Sudan: the Reconquest Reappraised* (London: Frank Cass, 1998) and 'Ismat Hasan Zulfo, *Karari* (London: Frederick Warne, 1980). For Omdurman, see Philip Ziegler, *Omdurman* (London: Collins, 1973). There are many books covering the South African War, but for those that focus more on Kitchener see André Wessels, ed., *Lord Kitchener and the War in South Africa 1899–1902* (Stroud: Sutton Publishing for Army Records Society, 2006); Keith Terrance Surridge, *Managing the South African War, 1899–1902* (Woodbridge: Boydell Press, 1998); Keith Surridge, 'The Politics of War: Lord Kitchener and the Settlement of the South African War, 1901–1902', in Greg Cuthbertson, Albert Grundlingh and Mary-Lynn Suttie, eds, *Writing a Wider War: Rethinking Gender, Race, and Identity in the South African War, 1899–1902* (Athens, OH: Ohio University Press, 2002), pp. 213–32; Keith Surridge, 'Lord Kitchener and the South African War 1899–1902', *Soldiers of the Queen: The Journal of the Victorian Military Society*, 101 (June 2000), 19–25.

Notes

1. Queen Victoria to Kitchener, 11 January 1901 in André Wessels, ed., *Lord Kitchener and the War in South Africa 1899–1902* (Stroud: Sutton Publishing for Army Records Society, 2006), p. 65; Keith Surridge, 'More than a great poster: Lord Kitchener and the image of the military hero', *Historical Research*, 74, 185 (2001), 298–313.

2. For more on Kitchener's early reputation see Surridge, 'More than a great poster', especially 307–10.

3. Trevor Royle, *The Kitchener Enigma* (London: Michael Joseph, 1985), pp. 138–41.

4. Lord Cromer, *Modern Egypt* (London: Macmillan, 1908), vol. II, pp. 87–88; Ian F W Beckett, 'Kitchener and the Politics of Command', in Edward Spiers, ed., *Sudan: the Reconquest Reappraised* (London: Frank Cass, 1998), p. 48.

5. The National Archives (hereafter TNA), Kitchener Mss, PRO 30/57/11/I13, Kitchener to Cromer, 18 October 1897.

6. Quoted in John Pollock, *Kitchener* (London: Constable & Robinson, 2002), p. 84; also ibid., pp. 82–84.

7. TNA, PRO 30/57/10/I4, Kitchener to Grenfell, 14 October 1897.

8. National Army Museum (hereafter NAM), Rawlinson Mss, 5201/33/5, Rawlinson letterbook, Rawlinson to Grenfell, 12 May 1898.

9. Lieutenant Colonel Charles à Court Repington, *Vestigia* (London: Constable, 1919), p. 101; Douglas Scott, ed., *Douglas Haig: The Preparatory Prologue 1861–1914. Diaries and Letters* (Barnsley: Pen & Sword, 2006), p. 71; General Sir Neville Lyttelton, *Eighty Years: Soldiering, Politics and Games* (London: Hodder & Stoughton, 1927), p. 186.

10. British Library (hereafter BL), Lansdowne Mss, Lan (5) 21, Cromer to Salisbury, 8 January 1898.

11. Lord Edward Cecil, *The Leisure of an Egyptian Official* (London: Hodder & Stoughton, 1921), pp. 184–87; Beckett, 'Kitchener and the Politics of Command', p. 48.

12. Archie Hunter, *Kitchener's Sword-arm: The Life and Campaigns of General Sir Archibald Hunter* (Staplehurst: Spellmount, 1996), p. 53.

13. Winston S Churchill, *The River War* (London: Longmans, Green & Co., 1900), II, p. 378; Randolph S Churchill, *Winston S Churchill, Vol. 1, Youth 1874–1900* (London: Heinemann, 1966), p. 424.

14. Ernest Bennett, 'After Omdurman', *Contemporary Review* 75 (1899), 20–21; NAM, 7404/36/3, Meiklejohn Mss, 'The Nile Campaign', pp. 19, 58; Surridge, 'More than a great poster', pp. 303–4.

15. NAM, Rawlinson Mss, 5201/33, Rawlinson diary, 14 January 1898; Repington, *Vestigia*, p. 157; Sir George Arthur, *General Sir John Maxwell* (London: John Murray, 1932), p. 59; NAM, Churcher Mss, 7804/53, Omdurman Diary, 14 August 1898, p. 5; Sir Horace Smith-Dorrien, *Memories of Forty-eight Years' Service* (London: John Murray, 1925), p. 101.

16. Major General Sir Frederick Maurice, *The Life of General Lord Rawlinson of Trent. From His Journals and Letters* (London: Cassell, 1928), pp. 31–32; Field Marshal Lord Grenfell, *Memoirs* (London: Hodder & Stoughton, n.d.), p. 154; P Harrington and F Sharf, eds, *Omdurman 1898: The Eyewitnesses Speak* (London: Greenhill Books, 1998), p. 72; H Alford and W Dennistoun Sword, *The Egyptian Soudan: Its Loss and Recovery* (London: Macmillan, 1898, reprinted by the Naval & Military Press, 1992), pp. 241, 289; G W Steevens, *With Kitchener to Khartum* (Edinburgh: Blackwood, 1898), pp. 22, 46.

17. Lieutenant Colonel E W C Sandes, *The Royal Engineers in Egypt and the Sudan* (Chatham: The Institution of Royal Engineers, 1937), pp. 222–36; Steevens, *With Kitchener*, p. 26; Royle, *Kitchener Enigma*, p. 116; Pollock, *Kitchener*, pp. 107–8.

18. Cromer, *Modern Egypt*, vol. II, pp. 98–102; See also TNA, PRO 30/57/10/I5, Wolseley to Kitchener, 14 April 1898, for his subsequent advice on the matter.

19. Wolseley to Kitchener, ibid.

20. P Ziegler, *Omdurman* (London: Collins, 1973), p. 28.

21. Beatrix Gatacre, *General Gatacre: The Story of the Life and Services of Sir William Forbes Gatacre 1843–1906* (London: John Murray, 1910), pp. 190–91. Edward Spiers, 'Campaigning with Kitchener', in Spiers, ed., *Sudan*, pp. 58, 62.

22. 'Ismat Hasan Zulfo, *Karari* (London: Frederick Warne, 1980), pp. 112–14; Hunter, *Kitchener's Sword-arm*, p. 93; Bennet Burleigh, *Khartoum Campaign 1898* (London: Chapman & Hall, 1899, reprinted by Ken Trotman Ltd, 1989), p. 150; Smith-Dorrien, *Memories*, p. 106; Repington, *Vestigia*, p. 154; Maurice, *Rawlinson*, p. 38; TNA, PRO 30/57/14/M11, Wingate, 3 March 1899, Note on the Dervish Wounded at Omdurman.

23. Zulfo, *Karari*, pp. 101–2.

24. Ibid., pp. 114–20.

25. John Meredith, ed., *Omdurman Diaries* (Barnsley: Leo Cooper, 1998), p. 183.

26. Zulfo, *Karari*, chapter 16, especially notes p. 189 for who was where, particularly Ali Wad Hilu.

27. NAM, Lewis Ms, 7503/9, Lewis Journal, 2 September 1898, p. 11; NAM, Rawlinson Mss, 5201/33/4; Rawlinson Diary, 2 September 1898.

28. Quoted in Spiers, 'Campaigning', in Spiers, ed., *Sudan*, p. 70.

29. TNA, WO 32/6143, Kitchener to Grenfell, 5 September 1898, p. 2A.

30. Ibid., p. 4A; Trevor Royle, *Fighting Mac* (Edinburgh: Mainstream, 1982), p. 97; Zulfo, *Karari*, p. 218.

31. NAM, Cameron Mss, 8305/55, Cameron to his father, 4 September 1898.

32. TNA, PRO 30/57/14/M11, Wingate, Note, 3 March 1899; Ziegler, *Omdurman*, pp. 215–16.

33. For a recent account of the fighting in 1884–85 see Michael Asher, *Khartoum* (London: Penguin, 2006), especially, pp. 28–33, 147–56.

34. Repington, *Vestigia*, p. 150.

35. Ibid., p. 169; Hunter, *Kitchener's Sword-arm*, p. 100; Ziegler, *Omdurman*, p. 164.

36. Repington, *Vestigia*, p. 111; Beckett, 'Kitchener and the Politics of Command', p. 49.

37. Keith Surridge, 'Lord Kitchener and the War in South Africa 1899–1902', *Soldiers of the Queen: the Journal of the Victorian Military Society* 101 (June 2000), 22; Wessels, ed., *Lord Kitchener*, pp. 13–14.

38. NAM, Marker Mss, 6803/4/4/7, Marker to his sister, 5 October 1900; H C B Cook, ed., 'Letters from South Africa 1899–1902', *Journal of the Society for Army Historical Research* LXIX, 278 (1991), 80.

39. TNA, PRO 30/57/22/Y4 & Y9, Brodrick to Kitchener and Kitchener to Brodrick, 24 November 1900 and 20 December 1900.

40. Quoted in Denis Judd and Keith Surridge, *The Boer War* (London: John Murray, 2002), p. 255; also, p. 217; Royle, *Kitchener Enigma*, p. 111.

41. TNA, PRO 30/57/22/Y95, Kitchener to Brodrick, 18 October 1901.

42. Brian Gardner, *Allenby* (London: Cassell, 1965), p. 48; Scott, *Haig*, p. 195.

43. TNA, PRO 30/57/22/Y101, Kitchener to Brodrick, 8 November 1901; TNA, CAB 37/59/124, Hamilton to Roberts, 3 December 1901; Royle, *Kitchener Enigma*, p. 181.

44. TNA, WO 108/405, Kitchener to De Wet, 14 February 1902; William Nasson, 'Africans at War', in John Gooch, ed., *The Boer War* (London: Frank Cass, 2000), pp. 126–40.

45. TNA, CO 417/307/40042/ff. 581-582, Brodrick to Kitchener and Kitchener to Brodrick, 4 and 5 December 1900; NAM, Roberts Mss, 7101/23/33/4, Kitchener to Roberts, 4 December 1900; TNA, PRO 30/57/22/Y30, Kitchener to Brodrick, 7 March 1901; Helen Bradford, 'Gentlemen and Boers: Afrikaner Nationalism, Gender, and Colonial Warfare in the South African War', in G Cuthbertson, A Grundlingh and M-L Suttie, eds, *Writing a Wider War: Rethinking Gender, Race, and Identity in the South African War, 1899–1902* (Athens, OH: Ohio University Press, 2002), pp. 37–66.

46. S B Spies, *Methods of Barbarism?* (Cape Town: Human & Rousseau, 1977), p. 183.

47. Bill Nasson, *The South African War 1899–1902* (London: Arnold, 1999), pp. 217–24; Royle, *Kitchener Enigma*, p. 179; Pollock, *Kitchener*, pp. 194–95; Spies, *Methods of Barbarism?*, pp. 143–260; Surridge, 'Lord Kitchener', pp. 23–25.

48. Nasson, *South African War*, pp. 215–18.

49. Keith Surridge, 'Rebellion, Martial Law and British Civil-Military Relations: The War in Cape Colony 1899–1902', *Small Wars and Insurgencies* 8, 2 (1997), 44–54; Richard Holmes, *The Little Field Marshal. Sir John French* (London: Jonathan Cape, 1981), pp. 112–16.

50. Quoted in Iain R. Smith, *The Origins of the South African War 1899–1902* (London: Longman, 1996), p. 148.

51. Keith Surridge, *Managing the South African War 1899–1902* (Woodbridge: Boydell Press, 1998), pp. 124–48.

52. Ibid., pp. 155–74; Judd and Surridge, *Boer War*, pp. 269–97; Keith Surridge, 'The Politics of War: Lord Kitchener and the Settlement of the South African War, 1901–1902', in Cuthbertson, Grundlingh and Suttie, eds, *Writing a Wider War*, pp. 213–32.

Appendix

Chronology of Victorian Wars

1837–38 Canadian Rebellion
1839–42 First Afghan War
1839–42 First China (Opium) War
1843 Conquest of Scinde
1843 Gwalior Campaign
1845–46 First Sikh War
1846–47 First Maori War
1846–47 Seventh Kaffir (Cape Frontier) War
1848–49 Second Sikh War
1850–53 Eighth Kaffir (Cape Frontier) War
1852–53 Second Burma War
1852 Black Mountain Expedition
1854–56 Crimean War
1856–57 Persian War
1856–57 Second China (Arrow) War
1857–58 Indian Mutiny
1858 Sittana Expedition
1860 Third China War
1860–61 Second Maori War
1861 Sikkim Expedition
1862–64 Taiping Rebellion
1863 Ambeyla Expedition
1863–66 Third Maori War
1864–66 Bhutan Expedition
1865–66 Jamaican Insurrection
1866 Fenian Raids into Canada
1867–68 Abyssinian Expedition
1868 Black Mountain Expedition
1870 Red River Expedition
1871–72 Lushai Expedition
1873–74 Second Ashanti (Asante) War
1874–75 Duffla Expedition
1875–1876 Perak Campaign
1877–78 Jowakhi Expedition
1877–78 Ninth Kaffir (Cape Frontier) War
1878 Dispatch of Indian Troops to

Malta and Cyprus
1878–80 Second Afghan War
1879 Zulu War
1879–80 Sekhkhuni Campaign
1880–81 First South African (Anglo-Transvaal) War
1882 Conquest of Egypt
1884–85 Bechuanaland Field Force
1884–85 Suakin Expeditions
1884–85 Gordon Relief Expedition
1885 Riel's Rebellion
1885–86 Third Burma War
1888 Sikkim Expedition
1888 Hazara and Black Mountain Expeditions
1888 Zululand Rebellion
1889–90 Chin-Lushai Expedition
1891 Manipur Expedition
1891 Miranzai Expedition
1891 Hunza and Nagar Expedition
1892 Tambi Expedition
1892–93 Chin Hills Expedition
1893 Matabeleland Rebellion
1894 Gambia Expedition
1894–95 Mahsud Expedition
1895 Relief of Chitral
1895–1900 Third Ashanti (Asante) War
1896 Mashonaland Rebellion
1896–98 Reconquest of the Sudan
1896–97 Bechuanaland Expedition
1897 Benin Expedition
1897–98 Tochi, Malakand, Buner, Mohmand and Tirah Expeditions
1898 Fashoda Incident
1898 Sierra Leone Hut Tax Rebellion
1899–1902 Second South African (Anglo-Boer) War
1900 Boxer Rebellion
1901–4 Somaliland Campaign

Index